Disparities in Health-Risk Behaviors and Health

Disparities in Health-Risk Behaviors and Health

Editors

Celia C. Lo
William Ash-Houchen
Tyrone C. Cheng

MDPI

Basel • Beijing • Wuhan • Barcelona • Belgrade • Novi Sad • Cluj • Manchester

Editors
Celia C. Lo
Texas Woman's University
Denton, TX
USA

William Ash-Houchen
Delta State University
Cleveland, MS
USA

Tyrone C. Cheng
University of Alabama
Tuscaloosa, AL
USA

Editorial Office
MDPI
St. Alban-Anlage 66
4052 Basel, Switzerland

This is a reprint of articles from the Special Issue published online in the open access journal *International Journal of Environmental Research and Public Health* (ISSN 1660-4601) (available at: https://www.mdpi.com/journal/ijerph/special_issues/Disparities_Health).

For citation purposes, cite each article independently as indicated on the article page online and as indicated below:

Lastname, A.A.; Lastname, B.B. Article Title. *Journal Name* **Year**, *Volume Number*, Page Range.

ISBN 978-3-7258-0147-3 (Hbk)
ISBN 978-3-7258-0148-0 (PDF)
doi.org/10.3390/books978-3-7258-0148-0

Contents

About the Editors

Celia C. Lo

Celia C. Lo is the manager of Research Science of the PERSEREC program at Peraton. She is a practiced researcher and project manager, skilled at designing, planning, and implementing complex and large-scale survey research. Furthermore, she is seasoned in managing and analyzing large administrative data sets. In the decades as an academic in the social sciences, she accrued expertise in research and teaching. Her work has emphasized the creation of measurable improvements in institutions and communities via the deployment of leadership in program building and program evaluation, along with sophistication in data analysis and innovation in budget management. Being the author of more than 150 peer-reviewed publications, during 2023, she drew on her long background in quantitative and qualitative research and her management experiences to lead four projects having USD 1.4M total funding and managed several other projects for Peraton—assignments having USD 1.5M total funding. Her knowledge of racial/ethnic and gender disparities, criminology, and public health, along with her advanced methodological and statistical skills, helped her team refine project execution strategies and deliver demonstrable mission success to customers, positioning PERSEREC well in terms of future contracts. She manages 11 direct reports. Ultimately, she strives to maintain an environment of trust and purposefulness in which each of us is able to succeed and grow.

William Ash-Houchen

William Ash-Houchen earned a PhD from Texas Woman's University in 2018. Currently, he is a Senior Research Analyst at the Oregon Criminal Justice Commission, where he provides research, planning, and policy support for state-level grant programs targeting the intersection of criminal justice and behavioral health issues. These grant programs provide a combined USD 40 million to county and federally recognized Indian tribal governments in Oregon biannually. Previously, he taught in criminal justice programs in Mississippi and Texas, publishing more than a dozen scholarly, peer-reviewed journal articles as part of an active research agenda examining substance use, mental health, and criminal behavior.

Tyrone C. Cheng

Tyrone C. Cheng earned his MSW and PhD from the University of Alabama in 1988 and 1993, respectively. His curriculum vitae lists 123 published works (sole or first author of 76). All but eight of the listed works were published in journals having impact factors. He has acquired an h-index score of 19, and his publications—to date—represent 1311 citations. His research has focused on topics in child welfare services, welfare policies, substance use, mental health and health service utilization, and intimate partner violence. He is the author of Case Examples in Child Welfare and Family Services for Social Workers, published in 2023 by Routledge. "Co-word analysis of first-authored publications written by top cited scholars of social work" (2023) in Research in Social Work indicates that he is among the top 2% most-cited social work researchers in the world. He served as associate editor for BMC Public Health in 2023, 2019, 2018, and 2017. Tyrone C. Cheng was in clinical practice as a licensed social worker for eight years after completing his doctoral studies in social work. His work with over 300 families from diverse ethnic backgrounds brought him wide-ranging experiences addressing child abuse and neglect, juvenile delinquency, mental health, and suicide issues affecting families in Ohio, Michigan, and Chicago. He also served as a community organizer in Chicago's Chinatown, charged with facilitating immigrant families' participation in reforming local schools.

Cheng taught and directed social work programs in different universities in Alabama, Georgia, Illinois, and New Jersey. In 2011, the School of Social Work, University of Alabama, honored him with its Dean's Faculty Award for Research, Teaching, and Service.

Preface

This reprint, derived from the Special Issue titled "Disparities in Health-Risk Behaviors and Health", is a comprehensive collection of novel papers that identifies and discusses the (1) social determinants of disparities in health-risk behaviors and health, (2) social mechanisms responsible for these persistent disparities, and (3) policies and practices recommended for reducing disparities. These papers were grounded firmly in the understanding that gender, racial/ethnic, immigration, LGBT, and socioeconomic statuses contribute to an individual's health status, providing the scientific community with paths to equity/equality that take more than the awareness and avoidance of blatant, explicit discrimination. We thank all the authors of the 12 papers in this Special Issue for challenging the coherence of the majority group attachment and fostering the social application of evidence-based ideas about diversity, inclusion, and equity.

Celia C. Lo, William Ash-Houchen, and Tyrone C. Cheng
Editors

International Journal of
Environmental Research and Public Health

MDPI

Article

Gender and Childhood Victimization: A Longitudinal Study of Heavy Drinking in Young Adulthood

William Ash-Houchen [1,*], Celia C. Lo [2], Heather M. Gerling [3] and Tyrone C. Cheng [4]

[1] Department of Justice Studies, Prairie View A&M University, Prairie View, TX 77446, USA
[2] PERSEREC, Peraton, Seaside, CA 93955, USA; celiaclo@yahoo.com
[3] Center for Depression Research and Clinical Care, UT Southwestern Medical Center, Dallas, TX 75390, USA; heather.gerling@utsouthwestern.edu
[4] School of Social Work, University of Alabama, Tuscaloosa, AL 35401, USA; tyronecheng@yahoo.com
* Correspondence: wiashhouchen@pvamu.edu

Abstract: The present longitudinal study, for 12 years, followed a group of young adults, examining (1) whether/how victimization in childhood increased the likelihood of heavy drinking; (2) whether depression mediated the strain–heavy drinking relationship; and (3) whether/how relationships among strain, depression, and heavy drinking differed across two gender groups. Data came from the National Longitudinal Survey of Youth 1997 cohort, dating 2004–2015 (5 interview waves and 22,549 person-wave measurements total). We linked consumption of 5+ drinks (during the month prior) to four discrete measures of violent victimization, to one measure of stressful events, and to depression. We needed to consider repeat measures of the same variables over time, so we used generalized estimating equations (GEE) to analyze data. Depression was found to increase heavy drinking uniformly. Empirical evidence confirmed that in the strain–heavy drinking relationship, depression plays a minor mediating role. Gender moderated heavy drinking's associations. Specifically, bullying in childhood raised risk for female respondents. The current strain was associated with a higher risk of heavy drinking among male respondents. Childhood victimization, as well as current life stress, play an important role in depression and heavy drinking. Future research should focus on the development of specific, targeted care to reduce heavy drinking's harm and promote equity among Americans.

Keywords: heavy drinking; victimization in childhood; depression; longitudinal study; gender

Citation: Ash-Houchen, W.; Lo, C.C.; Gerling, H.M.; Cheng, T.C. Gender and Childhood Victimization: A Longitudinal Study of Heavy Drinking in Young Adulthood. *Int. J. Environ. Res. Public Health* **2021**, *18*, 11089. https://doi.org/10.3390/ijerph182111089

Academic Editor: Paul B. Tchounwou

Received: 15 September 2021
Accepted: 12 October 2021
Published: 21 October 2021

1. Introduction

Most often defined as four or more drinks (for women) and five or more drinks (for men) in a relatively short window of time [1], heavy drinking remains a relatively common behavior among older adolescents and young adults, often tapering off after the transition to adulthood [2,3]. Close links are found in the literature between substance use and mental health symptomatology, such as depression, with some cases identifying substance use as a cause and others classifying substance use as an effect [4,5]. Heavy drinking during adolescence is associated with an array of harmful outcomes, from biological changes such as reductions in gray brain matter in the brain [6], greater risk of alcohol use disorder in adulthood [7], aggressive behavior and fighting [8,9], dating violence [10], reductions in health-related quality of life [11], other substance use [12], and socio-legal consequences (e.g., arrest) [13,14] and is thusly examined from public health and criminological contexts.

Recent research into heavy drinking behavior has elucidated nuances related to gender and race and still other statuses, often operating in tandem, that further refines our understanding of the complex interplay of social structure and lived experience. Heavy drinking occurs among all racial groups, with a general understanding that it is more common among male and White adolescents and young adults [15,16]. There is a significant body of research, however, examining gender differences in heavy drinking, finding that some statistical relationships (e.g., heavy drinking and fighting) act stronger for female respondents than males, making outcomes among female respondents worse [17,18]. Relatedly, while adolescents may be exposed to or model parental drinking behavior, parental heavy drinking may more powerfully impact young girls vs. boys in adolescence [19]. A significant and lasting relationship between victimization and substance use has been elucidated in the literature [20–23] explained using theoretical perspectives from public health and criminological disciplines, including the self-medication hypothesis, general strain theory, and the stress-process model. The effects of victimization, however, do not exist solely for those who are direct victims, such as in the case of a bullied child or adolescent. Instead, vicarious victimization, such as witnessing another person being shot or otherwise indirectly encountering victimization as a bystander, has become an increasingly powerful predictor of future substance use and depression in need of further examination [24–27].

1.1. Theoretical Frameworks

Three theoretical frameworks, the self-medication hypothesis, general strain theory, and the stress-process model, each posit overlapping elements of a stress and substance use coping relationship. Each shares a central tenet that stressful events in life can affect levels of substance use, although pathways differ among each. Rather than being seen as entirely competing perspectives on explaining heavy drinking behavior among adolescents, instead, these perspectives together help frame relevant predictors of adolescent heavy drinking, such as objective (e.g., poverty) and subjective stress/strain (e.g., victimization), mental health symptomatology, and a presence or lack of social support.

Khantzian's [28,29] self-medication hypothesis posits disruptions in affect and the ability to manage one's affect can induce a desire to reduce or eliminate such pain with substance use of a type that would diminish the experienced symptoms. If an individual were experiencing high levels of anxiety, they might then turn to depressant substances to help manage those symptoms. The self-medication hypothesis' associations with substance use have been tested in a variety of contexts in the historical literature [30–32]. Mentions of self-medication are now rarer, with some calls to retire the framework entirely in discussions of psychiatric conditions [33]. What remains trenchant from self-medication is the idea that painful affect can induce substance use, including heavy drinking [34].

Agnew's general strain theory [35–37] was developed to better explain violent delinquency, suggesting that the removal of positive stimuli, the introduction of negative stimuli, or a failure to achieve goals can each operate on a mediating negative affective state (often anger), and this negative affect can precipitate coping through criminal means such as substance use or delinquent behavior. General strain theory also confirms stressors' significance over time since stressors foster emotional or affective states (depression, anger, etc.) associated with deviance, including substance use [20,38]. For example, empirical research has found that use/misuse of alcohol can function as a coping strategy among children, adolescents, and adults exposed to stress from a variety of sources [39–41].

Pearlin's [42,43] stress-process model understands stressful events as a part of life, either acute or chronic, but often structured by race, gender, socioeconomic status, and still other forms of stratification leading to unequal distributions within and across communities. Social support, either from social networks or intimate partners, provides a critical cushion against these strains. Per the stress-process model, encountering stressors is a predictor of diminished mental health; at times, individuals respond to diminished mental health with drug use that constitutes self-medication [44].

1.2. Victimization, Depression, and Heavy Drinking

Victimization's relationship to increased risk of heavy drinking is documented in the literature [9,45,46], most often understood in the broader context of adverse childhood experiences (ACEs) and negative associations with mental health, across the lifespan, for both women and men [47–53]. Verbal, physical, and sexual abuse, as well as exposure to violence within the household, are all elements of adverse childhood experiences. While generally understood in the literature to increase the risk of engaging in heavy drinking, that victimization's effects are uniform for racial and ethnic minority groups or for women versus men cannot be taken for granted [52,53]. As a codifying example, sexual assault histories are widely reported among women, and ample research indicates these histories matter both as relevant risk factors but also avenues for heavy drinking treatment addressing underlying traumatic experiences [54,55]. Critically, coping with victimization may present further opportunities for additional or repeated victimization. Coping with the distress of an assault may lead one heavy drinking behaviors, in turn raising the risk of re-victimization [56].

Rich empirical evidence associates stressful and straining events with heavy drinking as an outcome in the short- and long-term [5,8,9,45,46,53,55,57,58]. Psychological distress, often assessed as depression, is a common predictor of heavy drinking [5,13,18,59], and the same stimuli driving levels of depression may also change the risk and protective factors for substance use behaviors [44]. Factors such as poverty and unemployment are related to heavy drinking throughout the literature, generally finding uniform effects leading toward higher levels of heavy drinking when unemployment and poverty levels are high [16,58,60]. That these periods are also associated with higher levels of depression is expected [61]. Higher levels of social support, often through an intimate partner, exert a protective effect against heavy drinking [16,55]. Protective resources may also exert differential and more powerful effects for women vs. men [62]. Previous research has also highlighted the positive effects of treatment, often brief motivational interviewing or interventions, with these efforts retaining the capacity for tailoring to specific audiences [17,18,55,63,64].

1.3. Hypotheses

The present study aimed at identifying a social mechanism that might connect childhood victimization to adulthood heavy drinking and depression using a framework including elements of the self-medication hypothesis, general strain theory, and the stress-process model. These perspectives suggest a general trajectory of higher risk of engaging in substance use, including heavy drinking, in the presence of current or former stressful events or strain, mental health symptomatology, and a lack of social support. Our prospective longitudinal design and multiple measures of respondents' heavy drinking as they aged allowed the study to track the impact of childhood victimization across a decade. The data collected in 2004, 2006, 2008, 2010, and 2015 described respondents as they reached ages anywhere from 19 to 36. That data meant we could take time into consideration as we observed what happened to effects of childhood victimization as adulthood progressed (e.g., their potential diminishment). We hypothesized (1) *direct* forms of childhood victimization, being bullied, and one *vicarious* form of childhood victimization, witnessing the shooting of a person, functioned as a mechanism linking victimization and adult heavy drinking and depression. (2) We further hypothesized depression mediates any relationship between childhood victimization and heavy drinking as is outlined in the criminological and mental health frameworks of stress-process, self-medication, and general strain. (3) Because we posited that a victim's age when victimized might be associated with differential impacts of victimization, we measured both of our childhood victimization variables twice: when respondents were preadolescents age 11 or younger and when they were 12–18. Moreover, we assigned a time factor to childhood victimization, namely, before or after age 12 (but no later than age 18). (4) We could find limited empirical evidence of gender's possible association with heavy drinking among individuals who experienced direct or vicarious victimization during preadolescence or adolescence [21,65] warranting further examination.

2. Materials and Methods

2.1. Data and Sample

The National Longitudinal Survey of Youth 1997 (NLSY97), funded by the Bureau of Labor Statistics, provided data for the present longitudinal study. The Ohio State University had begun the survey as an annual data collection, making it biennial after 2011. The survey sought to capture individuals' life experiences, notably, those involving family, crime, health, and substance abuse, over time. Its national representative sample comprised civilian, non-institutionalized people born between 1980 and 1984, who responded to items posed by an interviewer using computer-assisted personal interview (CAPI) technology, either in person or by phone. Respondents chose to be interviewed in English or in Spanish. A supplemental survey oversampling Black and Hispanic/Latino youth (born 1980–1984) was also included in the full sample of NLSY97. In 1997, the researchers interviewed 8984 persons age 12–18. Other descriptions of NLSY97 are included in previous research [41,66].

2.2. Measures

Our outcome variable, heavy drinking in the past month, was measured during 5 NLSY97 survey years between 2004 and 2015 (inclusive). We created for each respondent a longitudinal record that linked data from the 5 survey years. From each such record, we derived a number of person-waves, which provided our units of analysis; we applied the discrete-time method to analyze the data [67]. Within our final sample were 11,210 person-waves describing male respondents and 11,339 person-waves describing female respondents, for a total of 22,549 person-waves.

We measured the time-varying outcome variable, heavy drinking in the past month, for the NLSY97 survey years 2004, 2006, 2008, 2010, and 2015. Data from only these years made up the longitudinal records in our final sample, via which we measured respondent likelihood of recent heavy drinking. The measure reflected NLSY97 respondents' reports of how often (i.e., on how many days), in the 30 days preceding interview, they had consumed 5 or more drinks. A 1, indicating heavy drinking, was assigned to a respondent reporting consumption of 5 or more drinks on at least 1 day of the 30; the 0 assigned to respondents not reporting such consumption constituted the reference.

We employed 12 independent variables: gender, race/ethnicity, depression, recent stressful events, income-to-poverty ratio, education, age, marital status, parent's education, bullying victimization before age 12, bullying victimization at age 12–18, seeing the shooting of a person before age 12, and seeing the shooting of a person at age 12–18. Level of depression, income-to-poverty ratio, education, age, and marital status were treated as time-varying variables; all others were considered time-invariant. Depression was measured with a 5-item index asking how often, in the 30 days preceding survey, a respondent had felt nervous; calm or peaceful; down or blue; happy; and depressed. The index's offered responses ranged from 1 (all of the time) to 4 (none of the time); reversed coding allowed higher index scores to indicate higher levels of depression. The index's overall reliability is indicated by alpha scores ranging from 0.78–0.81 across the 5 survey years.

We used an index of 7 types of recent stressful events to describe respondents' experience over the previous 5 years of data collection in 2002, 2007, and 2013. The 7 included death of a close relative; becoming the victim of a violent crime; hospitalization of a member of one's household; incarceration of a member of one's household; a household member's becoming unemployed; one's parents divorcing; and one's family becoming homeless. Index scores ranged from 0 to 7; a relatively high number indicated the experience of relatively numerous stressful events.

Concerning education, the variable high school completion indicated possession of a high school diploma or GED, and the variable college completion indicated possession of an associate or baccalaureate degree; receipt of neither diploma nor degree provided the reference. At initial interviews conducted in 1997, NLSY97 respondents were ages 12–18. We used respondent age in 1997 to construct our variable age, which we measured in each of the 5 selected survey years. For each respondent, we recorded a continuous measure of household income-to-poverty ratio for the 12 months preceding each of the 5 interviews. For each, we measured marital status dichotomously, a 1 indicating being married, 0 otherwise.

We treated as time-invariant and measured dichotomously the variables bullying victimization before age 12, bullying victimization age 12–18, seeing the shooting of a person before age 12, and seeing the shooting of a person age 12–18. We assigned a 1 to indicate the presence of any of these forms of victimization, a 0 to indicate absence (the reference). We measured gender dichotomously, 1 indicating male, 0 female. We employed two dichotomous race/ethnicity measures, with 1 indicating a respondent self-reporting Hispanic ethnicity or non-Hispanic Black ethnicity and 0 indicating self-report of non-Hispanic White ethnicity. Parent's education was a time-invariant continuous variable stating the highest level of education attained by parents or, where mother's level differed from father's by that parent having the most formal education. Offered responses for this measure ranged from 0 (no education) to 7 (graduate or professional degree). Additionally, we employed dichotomous time factors describing each interview wave represented in our data: 2006, 2008, 2010, and 2015 (the 2004 survey year provided the reference).

2.3. Data Analysis

In light of our use of repeated measurements, we employed generalized estimating equations (GEE) to analyze the longitudinal data, estimating autocorrelations and autoregressive correlations using STATA (StataCorp, College Station, TX, USA) [68]. The analysis assessed, by gender, potential associations between the likelihood of heavy drinking and all independent variables. For the sample in its entirety, as well as for male respondents and female respondents separately, we completed a two-step multivariate analysis. For each of the three groups, Model 1 regressed heavy drinking on all independent variables except depression. We added depression to Model 1 to produce Model 2, the final multivariate model. In addition, we used the following procedure to examine gender's possible moderating role in heavy drinking's associations. First, we created a group of interaction terms between males and each of the other independent factors. Second, we ran a series of multivariate analyses that employed the entire sample and included (a) all independent variables, including the time factors and the dummy variable gender, and (b) interaction terms created between gender and each independent variable. Third, we tested for statistical significance to determine whether a given independent variable's association with heavy drinking likelihood differed for male versus female respondents, with all other independent variables controlled. If no coefficient for each of the two groups proved statistically significant, a moderating effect would not be sought.

3. Results

Concerning our heavy drinking outcome, data from 6303 respondents (3187 males, 3116 females) drove the results of the final multivariate analysis. Of the 6303, self-reported White respondents constituted 51.4%, self-reported Black respondents were 25.3%, and self-reported Hispanic respondents were 20.6%. For the sample as a whole, bullying victimization was more pervasive than the vicarious victimization of seeing a shooting: While 20.1% reported being bullied before age 12 and 15.2% reported being bullied at 12–18 years of age, just 10.5% reported seeing a shooting before age 12, and 9.7% reported seeing a shooting at between 12 and 18 years of age. Compared to females, males in our study were significantly more likely to have been subjected to bullying victimization before age 12, as well as to seeing a shooting both before age 12 and between the ages of 12 and 18.

Table 1 shows descriptive statistics for the time-varying heavy drinking outcome and independent variables. Statistics are presented both by gender and for the sample as a whole. Using chi-square and t-tests, we identified significant differences across gender groups for, respectively, the categorical and continuous variables. Across the 5 survey years, we considered, 44.4% of male respondents and 25.6% of female respondents reported consuming at least 5 drinks on at least one day in the preceding 30 days. For each independent variable except age and survey year, we observed statistically significant male–female differences.

Table 1. Descriptive statistics for time-varying heavy drinking outcome and independent variables.

	Whole Sample	Male	Female	*t*-Test	$\chi 2$
Variables	%/Mean (SD)	%/Mean (SD)	%/Mean (SD)	*p*	*p*
Heavy Drinking (0–1)	0.350	0.444	0.256		<0.01
Depression (5–20)	9.3 (2.4)	9.0 (2.3)	9.6 (2.4)	<0.01	
Stressful Events Index (0–6)	1.0 (0.9)	0.9 (0.9)	1.0 (0.9)	<0.01	
Age (19–36)	25.9 (4.0)	25.9 (4.1)	25.9 (4.0)	>0.05	
Completion of High School (0–1)	0.6150	0.6430	0.5870		<0.01
Completion of AA or Higher (0–1)	0.2940	0.2580	0.3300		<0.01
Income-to-Poverty Ratio (0–2627)	366.6 (380.0)	382.5 (390.4)	350.9 (368.7)	<0.01	
Married (0–1)	0.310	0.275	0.345	<0.01	
2004 Wave	0.195	0.193	0.197	>0.05	
2006 Wave	0.197	0.195	0.198	>0.05	
2008 Wave	0.204	0.203	0.207	>0.05	
2010 Wave	0.205	0.204	0.205	>0.05	
2015 Wave	0.200	0.201	0.198	>0.05	
n (person-waves)	22549	11210	11339		

Note: significance (*p*) of F-tests and significance of (*p*) of chi-square tests are presented on the right 2 columns.

Table 2 reflects our GEE model explaining heavy drinking likelihood for the full sample. Model 1 generated statistically significant associations between heavy drinking and seeing a shooting at 12–18 years of age. Moreover, Model 1 indicated that the likelihood of heavy drinking was higher for White respondents (versus Black or Hispanic), males, holders of an associate's or baccalaureate degree, high-income individuals, unmarried individuals, and individuals with a relatively well-educated parent(s). In turn, Model 2, which added to Model 1 the variable depression, yielded nearly identical results to Model 1. However, in Model 2, the relationship between seeing a shooting at 12–18 and heavy drinking in young adulthood did not achieve statistical significance. Nevertheless, in general, including depression did not substantially reduce the strength of the Model 1 coefficients. In this study, higher levels of depression were associated with a greater likelihood of engaging in heavy drinking in the 30 days preceding the interview. Models 1 and 2 alike exhibited significant improvement over the null model.

Table 3 presents multivariate results for male respondents and for female respondents separately. Again, our analysis included running Model 1 and then Model 2 discretely for each gender. In Model 1, male respondents were significantly less likely to report heavy drinking if they had experienced bullying before age 12, if they were Hispanic or Black if they were relatively low-income, if they reported relatively little stress, and if they were married. In Model 2, the variables that proved significant in Model 1 again proved significant, and a significant association was also found between depression and heavy drinking. In Model 2, moreover, coefficients' Model-1 strength generally persisted, as we have said, except that bullying victimization before age 12 showed a weaker significant association to heavy drinking once depression was included in the analysis.

Female respondents in our study were significantly more likely to report heavy drinking if they experienced bullying victimization before age 12; if they were White (rather than Black); if they held an associate's or baccalaureate degree (versus lacked a high school diploma); if their income was relatively high; if they were unmarried; or if they had a relatively well-educated parent(s). Model 2 indicated that for the females in our sample, reporting a relatively high level of depression was significantly associated with heavy drinking. Comparing Model 1 to Model 2, most coefficients did not exhibit substantial change; an exception was a slight change for the variable bullying victimization before 12. We obtained significant Wald chi-squares for all four of our models, signifying that the four represented significant improvements over the null models in the explanation of heavy drinking.

Table 2. Results of generalized estimating equation (GEE) explaining heavy drinking for the whole sample.

	Model 1		Model 2	
Explanatory Variables	**OR**		**OR**	
Depression			1.0756	**
Black	0.4005	**	0.4051	**
Hispanic	0.8431	**	0.8579	**
Male	2.2405	**	2.3680	**
Age	0.9967		0.9960	
High School Diploma	1.0668		1.1053	
Associate/College Degree	1.2142	*	1.2723	**
Income-to-Poverty Ratio	1.0002	**	1.0002	**
Parent's Education	1.0561	**	1.0553	**
Bully Victimization Younger Than 12	0.9796		0.9496	
Bully Victimization 12–18	1.0003		0.9657	
Seeing a Person Gunshot before 12	0.9910		0.9877	
Seeing a Person Gunshot 12–18	1.1323	*	1.1244	
Recent Stressful Events	1.0385	*	1.0300	*
Being Married	0.6441	**	0.6581	**
2006 Wave	1.0321		1.0406	
2008 Wave	0.9789		0.9719	
2010 Wave	0.8601		0.8715	
2015 Wave	0.77		0.78	
Constant	0	**	0.196771	**
Number of Person-Waves	22,549			
* $p < 0.05$; ** $p < 0.01$				

* indicates significant at the 0.05 level and ** indicates significant findings at the 0.01 level.

Table 3. Results of generalized estimated equations (GEE) explaining heavy drinking for each gender group among females versus males.

Explanatory Variables	**Male**				**Female**			
	Model 1		**Model 2**		**Model 1**		**Model 2**	
	OR		**OR**		**OR**		**OR**	
Depression			1.0742	**			1.0786	**
Black	0.4213	**	**0.4259**	**	0.3669	**	**0.3710**	**
Hispanic	0.8344	*	**0.8533**	*	0.8609		**0.8681**	
Age	1.0028		1.0033		0.9862		0.9842	
High School Diploma	1.0152		1.0378		1.1722		1.2463	
Associate/College Degree	1.1303		**1.1591**		1.3700	**	**1.4858**	**
Income-to-Poverty Ratio	1.0002	**	1.0002	**	1.0002	**	1.0002	**
Parent's Education	1.0351		1.0323		1.0864	**	1.0881	**
Bully Victimization Younger than 12	0.8762	*	**0.8517**	*	1.2000	*	**1.1604**	*
Bully Victimization 12–18	0.9896		0.9480		1.0269		1.0001	
Seeing a Person Gunshot Before 12	0.9338		0.9343		1.0698		1.0548	
Seeing a Person Gunshot 12–18	1.0829		1.0785		1.2345		1.2079	
Recent Stressful Events	1.0528	*	1.0447	*	1.0212		1.0117	
Being Married	0.7880	**	**0.8036**	**	0.5025	**	**0.5149**	**
2006 Wave	1.0316		1.0359		1.0412		1.0536	
2008 Wave	0.9273		0.9155		1.0570		1.0552	
2010 Wave	0.8049		0.8101		0.9487		0.9676	
2015 Wave	0.6967		0.6991		0.8830		0.9161	
Constant	0.8795		0.4502		0.4392		0.2054	**
Wald Chi-Square	282.26	**	342.20	**	388.25	**	437.79	**
Number of Person-Waves	11,210		11,210		11,339		11,339	
* $p < 0.05$; ** $p < 0.01$								

Note: Bold-faced, underlined figures signify significant interaction effects involving gender and the independent variable. * indicates significant at the 0.05 level and ** indicates significant findings at the 0.01 level.

Using the procedure detailed under "Data Analysis" above, we evaluated gender's moderating role in heavy drinking's associations with the included independent variables. Five significant gender differences demonstrate that gender moderated heavy drinking's associations. First, bullying victimization before age 12 reduced heavy drinking among males in our study, but it increased heavy drinking among females, according to our data analysis results. Second, Black respondents' relatively lower likelihood of heavy drinking, compared to Whites, was more pronounced among females compared to males. Third, in comparison with White respondents, we found Hispanic males to be at lower risk of heavy drinking versus White males, but heavy drinking risk for Hispanic females was about the same as that for White females. Fourth, among all females in our study, having an associate's or baccalaureate degree was associated with a relatively high likelihood of heavy drinking, to a degree surpassing the association found for males in the study. Finally, our study found heavy drinking to be much less likely among married respondents of either gender versus unmarried respondents of either gender, and this marriage–heavy drinking relationship was much more pronounced.

4. Discussion

Plainly, heavy drinking is a risky health behavior associated with many negative outcomes across the lifespan ranging from structural changes in the brain to criminal-legal interventions in adolescence and adulthood [16,45,69]. Our study examined multiple important features of heavy drinking, including its associations with powerful stressful events from childhood to adulthood and how gender modifies these statistical relationships. Findings can be interpreted as follows:

First, we acknowledge the outsized role played by victimization in patterning heavy drinking outcomes. Our study measured both direct and indirect victimization occurring in childhood and in adolescence, a total of four possible victimization measures early in the lifespan and their effects over time. This is an improvement to cross-sectional literature with more static measurements of victimization. With the control of more proximate traumatic and stressful events as indicated theoretically [37,70], the relationships among victimization and coping through heavy drinking as we hypothesized are made clearer. Our findings suggest that direct victimization in childhood is a critical predictor of later heavy drinking behavior for only female adolescents and young adults, and the same risk-generating effect was not found for our measure of vicarious or indirect victimization as expected for either gender group. Previous research outlines the role of victimization, among a tapestry of other adverse childhood experiences in generating conditions conducive to heavy drinking behavior [48,71–74] often through a pathway leading from the traumatic experience to lasting or lagged psychological distress [27,41,49,51,75]. Our findings are strongly suggestive of childhood as a major life stage in which direct victimization has powerful and lasting results for women and girls, acting on the risk of heavy drinking, even controlling for adolescent victimization and more recent stressful events. For men and boys, however, the significance was a reduction in the risk of heavy drinking. Gender socialization is a possible explanation for this difference, as young men and boys are often socialized to externalize negative effect, potentially leading to higher levels of fighting or aggressive behavior (though not in all cases) [76,77] while young women and girls may be more likely to internalize coping through substance use [78].

Second, our findings contribute to the theoretical knowledge of heavy drinking behavior. While the theoretical perspectives guiding this study have differences, a core of stressful or straining events potentially leading to coping through substance use in the absence of social support or other protective factors provides opportunities for interpretation across health and criminological disciplines. As the self-medication hypothesis suggests, substance use behavior may be a feature of coping [28], and results from our study indicated traumatic events experienced in childhood among female respondents could lead to heavy drinking. Our findings partially substantiate the most important underlying theme from the self-medication hypothesis, that stress and distress can lead to coping through substance use [29]. The second theoretical framework, general strain theory, has broadened from its original focus to encompass related behaviors such as substance use [35,70,79,80]. As expected, our findings can be partially interpreted through this trenchant criminological lens. Our results indicated that direct victimization in childhood among female respondents was associated with heavy drinking, as suggested in the general strain theory. Heavy drinking is associated with a host of criminal-legal outcomes such as arrest and aggressive behavior/fighting [8,81] making it an important avenue for future programming within the criminal and juvenile justice system and public health alike.

The final theoretical framework, the stress-process model, has a deeper understanding of the stressors and symptomology associated with negative coping [42,82,83]. Again, our findings are partially in concordance with the core of the theory; direct victimization in childhood among women and recent stressful events among male respondents are both associated with heavy drinking. Depression was also associated with heavy drinking. The stress-process model also provides a better understanding through the examination of the role of depression and psychological distress as powerful mediators of risky health behavior [84]. We found depression to increase risk uniformly for both gender groups. A similar effect also reinforces the role of depression as a mediating variable within the general strain and stress-process frameworks [42,79,85]. Social support provides a safeguard against negative effect, and heavy drinking [82,86], and marriage was found to exert a protective effect for both gender groups. Social support did demonstrate an interactive effect with gender, with female respondents seeing greater reductions in risk for being married. Taken together, our findings illustrate the relevance of public health and criminological theory in discussing risky health behaviors that may also be illegal or associated with illegal activity.

Third, the interpolation of gender alongside other social statuses enriches our understanding of the nuanced social structure elements leading to or protecting against heavy drinking as an outcome [52]. Our findings suggest that female adolescents and young adults may face a greater risk of engaging in heavy drinking than their male counterparts in cases where victimization has occurred in childhood. Importantly, the interactive effect with gender indicates the childhood victimization's effect is stronger (in generating heavy drinking risk) for female adolescents than for male adolescents for whom a decrease in risk was observed. Previous literature suggests that women's experiences with sexual assault may be leading to differences in levels of psychological distress as well as later heavy drinking behavior [54,55]. Traumatic events early in the lifespan may forge a critical link in a chain of events leading to psychological distress (e.g., depression) to adult alcohol use or other substance use [51,87]. Heavy drinking also shares a stronger link to psychological distress and depressive symptoms in general [5], and specifically in older women compared to older men [59]. Notably, two other relevant gendered differences deserve mention as both are related to the protective factors against the literature, and socioeconomic measures provided key context. Parental education and possessing an associate's or other college degree both exhibited an interactive effect with gender. Neither parental education nor possessing a college degree exerted any effect on male respondents' propensity to engage in heavy drinking, while each decreased risk for female adolescents significantly. Higher levels of women entering and graduating colleges and universities in the United States may be increasing their level of capital to protect against recent stressors that we found associated with men's heavy drinking in our study.

The picture becomes more complex when we interpolate race and gender, however. Our findings indicate that African American respondents are at significantly lower risk than their White counterparts, and Hispanic men are also at a significantly lower risk of heavy drinking. The interaction effect of race and gender is relevant, as the protective effect of race was weaker for Black males than Black females. The protective effect, however, is not found for Hispanic females, and again the results indicate an interactive effect among these two critical social status variables. The literature acknowledges African Americans generally have more risk factors for heavy drinking with lower rates of heavy drinking [62] than those who are White, but the risk is especially prominent for African American women [13]. Latino men and Latina women have also been found to have differential patterns and motivations (though psychological distress as a risk factor remains common among women) [88,89]. The literature and our results dovetail; gendered examinations of heavy drinking behavior remain relevant and are critical to engaging in meaningful prevention practices [8,52,53,87,90–92]. Future studies should make a careful study of social status modifying relationships between existing theoretical and thematic elements of heavy drinking.

Fourth, prevention efforts working at multiple levels must include modifying norms and beliefs about drinking behavior [93], including willingness and intention to engage in heavy drinking [3] and drinking contexts [14]. As well, research into emerging areas of neurobiology has led to better understandings of medical intervention models to reduce alcohol and other addictions in adulthood [94]. Heavy drinking prevention efforts in adolescents and young adults must acknowledge the social elements of drinking behavior that could be leading young adults through peer enticement or pressure to be successful [95]. The prevalence of cases in which depressive symptoms exist alongside heavy drinking points to the need for carefully constructed programming able to address the underlying traumatic experiences or other risk factors positioning these possibly endogenous outcomes [41,44]. Relatedly, trajectories for future programming require the careful inclusion of the intersection of sex, gender, sexual orientation, and gender identity, alongside but not instead of race [96–98]. Current programming may not yet be agile enough to address the specific needs of depressed women coping through heavy drinking [18]. Development of better programming remains important given these years of heavy drinking in adolescence, and early adulthood may lead to addictions in adulthood that are difficult to overcome without medical intervention [94]. Targeted prevention efforts, specifically addressing the adverse childhood experiences and other traumatic experiences leading to heavy drinking (and potentially greater negative outcomes) among women, remain a pressing need [62]. These must also meaningfully address how patterns of advantage and disadvantage structure the lives of women differently to address heightened risk among groups [13]. Previous research has demonstrated the effectiveness of brief motivational interventions or motivational interviews on drinking behavior, and these could be further refined to reach broader audiences, including adolescent and young women who are heavy drinking [17,18,63]. Another option that focuses on low-cost levels is text message or web-based programming aimed at reducing heavy drinking episodes or behaviors, which has demonstrated some effectiveness thus far in the literature for younger populations [54,99]. Promising approaches exist for treatment of heavy drinking behavior, and greater research and funding into both medical and other modalities would promote health equity in the United States and globally.

5. Conclusions

The current study extends the literature on victimization's long-term consequences, with direct victimization in childhood exerting an effect on heavy drinking later in the lifespan among female respondents and recent stressful events associated with heavy drinking among male respondents. The results suggest that gender remains an important variable to examine in analyses of substance use and victimization-related sequelae. Specific differences among gender groups in our findings suggest early childhood adverse experiences are powerful predictors of later heavy drinking for girls and women, while they are also more protected by their own education and parental education against heavy drinking. This suggests an educational pipeline generating capital for women, but not men, in a way that protects them from heavy drinking. Race, socioeconomic status, and other important statuses, alongside gender, may play substantial roles in structuring heavy drinking outcomes; these should be investigated thoroughly in order to promote health equity among Americans. Our study demonstrated several strengths, primarily related to the multiple measures of victimization, occurring at different points in the lifespan, and these effects across time. We were further able to draw from both public health and criminology theory to better explain the roles of victimization, depression, and heavy drinking behavior and how it differs for male and female gender groups. We also unearthed several gender-specific differences in the risk and protective factors associated with heavy drinking, which can enrich the already-deployed programming, helping make it more relevant to community audiences.

Our study had a few limitations to note. First, our measures of victimization, both direct and indirect, are imperfect. Victimization, particularly vicarious or indirect victimization, is not a well-studied concept empirically, and large, nationally representative surveys have only a few indicators for use. The inclusion of additional indicators in these large surveys would help better elucidate these further. Next, while longitudinal, limitations in the data collection did not allow us a perfect year-for-year measurement of each indicator. While the gaps in collection years are small, additional years of data may paint a clearer picture of the link between victimization in childhood and later heavy drinking. Next, a host of negative affective states are relevant to discussions of criminal coping, including substance use. While depression has demonstrated some support, other affective states such as anxiety or anger may also be leading to heavy drinking behavior and are in need of substantial investigation to better plan successful programming that will reach broad audiences and reduce the harm of heavy drinking.

Author Contributions: Conceptualization, C.C.L., W.A.-H., H.M.G. and T.C.C.; methodology, C.C.L.; validation, T.C.C., W.A.-H. and H.M.G.; formal analysis, C.C.L. and W.A.-H.; writing—original draft preparation, C.C.L. and W.A.-H.; writing—review and editing, T.C.C. and H.M.G. All authors have read and agreed to the published version of the manuscript.

Funding: This research received no external funding.

Institutional Review Board Statement: The study was conducted according to the guidelines of the Declaration of Helsinki and declared as not human subjects research and approval not needed by the Institutional Review Board of Prairie View A&M University (protocol code 2021-071; 27 August 2021).

Informed Consent Statement: Not applicable.

Data Availability Statement: Data from this study are publicly available and accessible through the United States Bureau of Labor Statistics. https://www.bls.gov/nls/nlsy97.htm (accessed on 11 October 2021).

Conflicts of Interest: The authors declare no conflict of interest.

References

1. NIAAA. NIAAA Council Approves Definition of Binge Drinking. 2004. Available online: https://pubs.niaaa.nih.gov/publications/Newsletter/winter2004/Newsletter_Number3.pdf (accessed on 11 October 2021).
2. Windle, M.; Mun, E.Y.; Windle, R.C. Adolescent-to-young adulthood heavy drinking trajectories and their prospective predictors. *J. Stud. Alcohol* **2005**, *66*, 313–322. [CrossRef]
3. Stevens, A.K.; Boyle, H.K.; Miller, M.B.; Carey, K.; Jackson, K.M.; Barnett, N.P.; Merrill, J.E. A qualitative examination of intentions and willingness for heavy drinking among young adult high-intensity drinkers. *Psychol. Addict. Behav.* **2021**. [CrossRef]
4. Cheng, T.; Lo, C. Risk and Protective Factors in Adult-Onset Drinking: Application of the Multiple Disadvantage Model. *Int. J. Heal. Wellness, Soc.* **2018**, *8*, 29–41. [CrossRef]
5. Acuff, S.F.; Soltis, K.E.; Luciano, M.T.; Meshesha, L.Z.; Pedrelli, P.; Dennhardt, A.A.; Murphy, J.G. Depressive symptoms as predictors of alcohol problem domains and reinforcement among heavy drinking college students. *Psychol. Addict. Behav.* **2018**, *32*, 792–799. [CrossRef]
6. Seo, S.; Beck, A.; Matthis, C.; Genauck, A.; Banaschewski, T.; Bokde, A.L.; Bromberg, U.; Buchel, C.; Quinlan, E.B.; Flor, H.; et al. Risk profiles for heavy drinking in adolescence: Differential effects of gender. *Addict. Biol.* **2018**, *24*, 787–801. [CrossRef]
7. Cheng, T.C.; Lo, C.C. Change in Adolescents' Alcohol-Use Patterns, from Non-Drinking to Non-Heavy Drinking or Heavy Drinking. *J. Drug Issues* **2015**, *45*, 447–459. [CrossRef]
8. Wells, S.; Speechley, M.; Koval, J.J.; Graham, K. Gender Differences in the Relationship between Heavy Episodic Drinking, Social Roles, and Alcohol-Related Aggression in a U.S. Sample of Late Adolescent and Young Adult Drinkers. *Am. J. Drug Alcohol Abus.* **2007**, *33*, 21–29. [CrossRef] [PubMed]
9. Smith, K.Z.; Smith, P.H.; Oberleitner, L.M.; Grekin, E.R.; McKee, S.A. Child Maltreatment and Physical Victimization: Does Heavy Drinking Mediate the Relationship? *Child Maltreatment* **2018**, *23*, 234–243. [CrossRef] [PubMed]

10. Stappenbeck, C.A.; Fromme, K. A longitudinal investigation of heavy drinking and physical dating violence in men and women. *Addict. Behav.* **2010**, *35*, 479–485. [CrossRef] [PubMed]
11. Monahan, C.J.; Bracken-Minor, K.L.; McCausland, C.M.; McDevitt-Murphy, M.E.; Murphy, J.G. Health-Related Quality of Life among Heavy-drinking College Students. *Am. J. Health Behav.* **2012**, *36*, 289–299. [CrossRef] [PubMed]
12. Littlefield, A.K.; Gottlieb, J.C.; Cohen, L.M.; Trotter, D.R.M. Electronic Cigarette Use among College Students: Links to Gender, Race/Ethnicity, Smoking, and Heavy Drinking. *J. Am. Coll. Health* **2015**, *63*, 523–529. [CrossRef] [PubMed]
13. Witbrodt, J.; Mulia, N.; Zemore, S.E.; Kerr, W.C. Racial/Ethnic Disparities in Alcohol-Related Problems: Differences by Gender and Level of Heavy Drinking. *Alcohol. Clin. Exp. Res.* **2014**, *38*, 1662–1670. [CrossRef] [PubMed]
14. Stanesby, O.; Labhart, F.; Dietze, P.; Wright, C.J.C.; Kuntsche, E. The contexts of heavy drinking: A systematic review of the combinations of context-related factors associated with heavy drinking occasions. *PLoS ONE* **2019**, *14*, e0218465. [CrossRef] [PubMed]
15. LaBrie, J.W.; Lac, A.; Kenney, S.R.; Mirza, T. Protective behavioral strategies mediate the effect of drinking motives on alcohol use among heavy drinking college students: Gender and race differences. *Addict. Behav.* **2011**, *36*, 354–361. [CrossRef]
16. Karlamangla, A.; Zhou, K.; Reuben, D.; Greendale, G.; Moore, A. Longitudinal trajectories of heavy drinking in adults in the United States of America. *Addiction* **2005**, *101*, 91–99. [CrossRef]
17. Polcin, D.L.; Nayak, M.B.; Korcha, R.; Pugh, S.; Witbrodt, J.; Salinardi, M.; Galloway, G.; Nelson, E. Heavy Drinking among Women Receiving Intensive Motivational Interviewing: 6-Month Outcomes. *J. Psychoact. Drugs* **2019**, *51*, 421–430. [CrossRef]
18. Merrill, J.E.; Reid, A.E.; Carey, M.P.; Carey, K.B. Gender and depression moderate response to brief motivational intervention for alcohol misuse among college students. *J. Consult. Clin. Psychol.* **2014**, *82*, 984–992. [CrossRef]
19. Homel, J.; Warren, D. The Relationship between Parent Drinking and Adolescent Drinking: Differences for Mothers and Fathers and Boys and Girls. *Subst. Use Misuse* **2019**, *54*, 661–669. [CrossRef]
20. Lo, C.C.; Kim, Y.S.; Ii, W.T.C. The Effects of Victimization on Drug Use: A Multilevel Analysis. *Subst. Use Misuse* **2008**, *43*, 1340–1361. [CrossRef]
21. Kritsotakis, G.; Papanikolaou, M.; Androulakis, E.; Philalithis, A.E. Associations of Bullying and Cyberbullying with Substance Use and Sexual Risk Taking in Young Adults. *J. Nurs. Scholarsh.* **2017**, *49*, 360–370. [CrossRef] [PubMed]
22. Maniglio, R. Bullying and Other Forms of Peer Victimization in Adolescence and Alcohol Use. *Trauma Violence Abus.* **2016**, *18*, 457–473. [CrossRef]
23. Priesman, E.; Newman, R.; Ford, J.A. Bullying Victimization, Binge Drinking, and Marijuana Use among Adolescents: Results from the 2013 National Youth Risk Behavior Survey. *J. Psychoact. Drugs* **2017**, *50*, 133–142. [CrossRef]
24. Baron, S.W. Street youths' violent responses to violent personal, vicarious, and anticipated strain. *J. Crim. Justice* **2009**, *37*, 442–451. [CrossRef]
25. Lee, Y.; Kim, J. Examining the Gendered Effect of Experienced and Vicarious Victimization: A General Strain Theory Perspective. *Am. J. Crim. Justice* **2017**, *43*, 181–196. [CrossRef]
26. Vogel, M.; Keith, S. Vicarious Peer Victimization and Adolescent Violence: Unpacking the Effects of Social Learning, General Strain, and Peer Group Selection. *Deviant Behav.* **2015**, *36*, 834–852. [CrossRef]
27. Lo, C.C.; Gerling, H.M.; Ash-Houchen, W.; Cheng, T.C. Violent Victimization, Stressful Events, and Depression: A Longitudinal Study of Young Adults in the U.S. *Community Ment. Health J.* **2020**, *57*, 502–511. [CrossRef]
28. Khantzian, E.J. The self-medication hypothesis of addictive disorders: Focus on Heroin and cocaine dependence. *Am. J. Psychiatry* **1985**, *142*, 1259–1264. [PubMed]
29. Khantzian, E.J. The self-medication hypothesis of substance use disorders: A reconsideration and recent applications. *Harv. Rev. Psychiatry* **1997**, *4*, 231–244. [CrossRef]
30. Harris, K.M.; Edlund, M.J. Self-Medication of Mental Health Problems: New Evidence from a National Survey. *Health Serv. Res.* **2005**, *40*, 117–134. [CrossRef]
31. Tronnier, C.D. Harnessing Attachment in Addiction Treatment: Regulation Theory and the Self-Medication Hypothesis. *J. Soc. Work Pract. Addict.* **2015**, *15*, 233–251. [CrossRef]
32. Wilkinson, A.L.; Halpern, C.T.; Herring, A.H.; Shanahan, M.; Ennett, S.T.; Hussey, J.M.; Harris, K.M. Testing Longitudinal Relationships Between Binge Drinking, Marijuana Use, and Depressive Symptoms and Moderation by Sex. *J. Adolesc. Health* **2016**, *59*, 681–687. [CrossRef]
33. Lembke, A. Time to Abandon the Self-Medication Hypothesis in Patients with Psychiatric Disorders. *Am. J. Drug Alcohol Abus.* **2012**, *38*, 524–529. [CrossRef] [PubMed]
34. Bachrach, R.L.; Read, J.P. Peer alcohol behavior moderates within-level associations between posttraumatic stress disorder symptoms and alcohol use in college students. *Psychol. Addict. Behav.* **2017**, *31*, 576–588. [CrossRef]
35. Agnew, R. Building on the Foundation of General Strain Theory: Specifying the Types of Strain Most Likely to Lead to Crime and Delinquency. *J. Res. Crime Delinquency* **2001**, *38*, 319–361. [CrossRef]
36. Agnew, R. Foundation for a General Strain Theory of Crime and Delinquency. *Criminology* **1992**, *30*, 47–88. [CrossRef]
37. Agnew, R. Experienced, vicarious, and anticipated strain: An exploratory study on physical victimization and delinquency. *Justice Q.* **2002**, *19*, 603–632. [CrossRef]
38. Lo, C.C.; Cheng, T.C.; Bohm, M.; Zhong, H. Rural-to-Urban Migration, Strain, and Juvenile Delinquency: A Study of Eighth-Grade Students in Guangzhou, China. *Int. J. Offender Ther. Comp. Criminol.* **2018**, *62*, 334–359. [CrossRef]

39. Yilmaz, M.; Lo, C.C.; Solakoğlu, Ö. Cigarette Use by Turkish Adolescents and Its Links to Strain, Depression, and Anger. *J. Drug Issues* **2015**, *45*, 396–408. [CrossRef]
40. Lo, C.C.; Cheng, T.C. The Impact of Childhood Maltreatment on Young Adults' Substance Abuse. *Am. J. Drug Alcohol Abus.* **2007**, *33*, 139–146. [CrossRef]
41. Ash-Houchen, W.; Lo, C.C. Racial/Ethnic Differences in Illicit Substance Use: A Temporal-Ordered Test of General Strain Theory. *J. Drug Issues* **2020**, *50*, 209–230. [CrossRef]
42. Pearlin, L.I. The sociological-study of stress. *J. Health Soc. Behav.* **1989**, *30*, 241–256. [CrossRef] [PubMed]
43. Pearlin, L.I.; Menaghan, E.G.; Lieberman, M.A.; Mullan, J.T. The Stress Process. *J. Health Soc. Behav.* **1981**, *22*, 337–356. [CrossRef] [PubMed]
44. Lo, C.C.; Cheng, T.C.; De La Rosa, I.A. Depression and Substance Use: A Temporal-Ordered Model. *Subst. Use Misuse* **2015**, *50*, 1274–1283. [CrossRef] [PubMed]
45. King, K.A.; Vidourek, R.A.; Merianos, A.L. School Violent Victimization and Recent Alcohol Use and Episodic Heavy Drinking among Youth. *J. Sch. Nurs.* **2014**, *30*, 187–195. [CrossRef] [PubMed]
46. Lee, C.; Cronley, C.; White, H.R.; Mun, E.-Y.; Stouthamer-Loeber, M.; Loeber, R. Racial Differences in the Consequences of Childhood Maltreatment for Adolescent and Young Adult Depression, Heavy Drinking, and Violence. *J. Adolesc. Health* **2012**, *50*, 443–449. [CrossRef]
47. King, S.M.; Burt, S.A.; Malone, S.M.; McGue, M.; Iacono, W.G. Etiological Contributions to Heavy Drinking from Late Adolescence to Young Adulthood. *J. Abnorm. Psychol.* **2005**, *114*, 587–598. [CrossRef]
48. Marks, L.R.; Acuff, S.F.; Withers, A.J.; MacKillop, J.; Murphy, J.G. Adverse childhood experiences, racial microaggressions, and alcohol misuse in Black and White emerging adults. *Psychol. Addict. Behav.* **2021**, *35*, 274–282. [CrossRef]
49. Merrick, M.T.; Ports, K.A.; Ford, D.C.; Afifi, T.O.; Gershoff, E.T.; Grogan-Kaylor, A. Unpacking the impact of adverse childhood experiences on adult mental health. *Child Abus. Negl.* **2017**, *69*, 10–19. [CrossRef]
50. Kisely, S.; Mills, R.; Strathearn, L.; Najman, J.M. Does child maltreatment predict alcohol use disorders in young adulthood? A cohort study of linked notifications and survey data. *Addiction* **2019**, *115*, 61–68. [CrossRef]
51. Thompson, M.P.; Kingree, J.B.; Lamis, D. Associations of adverse childhood experiences and suicidal behaviors in adulthood in a U.S. nationally representative sample. *Child Care Health Dev.* **2018**, *45*, 121–128. [CrossRef]
52. Forster, M.; Rogers, C.J.; Benjamin, S.M.; Grigsby, T.; Lust, K.; Eisenberg, M.E. Adverse Childhood Experiences, Ethnicity, and Substance Use among College Students: Findings from a Two-State Sample. *Subst. Use Misuse* **2019**, *54*, 2368–2379. [CrossRef]
53. Levine, E.C.; Martinez, O.; Mattera, B.; Wu, E.; Arreola, S.; Rutledge, S.; Newman, B.; Icard, L.; Muñoz-Laboy, M.; Hausmann-Stabile, C.; et al. Child Sexual Abuse and Adult Mental Health, Sexual Risk Behaviors, and Drinking Patterns among Latino Men Who Have Sex with Men. *J. Child Sex. Abus.* **2017**, *27*, 237–253. [CrossRef] [PubMed]
54. Stappenbeck, C.A.; Gulati, N.K.; Jaffe, A.E.; Blayney, J.A.; Kaysen, D. Initial efficacy of a web-based alcohol and emotion regulation intervention for college women with sexual assault histories. *Psychol. Addict. Behav.* **2021**. [CrossRef] [PubMed]
55. Stappenbeck, C.A.; Hassija, C.M.; Zimmerman, L.; Kaysen, D. Sexual assault related distress and drinking: The influence of daily reports of social support and coping control. *Addict. Behav.* **2014**, *42*, 108–113. [CrossRef] [PubMed]
56. Testa, M.; Hoffman, J.H.; Livingston, J.A. Alcohol and sexual risk behaviors as mediators of the sexual victimization–revictimization relationship. *J. Consult. Clin. Psychol.* **2010**, *78*, 249–259. [CrossRef]
57. Schwartz, S.J.; Unger, J.B.; Rosiers, S.E.D.; Lorenzo-Blanco, E.I.; Zamboanga, B.L.; Huang, S.; Baezconde-Garbanati, L.; Villamar, J.A.; Soto, D.W.; Pattarroyo, M.; et al. Domains of Acculturation and Their Effects on Substance Use and Sexual Behavior in Recent Hispanic Immigrant Adolescents. *Prev. Sci.* **2013**, *15*, 385–396. [CrossRef] [PubMed]
58. Mossakowski, K.N. Is the duration of poverty and unemployment a risk factor for heavy drinking? *Soc. Sci. Med.* **2008**, *67*, 947–955. [CrossRef]
59. Choi, N.G.; DiNitto, D.M. Psychological Distress, Binge/Heavy Drinking, and Gender Differences among Older Adults. *Am. J. Addict.* **2011**, *20*, 420–428. [CrossRef]
60. Lo, C.C.; Cheng, T.C. Heavy drinking during periods of high unemployment: 15-Year trend study of the role of race/ethnicity. *Drug Alcohol Depend.* **2013**, *133*, 383–390. [CrossRef]
61. Mossakowski, K.N. The Influence of Past Unemployment Duration on Symptoms of Depression among Young Women and Men in the United States. *Am. J. Public Health* **2009**, *99*, 1826–1832. [CrossRef]
62. Mulia, N.; Ye, Y.; Karriker-Jaffe, K.J.; Zemore, S.E.; Jones-Webb, R. Protective factors as an explanation for the 'paradox' of Black–White differences in heavy drinking. *Subst. Use Misuse* **2018**, *53*, 2003–2016. [CrossRef]
63. Magill, M.; Colby, S.M.; Orchowski, L.; Murphy, J.G.; Hoadley, A.; Brazil, L.A.; Barnett, N.P. How does brief motivational intervention change heavy drinking and harm among underage young adult drinkers? *J. Consult. Clin. Psychol.* **2017**, *85*, 447–458. [CrossRef]
64. Acuff, S.F.; Voss, A.T.; Dennhardt, A.A.; Borsari, B.; Martens, M.P.; Murphy, J.G. Brief Motivational Interventions Are Associated with Reductions in Alcohol-Induced Blackouts among Heavy Drinking College Students. *Alcohol. Clin. Exp. Res.* **2019**, *43*, 988–996. [CrossRef]
65. Nayak, M.B.; Lown, E.A.; Bond, J.C.; Greenfield, T.K. Lifetime victimization and past year alcohol use in a U.S. population sample of men and women drinkers. *Drug Alcohol Depend.* **2012**, *123*, 213–219. [CrossRef] [PubMed]

66. National Longitudinal Survey of Youth 1997 Cohort, 1997–2013 (rounds 3–13). 2015. Available online: https://www.norc.org/NewsEventsPublications/Pages/published-research.aspx?#Default=%7B%22k%22%3A%22%22%2C%22r%22%3A%5B%7B%22n%22%3A%22NORCProjectTags%22%2C%22t%22%3A%5B%22%5C%22%C7%82%C7%824e6174696f6e616c204c6f6e6769747564696e616c20537572766579206f6620596f757468202d2031393937%5C%22%22%5D%2C%22o%22%3A%22OR%22%2C%22k%22%3Afalse%2C%22m%22%3A%7B%22%5C%22%C7%82%C7%824e6174696f6e616c204c6f6e6769747564696e616c20537572766579206f6620596f757468202d2031393937%5C%22%22%3A%22National%20Longitudinal%20Survey%20of%20Youth%20-%201997%22%7D%7D%5D%7D (accessed on 11 October 2021).
67. Singer, J.D.; Willett, J.B. *Applied Longitudinal Data Analysis: Modeling Change and Event Occurrence*; Oxford University Press: Oxford, UK, 2003.
68. Hilbe, J.M.; Hardin, J.; Hardin, H. *Generalized Estimating Equations*; CRC Press: Boca Raton, FL, USA, 2003.
69. Evans-Polce, R.J.; Vasilenko, S.A.; Lanza, S.T. Changes in gender and racial/ethnic disparities in rates of cigarette use, regular heavy episodic drinking, and marijuana use: Ages 14 to 32. *Addict. Behav.* **2014**, *41*, 218–222. [CrossRef] [PubMed]
70. Akins, S.; Smith, C.L.; Mosher, C. Pathways to Adult Alcohol Abuse across Racial/Ethnic Groups: An Application of General Strain and Social Learning Theories. *J. Drug Issues* **2010**, *40*, 321–351. [CrossRef]
71. Crouch, E.; Radcliff, E.; Strompolis, M.; Wilson, A. Adverse Childhood Experiences (ACEs) and Alcohol Abuse among South Carolina Adults. *Subst. Use Misuse* **2017**, *53*, 1212–1220. [CrossRef]
72. Dube, S.R.; Anda, R.F.; Felitti, V.J.; Edwards, V.J.; Croft, J.B. Adverse childhood experiences and personal alcohol abuse as an adult. *Addict. Behav.* **2002**, *27*, 713–725. [CrossRef]
73. Fang, L.; McNeil, S. Is there a relationship between adverse childhood experiences and problem drinking behaviors? Findings from a population-based sample. *Public Health* **2017**, *150*, 34–42. [CrossRef]
74. Lee, R.D.; Chen, J. Adverse childhood experiences, mental health, and excessive alcohol use: Examination of race/ethnicity and sex differences. *Child Abus. Negl.* **2017**, *69*, 40–48. [CrossRef] [PubMed]
75. Lo, C.C.; Ash-Houchen, W.; Gerling, H.M.; Cheng, T.C. From Childhood Victim to Adult Criminal: Racial/Ethnic Differences in Patterns of Victimization–Offending among Americans in Early Adulthood. *Vict. Offenders* **2020**, *15*, 430–456. [CrossRef]
76. Galligan, S.B.; Barnett, R.V.; Brennan, M.A.; Israel, G.D. The Effects of Gender Role Conflict on Adolescent and Emerging Adult Male Resiliency. *J. Men's Stud.* **2010**, *18*, 3–21. [CrossRef]
77. O'Neal, C.R.; Weston, L.C.; He, X.; Huang, K.-Y.; Pine, D.S.; Kamboukos, D.; Brotman, L.M. Change in depression across adolescence: The role of early anger socialization and child anger. *J. Adolesc.* **2017**, *59*, 1–7. [CrossRef]
78. Achenbach, T.M. *Integrative Guide for the 1991 CBCL/4-18, YSR, and TRF Profiles*; Department of Psychiatry, University of Vermont: Burlington, VT, USA, 1991.
79. Agnew, R. When Criminal Coping is Likely: An Extension of General Strain Theory. *Deviant Behav.* **2013**, *34*, 653–670. [CrossRef]
80. Agnew, R.; White, H.R. An empirical test of general strain theory. *Criminology* **1992**, *30*, 475–500. [CrossRef]
81. Jun, H.-J.; Sacco, P.; Bright, C.; Cunningham-Williams, R.M. Gender Differences in the Relationship between Depression, Antisocial Behavior, Alcohol Use, and Gambling during Emerging Adulthood. *Int. J. Ment. Health Addict.* **2019**, *17*, 1328–1339. [CrossRef]
82. Pearlin, L.I.; Johnson, J.S. Marital Status, Life-Strains and Depression. *Am. Sociol. Rev.* **1977**, *42*, 704–715. [CrossRef] [PubMed]
83. Pearlin, L.I.; Schooler, C. The Structure of Coping. *J. Health Soc. Behav.* **1978**, *19*, 2–21. [CrossRef] [PubMed]
84. Pearlin, L.I.; Schieman, S.; Elena, M.F.; Stephen, C.M. Stress, Health, and the Life Course: Some Conceptual Perspectives. *J. Health Soc. Behav.* **2005**, *46*, 205–219. [CrossRef] [PubMed]
85. Aneshensel, C.S.; Avison, W.R. The Stress Process. *Soc. Ment. Health* **2015**, *5*, 67–85. [CrossRef]
86. Delucchi, K.L.; Kaskutas, L.A. Following Problem Drinkers over Eleven Years: Understanding Changes in Alcohol Consumption. *J. Stud. Alcohol Drugs* **2010**, *71*, 831–836. [CrossRef] [PubMed]
87. Karriker-Jaffe, K.J.; Witbrodt, J.; Mulia, N. Differential Consequences: Racial/Ethnic and Gender Differences in the Enduring Impact of Early Disadvantage on Heavy Drinking in Midlife. *Prev. Sci.* **2019**, *20*, 1009–1020. [CrossRef] [PubMed]
88. Lee, C.S.; Castro, F.G.; Nicholls, M.E.; O'Connor, B.; Marosi, S.; Colby, S.M. Gender differences in drinking behavior among Latino/a heavy drinkers. *Int. J. Drug Policy* **2018**, *64*, 79–86. [CrossRef] [PubMed]
89. Niño, M.D.; Cai, T.; Mota-Back, X.; Comeau, J. Gender differences in trajectories of alcohol use from ages 13 to 33 across Latina/o ethnic groups. *Drug Alcohol Depend.* **2017**, *180*, 113–120. [CrossRef]
90. Chen, P.; Jacobson, K.C. Developmental Trajectories of Substance Use From Early Adolescence to Young Adulthood: Gender and Racial/Ethnic Differences. *J. Adolesc. Health* **2012**, *50*, 154–163. [CrossRef] [PubMed]
91. Maag, J.W.; Irvin, D.M. Alcohol use and depression among African-American and Caucasian adolescents. *Adolescence* **2005**, *40*, 87–101.
92. Thrul, J.; Labhart, F.; Kuntsche, E. Drinking with mixed-gender groups is associated with heavy weekend drinking among young adults. *Addiction* **2017**, *112*, 432–439. [CrossRef]
93. Colby, S.M.; Swanton, D.N.; Colby, J.J. College Students' Evaluations of Heavy Drinking: The Influence of Gender, Age, and College Status. *J. Coll. Stud. Dev.* **2012**, *53*, 797–810. [CrossRef]
94. Gutman, S.A. Why Addiction Has a Chronic, Relapsing Course. The Neurobiology of Addiction. *Occup. Ther. Ment. Health* **2006**, *22*, 1–29. [CrossRef]

95. Skidmore, J.R.; Murphy, J.G. Relations between heavy drinking, gender, and substance-free reinforcement. *Exp. Clin. Psychopharmacol.* **2010**, *18*, 158–166. [CrossRef]
96. Peralta, R.L.; L. Mulhollem, M.; Blue, C.; Stewart, B.C. The Association between Heavy Episodic Drinking and Gender Orientation among U.S. College Students: The Significance of Masculinity. *Subst. Use Misuse* **2018**, *53*, 910–920. [CrossRef]
97. Veldhuis, C.B.; Hughes, T.L.; Drabble, L.A.; Wilsnack, S.C.; Matthews, A.K. Do relationships provide the same levels of protection against heavy drinking for lesbian and bisexual women? An intersectional approach. *Psychol. Sex. Orientat. Gend. Divers.* **2020**, *7*, 337–352. [CrossRef] [PubMed]
98. Törrönen, J.; Samuelsson, E.; Roumeliotis, F. Health, risk-taking and well-being: Doing gender in relation to discourses and practices of heavy drinking and health among young people. *Health Risk Soc.* **2020**, *22*, 305–323. [CrossRef]
99. Chavez, K.; Palfai, T.P. Reducing Heavy Episodic Drinking among College Students Using a Combined Web and Interactive Text Messaging Intervention. *Alcohol. Treat. Q.* **2021**, *39*, 82–95. [CrossRef]

International Journal of
Environmental Research and Public Health

Article

Support for Health Insurance Coverage for Legal Abortion in the United States

Charley Henderson and Philip Q. Yang *

Sociology Program, Texas Woman's University, Denton, TX 76204, USA; chenderson15@twu.edu
* Correspondence: pyang@twu.edu

Abstract: The use of health insurance to cover legal abortion is a controversial issue on which Americans are sharply divided. Currently, there is a lack of research on this issue as data became available only recently. Using data from the newly released General Social Survey in 2018, this study examines who is more or less likely to support health insurance coverage for legal abortion. The results show that the support and opposition were about evenly divided. The findings from the logistic regression analysis reveal that, holding other variables constant, Democrats, liberals, urban residents, the more educated, and the older were more likely to support health insurance coverage for legal abortion while women, Southerners, Christians, the currently married, and those with more children were less likely to favor it, compared to their respective counterparts. Additionally, the effect of education was stronger for liberals than for non-liberals. Race, family income, and full-time work status make no difference in the outcome. The findings have significant implications for research and practices in health insurance coverage for legal abortion.

Keywords: health insurance coverage; legal abortion; the United States; General Social Survey

Citation: Henderson, C.; Yang, P.Q. Support for Health Insurance Coverage for Legal Abortion in the United States. *Int. J. Environ. Res. Public Health* **2022**, *18*, 433. https://doi.org/10.3390/ijerph19010433

Academic Editor: Paul B. Tchounwou

Received: 10 November 2021
Accepted: 29 December 2021
Published: 31 December 2021

1. Introduction

The debate about restriction to legal abortion access is again taking a center stage in the United States. Germane to this debate, whether it is apropos to use health insurance to cover legal abortion is also a controversial issue facing American society today. Currently, there is little quantitative research on this issue to inform policy and practices because of a lack of data. It is important to understand where the American public stands on this issue, so we know what should be done next. It is also crucial to fathom who is more or less likely to support the use of health insurance for legal abortion so all sides of the debate know who to ally with, who to win over, and who to fight with in order to enact appropriate legislation and bring about social change.

One of the dilemmas women tend to encounter is the decision to have or not to have an abortion. Despite many social advances in feminism, abortion reforms and discussions are labelled as highly controversial in many parts of the United States [1]. Women's rights have been rallied for decades, yet the idea for a woman to receive an abortion remains stigmatized and hushed. As a society, we have constructed women's motherhood role, and it has become almost expected [2]. On the other hand, the right to abortion is also socially constructed. A denial of either the social construction of motherhood or the social construction of the right to abortion is overly simplistic and neglects the dual character of human nature. Currently, most research tends to focus on the policy of abortion, moral rights, and the mental health of women receiving an abortion, but not much about health insurance coverage for an abortion [1,3–5].

However, some state policies allow for abortion [1,3], but heavily regulate the procedure; thus, a new question concerning if women seeking a legal abortion should be able to use health insurance has arisen in recent years. In this paper, we focus on the research question of who is more or less likely to support using health insurance for legal abortion.

We address this question using the latest data from General Social Survey (GSS) collected in 2018. In the remainder of this paper, we review the historical background and current status of abortion and funding, propose hypotheses for testing, depict our data and methods, and present and discuss our findings.

1.1. Historical Background and Current Status

To understand the significance of legalizing abortion, one must first understand the history of abortion in the United States. The topic of abortion has had a long-disputed history in the U.S., which has witnessed the development of many of the policies in today's society.

Planned Parenthood provides a list of procedures and expectations for performing an abortion in their clinics [6]. The procedure itself only takes around five to ten minutes, and they provide onsite counseling, examination, and medication to ease any pain during and after the procedure [6]. Currently, the United States consistently allows an abortion before twenty weeks, but with extenuating circumstance a late term abortion is permissible when the fetus is nearly fully developed [6]. The first step consists of an ultrasound to confirm that the woman is within the legal time frame to receive an abortion.

Once the ultrasound is completed, the health care provider will provide information to determine which form of abortion will be performed. The most common is the suction abortion [6]. The health professional will administer an over-the-counter pain medication to help with cramping, a sedation to keep the woman relaxed, and an antibiotic to help in preventing an infection [6]. Next, after numbing and widening the cervix, a small tube is inserted with a hand-held suction machine to remove any pregnancy tissue.

However, the organization also states they perform a dilation and evacuation procedure, which is the method typically used after sixteen weeks. This form of abortion usually takes a couple of days versus just the five-to-ten-minute procedure. To open the cervix for the procedure, the health care professional will insert a laminaria to help absorb the fluid from the body, and widen the cervix [6]. Just like in the suction procedure, the woman is issued over-the-counter pain medications for cramping, a sedative, and antibiotics to prevent infection [6]. From here, the same steps are taken as the suction abortion.

These are the currently allowed procedures in most of the United States. However, the question is: how did we as a society get our opinions in which most hold today about abortion? The first recorded abortion occurred in colonial America, and was a practiced, legal procedure [7]. According to Dine [7]), the procedure was common enough that it was added through legal and medical records. In fact, abortion helped boom early pharmaceutical companies for drugs to help induce abortion [8,9]. Newspapers raved about abortion medication, mailed flyers were used, and it was even advertised that if the home remedy did not work, a practitioner would be able to perform "instrumental procedures" [8,9]. At the time, the only attempt to govern the abortion was to reduce the poisoning side effects from the home medications [8,9].

However, the politicization of abortion began in the late 1800s [8,9]. When the term "quickening" (i.e., feeling the fetus moving) became widely used, then the medical establishments urged the banning of abortion unless deemed necessary to save a woman's life [8,9]. By the early 1900s, abortion had been related to female independence, threatening male dominance [7]. One of the biggest pushes for the illegalization of abortion and the abortion drugs was led by OB-GYN Dr. Horatio Storer [8,9]. Many believe his opposing rally against abortion was centered around females aspiring to become doctors at Harvard Medical School where he devoted much of his medical practice [9]. He virtually succeeded criminalizing abortion and abortion drugs in the majority of the United States. Other opponents to abortion included female physicians such as Elizabeth Blackwell and Charlotte Loziėr, who both believed abortions were sinful and dangerous [10]. It is also worth mentioning that many of the early leaders of the U.S. women's suffrage movement (e.g., Susan B. Anthony, Elizabeth Cady Stanton, Victoria Woodhull, Elizabeth Blackwell) deemed abortion as "infanticide" [10]. They believed that the rights of mother and child are intricately tied and that the right to life and the right to vote are rooted in the inherent dignity of each human person. However, they were skeptical about the criminalization of abortion [10].

Despite the illegalization of abortion, many continued to have underground, dangerous, life-threatening procedures [7–9]. One of the physicians performing abortions behind closed doors stated that the majority of those receiving an abortion were middle to upper class, Protestant, married women [8,9]. However, it was not until the 1973 Supreme Court Case *Roe* vs. *Wade* that abortion once again became legal in the United States [7–9]. Nevertheless, in 1977, the Hyde Amendment prohibited the use of federal funds for an abortion unless the pregnancy was determined to be the result of "rape, incest, or if it is determined to endanger the woman's life" [11].

Currently, abortion is legal in every state; however, there is a push to overturn the *Roe* vs. *Wade* decision [12]. With repeated failures at the national level, anti-abortion forces have shifted the focus to the state level. As a result, many laws have been enacted at the state level, heavily regulating and restricting the access to abortion [12]. Despite the heavy regulation, there are still some states that allow for health insurance coverage of legal abortion. The median cost for an out-of-pocket abortion between ten and twenty weeks is between USD 500 and USD 1200 [11]. As previously mentioned, the Hyde Amendment banned the use of federal funds, such as Medicaid, to help cover the costs of legal abortion. Around two-thirds of American women use Medicaid to help cover the costs of reproductive health, and many of these women are of lower income status [11]. One of the provisions for federally funded abortion is that the state can opt to cover all or part of an abortion [11]. However, less than twenty states choose to help cover the cost.

Private insurances are also heavily regulated by the state, and the majority choose the same provisions as federal programs, or have even stricter regulations for health insurance coverage for abortion [11]. Only California, Oregon, New York, and Washington State require private plans to have coverage for abortion with none or very light regulations [11].

1.2. Hypotheses

Since our research question is quite new, there is not much direct empirical evidence from the existing literature that can be used to shore up our hypotheses. Thus, we largely rely on theorization and some indirect evidence. We propose a number of hypotheses for testing. Survey data show women tend to be on the side of pro-choice on the abortion issue compared to men [13,14]. Since women are the ones who undergo abortion and may experience physical suffering, mental stress, and financial difficulty, they will benefit from health insurance coverage for an abortion. Thus, we hypothesize that, *all else being equal, women are more likely than men to support the use of health insurance to cover an abortion* for the interest of themselves and their families. Evidence indicates that younger people are more likely to support legal abortion than older people, but direct evidence between age and support for abortion health insurance coverage does not exist [14]. We anticipate *an inverse relationship between age and the likelihood of support for using health insurance to help with the costs of legal abortion, holding other variables constant,* because older people are generally more conservative than younger ones. Earlier studies of abortion attitudes found that blacks were less likely than whites to support legal abortion [15,16]. Furthermore, traditionally abortions were more likely to occur among white women than among black or other minority women. As of 2016, the overall rate of abortion based on race in the United States was highest among whites than among blacks or other races [17]. This suggests whites will benefit more from health insurance coverage for abortion than minorities. Hence, we expect that *racial minorities are less likely than whites to support health insurance coverage for abortion, ceteris paribus.*

The South is the hub of anti-abortion fervor [18]. Given the conservative tradition and environment in the South, we predict that *Southerners are less likely than residents in other regions to support health insurance coverage for legal abortion, controlling for other variables.* In the United States, urban areas tend to be more liberal than rural areas. Hence, we hypothesize that *urban residents are more likely than rural residents to favor the use of health insurance to cover legal abortion, other things being equal.*

Religion was generally considered the strongest predictor of abortion attitudes [19]. In the U.S., Christians are the religious majority and tend to be more conservative. A large majority of Evangelical Protestants oppose legal abortion [14,19,20]. Christians also include Catholics whose religious tenets prohibit an abortion [19]. Orthodox Christians also condemn abortion. Despite some variation among Christian groups, Christianity advocates the "sanctity of human life" and generally opposes abortion more than other religions and the religious unaffiliated. Thus, we expect *Christians to be less likely than non-Christians to support using health insurance to cover legal abortion, holding other variables constant.*

Marriage and family can impact support for health insurance coverage for legal abortion. Available empirical evidence indicates that marriage reduces the likelihood of support for abortion [20]. Compared to their unmarried counterparts, married individuals are much less likely to opt for an abortion if pregnancy occurs. The need to cover an abortion is relatively lower for married people. Thus, we predict that *individuals who are currently married are less likely than those who are not currently married to support using health insurance to cover the cost of legal abortion.* Individuals who desire a larger family or have more children are less likely to need an abortion. Hence, we hypothesize *a negative relationship between the number of children and the probability to support health insurance coverage for legal abortion.*

Socioeconomic status can also influence support for the use of health insurance to cover legal abortion. Education makes people more open-minded [21,22]. Many studies have documented that more educated people are more likely to support legal abortion than less educated ones [23–25]. By extension, we hypothesize that *education is positively associated with the probability to support health insurance coverage for legal abortion.* Some prior studies reveal links between employment status and abortion attitudes [24,26]. A full-time job is normally associated with health insurance. Hence, it is reasonable to expect *individuals who hold a full-time job to be more likely than individuals who do not have a full-time job to support health insurance coverage for legal abortion* because they can benefit from their job-related insurance to cover an abortion should it happen. Family income means financial ability. Some evidence indicates an inverse association between income and support for abortion [24,27]. As an extension, we anticipate that *individuals with a higher family income are less likely to support health insurance coverage for abortion than those with a low family income* because they are more likely to be able to afford it if needed.

Abortion is a political issue, so political factors matter. It is well known that Democrats are generally more supportive of pro-choice than other parties [14,28–31]. Thus, we predict that to be consistent with their pro-choice stance, *Democrats are more likely to support health insurance coverage for abortion than non-Democrats.* It is also common knowledge that liberals tend to be pro-choice [14,29,30]. As an extension, liberals should be more supportive of health insurance coverage for abortion than non-liberals. Hence, we hypothesize that *liberals are more likely than non-liberals to support health insurance coverage for abortion.* We found that the correlation between the dummy variable for Democrat and the dummy variable for Liberal in our sample is 0.365. Thus, multicollinearity is not a concern, and the independent effects of both party affiliation and political ideology can be assessed simultaneously.

2. Materials and Methods

For this study, we used the GSS conducted in 2018 [32]. The GSS has surveyed non-institutionalized U.S. adult population aged 18 or older since 1972, covering demographic, behavioral, and attitudinal topics along with special topics of interest. We used GSS 2018 not only because it is the latest available GSS data but more importantly because the 2018 survey added for the first time the following new survey question: "People use their health insurance to help cover the cost of receiving health care. Do you think people should be able to use their health insurance to help cover the cost of receiving an abortion"? This new question provides the necessary information for us to study the current topic and to contribute to the continuous debate over abortion in the United States.

GSS 2018 is a full probability sample based on a multistage probability sampling design. Since the GSS only selected one respondent per household for survey, respondents in a larger household had a smaller chance of being selected than those in a smaller household. To address this bias, we used the weight variable designed by the GSS to weight the data, so that the findings can be generalized to the U.S. adult population. Our GSS sample statistics are similar to the available estimates of the U.S. population characteristics from the 2018 American Community Survey (ACS) collected by the U.S. Census Bureau. For example, in terms of gender composition, our GSS 2018 showed 53% female and 47% male for the U.S. adult population as compared to the estimates of ACS 2018 at 50.8% female and 49.2% male for the entire U.S. population. In terms of race, our GSS 2018 U.S. adult sample recorded 72.2% white, 15.1% black, and 12.7% other race, in comparison with 72.2% white, 12.7% black, and 15.1% other races combined (including 3.4% for two or more races) estimated by ACS 2018. GSS 2018 contained 49% of the currently married, which was similar to 47.8% of the currently married in ACS 2018. We restricted the analysis to the valid cases of the dependent variable on the use of health insurance to cover the cost of an abortion. The restricted sample contains 2,134 cases.

Table 1 provides the descriptions of the variables and their measurements used in the study. Since they are straightforward, only brief necessary notes are presented in order to conserve space. The dichotomous dependent variable measures whether the respondent supports or opposes using health insurance to cover legal abortion. Our independent variables include demographic characteristics (i.e., gender, age, race, region, urban/rural residency, religion, marital status, and number of children), socioeconomic status (i.e., education, employment, and family income), and political variables (i.e., political party affiliation, and political ideology). Family income is inflation-adjusted and converted to the 2000 constant U.S. dollar.

Table 1. Description of Variables Used in the Analysis.

Variable	Measurement	Mean	Standard Deviation
Dependent Variable			
Support for health insurance to cover abortion	1 = Support, 0 = Oppose	0.498	0.50
Independent variables			
Gender	1 = Female, 0 = Male	0.530	0.499
Race			
Black	1 = Black, 0 = Else	0.151	0.358
Other	1 = Other, 0 = Else	0.127	0.333
Age	Years	46.302	17.755
Region	1 = South, 0 = Else	0.390	0.488
Urban	1 = Urban, 0 = Rural	0.890	0.310
Religion	1 = Christian, 0 = Else	0.710	0.452
Marital status	1 = Currently married, 0 = Else	0.490	0.500
# of Children	Number	1.820	1.677
Education	Years of schooling	13.720	2.989
Full-time job	1 = Full-time, 0 = Else	0.500	0.500
Family income	USD in constant 2000 U.S. dollars	54,230.75	43,971.079
Party affiliation	1 = Democrat, 0 = Else	0.300	0.459
Political ideology	1 = Liberal, 0 = Else	0.300	0.458

We first performed crosstabulations and χ^2 tests for each predictor and the dependent variable. Since our dependent variable is dichotomous with many predictors, binary logistic regression is most appropriate to determine who is more or less likely to support using health insurance for legal abortion. The model takes on the form:

$$\ln\left(\frac{p_i}{1-p}\right) = a + \sum Bi\ X_i$$

where $\ln\left(\frac{p_i}{1-p}\right)$ is the logged odds ratio of supporting the use of health insurance to help cover legal abortion, a denotes the intercept, B_i is the logistic coefficient for variables X_i and X_i represents the independent variables in the analysis. Some advantages of using a logistic regression model compared to a χ^2 test include that multiple predictors can be included and explanatory variables can be discrete or continuous [33].

3. Results

3.1. Descriptive and Bivariate Analysis

Table 1 also displays the means and standard deviations of the variables used in the analysis. For a dummy coded variable, the mean can be interpreted as a percentage by multiplying the value by 100. Based on our sample statistics evident in Table 1, in 2018, roughly 50% (49.8% to be precise) of the Americans supported the use of health insurance to cover a legal abortion while the other half (50.2% to be exact) were against it. Note that our sample included 53% of women and 47% of men. Our sample comprised 15% blacks and 13% other race, versus 72% whites. On average, the respondents were about 46 years old with a standard deviation of 17.8 years. Almost two out of five resided in the South. Nearly 90% were urban dwellers. A large majority (71%) of the respondents were Christian versus 29% non-Christian. Nearly half were currently married. On average, the respondents reported almost 2 children. They also reported an average of 13.7 years of schooling, which equated to some college. Half of the respondents held a full-time job. On average, the respondents reported an annual family income of approximately USD 54,231 in the 2000 constant dollars. The sample was composed of 30% Democrats versus 70% non-Democrats, and 30% liberals versus 70% non-liberals.

To gain a further understanding of the relationships between the predictors and support for using health insurance to cover legal abortion, we cross-tabulated each predictor and the dependent variable and conducted chi-squared tests. For the feasibility of these analyses, we collapsed several continuous variables including age, education, number of children, and family income. The results are shown in Table 2. Except for age, race, employment status, and family income, all other predictors display a significant relationship with the dependent variable because the χ^2 values are significant at least at the 0.05 level. Among the significant predictors, most relationships are congruent with our hypotheses. One exception is gender, as surprisingly women (47.6%) were somewhat less likely to favor the use of health insurance for abortion than men (52.2%). However, the results of these bivariate analyses are tentative because other factors that could affect the dependent variable have not been controlled. In order to ascertain the true relationships, multivariate analysis is called for.

Table 2. Percentage Distributions of Support for Using Health Insurance Coverage for Legal Abortion by Predictors, GSS 2018.

Variable	Support for Health Insurance to Cover Abortion (%)	N	χ^2
Gender		2134	4.458 *
Female	47.6		
Male	52.2		
Age		2134	3.941
18–29	53.6		
30–64	48.3		
65 or older	50.3		
Race		2134	5.542
White	48.9		
Black	55.8		
Other	47.8		
Region		2134	53.779 ***
South	56.1		
Non-South	39.8		
Urban/rural residency		2134	29.706 ***
Urban	51.8		
Rural	32.8		
Religion		2120	96.531 ***
Christian	42.9		
Not Christian	66.4		
Marital Status		2,134	40.046 ***
Currently married	42.7		
Not curr. married	56.4		
# of children		2130	15.681 ***
2 or less	52.5		
3 or more	43.1		
Education		2132	59.642 ***
College educated	56.6		
Not coll. educated	39.6		
Work Status		2132	0.604
Full-Time	50.6		
Not full time	48.9		
Family income		1940	2.722
Less than average	47.9		
Average or more	51.7		
Party affiliation		2106	94.114 ***
Democrat	65.8		
Non-Democrat	42.7		
Political ideology		2051	138.761 ***
Liberal	70.4		
Non-Liberal	42.0		

* $p \leq 0.05$, ** $p \leq 0.01$, *** $p \leq 0.001$.

3.2. *Multivariate Analysis*

Table 3 presents the results of the two logistic regression models. Model 1 is the full model including all predictors. Model 2 adds the interaction term Education x Liberal to Model 1.

Table 3. Logistic Regression Estimates Predicting Support for the Use of Health Insurance to Cover Abortion, U.S. Adults, GSS 2018.

Predictor	Model 1		Model 2	
	B	Odds Ratio	B	Odds Ratio
Female	−0.215 * (0.105)	0.806	−0.215 * (0.0105)	0.807
Age	0.007 * (0.004)	1.007	0.007 * (0.004)	1.007
Race (Ref. = White)				
Black	0.079 (0.158)	1.082	0.082 (0.158)	1.085
Other	−0.117 (0.168)	0.889	−0.093 (0.169)	0.912
South	−0.395 *** (0.110)	0.674	−0.388 *** (0.110)	0.678
Urban	0.392 * (0.174)	1.480	0.378 * (0.174)	1.460
Christian	−0.0744 *** (0.112)	0.475	−0.725 *** (0.122)	0.484
Married	−0.573 *** (0.115)	0.564	−0.565 *** (0.115)	0.569
# of Children	−0.083 * (0.036)	0.920	−0.079 * (0.036)	0.924
Education	0.109 *** (0.020)	1.115	0.081 *** (0.024)	1.085
Full-time job	0.062 (0.110)	1.064	0.067 (0.110)	1.069
Family income in USD 1000	0.001 (0.001)	1.001	0.001 (0.001)	1.001
Democrat	0.727 *** (0.125)	2.069	0.698 *** (0.126)	2.010
Liberal	0.772 *** (0.124)	2.164	0.478 (0.580)	0.620
Education x Liberal			0.091 * (0.041)	1.095
Constant	−1.467 *** (0.359)	0.231	−1.097 (0.393)	0.334
−2 Log Likelihood	2218.904		2213.882	
Model χ^2	356.048 ***		361.071 ***	
Pseudo R^2	0.233		0.236	
df	14		15	
N	1895		1895	

* $p \leq 0.05$, ** $p \leq 0.01$, *** $p \leq 0.001$. Notes: The odds ratio is the antilog of the B, and the standard errors are in parentheses.

The model fit statistics indicate that Model 1 fits the data very well as indicated by the highly significant model χ^2 (=0.356). The pseudo R^2 indicates that Model 1 explains 23.3% of the variation in the probability of support for using health insurance for legal abortion.

The parameter estimates in Model 1 represent the independent effects of the predictors on the dependent variable. As shown in Model 1, except for race all demographic variables have a significant effect on support for the use of health insurance for legal abortion. The logistic regression coefficient for the female dummy variable is significant at the 0.05 level, but the sign is in the unexpected opposite direction. The odds ratio (=0.806) indicates that women were 19.4% (=0.806 − 1 = −0.194) less likely than men to support the use of health insurance for legal abortion. These results are at odds with our hypothesis. To test the possibility that an inadequate control of political orientation may have impacted the gender difference in support for the use of health insurance for abortion, we created another dummy "middle of the road" for political orientation, used conservative as the reference category, and reran the model. The result of a greater propensity of men over women in favor of insurance coverage for abortion remains unchanged. In addition, we created two interaction terms: Female x Liberal, and Female x Democrat and reran the model separately one at a time for each of the two interaction terms. Both interaction terms are not significant at the 0.05 level. However, among both liberals and non-liberals, women were still less likely than men to support health insurance for abortion; this was also true among Democrats and non-Democrats. Thus, women's lower propensity than men to favor health insurance for legal abortion is not very likely to be a statistical artifact.

Age is also significant at the 0.05 level, but the effect contradicts our expectation since both the B and odds ratio show older people were more likely to support the use of health insurance for legal abortion. The dummy variable South is highly significant at the 0.001 level. As hypothesized, Southerners were about 33% (=0.674 − 1 = −0.326) less likely than residents in other regions to support the use of health insurance coverage for legal abortion. Additionally, as expected, urban residents were 1.48 times as likely as rural residents to support the use of health insurance for legal abortion.

Coinciding with our hypothesis, Christians were about 53% (0.475 − 1 = −0.525) less likely to support the use of health insurance coverage for legal abortion. We understand Christians encompass various groups. To test the differences among various Christian groups in support for the use of health insurance for abortion, we replaced the Christian dummy variable by three dummy variables for Christian groups with non-Christians as the reference category: Protestant, Catholic, and other Christian (Note: Since the number of Orthodox Christians was too small, we had to lump Orthodox Christian into the other Christian category), and we then reran Model 1. The results show that each of these three Christian groups was less likely than non-Christians to support health insurance for abortion with trivial changes in the effects of other predictors. Because of these results, we decided to merge all Christian groups into one category Christian for the efficiency of analysis and presentation.

Consistent with our hypothesis, currently married people were significantly less likely to support the use of health insurance to cover legal abortion than their not currently married counterparts. The effect of the number of children is also expected and significant at the 0.05 level. For each additional child, the odds of supporting the use of health insurance for abortion were predicted to decrease by 8% (0.920 − 1 = −0.08), holding all other variables constant. There were no significant differences between racial minorities and whites in support for the use of health insurance to cover legal abortion.

The effects of socioeconomic variables are mixed. As hypothesized, education has a highly significant positive effect on the dependent variable. For each additional year of schooling, the odds of supporting the use of health insurance for legal abortion were predicted to increase by 11.5% (1.115 − 1 = 0.115). However, full-time employment and family income had no significant effect on support for the use of health insurance to cover abortion.

Coinciding with common sense and our hypotheses, both party affiliation and political ideology are proven to be highly significant predictors of support for the use of health insurance to cover legal abortion. Significant at the 0.001 level, Democrats were twice as likely as non-Democrats to support the use of health insurance to cover legal abortion. We reran Model 1 by replacing the Democrat dummy variable by three dummy variables for Republican, Independent, and other party. The results confirmed that Republicans, Independents, and other party were all less likely than Democrats (the reference category) to support health insurance for abortion. Because of these results, we decided to keep one dummy variable for Democrat for the efficiency of analysis and presentation. Similarly, as shown by the odds ratio in Model 1 liberals were 2.164 times as likely as non-liberals to support the use of health insurance for abortion.

Are effects of certain predictors (e.g., education, party affiliation) moderated by other predictors (e.g., political ideology, gender, religion, region)? To address this question, we created many cross-product terms to test the possible interaction or moderating effects.

None of the interaction effects were significant at the 0.05 level, except for the interaction between education and being liberal. The results are presented in Model 2 of Table 3. Compared to Model 1, Model 2 fits the data significantly better with a significantly smaller −2 log likelihood, a significantly greater model χ^2 (=0.361), and a significantly greater pseudo R^2 (=0.236) with one additional degree of freedom. The interaction term Education x Liberal is significant at the 0.05 level. The B indicates that the effect of education on support for the use of health insurance to cover abortion is greater for liberals than for non-liberals.

4. Discussion

Our findings have significant implications for research on this issue and for practices. Our findings confirm the conventional wisdom and our hypotheses regarding the effects of political party affiliation and political ideology on support for health insurance coverage for abortion [14,29–32]. They suggest that political divides serve as the most important considerations for coalition, operation, or opposition in dealing with the abortion health insurance issue. Earlier studies of abort attitudes [24,28] only found weak associations between political variables and abortion attitudes. Perhaps time is different now as the battles for legal abortion have intensified and partisan and ideological divides have deepened in more recent years.

Our result of a significant positive relationship between education and the dependent variable is consistent with the findings about the relationship between education and abortion attitudes in the literature [23,27]. It suggests that educational attainment will help increase support for the use of health insurance to cover abortion [23–25]. The significant interaction effect between education and political ideology implies that the more educated liberals tend to be the strongest advocates for abortion health insurance coverage.

The result that women are significantly less likely to support health insurance coverage for abortion than men before and after controlling for other factors seems to be a conundrum but may have a reason. Past studies of abortion attitudes generate mixed results about the gender difference. While some studies [23,34] found men were more likely to support abortion than women, Legge's research [27] detected the opposite to some extent after holding other predictors constant. Of course, our dependent variable is not the same as theirs but these dependent variables all pertain to support for legal abortion or the use of insurance to cover legal abortion. One probable explanation offered by Blake and Del Pinal dubbed the "motherhood hypothesis" postulates that women place more importance on motherhood than on reproductive freedom than men [35]. This proposition may also help explain the gender difference in support for health insurance coverage for abortion. This result also suggests that one cannot assume women will automatically support health insurance coverage for abortion and that men can also support abortion insurance coverage.

Legge found that older people were less likely to be associated with support for abortion [27], but Baker et al.'s earlier study [34] concluded that age is not a particularly strong predictor of abortion attitudes. Nevertheless, our finding about a positive relationship between age and support for health insurance coverage for abortion is not in line with the findings of both studies and challenges the conventional expectation. This result suggests that older people may be a group to win over for support for abortion insurance coverage.

Prior research points to the most preponderant role of religion in shaping abortion attitudes [19,27,35]. The finding in our study suggests that, albeit not most important, religion remains a very important determinant of attitudes toward abortion insurance coverage as it impacts nearly every aspect and moral decision [14,19,36]. Opposition to the use of health insurance coverage for abortion can be expected to hail from the bulk of the Christian groups. The South is another base of opposition. Resistance to abortion insurance coverage can also come from those who are married and have more children.

The data provided in this study are particularly important because as of 2021, some southern states now prevent abortions as soon as the doctors are able to find a fetal heartbeat [37]. Often, this is before the woman even starts experiencing pregnancy symptoms, leading to finding out about the pregnancy past the allotted abortion time frame. Women who are impregnated as a result of rape and incest are no longer excluded from abortion laws. It is imperative to understand that many parties are involved on both sides of the debate. The battle over abortion and its coverage by health insurance is not only about civil rights and women's rights but also about profit as medicalization of abortion is a huge business industry. Consequently, many parties have a stake in medicalization of abortion and its coverage by one's health insurance, including physicians, birth control clinics, pharmaceutical companies, and the health insurance industry [38].

5. Conclusions

There is a dearth of quantitative data on support for the use of health insurance to access abortion, instead of paying out of pocket for the procedure. To provide policymakers and practitioners with useful information on this issue, this study examines American attitudes toward support for health insurance coverage for abortion, using the latest new data from GSS 2018. The results show that the support and opposition were about evenly divided. The findings from the logistic regression analysis reveal that, holding other variables constant, Democrats, liberals, urban residents, the more educated, and the older were more likely to support health insurance coverage for legal abortion while women, Southerners, Christians, the currently married, and those with more children were less likely to favor it, compared to their respective counterparts. Additionally, the effect of education was stronger for liberals than for non-liberals. Race, family income, and full-time work status make no difference in the outcome.

Health insurance coverage for abortion is emerging as a critical issue that calls for additional research. Some of our findings, especially with regard to the effects of gender and age, will require verification from other data sources. Since our data are cross-sectional, longitudinal data will help capture the changing American attitudes toward this issue.

Author Contributions: Conceptualization, C.H. and P.Q.Y.; methodology, P.Q.Y. and C.H.; validation, P.Q.Y.; formal analysis, C.H. and P.Q.Y.; writing—original draft preparation, C.H.; writing—review, editing, and most revisions, P.Q.Y.; supervision, P.Q.Y. All authors have read and agreed to the published version of the manuscript.

Funding: This research received no external funding.

Institutional Review Board Statement: Ethical review and approval were waived for this study because it uses public-use data that require no approval.

Informed Consent Statement: Not applicable.

Data Availability Statement: Publicly available data were used for this study. The data set can be found here: https://gss.norc.org/ accessed on 28 August 2020.

Acknowledgments: An earlier version of this paper was presented at the 2021 Annual Conference of the Southwestern Social Science Association, New Orleans, 15–17 April 2021. We greatly appreciate the very helpful comments and suggestions of the three IJERPH anonymous reviewers on an earlier version of this manuscript for their contributions.

Conflicts of Interest: The authors declare no conflict of interest.

References

1. Boyle, E.; Minzee, K.; Longhofer, W. Abortion liberalization in world society, 1960–2009. *Am. J. Sociol.* **2015**, *121*, 882–913. [CrossRef] [PubMed]
2. Stabile, B. Reproductive policy and the social construction of motherhood. *Politics Life Sci.* **2016**, *35*, 18–29. [CrossRef] [PubMed]
3. De Londras, F.; Enright, M. *Repealing the 8th—Reforming Irish Abortion Law: A Rights-Based Approach to Abortion*; Policy Press: Brristol, UK, 2018.
4. Hurst, R.A.J. Abortion as a feminist pedagogy of grief in Marianna Apostolides's Deep Salt Water. *Fem. Stud.* **2020**, *46*, 43–73. [CrossRef]
5. Johnston, B.R.; Keogh, L.; Norman, W.V. *Decriminalizing Abortion in the UK: What Would It Mean?* Policy Press: Brristol, UK, 2020.

6. Planned Parenthood. What Happens during an In-Clinic Abortion? 2020. Available online: https://www.plannedparenthood.org/learn/abortion/in-clinic-abortion-procedures/what-happens-during-an-in-clinic-abortion (accessed on 5 December 2020).
7. Dine, R. Scarlet Letters: Getting the History of Abortion and Contraception Right. 2013. Available online: https://www.americanprogress.org/issues/religion/news/2013/08/08/71893/scarlet-letters-getting-the-history-of-abortion-and-contraception-right/ (accessed on 6 December 2020).
8. Reagan, L.J. *When Abortion Was a Crime: Women, Medicine, and Law in the United States, 1867–1973*; University of California Press: Berkeley, CA, USA, 1998.
9. Ravitz, J. The Surprising History of Abortion in the United States. 2016. Available online: https://www.cnn.com/2016/06/23/health/abortion-history-in-united-states/index.html (accessed on 4 December 2020).
10. Dudden, F.E. Women's rights advocates and abortion laws. *J. Women's Hist.* **2019**, *31*, 102–123. [CrossRef]
11. Salganicoff, A.; Sobel, L.; Ramaswamy, A. Coverage for Abortion Services in Medicaid, Marketplace Plans and Private Plans. 2019. Available online: https://www.kff.org/womens-health-policy/issue-brief/coverage-for-abortion-services-in-medicaid-marketplace-plans-and-private-plans/ (accessed on 6 December 2020).
12. Ellmann, N. State Actions Undermining Abortion Rights in 2020. 2020. Available online: https://www.americanprogress.org/issues/women/reports/2020/08/27/489786/state-actions-undermining-abortion-rights-2020/ (accessed on 5 December 2020).
13. Gallup. Abortion Trends by Gender. 2021. Available online: https://news.gallup.com/poll/245618/abortion-trends-gender.aspx (accessed on 31 October 2021).
14. Pew Research Center. Public Opinion on Abortion. 2021. Available online: https://www.pewforum.org/fact-sheet/public-opinion-on-abortion/ (accessed on 31 October 2021).
15. Coombs, M.; Welch, S. Blacks, whites, and attitudes toward abortion. *Public Opin. Q.* **1982**, *46*, 510–520. [CrossRef] [PubMed]
16. Hall, E.; Ferree, M. Race differences in abortion attitudes. *Public Opin. Q.* **1986**, *50*, 193–207. [CrossRef] [PubMed]
17. KFF. Reported Legal Abortions by Race of Women who Obtained Abortion by the State of Occurrence. 2016. Available online: https://www.kff.org/womens-health-policy/state-indicator/abortions-by-race/?currentTimeframe=0&sortModel=%7B%22colId%22:%22Location%22,%22sort%22:%22asc%22%7D (accessed on 9 December 2020).
18. Varney, S. Why Is the South the Epicenter of Anti-Abortion Fervor? 2021. Available online: https://khn.org/news/article/qa-why-south-is-anti-abortion-epicenter/ (accessed on 31 October 2021).
19. Jelen, T.G.; Wilcox, C. 2003. Causes and consequences of public attitudes toward abortion: A review and research agenda. *Political Res. Q.* **2003**, *56*, 489–500. [CrossRef]
20. Hoffmann, J.P.; Johnson, S.M. Attitudes toward abortion among religious traditions in the United States: Change or continuity? *Sociol. Relig.* **2005**, *66*, 161–182. [CrossRef]
21. Hare, W. *Open-Mindedness and Education*; McGill-Queen's University Press: Kinston, ON, Canada; Montreal, QC, Canada, 1979.
22. Verducci, S. Open-Mindedness and education. In *The Oxford Encyclopedia of Philosophy of Education*; Oxford University Press: Oxford, UK, 2021. [CrossRef]
23. Granberg, D.; Granberg, B.W. Abortion attitudes, 1965-1980: Trends and determinants. *Fam Plann Perspect.* **1980**, *12*, 250–261. [CrossRef] [PubMed]
24. Jelen, T.G.; Damore, D.F.; Lamatsch, T. Gender, employment status, and abortion: A longitudinal analysis. *Sex Roles* **2002**, *47*, 321–330. [CrossRef]
25. Wang, G.Z.; Buffalo, M.D. Social and cultural determinants of attitudes toward abortion: A test of Reiss' hypotheses. *Soc. Sci. J.* **2004**, *41*, 93–105. [CrossRef]
26. Luker, K. *Abortion and the Politics of Motherhood*; University of California Press: Berkeley, CA, USA, 1984.
27. Legge, J.S., Jr. The determinants of attitudes toward abortion in the American electorate. *West. Political Q.* **1983**, *36*, 479–490. [CrossRef]
28. Hess, J.A.; Rueb, J.D. Attitudes toward abortion, religion, and party affiliation among college students. *Curr. Psychol.* **2005**, *24*, 24–42. [CrossRef]
29. Statista Research Department. Support for Abortion by Party and Level of Legalization U.S. 2021. Available online: https://www.statista.com/statistics/1079467/abortion-support-party-level-legalization-us/ (accessed on 31 October 2021).
30. Gallup. Abortion Trends by Party Identification. 2021. Available online: https://news.gallup.com/poll/246278/abortion-trends-party.aspx (accessed on 20 December 2021).
31. Adams, G.D. Abortion: Evidence of an issue evolution. *Am. J. Political Sci.* **1997**, *41*, 718–737. [CrossRef]
32. Smith, T.; Davern, M.; Freese, J.; Hout, M. *General Social Surveys, 1972–2018*; NORC: Chicago, IL, USA, 2019.
33. Afifi, A.; Clark, V. *Computer-Aided Multivariate Analysis*, 2nd ed.; Van Nostrand Reinhold: New York, NY, USA, 1990.
34. Baker, R.K.; Epstein, L.K.; Forth, R.D. Matters of life and death: Social, political, and religious correlates of attitudes on abortion. *Am. Politics Q.* **1981**, *9*, 89–102. [CrossRef] [PubMed]
35. Blake, J.; del Pinal, J.H. Predicting polar attitudes toward abortion in the United States. In *Abortion Parley*; Burtchael, J.T., Ed.; Andrews and McMeel: Kansas City, MO, USA, 1980; pp. 28–56.
36. Brunn, S.D.; Webster, G.R.; Archer, J.C. The Bible belt in a changing South. *Southeast Geogr.* **2011**, *51*, 513–549. [CrossRef]

37. Najmadadi, S. Greg Abbott Signs into Law one of Nation's Strictest Abortion Measures, Banning Procedure as Early as Six Weeks into a Pregnancy. 2021. Available online: https://www.texastribune.org/2021/05/18/texas-heartbeat-bill-abortions-law/ (accessed on 25 June 2021).
38. Halfmann, D. Political institutions and the comparative medicalization of abortion. *J. Health Soc. Behav.* **2019**, *60*, 138–152. [CrossRef] [PubMed]

International Journal of
Environmental Research and Public Health

MDPI

Article

An Epidemiologic Analysis of Associations between County-Level Per Capita Income, Unemployment Rate, and COVID-19 Vaccination Rates in the United States

Yuqi Guo [1,2,*], Andrea R. Kaniuka [3], Jingjing Gao [4] and Omar T. Sims [5,6,7,8,*]

1 School of Social Work, College of Health and Human Services, University of North Carolina at Charlotte, Charlotte, NC 28262, USA
2 School of Data Science, University of North Carolina at Charlotte, Charlotte, NC 28262, USA
3 Department of Public Health Sciences, College of Health and Human Services, University of North Carolina at Charlotte, Charlotte, NC 28262, USA; akaniuka@uncc.edu
4 Public Policy Program, College of Arts and Sciences, University of North Carolina at Charlotte, Charlotte, NC 28262, USA; jgao9@uncc.edu
5 Department of Social Work, College of Arts and Sciences, University of Alabama at Birmingham, Birmingham, AL 35222, USA
6 Department of Health Behavior, School of Public Health, University of Alabama at Birmingham, Birmingham, AL 35222, USA
7 Center for AIDS Research, School of Medicine, University of Alabama at Birmingham, Birmingham, AL 35222, USA
8 African American Studies, College of Arts and Science, University of Alabama at Birmingham, Birmingham, AL 35222, USA
* Correspondence: yguo16@uncc.edu (Y.G.); osims@uab.edu (O.T.S.)

Abstract: The purpose of this longitudinal study was to examine associations between per capita income, unemployment rates, and COVID-19 vaccination rates at the county-level across the United States (U.S.), as well as to identify the interaction effects between county-level per capita income, unemployment rates, and racial/ethnic composition on COVID-19 vaccination rates. All counties in the U.S. that reported COVID-19 vaccination rates from January 2021 to July 2021 were included in this longitudinal study (n = 2857). Pooled ordinary least squares (OLS) with fixed-effects were employed to longitudinally examine economic impacts on racial/ethnic disparities on county-level COVID-19 vaccination rates. County-level per capita income and county-level unemployment rates were both positively associated with county-level COVID-19 vaccination rates across the U.S. However, the associations were divergent in the context of race/ethnicity. Public health efforts to bolster COVID-19 vaccination rates are encouraged to consider economic factors that are associated with decreases in COVID-19 vaccination rates.

Keywords: COVID-19 vaccination rates; race/ethnicity; per capita income; unemployment rate; racial disparities

Citation: Guo, Y.; Kaniuka, A.R.; Gao, J.; Sims, O.T. An Epidemiologic Analysis of Associations between County-Level Per Capita Income, Unemployment Rate, and COVID-19 Vaccination Rates in the United States. *Int. J. Environ. Res. Public Health* **2022**, *19*, 1755. https://doi.org/10.3390/ijerph19031755

Academic Editor: Fred Paas

Received: 16 December 2021
Accepted: 28 January 2022
Published: 3 February 2022

1. Introduction

In February 2020, the novel coronavirus (COVID-19) was declared a public health emergency in the United States (U.S.), and in March 2020 it was declared a pandemic by the World Health Organization (WHO) [1]. Soon after, states in the U.S. began implementing various community mitigation strategies (e.g., mandatory stay at home orders and business closures) to curb the spread of COVID-19. In total, 42 U.S. states and territories issued mandatory stay-at-home orders, covering 73% of U.S. counties [2]. Community mitigation strategies were effective in their aim of reducing close contact and movement outside of households [2], and consequently reduced the number of COVID-19 cases [3]; however, these public health strategies were associated with an array of negative economic impacts, including higher unemployment rates, decreased participation in the labor force, and reductions in income. For example, the most recent estimates indicate that the unemployment rate peaked in April 2020 (14.8%) during the pandemic, and the current unemployment rate remains higher than the pre-pandemic unemployment rate (5.4% vs. 3.5%) [4]. Since the start of the pandemic, over 100 million unemployment claims have been filed, with one in four workers accessing unemployment aid at some point during the pandemic [5]. Furthermore, approximately one in five U.S. adults reported a drop in income during the pandemic, resulting in difficulty covering various expenses (e.g., rent or mortgage payments, medical care, and food costs) [6].

Certain demographic groups in the U.S. have been disproportionately affected by the economic impacts of COVID-19. Socio-economic status is significantly associated with health status and socio-economic factors represent important risk factors for disparities in health status [7]. In the U.S., individuals who are Black, Indigenous, People of Color (BIPOC) are more likely to experience unemployment or a reduction in income during the pandemic [6,8]. This trend is likely due to the racial/ethnic composition of workers in the sectors hardest hit during the COVID-19 pandemic. For example, the leisure (e.g., travel industry) and hospitality (e.g., restaurant workers) sectors, industries in which BIPOC individuals are more likely to work, saw the largest increases in unemployment [9]. Further, compared to White individuals, BIPOC individuals, who are already more likely to work in lower paying jobs [6], were more likely to report reductions in income and to have difficulty paying their bills [9]. As well, BIPOC individuals are reporting slower job recovery than White individuals [10]. The economic impacts of COVID-19 further exacerbated wealth and income gaps between White and BIPOC Americans [11] and compounded issues of access to a paramount public health prevention strategy—COV ID-19 vaccination.

In order to curb the spread of COVID-19, multiple COVID-19 vaccinations were rapidly developed and eventually emerged as the primary public health approach to combat the COVID-19 pandemic [12]. Three COVID-19 vaccinations were granted emergency use authorization: the Pfizer-BioNTech and Moderna COVID-19 vaccines (December 2020) and the Johnson & Johnson (J&J) COVID-19 vaccine (February 2021) [13]. In August 2021, the Pfizer-BioNTech vaccine became the first to receive full FDA approval [14]. All three COVID-19 vaccines are effective, with twice vaccinated individuals being five times less likely to acquire COVID-19 infection and ten times less likely to experience hospitalization and death compared to unvaccinated individuals [15]. Despite their effectiveness as a primary prevention strategy, rates of vaccination lag behind desired targets set by the federal government [16]. The administration of vaccines began in December 2020, and by 24 January 2022, approximately 63.4% of Americans (~210.5 million) have been twice vaccinated (i.e., one shot of J&J vaccine, two doses of Pfizer or Moderna vaccine) [17].

Vaccination rates among BIPOC persons are lagging compared to their non-Hispanic White counterparts, with non-Hispanic Black and Hispanic Americans being less likely than non-Hispanic Whites to be twice vaccinated against COVID-19 [18]. Disparities in vaccination rates may be due to issues of access (e.g., lack of accessible clinic, inability to take time off of work), as well as vaccine hesitancy potentially rooted in mistrust in the medical field due to historical and contemporary experiences of healthcare discrimination [19,20]. This is of particular concern given that BIPOC persons have a high frequency of several COVID-19 risk factors (e.g., diabetes, heart disease, and obesity) [21]. As well, BIPOC individuals are more likely to work in "essential" jobs (e.g., factories, health care), and thus are less likely to be able to telework, ultimately increasing their exposure to COVID-19 [22]. As a result, compared to White Americans, BIPOC Americans have higher rates of COVID-19 infection and death [23], highlighting the importance of COVID-19 vaccination for this population and underscoring the need to address factors contributing to inequities in vaccine distribution.

As such, the Centers for Disease Control and Prevention (CDC) has identified COVID-19 vaccine equity for BIPOC individuals as a top priority, highlighting income and wealth gaps and employment as barriers to vaccination [24]. Burgeoning evidence suggests that at the individual and county level, household income and employment impact vaccination rates [25–27]. Furthermore, the extant literature suggests that social vulnerability, which takes into account the racial/ethnic composition of an area, is associated with lower vaccination rates [28].

However, social vulnerability is an aggregate score of all three factors which fails to allow for an examination of how unemployment rates and income may impact racial/ethnic disparities on COVID-19 vaccination rates. As such, using longitudinal data from the U.S. Census Bureau and the CDC, this study conducted a longitudinal analysis across the U.S. at the county-level (1) to examine the relationship between county-level per capita income and county-level COVID-19 vaccination rates, (2) to examine the relationship between county-level unemployment rates and county-level COVID-19 vaccination rates, and (3) to identify interaction effects between county-level per capita income, county-level unemployment rates, and county-level racial/ethnic composition on county-level COVID-19 vaccination rates.

2. Materials and Methods

2.1. Study Design

An analysis of publicly available, secondary data was conducted in the U.S. at the county-level. County-level socio-economic demographics and county-level vaccination rates were extracted from the U.S. Census Bureau [29] and the CDC's COVID-19 vaccine tracker [29], respectively. All U.S. counties that reported COVID-19 vaccination rates from January 2021 to July 2021 were included in the sample (n = 2857). This time span included seven time points, namely the first day of the month spanning January 2021 to July 2021. In total, the present study analyzed 19,999 county-time waves.

2.2. Dependent Variable

The dependent variable was the county-level adult vaccination rate, defined as the percentage of twice vaccinated adults (age 18 or older) per county on the first day of each month (January 2021 to July 2021), as reported by the CDC's COVID-19 vaccine tracker [30].

2.3. Independent Variables

County-level unemployment rates were measured by the number of unemployed adults in each county divided by the number of adults in the labor force in each county, as indicated by U.S. Census Bureau data. Using U.S. Census Bureau data [29], county-level per capita income was calculated by dividing the county's total income by its population.

2.4. Moderating Variable

County-level racial/ethnic composition was measured by the percentage of BIPOC adults in each county as reported by the U.S. Census Bureau [28]. This percentage was then dichotomized into the top and bottom 5% of the distribution by county-level racial/ethnic composition. In this study, BIPOC refers to all people of color including but not limited to Black, Hispanic, and Asian individuals.

2.5. Covariates

Covariates included access to the COVID-19 vaccine (i.e., number of days the COVID-19 vaccine was available in each county), the number of nurse practitioners in each county—a proxy for healthcare availability at the county-level, gender (male or female), education (percentage of adults with a bachelor's degree or higher), and the percentage of individuals who were older adults ($\geq$65 years old).

2.6. Data Analysis

Measures of central tendency and frequency distributions were used to characterize the study sample. Pooled ordinary least squares (OLS) with fixed-effects were employed to longitudinally examine economic impacts on racial/ethnic disparities on county-level

COVID-19 vaccination rates. Interaction effects between the percentage of BIPOC adults and economic factors (i.e., unemployment, per capita income) on county-level vaccination rates were analyzed using OLS models with fixed-effects.

3. Results

Table 1 contains descriptive statistics across 19,999 county-time-waves (2857 counties from January 2021 to July 2021). Across time-waves, the average county-level COVID-19 vaccination rate was 14.82% (SD = 15.22), the mean racial/ethnic composition of counties with BIPOC was 15.45% (SD = 0.16), and the average number of days that the COVID-19 vaccine was available to the general population was 25.29 (SD = 33.35). The average unemployment rate was 6.71% across time-waves (SD = 2.24), while the average per capita income was $25,000.92 (SD = $5921.20).

Table 1. Descriptive Statistics.

n = 19,992				
County-Level Variables	**Mean**	**Std. Dev.**	**Min**	**Max**
Panel time range			1 January 2021	7 January 2021
COVID-19 vaccination rate	14.82	15.22	0.00	99.90
Percentage of Black and Indigenous People of Color (BIPOC)	15.45	16.12	0.91	93.71
Females	49.99	2.12	26.84	56.87
Number of days of COVID-19 vaccine availability	25.29	33.35	0.00	107.00
Number of nurse practitioners	53.04	154.49	1.00	3938.00
Unemployment rate	6.71	2.24	1.70	22.50
Per capita income	25,000.92	5921.20	9688.43	66,518.36
Percent of adults with bachelor's degree	21.82	9.55	5.40	78.50
Percentage of older adults population aged (≥65 years old)	19.42	4.58	4.83	57.59

3.1. Associations between County-Level Per Capita Income, County-Level Unemployment Rate and County-Level Vaccination Rates

Table 2 presents the results of the pooled OLS with fixed-effects. Aim 1 was to assess the relationship between county-level per capita income and county-level COVID-19 vaccination rates. Per capita income was positively associated with COVID-19 vaccination rates. For every $10,000 dollar increase in per capita income, county-level COVID-19 vaccination rates increased by 0.01%. Aim 2 was to assess the relationship between county-level unemployment and county-level COVID-19 vaccination rates. The unemployment rate was positively associated with COVID-19 vaccination rates. For every 1% increase in unemployment rate, county-level COVID-19 vaccination rates increased by 0.41%.

3.2. Interaction Effects

Aim 3 was to analyze interaction effects among county-level per capita income and unemployment rates with racial/ethnic composition (% of BIPOC adults) on county-level COVID-19 vaccination rates. Significant interaction effects were found between the unemployment rates and the percentage of racial minorities. A graph of the interaction effect is presented in Figure 1. In counties with greater racial/ethnic minority populations, increases in per capita income were associated with lower vaccination rates; however, in counties with lower racial/ethnic minority populations, increases in per capita income were associated with higher vaccination rates. Significant interaction effects were also found between the unemployment rate and the percentage of racial/ethnic minorities. A graph of the interaction effect is presented in Figure 2. In counties with greater racial/ethnic minority populations, increases in unemployment rates were related to higher COVID-19 vaccination rates; however, in counties with lower racial/ethnic minority populations, increases in unemployment rates were related to lower COVID-19 vaccination rates.

Table 2. Ordinal Least Squared Analysis Examining Associations with County-level COVID-19 Vaccination Rates and Interaction Effects.

	County-Level COVID-19 Vaccination Rates		
County-Level Variables	**Time-Fixed Effects**	**Unemployment Rate**	**Per Capita Income**
Rates of racial minorities	−4.583 ***	−10.50 ***	14.96 ***
Number of nurse practitioners	0.00276 ***	0.00268 ***	0.00431 ***
Unemployment rate	0.413 ***	0.296 ***	0.421 ***
Per capita income	0.000132 ***	0.000130 ***	0.000291 ***
Percent of adults with bachelor's degree	0.150 ***	0.152 ***	0.155 ***
Percentage of population aged 65 and above	14.84 ***	14.38 ***	12.71 ***
Rates of Female	−10.99 ***	−11.73 ***	−7.695 **
Number of days of COVID-19 vaccine availability	−0.118 ***	−0.121 ***	−0.135 ***
1 February 2021	1.352 ***	1.352 ***	1.352 ***
1 March 2021	6.718 ***	6.718 ***	6.718 ***
1 April 2021	15.37 ***	15.38 ***	15.40 ***
1 May 2021	28.47 ***	28.54 ***	28.91 ***
2 June 2021	37.59 ***	37.75 ***	38.54 ***
2 July 2021	44.25 ***	44.49 ***	45.69 ***
Racial minorities *Unemployment rate		0.737 ***	
Racial minorities * Per capita income			−0.000915 ***
Constant	−6.185 ***	−4.843 ***	−11.31 ***
Observations	19,999	19,999	19,999
R-squared	0.758	0.758	0.761

*** $p < 0.001$, ** $p < 0.01$, * $p < 0.05$.

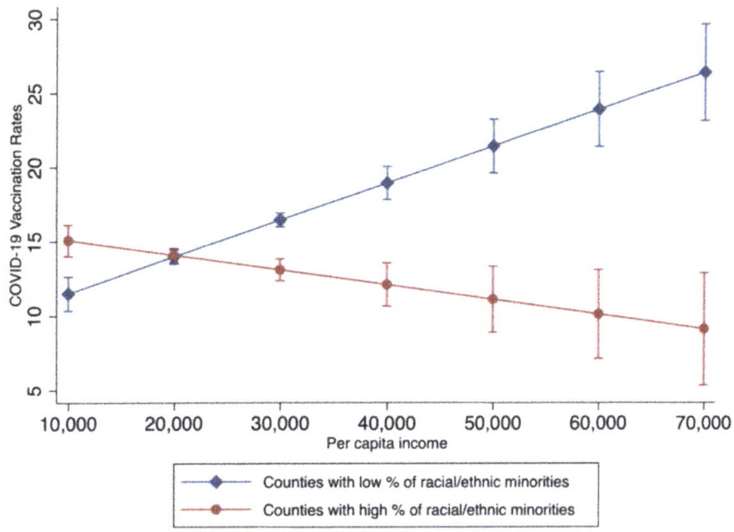

Figure 1. Interaction effects between County-level Per Capita Income, Racial/Ethnic Minorities, and COVID-19 Vaccination Rates. Counties with low and high percent of racial/ethnic minorities: the percentage of adults who are Black, Indigenous, People of Color adults was dichotomized into the top and bottom 5% of the distribution by county-level racial/ethnic composition.

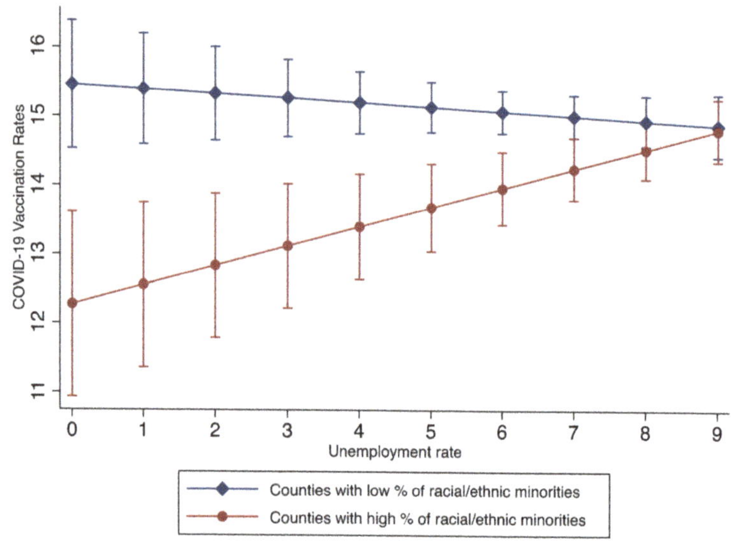

Figure 2. Interaction effects between County-level Unemployment Rate, Racial/Ethnic Minorities, and COVID-19 Vaccination Rates. Counties with low and high percent of racial/ethnic minorities: the percentage of adults who are Black, Indigenous, People of Color adults was dichotomized into the top and bottom 5% of the distribution by county-level racial/ethnic composition.

4. Discussion

This study longitudinally examined county-level relationships between county-level economic factors (i.e., per capita income and unemployment rate) and racial/ethnic composition and county-level COVID-19 vaccination rates in the U.S. Several notable findings emerged from the longitudinal analysis. First, county-level per capita income was positively associated with county-level COVID-19 vaccination rates across U.S counties, and similar findings have been found elsewhere at the county level [28]. Interestingly, we found that this trend (i.e., increases in per capita income being associated with increases in COVID-19 vaccination rates) was divergent in the context of interactive effects with race/ethnicity. We found that increases in per capita income were associated with decreases in COVID-19 vaccination rates in counties with higher proportions of BIPOC adults. It is plausible that race-based political ideology, unequal health care resource distribution, lack of culture-sensitive public health policies, medical distrust, and contemporary healthcare discrimination may contribute to this negative association between per capita income and COVID-19 vaccination rates in counties with higher proportions of BIPOC adults [19,20,31–34]. More studies are needed to explore reasons why COVID-19 vaccination rates in counties with higher proportions of BIPOC adults decrease with increasing per capita income. Despite state and national efforts to address racial inequalities in COVID-19 vaccination, without developing policy interventions that consider economic factors, lagging vaccination rates among BIPOCs will worsen.

Second, county-level unemployment rates were positively associated with county-level COVID-19 vaccination rates. This finding is consistent with a prior study during the first 100 days of COVID-19 vaccination in the U.S., which found that higher state-level unemployment rates were associated with higher state-level vaccination rates [27]. However, we found that county-level proportions of BIPOC adults moderated the effects of county-level unemployment rates on county-level COVID-19 vaccination rates. Increases in unemployment rates were associated with increases in COVID-19 vaccination rates in counties with a higher proportion of BIPOC, but increases in unemployment rates were associated with decreases in COVID-19 vaccination rates in counties with lower proportions of BIPOC (i.e., predominantly non-Hispanic White). In general, unemployment is known to negatively impact vaccination rates for other viral infections (e.g., influenza), but findings from this study suggest that unemployment does not impact COVID-19 vaccination rates in a similar fashion between BIPOC and non-BIPOC individuals at the population-level [35,36]. Interestingly, since BIPOC individuals have faced higher risks of unemployment during the COVID-19 pandemic [9], they may be more motivated to vaccinate against COVID-19 in order to return to the workforce [37]. Equally important, unlike other types of vaccinations, the need for COVID-19 vaccination is not driven by the presence of a pressing pandemic, and the COVID-19 vaccination is widely available at no cost for those who are unemployed or without health insurance [38]. It is plausible that no-cost access to the COVID-19 vaccine for those unemployed and likely without health insurance in some way may provide a means for those with increased risk of unemployment, in particular BIPOC individuals, to secure employment, especially provided that many employers are starting to require COVID-19 vaccination. However, future studies are needed to explore and determine what situational or underlying mechanisms of the COVID-19 pandemic lead to increases in COVID-19 vaccination at the population-level among BIPOC individuals who are unemployed.

This study had notable limitations and strengths. Causality cannot be inferred given the study design and statistical approach. Vaccine incentive programs may bolster vaccination, and the current analysis did not include vaccine incentive programs in the analysis. Also, the study did not explore other social factors, such as index of deprivation and geographical (including but not limited to urban and rural) differences. Future studies may consider comparing COVID-19 vaccination differences based on geographics and socio-economic classifications. However, all counties in the U.S. were included in the study, which considerably increased the study's generalizability. Unlike many studies, the study aimed to examine ways in which economic factors may contribute to disparities and impact outcomes in the context of race/ethnicity versus an examination of disparities and outcomes only based on race/ethnicity.

5. Conclusions

Our findings indicate that county-level per capita income is negatively associated with county-level COVID-19 vaccination rates in counties with higher proportions of BIPOC individuals, while the county-level unemployment rate is negatively associated with county-level vaccination rates in counties with higher proportions of non-Hispanic White individuals. Taken together, it is critical to develop policy interventions to increase vaccination rates in racial/ethnic minority communities in order to stimulate economic recovery. Public health efforts to bolster COVID-19 vaccination rates are encouraged to consider and respond to economic factors that are associated with decreases in COVID-19 vaccination rates. Future research exploring factors underlying these disparate findings at the county-level across the U.S. in the context of race/ethnicity are needed.

Author Contributions: Y.G., Formal Analysis: Y.G. and J.G. Writing—original draft preparation: Y.G. and A.R.K. Writing—Review & Editing: O.T.S. Supervision: O.T.S. All authors have read and agreed to the published version of the manuscript.

Funding: This research received no external funding.

Institutional Review Board Statement: Not applicable.

Informed Consent Statement: This study did not involve humans.

Data Availability Statement: Publicly available datasets were analyzed in this study. This data can be found here: https://www.census.gov/programs-surveys/ces/data/restricted-use-data/demographic-data.html (accessed on 30 May 2021) and here https://data.cdc.gov/Vaccinations/COVID-19-Vaccinations-in-the-United-States-County/8xkx-amqh (accessed on 30 May 2021).

Acknowledgments: Not applicable.

Conflicts of Interest: The authors declare that they have no conflicts of interest.

References

1. A Timeline of COVID-19 Developments in 2020. Available online: https://www.ajmc.com/view/a-timeline-of-covid19-developments-in-2020 (accessed on 13 December 2021).
2. Moreland, A.; Herlihy, C.; Tynan, M.A.; Sunshine, G.; McCord, R.F.; Hilton, C.; Poovey, J.; Werner, A.K.; Jones, C.D.; Fulmer, E.B.; et al. Timing of state and territorial COVID-19 stay-at-home orders and changes in population movement—United States, March 1–May 31, 2020. *Morb. Mortal. Wkly. Rep.* **2020**, *69*, 1198–1203. [CrossRef] [PubMed]
3. Fowler, J.H.; Hill, S.J.; Levin, R.; Obradovich, N. Stay-at-home orders associate with subsequent decreases in COVID-19 cases and fatalities in the United States. *PLoS ONE* **2021**, *16*, e0248849. [CrossRef] [PubMed]
4. Falk, G.; Romero, P.D.; Micchitta, I.A.; Nyhof, E.C. Unemployment Rates during the COVID-19 Pandemic. Congressional Research Service. 20 August 2021. Available online: https://crsreports.congress.gov/product/details?prodcode=R46554 (accessed on 25 July 2021).
5. 1 in 4 Workers Relied on Unemployment Aid during the Pandemic. Available online: https://tcf.org/content/commentary/1-in-4-workers-relied-on-unemployment-aid-during-the-pandemic/ (accessed on 13 December 2021).
6. Economic Fallout from COVID-19 Continues to Hit Lower-Income Americans the Hardest. Available online: https://www.pewresearch.org/social-trends/2020/09/24/economic-fallout-from-covid-19-continues-to-hit-lower-income-americans-the-hardest/ (accessed on 13 December 2021).
7. Nisticò, F.; Troiano, G.; Nante, N.; Piacentini, P. Socioeconomic factors and mortality: Evidences from an Italian study. *Int. J. Healthc. Manag.* **2018**, *13*, 234–239. [CrossRef]
8. Black Workers Face Two of the Most Lethal Preexisting Conditions for Coronavirus—Racism and Economic Inequality. Available online: https://www.epi.org/publication/black-workers-covid/ (accessed on 13 December 2021).
9. Low-Wage, Low-Hours Workers Were Hit Hardest in the COVID-19 Recession. Available online: https://www.epi.org/publication/swa-2020-employment-report/ (accessed on 13 December 2021).
10. Tracking the COVID-19 Economy's Effects on Food, Housing, and Employment Hardships. Available online: https://www.cbpp.org/research/poverty-and-inequality/tracking-the-covid-19-economys-effects-on-food-housing-and (accessed on 13 December 2021).
11. COVID-19's Impact on US Income Inequality: It's Going to Get Worse before It Gets Better. Available online: https://www2.deloitte.com/us/en/insights/economy/issues-by-the-numbers/covid-19-impact-on-income-inequality.html/#deloitte-services (accessed on 13 December 2021).
12. Developing COVID-19 Vaccines. Available online: https://www.cdc.gov/coronavirus/2019-ncov/vaccines/distributing/steps-ensure-safety.html (accessed on 13 December 2021).
13. COVID-19 Frequently Asked Questions. Available online: https://www.fda.gov/emergency-preparedness-and-response/coronavirus-disease-2019-covid-19/covid-19-frequently-asked-questions#:~{}:text=On%20December%2011%2C%202020,)%20of%20a%20vaccine (accessed on 13 December 2021).
14. FDA Approves First COVID-19 Vaccine. Available online: https://www.fda.gov/news-events/press-announcements/fda-approves-first-covid-19-vaccine (accessed on 13 December 2021).
15. Scobie, H.M.; Johnson, A.G.; Suthar, A.B.; Severson, R.; Alden, N.B.; Balter, S.; Bertolino, D.; Blythe, D.; Brady, S.; Cadwell, B.; et al. Monitoring incidence of COVID-19 cases, hospitalizations, and deaths, by vaccination status—13 U.S. Jurisdictions, 4 April–17 July 2021. *Morb. Mortal. Wkly. Rep.* **2021**, *70*, 1284–1290. [CrossRef] [PubMed]
16. President Biden to Announce Goal to Administer at Least One Vaccine Shot to 70% of the U.S. Adult Population by 4 July. Available online: https://www.whitehouse.gov/briefing-room/statements-releases/2021/05/04/fact-sheet-president-biden-to-announce-goal-to-administer-at-least-one-vaccine-shot-to-70-of-the-u-s-adult-population-by-july-4th/ (accessed on 13 December 2021).
17. COVID-19 Vaccinations in the United States. Available online: https://covid.cdc.gov/covid-data-tracker/#vaccinations_vacc-total-admin-rate-total (accessed on 13 December 2021).
18. Demographic Trends of People Receiving COVID-19 Vaccinations in the United States. Available online: https://covid.cdc.gov/covid-data-tracker/#vaccination-demographics-trends (accessed on 13 December 2021).
19. Khubchandani, J.; Macias, Y. COVID-19 vaccination hesitancy in Hispanics and African-Americans: A review and recommendations for practice. *Brain Behav. Immun. Health* **2021**, *15*, 100277. [CrossRef] [PubMed]
20. Momplaisir, F.M.; Kuter, B.J.; Ghadimi, F.; Browne, S.; Nkwihoreze, H.; Feemster, K.A.; Frank, I.; Faig, W.; Shen, A.K.; Offit, P.A.; et al. Racial/ethnic differences in COVID-19 vaccine hesitancy among health care workers in 2 large academic hospitals. *JAMA Netw. Open* **2021**, *4*, e2121931. [CrossRef] [PubMed]
21. Health Equity Considerations and Racial and Ethnic Minority Groups. Available online: https://www.cdc.gov/coronavirus/2019-ncov/community/health-equity/race-ethnicity.html (accessed on 13 December 2021).
22. Hawkins, D. Differential occupational risk for COVID-19 and other infection exposure according to race and ethnicity. *Am. J. Ind. Med.* **2020**, *63*, 817–820. [CrossRef] [PubMed]
23. Risk for COVID-19 Infection, Hospitalization, and Death by Race/Ethnicity. Available online: https://www.cdc.gov/coronavirus/2019-ncov/covid-data/investigations-discovery/hospitalization-death-by-race-ethnicity.html (accessed on 13 December 2021).

24. COVID-19 Vaccine Equity for Racial and Ethnic Minority Groups. Available online: https://www.cdc.gov/coronavirus/2019-ncov/community/health-equity/vaccine-equity.html (accessed on 13 December 2021).
25. Baack, B.N.; Abad, N.; Yankey, D.; Kahn, K.E.; Razzaghi, H.; Brookmeyer, K.; Kolis, J.; Wilhelm, E.; Nguyen, K.H.; Singleton, J.A. COVID-19 vaccination coverage and intent among adults aged 18–39 years—United States, March–May 2021. *MMWR Morb. Mortal. Wkly. Rep.* **2021**, *70*, 928–933. [CrossRef] [PubMed]
26. Barry, V.; Dasgupta, S.; Weller, D.L.; Kriss, J.L.; Cadwell, B.L.; Rose, C.; Pingali, C.; Musial, T.; Sharpe, J.D.; Flores, S.A.; et al. Patterns in COVID-19 vaccination coverage, by social vulnerability and urbanicity—United States, 14 December 2020–1 May 2021. *MMWR Morb. Mortal. Wkly. Rep.* **2021**, *70*, 818–824. [CrossRef] [PubMed]
27. Roghani, A.; Panahi, S. Higher COVID-19 vaccination rates among unemployed in the United States: State level study in the first 100 days of vaccine initiation. *medRxiv* **2021**. [CrossRef]
28. Hughes, M.M.; Wang, A.; Grossman, M.K.; Pun, E.; Whiteman, A.; Deng, L.; Hallisey, E.; Sharpe, J.D.; Ussery, E.N.; Stokley, S.; et al. County-level COVID-19 vaccination coverage and social vulnerability—United States, 14 December 2020–1 March 2021. *MMWR Morb. Mortal. Wkly. Rep.* **2021**, *70*, 431–436. [CrossRef] [PubMed]
29. Demographic Data. Available online: https://www.census.gov/programs-surveys/ces/data/restricted-use-data/demographic-data.html (accessed on 13 December 2021).
30. COVID-19 Vaccinations in the United States, County. Available online: https://data.cdc.gov/Vaccinations/COVID-19-Vaccinations-in-the-United-States-County/8xkx-amqh (accessed on 13 December 2021).
31. Schneider, E.C.; Cleary, P.D.; Zaslavsky, A.M.; Epstein, A.M. Racial disparity in influenza vaccination: Does managed care narrow the gap between African Americans and whites? *JAMA* **2001**, *286*, 1455–1460. [CrossRef] [PubMed]
32. Smith, A.C.; Woerner, J.; Perera, R.; Haeny, A.M.; Cox, J.M. An investigation of associations between race, ethnicity, and past experiences of discrimination with medical mistrust and COVID-19 protective strategies. *J. Racial Ethn. Health Disparities* **2021**, 1–13. [CrossRef] [PubMed]
33. Bendau, A.; Plag, J.; Petzold, M.B.; Ströhle, A. COVID-19 vaccine hesitancy and related fears and anxiety. *Int. Immunopharmacol.* **2021**, *97*, 107724. [CrossRef] [PubMed]
34. Ullah, I.; Khan, K.S.; Tahir, M.J.; Ahmed, A.; Harapan, H. Myths and conspiracy theories on vaccines and COVID-19: Potential effect on global vaccine refusals. *Vacunas* **2021**, *22*, 93–97. [CrossRef] [PubMed]
35. Demenech, L.M.; Dumith, S.D.; Vieira, M.E.; Neiva-Silva, L. Income inequality and risk of infection and death by COVID-19 in Brazil. *Rev. Bras. Epidemiol.* **2020**, *23*, e200095. [CrossRef] [PubMed]
36. Malik, A.A.; McFadden, S.M.; Elharake, J.; Omer, S.B. Determinants of COVID-19 vaccine acceptance in the US. *EClin-icalMedicine* **2020**, *26*, 100495. [CrossRef] [PubMed]
37. Pieroni, V.; Facchini, A.; Riccaboni, M. COVID-19 vaccination and unemployment risk: Lessons from the Italian crisis. *Sci. Rep.* **2021**, *11*, 18538. [CrossRef] [PubMed]
38. Fairlie, R.W.; Couch, K.; Xu, H. The Impacts of COVID-19 on Minority Unemployment: First Evidence from April 2020 CPS Microdata. National Bureau of Economic Research. 25 May 2020. Available online: https://www.nber.org/system/files/working_papers/w27246/w27246.pdf (accessed on 25 July 2021).

International Journal of
Environmental Research and Public Health

Article

Local Ties, Trans-Local Ties, and Substance Use among Rural-to-Urban Migrants in China

Xi Chen [1], Hua Zhong [2,*] and Serena Yunran Zhang [2]

[1] The Jockey Club School of Public Health and Primary Care, The Chinese University of Hong Kong, Hong Kong, China; chenxi424@gmail.com
[2] Department of Sociology, The Chinese University of Hong Kong, Hong Kong, China; yunranzhang@link.cuhk.edu.hk
* Correspondence: sarazhong@cuhk.edu.hk

Abstract: China has witnessed unprecedented rural-to-urban migration since the early 1980s. While trying to assimilate into the city, rural-to-urban migrants still maintain close ties with their home communities. This study examines how local ties and trans-local ties of rural-to-urban migrants affect their alcohol and tobacco use. Data were obtained from the 2016 and 2018 China Labor-force Dynamics Survey, a nationally representative sample of adults aged over 15 in 29 provinces in China. Participants included 1426 rural-to-urban migrant workers and 6438 urban residents in China. We found that compared to urban natives, rural-to-urban migrants had higher tobacco use prevalence (logit = 0.19, 95% CI = [0.03, 0.35]; $p < 0.05$) and more frequent alcohol use (logit = 0.27, 95% CI = [0.11, 0.42]; $p < 0.001$) after adjusting for sociodemographic characteristics. Migrants with more local social ties engaged in more frequent drinking (having >10 local friends vs. having 0 local friends: logit = 0.58, [0.10, 1.06], $p < 0.05$), whereas trans-local ties were not a significant correlate. In contrast, migrants who returned to their hometown more times (an indicator of trans-local ties) were more likely to be current tobacco users (logit = 0.01, 95% CI = [0.00, 0.02], $p < 0.01$) after adjusting for sociodemographic variables. These findings extended the research on social networks and health behaviors by identifying how local and trans-local ties differentially affected the vulnerabilities of tobacco and alcohol use among rural-to-urban migrants in China. The findings suggested that policies and interventions on reducing migrants' health risk behaviors should focus on the role of different types of social ties.

Keywords: local ties; trans-local ties; alcohol use; tobacco use; rural-to-urban migrants; China

Citation: Chen, X.; Zhong, H.; Zhang, S.Y. Local Ties, Trans-Local Ties, and Substance Use among Rural-to-Urban Migrants in China. *Int. J. Environ. Res. Public Health* **2022**, *19*, 4233. https://doi.org/10.3390/ijerph19074233

Academic Editor: William Ash-Houchen

Received: 24 January 2022
Accepted: 29 March 2022
Published: 1 April 2022

1. Introduction

1.1. Tobacco and Alcohol Use among Rural-to-Urban Migrants in China

Although Western developed countries have completed urbanization in a much earlier historical period, there is large-scale ongoing rural-to-urban migration in most of the developing countries. The effects of such internal migration on migrants' well-being have aroused substantial attention from researchers. As a typical developing society, China has witnessed unprecedented rural-to-urban migration along with its rapid modernization and urbanization process since the early 1980s. In the 1990s, China gradually became the "World Factory", and brought a soaring demand for rural-to-urban workers; such demand continued in the 21st century [1]. Figure 1 shows that the number of rural migrant workers in China kept increasing and reached 173 million in 2018, a population even larger than the entire working population in the United States. Compared with rural-to-urban migrants in other developing countries, these Chinese migrant workers might be more vulnerable since they have been regarded as second-class citizens in their own country [2]. Although rural migrants are allowed to work in Chinese cities, they face difficulty in changing their official residency status from "rural" to "urban" due to the household registration (*hukou*) system [3]. *Hukou* is a discriminatory institutional arrangement in China established in the late 1950s to distinguish "urban" (non-agriculture) and "rural" (agriculture) residents so that urban residents have priorities in resource competition. For instance, the urban welfare system in China is more comprehensive and more generous than the rural one. Holding a "rural" *hukou* restricts rural migrants' employment opportunities in a better-paid labor market, excludes them from the urban housing benefits, limits their rights to enjoy urban medical care and a pension, and causes identity discrimination against them [4–7]. Previous studies have documented a high level of psychological and social stress among rural-to-urban migrants in China due to their lower socioeconomic status (SES), unstable living and employment conditions, and insufficient social protection [8,9]. Such mental stress may result in elevated levels of health risk behaviors, particularly increasing their susceptibility to substance use as a way to cope with the stress [10,11].

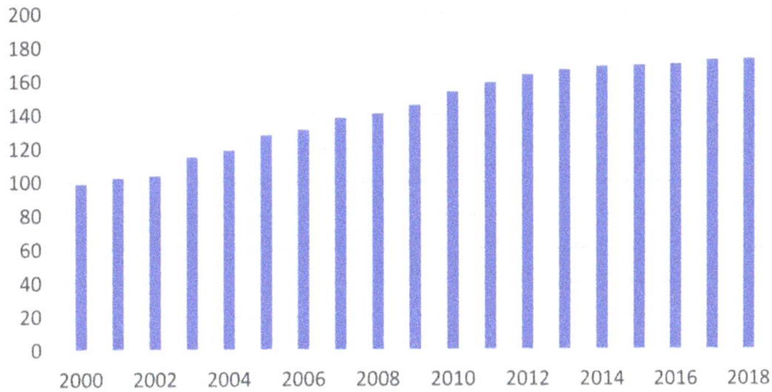

Figure 1. The rising number of rural migrants who left their rural hometown from 2000 to 2018 (million). Source: National Bureau of Statistics, China.

Both tobacco and alcohol use are prevalent among Chinese rural-to-urban migrants. A meta-analysis in 2016 showed that the prevalence of tobacco use among Chinese internal migrants ranged from 17.03% to 41.42% (for studies including both female and male migrants), and the pooled prevalence of tobacco use was 27.75% (46.71% for males and 5.34% for females) [12]. Alcohol misuse was also reported to increase among rural-to-urban migrants [13]. A study of 2153 young rural-to-urban migrants found that about one-third (34.6%) of participants had experienced alcohol intoxication at least once during the past month [14]. However, the results were mixed regarding whether rural-to-urban migrants engage in higher levels of substance use than their urban counterparts. Several studies found that the prevalence of tobacco use is greater among rural-to-urban migrants than urban residents [10,15,16], whereas others have found that the prevalence of tobacco use was lower than that of urban residents [17–19]. Such inconsistent findings may be partly due to the variations in the selection of samples and control groups. National-level representative data are thus needed to ascertain whether rural-to-urban migrants engage in higher levels of substance use than urban residents in China.

1.2. Social Ties and Immigrants' Health Behaviors

Previous studies on substance use among internal migrants in China mostly focus on their low SES and psychological distress as risk factors (e.g., [10,11]). However, substance use, as well as migration, are not only an individual choice but a network-based behavior, which are subject to interpersonal influence. Social ties may have a dualistic effect on health by either preventing or promoting health risk behaviors through psychological and behavioral mechanisms. On the positive side, social ties may generate social support that can help buffer stress, affect appraisals of stress, and alter the perceived capacity to cope [20]. Social connectedness can also create a sense of belonging and a positive psychological state that produce positive physiological responses and promote positive health behaviors [20].

On the negative side, however, social connections can expose individuals to environmental cues of health risk behaviors and possibly boost their engagement of risk behaviors due to behavioral contagion [21,22]. Additionally, social ties may produce psychological stress when social interactions involve excessive demands, restrict freedom, and require group conformity [23], which may, in turn, increase health risk behaviors.

Prior studies on international immigrants have identified that disrupted social networks and social isolation following migration may lead to health risk behaviors among immigrants [24,25]. However, these immigrants may maintain connections with home countries through transnational ties while at the same time building social ties in the receiving society. To date, only a few studies have examined how locations of social ties may affect substance use among immigrants. A study of Latino immigrants in the US found that greater perceived neighborhood social cohesion (local neighborhood ties) was associated with a decreased possibility of being a current smoker; however, the number of past-year return visits to the country-of-origin (transnational ties) was positively associated with their current smoker status [26]. Another study on Latino and Asian origin immigrants in the US found that cross-border ties were associated with a greater likelihood of past-year alcohol use for Latina women, whereas such ties were related to lower probabilities of past-year alcohol use among Asian immigrants [27]. Such findings highlight the importance of differentiating the locality of social ties when considering how ties to migrants' host society and ties to the sending areas may affect their health behaviors. Beyond the international migration milieu, what has yet to be considered is whether trans-local ties matter in the internal migration setting.

1.3. Local Ties, Trans-Local Ties, and Health of Rural-to-Urban Migrants in China

Despite some relaxation of the *hukou* system in recent years, it remains difficult for rural-to-urban migrant workers in China to obtain an urban *hukou* and settle in the city permanently. Most rural migrants still engage in high circular mobility between urban areas and rural communities and sustain close ties with their home communities [9]. Moreover, taking advantage of the low-cost internet and communication technology, rural migrants in cities can keep social, emotional, and economic ties with their family and friends in the home community easily.

Some studies have examined the effect of local ties and trans-local ties on Chinese internal migrants' health, focusing exclusively on their psychological well-being. Jin et al.'s (2012) [9] survey of migrant adults in Shanghai found that more trans-local ties were associated with better mental health among rural migrants, whereas the number of local ties was not a significant correlate of their mental health. The beneficial role of trans-local ties in migrants' psychological well-being may be due to the social support and positive social comparison generated from the trans-local ties. Compared to local ties, trans-local ties tend to strengthen migrants' social comparison with residents in the rural communities from which they migrate and can produce a more favorable evaluation of their social status as they generally make more money in cities. Similarly, research on rural-to-urban migrant children in China found that both local ties and trans-local ties enhanced migrant adolescents' mental well-being, with trans-local ties being somewhat more useful in moderating social stress they experienced [28,29]. In contrast, other studies have identified certain negative or nonsignificant effects of local ties on migrant workers' victimization and life satisfaction since their close interactions with urban natives may increase their risky lifestyles (e.g., more entertainment activities at night) or experience more discriminations from urban natives [6,30]; Yue et al.'s (2019) also pointed out the nonsignificant relationship between trans-local ties and migrant workers' life satisfaction since trans-local contacts are also socially vulnerable and could not provide the help and support that migrants need [31].

Despite emerging evidence of the effect of local and trans-local ties on migrants' health in China, two research gaps remain in the past literature. First, to the best of our knowledge, no studies have examined how local and trans-local ties may affect health risk behaviors among rural-to-urban migrants in China. Second, previous measures of the trans-local relations of rural-to-urban migrants in China either used the number of close friends and relatives outside the host cities [9] or the frequency of contact with home friends and relatives [28,29], which did not directly assess the social and economic activities of migrants in the home communities. We address that gap in this study by gauging migrants' trans-local ties with the number of return visits, their economic contribution to rural communities where they migrated, and the help they offered to village fellows in their sending areas.

1.4. The Present Study

Based on the national-representative China Labor-Force Dynamics Survey (2016 and 2018), this study aims to examine the prevalence and correlated social factors of tobacco and alcohol use among rural-to-urban migrant workers in China, with a special focus on their social ties to host cities and to home communities. Although we target rural-to-urban migrants, we also include a sample of native urban residents for comparison, which may help us identify the unique features of substance use and the effects of social ties among migrants. We have two specific research questions in this study: (1) to explore whether rural-to-urban migrants in China have higher levels of tobacco and alcohol use than their urban counterparts, after adjusting for sociodemographic variables; and (2) to analyze how local and trans-local ties affect rural-to-urban migrants' tobacco and alcohol use in China. Due to the inconsistent evidence of the prevalence of substance use among rural migrants in China and virtually nonexistent research on the effects of local and trans-local ties on their health risk behaviors, we raised research questions instead of proposing specific hypotheses. We organize the paper as follows: first, we outline the research methods and analytical strategies; we then describe the main results and discuss their theoretical and policy implications.

2. Materials and Methods

2.1. Data

This study used data from China Labor-force Dynamics Survey (CLDS), a nationwide multiple cross-sectional survey conducted biannually by the Sun Yat-Sen University in China since 2012 [32]. With a focus on labor force issues, the CLDS is a nationally representative study of individuals aged over 15, families, and communities in urban and rural areas across 29 of the 31 provinces of mainland China (excluding Tibet and Hainan). The survey applied multistage cluster proportionate probability sampling methods. The 29 provinces were first classified into six strata based on population size and geographic location. Rural counties, county-level cities, and county-level urban districts (primary sampling units, PSUs) within each stratum were then randomly selected according to their GDP rankings. The quantity of PSUs in each geographic stratum was determined by the size of their labor force. Within each PSU, urban and rural communities (secondary sampling units, SSUs) were randomly drawn based on their GDP rankings and the proportion of the internal migrant population. Finally, the households were selected at random from each SSU, and all family members aged over 15 were sampled. Detailed information of the CLDS data was shown elsewhere (e.g., [33,34]).

To reflect the recent pattern of substance use among rural-to-urban migrants in China, we analyzed the latest two waves of data available that were collected in 2016 and 2018. The 2016 CLDS included 7767 respondents in urban districts, among which 1234 were rural-to-urban migrants. The 2018 CLDS contained 4924 respondents in urban districts and 714 of them were rural-to-urban migrants. As the present study focused only on the working population, respondents who reported being unemployed since the last year were excluded from the analysis (n = 4827). The final sample size was 7864 respondents, including 1426 rural-to-urban migrants (without an urban *hukou*) and 6438 urban native residents (with an urban *hukou*).

2.2. *Measurement*

2.2.1. Dependent Variables

Tobacco Use. The participants were first asked whether they have a tobacco use history ("Have you smoked one or more cigarettes per day for at least one year?"). For those who had a tobacco use history, they were further asked whether they were still smoking cigarettes currently ("Have you quit smoking or do you still smoke cigarettes currently?"). The tobacco use in our study thus was recoded as a binary variable (0 = current non-smoker; 1 = respondents with a tobacco use history and are currently using tobacco).

Alcohol Use. It was gauged by first asking the respondents whether they engaged in drinking alcohol (at least once a week). Respondents who reported "yes" to this question were further asked to report the frequency of drinking. The variable of drinking behavior was an ordinal variable that included four categories of response (1 = never/less than once a week, 2 = 1–2 times per week, 3 = 3–4 times per week, and 4 = almost every day).

2.2.2. Independent Variables

Local social ties were measured by asking respondents to indicate the number of local friends they had in cities. We categorized the responses into four categories, i.e., no local friends, 1–5 local friends, 6–10 local friends, and more than 10 local friends.

Local neighborhood cohesion was assessed by three questions about perceptions of neighborhood support and trust: (1) "Do you know your neighbors?" (1 = very little; 5 = very well); (2) "Do you trust your neighbors?" (1 = very little; 5 = very much); and (3) "Is there mutual support between you and your neighbors and other residents in this urban community?" (1 = very little; 5 = very much). The mean of the three items was calculated, with higher scores representing a stronger perception of neighborhood cohesion (three-item scale, alpha = 0.82).

Trans-local ties were measured by three questions. The first question asked respondents about the number of times that they went back to their home communities in the past year. The second question asked respondents whether they had donated money to their home communities. The third question asked respondents whether they had helped people in their home communities.

2.2.3. Control Variables

The control variables included age, sex (male vs. female), marital status (single, cohabitate, married, and divorced/widowed), education (primary school or below, secondary school, and college or above), occupation (manufacture industry, service industry, and other), logged annual income, and the region (East, Middle, and West).

2.3. *Analytical Strategies*

We first conducted descriptive analysis for all variables among the full sample and subsamples of rural-to-urban migrants and urban native residents. We also tested the differences in these variables between migrants and native urban residents using two-sided *t*-tests or *chi*-square tests. Next, we performed logistic regression to examine the effect of migration status on tobacco use and used ordinal logistic regression to estimate the effect of migration status on the frequency of drinking after controlling for other sociodemographic variables. We then investigated the associations between sociodemographic characteristics and tobacco and alcohol use among migrants and urban native residents using either logistic regression (for tobacco use) or ordinal logistic regression (for alcohol use) models. Lastly, we ran appropriate regression models to examine the effect of local ties and trans-local ties on tobacco and alcohol use among rural-to-urban migrants and native urban residents. We performed a formal test of multicollinearity. The variance inflation factor for each of the predictors was well below 10 (ranged from 1.02 to 2.36); thus, there were no extreme interrelations between predictor variables. All analyses were performed in Stata 16.0. The coefficients with 95% confidence intervals were reported. A p value of 0.05 was set as the level of statistical significance.

3. Results

3.1. Sample Characteristics

The descriptive statistics are displayed in Table 1. The mean age of the full sample was 43 (SD = 11.33). There were slightly more males (53.08%) than females (46.92%). A majority of respondents were married (81.37%), had secondary education (52.74%) or above (34.92%), and worked in the service industry (51.04%). More than half of the respondents were in East China (53.62%), with the remaining in the Middle (21.43%) and the West (24.95%). The comparisons between rural-to-urban migrants and local workers showed that migrant workers were younger, lower-educated, more likely to be single, more likely to work in the manufacturing industry, and more likely to be located in the East. There were no significant differences in sex and annual income between the two samples.

Table 1. Descriptive statistics.

	Full Sample (N = 7864)		Rural-to-Urban Migrants (N = 1426)		Urban Native Residents (N = 6438)		*t/chi*-Square Test
	Mean/%	SD	Mean/%	SD	Mean/%	SD	
Age, mean (SD)	42.79	−11.33	39.34	−11.25	43.56	−11.21	12.83 ***
Sex							
Male	53.08		52.1		53.29		0.66
Female	46.92		47.9		46.71		
Marital status							
Single	13.83		17.81		12.95		42.39 ***
Cohabitate	0.85		1.47		0.72		
Married	81.37		78.47		82.01		
Divorced/widowed	3.94		2.24		4.32		
Education							
Primary school or below	12.35		17.56		11.19		50.34 ***
Secondary school	52.74		62.99		50.47		
College or above	34.92		19.45		38.34		
Occupation							
Manufacturing industry	27.9		35.2		26.28		50.38 ***
Service industry	51.04		47.76		51.77		
Other	21.06		17.04		21.95		
Annual income (logged), mean (SD)	10.1	−2.49	10.1	−2.59	10.1	−2.47	−0.04
Region							
East	53.62		61.36		51.91		42.23 ***
Middle	21.43		18.3		22.12		
West	24.95		20.34		25.97		
Current tobacco use							
Yes	24.42		26.95		23.86		6.02 *
No	75.58		73.05		76.14		
Frequency of drinking							
Less than once per week	78.44		76.05		78.97		12.49 **
1–2 times per week	12.7		14.04		12.4		
3–4 times per week	4.28		3.86		4.37		
Almost everyday	4.58		6.04		4.26		

Table 1. *Cont.*

	Full Sample (N = 7864)		Rural-to-Urban Migrants (N = 1426)		Urban Native Residents (N = 6438)		t/chi-Square Test
	Mean/%	SD	Mean/%	SD	Mean/%	SD	
Local ties							
Number of local friends							
0	12.43		11.72		15.59		35.96 ***
1—5	40.36		39.75		43.09		
6—10	27.11		27.41		25.74		
>10	20.11		21.12		15.59		
Perceived neighborhood cohesion, mean (SD)	3.26	−0.81	2.93	−0.82	3.33	−0.79	17.11 ***
Trans-local ties							
Number of times going back to the home community, mean (SD)			5.6	−23.44			
Donation to the home community							
Yes			23.29				
No			76.71				
Help people in the home community							
Yes			37.48				
No			62.52				

* $p < 0.05$, ** $p < 0.01$, *** $p < 0.001$.

3.2. Differences in Local/Trans-Local Ties and Substance Use between Rural-to-Urban Migrants and Urban Natives

Nearly one in four respondents (24.42%) in the full sample were current smokers, with rural-to-urban migrants being significantly more likely to report current smoker status than local workers (26.95% vs. 23.86%, $p < 0.05$). About 80% (78.44%) of respondents never drank or drank less than once per week. Rural-to-urban migrant workers tended to drink more frequently than their urban counterparts. As for local ties, rural-to-urban migrants seemed to report more friends in the city than urban native residents. However, urban residents perceived a significantly higher level of neighborhood cohesion than migrants. On average, rural-to-urban migrants went back to their hometown about 5.6 times in the past year. Nearly one in four rural-to-urban migrants (23.29%) donated money to their home communities, and more than one-third of migrants (37.48%) helped people in the home communities.

3.3. Associations between Migration Status and Substance Use

Table 2 presents the effect of migration status on tobacco and alcohol use. The results revealed that being a rural-to-urban migrant was positively associated with both tobacco use (logit = 0.19, 95% CI = [0.03, 0.35]; $p < 0.05$) and alcohol use (logit = 0.27, 95% CI = [0.11, 0.42]; $p < 0.001$), after controlling for other sociodemographic variables.

Table 2. The effect of migration status on tobacco use and alcohol use.

	Tobacco Use		Alcohol Use	
	Logit	[95% CI]	Logit	[95% CI]
Rural-to-urban migrants	0.19 *	[0.03, 0.35]	0.27 ***	[0.11, 0.42]
Age	0.01 ***	[0.01, 0.02]	0.02 ***	[0.01, 0.02]
Sex (ref: male)				
Female	−4.06 ***	[−4.34, −3.77]	−2.52 ***	[−2.70, −2.35]

Table 2. *Cont.*

	Tobacco Use		Alcohol Use	
	Logit	**[95% CI]**	**Logit**	**[95% CI]**
Marital status (ref: single)				
Cohabitate	−0.05	[−0.73, 0.62]	0.19	[−0.44, 0.82]
Married	−0.02	[−0.23, 0.19]	0.06	[−0.14, 0.27]
Divorced/widowed	0.43 *	[0.04, 0.83]	0.33	[−0.03,0.69]
Education (ref: primary or below)				
Secondary	0.14	[−0.06, 0.35]	0.13	[−0.07, 0.33]
College or above	−0.52 ***	[−0.76, −0.29]	−0.10	[−0.32, 0.13]
Annual income (logged)	0.01	[−0.02, 0.04]	0.04 **	[0.01, 0.07]
Occupation (ref: other)				
Manufacturing industry	0.27 **	[0.10, 0.44]	0.19 *	[0.02, 0.35]
Service industry	0.19 *	[0.02, 0.36]	0.07	[−0.09, 0.24]
Region (ref: East)				
Middle	−0.09	[−0.25, 0.06]	0.03	[−0.12, 0.18]
West	0.11	[−0.04, 0.26]	0.21 **	[0.07, 0.35]

* $p < 0.05$, ** $p < 0.01$, *** $p < 0.001$.

3.4. Associations between Background Variables and Substance Use

Table 3 shows the associations between sociodemographic variables and tobacco and alcohol use. Results in Model 1a revealed that among the rural-to-urban migrant workers, female sex (b = −4.51, 95% CI = [−5.24, −3.79]; $p < 0.001$) and college education or above (b = −0.62, 95% CI = [−1.18, −0.06]; $p < 0.05$) were associated with lower likelihood of tobacco use. The same pattern held for urban native workers (Model 1b). Migrant workers who were employed in the service sector were more likely to use tobacco (b = 0.53, 95% CI = [0.09, 0.97]; $p < 0.05$). However, urban residents who worked in the manufacturing industry were more likely to report tobacco use (b = 0.25, 95% CI = [0.06, 0.44]; $p < 0.01$). As for the alcohol use, Models 2a and 2b showed that females report less frequency of drinking among rural-to-urban migrants and urban native residents. Urban residents with higher annual income and who lived in the West tend to have a higher frequency of drinking, whereas socioeconomic variables were not significantly associated with alcohol use among rural-to-urban migrant workers.

Table 3. The association between sociodemographic variables and tobacco use and alcohol use among migrants and urban native residents.

	Current Tobacco Use				Frequency of Drinking			
	Model 1a Rural-to-Urban Migrants		Model 1b Urban Native Residents		Model 2a Rural-to-Urban Migrants		Model 2b Urban Native Residents	
	Logit	**[95% CI]**	**Logit**	**[95% CI]**	**Logit**	**[95% CI]**	**Logit**	**[95% CI]**
Age	0.01	[−0.01, 0.02]	0.01 ***	[0.01, 0.02]	0.01	[−0.01, 0.02]	0.02 ***	[0.01, 0.03]
Sex (ref: male)								
Female	−4.51 ***	[−5.24, −3.79]	−3.97 ***	[−4.28, −3.65]	−2.62 ***	[−3.01, −2.22]	−2.50 ***	[−2.70, −2.31]
Marital status (ref: single)								
Cohabitate	0.72	[−0.58, 2.02]	−0.40	[−1.22, 0.42]	0.80	[−0.24, 1.84]	−0.17	[−0.97, 0.63]
Married	−0.02	[−0.47, 0.43]	−0.02	[−0.26, 0.22]	0.09	[−0.33, 0.51]	0.06	[−0.18, 0.29]
Divorced/widowed	0.31	[−1.02, 1.64]	0.44 *	[0.02, 0.86]	−0.24	[−1.47, 0.99]	0.37	[−0.02, 0.76]

Table 3. *Cont.*

	Current Tobacco Use				Frequency of Drinking			
	Model 1a Rural-to-Urban Migrants		Model 1b Urban Native Residents		Model 2a Rural-to-Urban Migrants		Model 2b Urban Native Residents	
	Logit	[95% CI]	Logit	[95% CI]	Logit	[95% CI]	Logit	[95% CI]
Education (ref: primary or below)								
Secondary	−0.21	[−0.65, 0.22]	0.25 *	[0.01, 0.49]	−0.13	[−0.52, 0.26]	0.21	[−0.02, 0.44]
College or above	−0.62 *	[−1.18, −0.06]	−0.45 **	[−0.71, −0.18]	−0.35	[−0.85, 0.16]	−0.02	[−0.28, 0.24]
Annual income (logged)	0.02	[−0.04, 0.09]	0.01	[−0.02, 0.04]	0.02	[−0.04, 0.08]	0.05 **	[0.01, 0.08]
Occupation (ref: other)								
Manufacturing industry	0.35	[−0.09, 0.79]	0.25 **	[0.06, 0.44]	0.15	[−0.26, 0.55]	0.17	[−0.01, 0.36]
Service industry	0.53 *	[0.09, 0.97]	0.12	[−0.06, 0.31]	0.05	[−0.35, 0.45]	0.06	[−0.12, 0.24]
Region (ref: East)								
Middle	−0.37	[−0.78, 0.03]	−0.04	[−0.21, 0.13]	−0.17	[−0.55, 0.21]	0.08	[−0.08, 0.24]
West	0.16	[−0.21, 0.53]	0.11	[−0.06, 0.27]	0.24	[−0.08, 0.57]	0.22 **	[0.06, 0.37]

* $p < 0.05$, ** $p < 0.01$, *** $p < 0.001$.

3.5. Associations between Local/Trans-Local Ties and Substance Use among Rural-to-Urban Migrants and Urban Natives

The effects of local/trans-local ties on tobacco use were shown in Table 4. Model 3a demonstrated no significant association between the strength of local ties and tobacco use among the rural-to-urban migrant sample. In contrast, migrants who had more return visits to sending areas were more likely to use tobacco (Model 3b: b = 0.01, 95% CI = [0.00, 0.02]; $p < 0.01$). Model 4 in Table 4 shows that native urban residents having more than 10 local friends were more likely to be current smokers (b = 0.36, 95% CI = [0.11, 0.61], $p < 0.01$) than those with no local friends. Perceived neighborhood cohesion had no significant effect on tobacco use among either rural-to-urban migrants or native urban residents.

Table 4. The effect of local ties and trans-local ties on tobacco use.

	Rural-to-Urban Migrants				Native Urban Residents	
	Model 3a		Model 3b		Model 4	
	Logit	[95% CI]	Logit	[95% CI]	Logit	[95% CI]
Local ties						
Number of local friends (ref: =0)						
1—5	−0.03	[−0.48, 0.41]	−0.18	[−0.67, 0.31]	0.09	[−0.14, 0.32]
6—10	−0.24	[−0.72, 0.24]	−0.28	[−0.81, 0.24]	0.10	[−0.14, 0.34]
>10	0.30	[−0.22, 0.82]	0.12	[−0.46, 0.70]	0.36 **	[0.11, 0.61]
Perceived neighborhood cohesion	−0.00	[−0.19, 0.18]	0.04	[−0.16, 0.25]	0.00	[−0.09, 0.09]
Trans-local ties						
Number of times going back to the sending community			0.01 **	[0.00, 0.02]		
Donation to the sending communities (ref: no)						
Yes			−0.02	[−0.42, 0.39]		
Help people in the sending community (ref: no)						
Yes			0.15	[−0.21, 0.51]		

** $p < 0.01$. All models adjusted for sociodemographic variables, including age, sex, marital status, education, annual income, occupation, and region.

Table 5 presents the results of the relationship between local/trans-local ties and alcohol use. Model 5a showed that for rural-to-urban migrants, having more local friends were associated with higher frequency of drinking (b = 0.58, 95% [0.10, 1.06]; $p < 0.05$); this association remained marginally significant even when trans-local ties were included

(Model 5b: b = 0.47, 95% CI = [−0.06, 0.99]; p = 0.08). Similarly, we observed that native urban residents with more local friends had significantly higher drinking frequencies (Model 6). Perceived neighborhood cohesion in the city and trans-local ties with migrants' home communities were not associated with alcohol use. However, perceived neighborhood cohesion was negatively associated with drinking frequency among urban residents (b = −0.14, 95% CI = [−0.23, −0.06]; $p < 0.01$).

Table 5. The effect of local ties and trans-local ties on alcohol use.

	Rural-to-Urban Migrants				Native Urban Residents	
	Model 5a		Model 5b		Model 6	
	b	[95% CI]	b	[95% CI]	b	[95% CI]
Local ties						
# of local friends (ref: =0)						
1—5	0.18	[−0.24, 0.60]	0.06	[−0.40, 0.52]	0.18	[−0.05, 0.41]
6—10	0.06	[−0.40, 0.52]	0.01	[−0.49, 0.51]	0.43 ***	[0.19, 0.67]
>10	0.58 *	[0.10, 1.06]	0.47	[−0.06, 0.99]	0.54 ***	[0.29, 0.79]
Perceived community cohesion	−0.06	[−0.23, 0.11]	0.00	[−0.18, 0.19]	−0.14 **	[−0.23, −0.06]
Trans-local ties						
Number of times going back to the sending community			0.00	[−0.00, 0.01]		
Donation to the sending communities (ref: no)						
Yes			−0.09	[−0.45, 0.28]		
Help people in the sending community (ref: no)						
Yes			0.15	[−0.18, 0.48]		

* $p < 0.05$, ** $p < 0.01$, *** $p < 0.001$. All models adjusted for sociodemographic variables, including age, sex, marital status, education, annual income, occupation, and region.

4. Discussion

While assimilating into the city and building local ties, rural-to-urban migrants in China maintain close social ties to their home communities. However, limited studies have examined the effects of local and trans-local ties on the health risk behaviors among migrant workers in China. Using nationally representative data, this study presented an overview and comparative analyses of the alcohol and tobacco use among rural-to-urban migrants and urban native residents and investigated how local and trans-local ties might affect substance use among the two populations in China. The results extended the research on social networks and health risk behaviors and provided evidence for further research and the development of public health policy on alcohol and tobacco use. We discuss the main findings below.

First, our findings revealed that rural-to-urban migrant workers had greater levels of tobacco and alcohol use than their urban counterparts after adjusting for sociodemographic variables. Such findings were not consistent with some previous studies showing that rural-to-urban migrants tended to report less substance use than urban residents [17–19]. However, these studies were mostly conducted in only one province in China and collected data more than 15 years ago (e.g., in 2004–2005 for [17,18]), which may not reflect current situations of substance use among rural-to-urban migrant workers in China. Based on the national-representative data from the 2012 Migrant Dynamics Monitoring Survey in China, one study found that the prevalence of migrants' tobacco use was slightly lower than that in the general population [19]. However, the data of substance use in the general population they compared to were from another survey (i.e., 2010 Global Adult Tobacco Survey). Given the data collection of the two surveys was at different times and used different sampling methods and measures, results from such a comparison may not be conclusive. To understand the above substance use disparities between rural-to-urban migrants and urban natives, we could seek hints from prior studies on urban-rural inequalities in China.

Modern alcohol and tobacco consumption have been consistently high in China since the 1980s (when China opened its door to the whole world). Among all countries, China continues to be the largest manufacturer and consumer of cigarettes in recent decades; drinking alcohol, as a cultural symbol of happiness/celebrity and recently as necessary skills for career advancement, has been even widely accepted in China for thousands of years, which is rarely seen in other countries [35,36]. Fortunately, with rapid modernization and social development, awareness of the negative health effects of alcohol and tobacco use has been largely improved among well-educated Chinese people. However, due to the long-term rural-urban division in China, rural areas are generally less developed and have lower levels of education. It is thus understandable that compared with urban elites, rural people have much less exposure to information about the harms of smoking and drinking [37]. Such lagged awareness might be partially attributable to the greater levels of rural-to-urban migrants' tobacco and alcohol use since they are coming from rural areas. Future studies could directly examine the differential awareness of the substance use harm among rural peasants, migrant workers, and various social classes of urban natives.

Second, our findings showed that local and trans-local ties were differentially associated with rural-to-urban migrants' tobacco and alcohol use. Specifically, more local friends were associated with more frequent drinking behaviors among rural-to-urban migrant workers, whereas the strength of trans-local ties was positively related to their tobacco use. The positive association between local social ties and alcohol use may reflect the adverse consequences of assimilating into the host society among rural-to-urban migrants in China. Chinese drinking culture encourages social drinking, and drinking alcohol is a means for individuals to establish and express relationships with one another [38]. Rural-to-urban migrants with more local friends tend to drink more frequently to cultivate "guanxi" (the Chinese expression of sentimental and instrumental interpersonal connections) and strengthen social connections in the receiving city. We also conjectured that a large network of local friends might indicate greater adherence to behavioral norms in cities that seem less restrictive of drinking. Studies have shown that urban residents have greater levels of alcohol consumption affordability and more access to drinking-related activities/events [39,40]. In this context, rural-to-urban migrants with more local friends may be subject to a higher level of social pressure to adopt group-specific normative health behaviors and to drink more frequently with their local contacts (e.g., to discuss work-related business or to strengthen "*guanxi*" in dining tables). In other words, although local ties might provide positive instrumental and emotional support for migrant workers, such ties could foster a type of negative assimilation and increase health risks among migrant workers. Both pros and cons of local ties need to be carefully examined in future research.

Additionally, it is worth noting that perceived neighborhood cohesion was associated with less frequent alcohol use only among urban residents, but not among the migrant workers. A growing body of research has suggested that higher neighborhood social cohesion is associated with better health and well-being outcomes. Neighborhood social cohesion may promote health and health behavior by distributing health information, providing social and psychological support, and reinforcing healthy norms that certain behaviors (e.g., not heavy drinking) are desirable. Our finding of the beneficial role of neighborhood cohesion in reducing alcohol use among urban residents was consistent with prior studies. However, the insignificant effect of neighborhood cohesion for rural migrants may be due to the residential segregation they experienced in cities [6]. Chinese internal migrants are often excluded from mainstream urban neighborhoods with a beautiful and clean environment, good public order, and harmonious neighborhood relationships. Instead, Chinese rural-to-urban migrants tend to reside in poor urban enclaves (e.g., urban villages) characterized by high population density, low level of regulation, unhealthy living environment, and frequent safety problems [41,42]. Despite the adverse environment of these migrant-concentrated neighborhoods, the majority of rural migrants do not want to move out because of the low living cost. To some extent, they are stuck in these enclaves that can provide limited resources to develop healthy behaviors. Future studies could conduct surveys and interviews in such migrant-concentrated neighborhoods to examine the unique effects of neighborhoods on migrant workers' health and health behaviors.

Different from the analysis of alcohol use, we found that the number of past-year return visits to migrants' sending areas (trans-local ties) was positively associated with their current smoker status, while the number of local ties was not a significant correlate. The positive relationship between the number of return visits and current smoker status was consistent with overseas evidence [26]. We interpreted the findings from two perspectives. First, visits back home were behavioral indicators of connections to home communities, which may reinforce adherence to social norms and health behaviors prevalent in the home communities. As the prevalence of tobacco use and tobacco abuse was higher among rural residents than urban residents in China [40,43], rural-to-urban migrants who went back to home communities more frequently were more likely to be exposed to the tobacco-promoting norms and context. Additionally, the price of cigarettes is generally lower in rural areas, so people who return to rural communities have more opportunities to purchase cheaper cigarettes and bring them back to cities. Second, maintaining trans-local ties in the sending communities (e.g., travel and gift expenses) may result in financial and emotional stress. Such stress may, in turn, increase the propensity for engaging in health risk behaviors. However, we did not have information about the specific reasons or detailed context for the return visits among rural-to-urban migrants (e.g., taking care of left-behind children or the death of a family member). Future research could further examine the reasons for the return visits and their associations with health risk behaviors.

Realizing the huge health burden (e.g., lung cancer and liver cancer) related to tobacco and alcohol use, the Chinese government has developed an ambitious action plan ("Health China 2030 Strategy") and aimed to substantially reduce the prevalence of alcohol and tobacco use by 2030 [35–39]. However, due to the vast development gap between rural and urban areas, all tobacco and alcohol control/prevention measures progressed slowly for the rural population, including rural-to-urban migrants. Our findings suggested that we should spend immense efforts on promoting citizens' awareness of the negative health effects of tobacco use, especially in rural China, since migrant tobacco users continued to be significantly influenced by their rural ties; for reducing their alcohol use, the receiving societies need to provide migrant workers more healthy access to establish and expand their urban local ties and fundamentally reduce their institutional social exclusion in urban areas. As latecomers of modernization, many other developing countries, similar to China, began developing their industrialization and urbanization rapidly in recent decades, leading to large-scale rural-to-urban migration within their countries. The models and results of the present research could inspire future cross-cultural studies to extend our understandings on the nexus between internal migration and health, plus providing more generalizable evidence for global policy shifts on how to improve migrant workers' well-being.

Despite significant findings, this study was not without limitations. First, the study was cross-sectional, and causality could not be inferred from the results. Longitudinal investigations are warranted to elucidate whether social ties predict substance use among the migrant population. Second, we did not control for tobacco and alcohol use before migration in our models since such data were not available. More sophisticated measures on migrant workers' prior tobacco and alcohol use thus need to be designed in future examinations. Third, we used self-report data of tobacco and alcohol use, which may be subject to certain reporting biases. Although the data were anonymous to reduce the potential inaccuracies, it will be helpful to adopt other measures (e.g., biochemical markers) to examine the criterion-related validity of self-report substance use data. Fourth, we included a single-item measure of current tobacco use status and drinking frequency. More comprehensive assessments of tobacco and alcohol use (e.g., quantity and duration of tobacco use/binge drinking) are needed to capture different types of substance use (e.g., light users vs. substance abusers). Fifth, we assessed trans-local ties using behavioral indicators of connectedness to the migrants' sending areas. Although behavioral indicators of transnationalism were widely used and have been validated in previous studies [44], future studies may include additional indicators of trans-local ties, such as perceived connectedness to the home communities. Lastly, constrained by the lack of provincial-representative data, we did not conduct a provincial-level analysis on migrant workers' tobacco and alcohol use, despite that we have controlled for the region in our analysis. Future studies may conduct a more comprehensive regional and provincial analysis on migrant workers' tobacco and alcohol use, considering the great levels of internal inequality within China.

5. Conclusions

This study was a pioneering one which examined the roles of local and trans-local ties in health risk behaviors among rural-to-urban migrants, the largest disadvantaged social group in China. Based on a nationally representative survey of rural-to-urban migrants and their urban counterparts, our results revealed that migrant workers' higher risks in terms of tobacco and alcohol use were embedded into their relationships with both sending societies and receiving societies. Among all rural-to-urban migrants, those with a larger local network tended to drink alcohol more frequently since they might form a risky lifestyle to actively socialize with their urban native contacts, aiming to overcome their social segregation and resource constraints experienced in urban areas. Migrant workers with stronger trans-local ties were more likely to be current tobacco users due to their continuing adoption of tobacco tolerance in their rural hometowns, which could be linked with the insufficient health knowledge and awareness in less developed rural China. To lower the health risks of these migrant workers, it calls for essential actions to reduce the exclusion they experience in urban areas and improve health-related education in rural areas.

Author Contributions: Conceptualization, X.C. and H.Z.; Methodology, S.Y.Z. and X.C.; Formal Analysis, X.C., H.Z. and S.Y.Z.; Data Curation, H.Z.; Writing—Original Draft Preparation, X.C.; Writing—Review and Editing, H.Z. All authors have read and agreed to the published version of the manuscript.

Funding: This research received no external funding. The author(s) received no financial support for the research, authorship, and/or publication of this article.

Institutional Review Board Statement: Ethical review and approval were waived for this study due to publicly open data from the CLDS.

Informed Consent Statement: Informed consent was obtained from all subjects involved in the study.

Data Availability Statement: The overview and documents of the CLDS can be found at http://css.sysu.edu.cn/Data (accessed on 15 November 2021).

Acknowledgments: The data analyzed in this study was collected by the research project "China Labor-force Dynamics Survey (CLDS)" carried out by the Center for Social Survey, Sun Yat-sen University. The authors appreciate the assistance of the institute when we applied for the use of the data.

Conflicts of Interest: The authors declare no conflict of interest.

References

1. Zhao, S. What determines migrant workers' life chances in contemporary China? Hukou, social exclusion and the market. *Mod. China* **2011**, *37*, 243–285.
2. Zhang, L. *Strangers in the City: Reconfigurations of Space, Power, and Social Networks within China's Floating Population*; Stanford University Press: Stanford, CA, USA, 2001.
3. Ma, L.J.C.; Xiang, B. Native place, migration and the emergence of peasant enclaves in Beijing. *China Q.* **1998**, *155*, 546–581. [CrossRef]
4. Solinger, D. *Contesting Citizenship*; The University of California Press: Berkeley, CA, USA, 1999.
5. Fan, C.C. *China on the Move: Migration, the State, and the Household*; Routledge: London, UK, 2007.
6. Zhong, H.; Xu, J.; Piquero, A.R. Internal migration, social exclusion, and victimization: An analysis of Chinese rural-to-urban migrants. *J. Res. Crime Delinq.* **2017**, *54*, 479–514. [CrossRef]

7. Chen, X. Strain, school type, and delinquent behavior among migrant adolescents in China. *Asian J. Criminol.* **2021**, *16*, 357–376. [CrossRef]
8. Ji, P.; Liu, J.; Cheng, J.; Yang, D.; Xia, T.; Zhang, D.; Lu, Z. The analysis of main health problems and policy orientation in Shenzhen city. *Med. Soc.* **2002**, *15*, 4–7.
9. Jin, L.; Wen, M.; Fan, J.X.; Wang, G. Trans-local ties, local ties and psychological well-being among rural-to-urban migrants in Shanghai. *Soc. Sci. Med.* **2012**, *75*, 288–296. [CrossRef]
10. Chen, X.; Li, X.; Stanton, B.; Fang, X.; Lin, D.; Cole, M.; Liu, H.; Yang, H. Cigarette tobacco use among rural-to-urban migrants in Beijing, China. *Prev. Med.* **2004**, *39*, 666–673. [CrossRef]
11. Xie, S. The migration, mental stress, and tobacco use of internal migrants in China: The moderating effect of the social context of the host society. *Subst. Use Misuse* **2017**, *52*, 1733–1743. [CrossRef]
12. Liu, Y.; Gao, J.; Shou, J.; Xia, H.; Shen, Y.; Zhu, S.; Pan, Z. The prevalence of cigarette tobacco use among rural-to-urban migrants in China: A systematic review and meta-analysis. *Subst. Use Misuse* **2016**, *51*, 206–215. [CrossRef]
13. Mou, J.; Griffiths, S.M.; Fong, H.; Dawes, M.G. Health of China's rural–urban migrants and their families: A review of literature from 2000 to 2012. *Br. Med. Bull.* **2013**, *106*, 19–43. [CrossRef]
14. Lin, D.; Li, X.; Yang, H.; Fang, X.; Stanton, B.; Chen, X.; Abbey, A.; Liu, H. Alcohol intoxication and sexual risk behaviors among rural-to-urban migrants in China. *Drug Alcohol Depend.* **2005**, *79*, 103–112. [CrossRef] [PubMed]
15. Wan, X.; Shin, S.S.; Wang, Q.; Raymond, H.F.; Liu, H.; Ding, D.; Yang, G.; Novotny, T.E. Tobacco use among young rural to urban migrant women in China: A cross-sectional survey. *PLoS ONE* **2011**, *6*, e23028. [CrossRef] [PubMed]
16. Cui, X.; Rockett, I.R.; Yang, T.; Cao, R. Work stress, life stress, and tobacco use among rural-urban migrant workers in China. *BMC Public Health* **2012**, *12*, 979. [CrossRef] [PubMed]
17. Hesketh, T.; Lu, L.; Jun, Y.X.; Mei, W.H. Tobacco use, cessation and expenditure in low income Chinese: Cross sectional survey. *BMC Public Health* **2007**, *7*, 29. [CrossRef]
18. Chen, X.; Stanton, B.; Li, X.; Fang, X.; Lin, D.; Xiong, Q. A comparison of health-risk behaviors of rural migrants with rural residents and urban residents in China. *Am. J. Health Behav.* **2009**, *33*, 15–25. [CrossRef] [PubMed]
19. Ji, Y.; Liu, S.; Zhao, X.; Jiang, Y.; Zeng, Q.; Chang, C. Tobacco use and its determinants in Chinese internal migrants: Nationally representative cross-sectional data analyses. *Nicotine Tob. Res.* **2016**, *18*, 1719–1726. [CrossRef] [PubMed]
20. Villalonga-Olives, E.; Kawachi, I. The dark side of social capital: A systematic review of the negative health effects of social capital. *Soc. Sci. Med.* **2017**, *194*, 105–127. [CrossRef]
21. Seid, A.K.; Hesse, M.; Bloomfield, K. 'Make it another for me and my mates': Does social capital encourage risky drinking among the Danish general population? *Scand. J. Public Health* **2016**, *44*, 240–248. [CrossRef]
22. Takakura, M. Relations of participation in organized activities to tobacco use and drinking among Japanese youth: Contextual effects of structural social capital in high school. *Int. J. Public Health* **2015**, *60*, 679–689. [CrossRef]
23. Portes, A. Social capital: Its origins and applications in modern sociology. *Annu. Rev. Sociol.* **1998**, *24*, 1–24. [CrossRef]
24. Mulvaney-Day, N.E.; Alegría, M.; Sribney, W. Social cohesion, social support, and health among Latinos in the United States. *Soc. Sci. Med.* **2007**, *64*, 477–495. [CrossRef] [PubMed]
25. Finch, B.K. Acculturation stress, social support, and self-rated health among Latinos in California. *J. Immigr. Health* **2003**, *5*, 109–117. [CrossRef] [PubMed]
26. Alcántara, C.; Molina, K.M.; Kawachi, I. Transnational, social, and neighborhood ties and tobacco use among Latino immigrants: Does gender matter? *Am. J. Public Health* **2015**, *105*, 741–749. [CrossRef] [PubMed]
27. Torres, J.M.; Ro, A.; Sudhinaraset, M. Reconsidering the relationship between age at migration and health behaviors among US immigrants: The modifying role of continued cross-border ties. *Immigr. Health* **2019**, *19*, 17–45.
28. Cheung, N.W. Rural-to-urban migrant adolescents in Guangzhou, China: Psychological health, victimization, and local and trans-local ties. *Soc. Sci. Med.* **2013**, *93*, 121–129. [CrossRef] [PubMed]
29. Cheung, N.W. Social stress, locality of social ties and mental well-being: The case of rural migrant adolescents in urban China. *Health Place* **2014**, *27*, 142–154. [CrossRef] [PubMed]
30. Wang, B.; Li, X.; Stanton, B.; Fang, X. The influence of social stigma and discriminatory experience on psychological distress and quality of life among rural-to-urban migrants in China. *Soc. Sci. Med.* **2010**, *71*, 84–92. [CrossRef]
31. Yue, Z.; Fong, E.; Yuan, Y.; Li, S. Life satisfaction and internal migration experience: Migrant workers in Guangzhou, China. *Asian Popul. Stud.* **2019**, *15*, 302–318. [CrossRef]
32. Wang, J.; Zhou, Y.; Liu, S. China Labor-force Dynamics Survey: Design and practice. *Chin. Sociol. Dialogue* **2017**, *2*, 83–97. [CrossRef]
33. Wang, R.; Xue, D.; Liu, Y.; Chen, H.; Qiu, Y. The relationship between urbanization and depression in China: The mediating role of neighborhood social capital. *Int. J. Equity Health* **2018**, *17*, 105. [CrossRef]
34. Yi, Y.; Liao, Y.; Zheng, L.; Li, M.; Gu, J.; Hao, C.; Hao, Y. Health selectivity and rural-urban migration in China: A nationwide multiple cross-sectional study in 2012, 2014, 2016. *Int. J. Environ. Res. Public Health* **2019**, *16*, 1596. [CrossRef] [PubMed]
35. Zhang, G.; Zhan, J.; Fu, H. Trends in Smoking Prevalence and Intensity between 2010 and 2018: Implications for tobacco control in China. *Int. J. Environ. Res. Public Health* **2022**, *19*, 670. [CrossRef]
36. Jiang, H.; Room, R.; Hao, W. Alcohol and related health issues in China: Action needed. *Lancet Glob. Health* **2015**, *3*, e190–e191. [CrossRef]

37. Parascandola, M.; Xiao, L. Tobacco and the lung cancer epidemic in China. *Transl. Lung Cancer Res.* **2019**, *8* (Suppl. S1), S21. [CrossRef] [PubMed]
38. Cochrane, J.; Chen, H.; Conigrave, K.M.; Hao, W. Alcohol use in China. *Alcohol Alcohol.* **2003**, *38*, 537–542. [CrossRef] [PubMed]
39. Im, P.K.; Millwood, I.Y.; Guo, Y.; Du, H.; Chen, Y.; Bian, Z.; Tan, Y.; Guo, Z.; Wu, S.; Hua, Y.; et al. Patterns and trends of alcohol consumption in rural and urban areas of China: Findings from the China Kadoorie Biobank. *BMC Public Health* **2019**, *19*, 217. [CrossRef] [PubMed]
40. Zhou, X.; Su, Z.; Deng, H.; Xiang, X.; Chen, H.; Hao, W. A comparative survey on alcohol and tobacco use in urban and rural populations in the Huaihua District of Hunan Province, China. *Alcohol* **2006**, *39*, 87–96. [CrossRef]
41. Liu, Y.; He, S.; Wu, F.; Webster, C. Urban villages under China's rapid urbanization: Unregulated assets and transitional neighbourhoods. *Habitat Int.* **2010**, *34*, 135–144. [CrossRef]
42. Zhou, M.; Cai, G. Trapped in neglected corners of a booming metropolis: Residential patterns and marginalization of migrant workers in Guangzhou. In *Urban China in Transition*; Logan, J.R., Ed.; Blackwell Publishing: Oxford, UK, 2008; pp. 226–249.
43. Li, Q.; Hsia, J.; Yang, G. Prevalence of tobacco use in China in 2010. *N. Engl. J. Med.* **2011**, *364*, 2469–2470. [CrossRef]
44. Kim, Y.N.; Urquia, M.; Villadsen, S.F.; Merry, L. A scoping review on the measurement of transnationalism in migrant health research in high-income countries. *Glob. Health* **2021**, *17*, 126. [CrossRef]

International Journal of
Environmental Research and Public Health

MDPI

Article

Exploring Preventive Healthcare in a High-Risk Vulnerable Population

Trisha L. Amboree [1,2], Jane R. Montealegre [3,4], Kayo Fujimoto [5], Osaro Mgbere [6,7], Charles Darkoh [2,8,*] and Paige Padgett Wermuth [1]

1 Department of Management, Policy, and Community Health, The University of Texas Health Science Center School of Public Health, Houston, TX 77030, USA; trish.amboree@bcm.edu (T.L.A.); paige.m.padgett@uth.tmc.edu (P.P.W.)
2 Department of Epidemiology, Human Genetics and Environmental Sciences, The University of Texas Health Science Center School of Public Health, Houston, TX 77030, USA
3 Dan L Duncan Comprehensive Cancer Center, Baylor College of Medicine, Houston, TX 77030, USA; jrmontea@bcm.edu
4 Department of Pediatrics, Baylor College of Medicine, Houston, TX 77030, USA
5 Department of Health Promotion and Behavioral Sciences, The University of Texas Health Science Center School of Public Health, Houston, TX 77030, USA; kayo.fujimoto@uth.tmc.edu
6 Disease Prevention and Control Division, Houston Health Department, Houston, TX 77054, USA; osaro.mgbere@houstontx.gov
7 Institute of Community Health, University of Houston College of Pharmacy, Houston, TX 77204, USA
8 Microbiology and Infectious Diseases Program, University of Texas MD Anderson Cancer Center UTHealth Graduate School of Biomedical Sciences, Houston, TX 77030, USA
* Correspondence: charles.darkoh@uth.tmc.edu; Tel.: +1-713-500-9368

Citation: Amboree, T.L.; Montealegre, J.R.; Fujimoto, K.; Mgbere, O.; Darkoh, C.; Wermuth, P.P. Exploring Preventive Healthcare in a High-Risk Vulnerable Population. *Int. J. Environ. Res. Public Health* **2022**, *19*, 4502. https://doi.org/10.3390/ijerph19084502

Academic Editors: Celia C. Lo, William Ash-Houchen and Tyrone C. Cheng

Received: 8 March 2022
Accepted: 6 April 2022
Published: 8 April 2022

Abstract: This study describes preventive care behaviors and explores opportunities to deliver preventive sexual healthcare to a high-risk vulnerable population. Data from the National HIV Behavioral Surveillance (NHBS) system high-risk heterosexuals (HET) cycle (2019) in Houston, Texas, was used to describe preventive care utilization and assess the relationship between healthcare utilization and sociodemographic characteristics. More than 47% reported having no usual source of healthcare, and 94.6% reported receiving no non-HIV STI testing in the past 12 months. Additionally, many sociodemographic factors were associated with healthcare utilization and having a usual source of healthcare. Future efforts should be targeted at increasing preventive healthcare utilization among high-risk vulnerable populations as well as implementing more preventive sexual healthcare services in the community health centers where these populations most frequently encounter healthcare.

Keywords: preventive healthcare; sexual health; preventive medicine; public health

1. Introduction

The term "vulnerable populations" has historically been used in research to refer to populations comprising a disadvantaged portion of the community that require specific consideration and protection [1]. However, this also includes a broader population that is of low socioeconomic status, those who are underinsured, and those who are a part of racial/ethnic minority groups [1,2]. Health risks, specifically disease acquisition and treatment, of these populations are exacerbated by lack of access to healthcare and preventive services, as adequate healthcare access is vitally important to prevent and treat illnesses [2,3]. These populations are also at increased risk for poor health outcomes [2,4]. The use of preventive healthcare services, such as screening, testing, and vaccination, is multidimensional and has been associated with different factors [5]. Racial/ethnic minority populations have historically reported not having usual sources of medical care, no health insurance or under-insurance, and low socioeconomic status [5]. The vulnerability of these higher-risk populations contributes to the disparate burden of morbidity and mortality that racial/ethnic minorities, specifically Black/African American and Hispanic/Latinx populations, tend to carry in regard to chronic illnesses and other poor health outcomes [5]. Furthermore, this leads to differing health-seeking behaviors among populations that are at increased risk of poor health outcomes [5].

One widely recommended and available preventive health service is routine testing for human immunodeficiency virus (HIV) and other sexually transmitted infections (STIs). Globally, the vast majority of HIV infections occur in low- and middle-income countries [6,7]. In the U.S., high-risk racial/ethnic minority populations tend to carry a higher disease burden in terms of HIV and other STIs [8]. Specifically, those who identify as Black/African American accounted for 42% of all new HIV diagnoses in the U.S. in 2019, and 29% were among those who identified as Hispanic/Latinx [9]. STIs as a group are also more prevalent in the U.S. among racial/ethnic minorities [10,11], with these disparities being the result of social factors such as poverty, lack of employment, and low education [12]. Preventive healthcare utilization, such as routine HIV and other STI testing, could greatly help in reducing the disease burden by decreasing transmission within these communities.

Another available and recommended preventive health service is vaccination against human papillomavirus (HPV). While HPV, the most common STI globally, is nearly ubiquitous among sexually active adults, Black and Hispanic women exhibit higher rates of HPV-associated cervical cancer compared with women of other races/ethnicities [13]. Vaccine coverage against preventable infections, such as HPV, may reduce the risk of persistent HPV infections within these high-risk populations. While the HPV vaccine is recommended routinely for young people aged 9–26 years, the catch-up vaccine is licensed for adults through the age of 45 years, for whom joint decision-making between providers and patients is recommended [14].

Efforts to increase preventive healthcare utilization among high-risk populations have included identifying key barriers to healthcare access and recognizing access to health services as a key social determinant of health in Healthy People 2030; however, much work needs to be completed to actively reduce health disparities [15]. To our knowledge, a representative study assessing preventive healthcare utilization has not been conducted in a mostly racial/ethnic minority population living in medically underserved areas of high socioeconomic deprivation. Thus, the objective of this study was to describe preventive healthcare behaviors among a high-risk vulnerable population as well as to explore opportunities to deliver preventive healthcare, specifically regarding HPV vaccination and HIV and other STI testing behaviors, to high-risk vulnerable populations.

2. Materials and Methods

This study utilizes data obtained from the Centers for Disease Control and Prevention (CDC) National HIV Behavioral Surveillance (NHBS) system in Houston, Texas. The NHBS collects data every year in populations at high risk for HIV infection—specifically, men who have sex with men (MSM), people who inject drugs (PWID), and heterosexually active adults at increased risk for HIV (HET)—and uses a standardized, interviewer-administered survey instrument to gather information on participant demographics, sexual behaviors, alcohol and drug use history, HIV and other STI testing and use of prevention services, and health conditions as well as site-specific questions of interest [16,17]. The HET population was utilized in this analysis and represents a highly vulnerable population, as defined by living in a census track with high levels of economic deprivation and disproportionately high rates of HIV infection, with the majority being from racial/ethnic minority groups.

Respondent Driven Sampling (RDS) methods were used to recruit participants in the high-risk heterosexual population. This hard-to-reach population is not usually captured by traditional sampling methods; thus, to obtain an adequate sample, RDS utilizes participants' social networks [18]. Furthermore, RDS allows the sampling of a population that does not have an existing sampling frame [19]. RDS methods specific to NHBS have been described in detail elsewhere [20–22]. Briefly, this sampling utilizes a social network-based recruitment method that begins with initial recruits or "seeds" who are identified before the start of data collection. After the seeds complete the study activities, they are asked to recruit up to five other people they know or associate with. These recruited persons then complete the study activities and recruit others. This adaptive sampling technique is commonly used to sample hidden populations, such as high-risk heterosexual populations, and yields efficient estimates [19–23]. NHBS participants received incentives for their participation in study activities, including monetary compensation for time spent completing the survey and for providing specimens for HIV and STI testing [16].

2.1. Study Sample

The current study utilized data from the NHBS–HET cycle with data collection from July to December of 2019. The target sample was made up of individuals aged 18–60 years who lived in Houston or Harris County, identified as male or female, had vaginal or anal sex with someone of the opposite sex in the past 12 months, and were able to complete the NHBS interview in English or Spanish. NHBS also defines heterosexually active adults at increased risk for HIV as having low household incomes, defined as at or below 150% of the poverty guidelines adjusted for geographic differences in the cost of living. However, for the purposes of this paper, we did not exclude those who did not meet the low-income definition because all participants lived in areas with high socioeconomic deprivation and increased HIV prevalence. Additionally, those who reported non-prescription injection drug use in the past 12 months were excluded from the study. Furthermore, males who reported having other male sexual partners in the past 12 months were excluded, as both these populations are assessed in a different NHBS cycle of data collection [16].

The current study's population was a subset of eligible NHBS study participants. NHBS participants were included in this study if they were aged 18–60 years at the time of their interview and completed the NHBS interview in 2019. Participants were excluded if they did not meet NHBS inclusion criteria or did not complete the interview. A total of 591 NHBS–HET participants met these criteria. The study protocol was reviewed and approved as "exempt" by the Committee for the Protection of Human Subjects at the University of Texas Health Science Center at Houston.

2.2. Measures

The main outcome, healthcare utilization, was determined by assessing whether participants had a usual source of healthcare and their last healthcare encounter. The presence of a usual source of healthcare was assessed by asking participants "*Is there a place that you usually go when you are sick, or you need advice about your health? Do NOT include internet web sites*". Furthermore, the time from the last healthcare encounter was assessed by asking the participants "*About how long has it been since you last saw a doctor, nurse, or other health care provider about your own health?*". Having a usual source of healthcare was categorized as no usual source of healthcare, clinic or healthcare center, or doctor's office or HMO. The time from the last healthcare encounter was categorized as within the past 12 months, 1–2 years ago, 2–5 years ago, or more than 5 years ago.

Testing behaviors assessed included receiving an HIV test in the past 12 months, HIV testing frequency, HIV testing location, and receiving an STI test other than HIV in the past 12 months. HIV testing in the past 12 months was assessed by asking participants "*Was your most recent HIV test in the past 12 months, that is, since [fill with interview month] of last year?*". HIV testing frequency was assessed by asking participants "*When did you have your most recent HIV test? Please tell me the month and year*". HIV testing frequency was categorized as never tested, tested 0–6 months ago, tested 7–12 months ago, tested 13–24 months ago, tested 25–60 months ago, or tested more than 60 months ago. HIV testing location was assessed by asking participants "*When you got tested [if month & year of last test are known, fill with response] where did you get tested?*". HIV test location was categorized as HIV counseling and testing site, HIV/AIDs street outreach or mobile unit, drug treatment program, correctional facility, family planning or obstetrics clinic, community health center, private doctor's office, emergency room, hospital inpatient, at home, or unspecified other.

Other STI testing in the past 12 months was assessed by asking participants *"In the past 12 months, that is, since <interview month, [interview year-1]>, were you tested by a doctor or other health care provider for a sexually transmitted disease like gonorrhea, chlamydia, or syphilis? Do NOT include tests for HIV or hepatitis"*. Uptake of the HPV vaccine was assessed by the item *"Have you ever received a shot that protects against HPV, for example Gardasil?"* and was categorized as yes or no in the analyses.

For the analyses, HIV testing in the past 12 months was categorized as yes or no. Other STI testing in the past 12 months was categorized as yes or no. The participants' sociodemographic variables included age in years (continuous and ranged from 18 years to 60 years), sex (dichotomized as female and male), and self-reported race/ethnicity (categorized as non-Hispanic White, non-Hispanic Black, Hispanic, or non-Hispanic other). The non-Hispanic other category refers to participants who reported being Asian, Alaskan Native, or Pacific Islander. Furthermore, sociodemographic variables included education (categorized as less than a high school diploma, high school diploma or equivalent, or at least some college education), health insurance type (categorized as no health insurance, private health insurance, public health insurance, or some other insurance coverage), and poverty level (categorized as above the poverty level or below the poverty level). Poverty was determined by assessing the participant's self-reported annual household income and the number of dependents that relied on that income and comparing it with federal poverty guidelines. Additionally, homelessness (categorized as never homeless, currently homeless, or previously homeless but not currently homeless) and incarceration status (categorized as never incarcerated, incarcerated but not within the past 12 months, or incarcerated within the past 12 months) were included.

For regression analyses, healthcare utilization was assessed by collapsing the variable for the time from the last healthcare encounter into two categories: had a healthcare encounter within the past 12 months or did not have a healthcare encounter within the past 12 months. The usual source of healthcare was assessed by collapsing the variable into two categories: has a usual source of healthcare and does not have a usual source of healthcare.

2.3. Statistical Analysis

Data were cleaned, prepared, and formatted in SAS 9.4 (SAS Institute, Cary, NC, USA), exported as a comma-separated value file, and converted into an RDS object for analysis in RDS Analyst [24]. Questions about network size and characteristics of participants' networks were used to create population weights to account for sources of bias inherent to RDS methodology and to calculate population estimates and sample variances [25]. RDS Analyst was utilized to generate population prevalence estimates along with 95% confidence intervals and standard errors. Furthermore, population cross-tabulations were conducted in RDS Analyst. Bivariable and multivariable regression analyses were conducted in SAS 9.4 using the modified Poisson regression approach with the log link function and robust variance estimation clustered on the recruitment chain (SAS Institute, Cary, NC, USA) [26]. Estimates from regression analyses were RDS-adjusted using Gile's sequential sampling weights with an estimated population size of 53,690. The unweighted multivariable estimates were also included. The PROC GENMOD was used to generate unadjusted and adjusted prevalence ratios and 95% confidence intervals to assess the association between sociodemographic characteristics and indicators of healthcare access and utilization. Sociodemographic variables included age, sex, race/ethnicity, education, health insurance type, poverty, homelessness, and incarceration status. All statistical tests performed were two-tailed with a probability value of 0.05 used as the threshold for declaring statistical significance.

3. Results

Table 1 summarizes the sociodemographic characteristics of this study population. The 591 respondents examined had an average age of 38.7 years, 55% were female, 78.3% were non-Hispanic Black, 52.5% had a high school diploma or equivalent, 51.3% reported having no health insurance, 83.5% had a household income below the poverty level, 21.3% were currently homeless, and 51.1% had a history of incarceration.

Table 1. Demographic characteristics of the study population.

	N	Weighted % (95% CI)	SE
Age, Continuous (mean, SD)	591	—	38.7, 12.7
Sex			
Male	290	45.0 (37.5–52.4)	3.8
Female	301	55.0 (47.6–62.5)	3.8
Race/Ethnicity			
White	39	5.1 (2.2–8.0)	1.5
Black	465	78.3 (72.1–84.6)	3.2
Hispanic	75	14.9 (9.6–20.3)	2.7
Other	10	1.7 (0.1–3.3)	0.8
Education			
Less than HS diploma	155	27.1 (20.9–33.2)	3.1
HS diploma or equivalent	282	52.5 (45.7–59.3)	3.5
Some college or above	154	20.4 (15.6–25.2)	2.4
Health Insurance Type			
No health insurance	309	51.3 (44.7–58.0)	3.4
Private plan	39	6.8 (4.2–9.4)	1.3
Public plan	228	40.3 (33.8–46.7)	3.3
Other	9	1.6 (0.2–3.0)	0.7
Poverty			
Above poverty level	104	16.5 (12.1–20.9)	2.2
Below poverty level	487	83.5 (79.2–87.9)	2.2
Homelessness			
Never homeless	364	67.1 (60.1–74.0)	3.6
Currently homeless	135	21.3 (15.3–27.4)	3.1
Previously but not currently homeless	91	11.7 (8.1–15.2)	1.8
Incarcerated			
Never incarcerated	163	31.7 (25.7–37.6)	3.0
Incarcerated, but not within past 12 months	303	51.1 (44.4–58.0)	3.5
Incarcerated within past 12 months	125	17.2 (13.0–21.4)	2.1

Abbreviations: CI = Confidence Interval; SE = Standard Error; SD = Standard Deviation.

Table 2 describes the primary care utilization of this study population. Of the 591 respondents, 47.7% reported having no usual source of healthcare; however, 68.6% had a healthcare encounter within the past 12 months. The primary sources of healthcare among those who reported having a usual source were family planning and obstetrics clinics and community healthcare centers (70.2%) (data not shown in tables). Furthermore, 58.3% reported not having received an HIV test within the past 12 months, and 20.9% reported never being tested for HIV. Of those who had received an HIV test, 39% received their most recent test from a community health center. Additionally, 94.6% reported not being tested for other STIs in the past 12 months. Lastly, only 8.3% reported having received at least one dose of the HPV vaccine. In those who were age-eligible, only 11.5% had received at least one dose of the HPV vaccine (data not shown in tables).

Table 3 shows the weighted unadjusted prevalence ratios and the weighted and unweighted adjusted prevalence ratios from the modified Poisson regression models of healthcare utilization and sociodemographic factors. There were 10 recruitment chains with a minimum cluster size of 1 and a maximum cluster size of 320. Age, educational attainment, poverty, and incarceration history were not statistically significant in the bivariable models.

However, age, education, and poverty were retained in multivariable models due to a priori knowledge [5]. In the weighted multivariable model, being female ($p < 0.0001$), of Black race/ethnicity ($p = 0.04$), having at least some college education ($p = 0.01$), and having a private or public health insurance plan ($p = 0.0003$ and $p < 0.0001$, respectively) were all significantly associated with a higher prevalence of having had a healthcare encounter in the past 12 months. On the other hand, having a history of homelessness but not being currently homeless ($p < 0.0001$) was significantly associated with a lower prevalence of a healthcare encounter in the past 12 months.

Table 2. Testing behaviors and primary care utilization among the study population.

	N	Population % (95% CI)	SE
Usual Source of Healthcare			
No usual source of healthcare	291	47.7 (40.8–54.5)	3.5
Clinic or healthcare center	203	34.2 (28.1–40.3)	3.1
Doctor's office or HMO	86	18.1 (13.6–22.7)	2.3
Last Healthcare Visit			
Within past year	394	68.6 (62.5–74.8)	3.1
1–2 years ago	103	14.7 (10.9–18.5)	2.0
2–5 years ago	76	14.5 (9.5–19.3)	2.5
5+ years ago	16	2.3 (0.7–3.8)	0.8
HIV Test in Past 12 Months			
Yes	223	41.7 (34.9–48.7)	3.5
No	358	58.3 (51.3–65.1)	3.5
HIV Testing Frequency			
0–6 months	125	27.5 (20.3–34.8)	3.7
7–12 months	88	17.3 (12.2–22.4)	2.6
13–24 months	86	18.7 (12.7–24.6)	3
25–60 months	55	8.2 (5.4–11.1)	1.5
60+ months	39	7.4 (4.4–10.4)	1.5
Never tested	114	20.9 (15.9–26.0)	2.6
Most Recent HIV Test Location			
HIV counseling and testing site	12	2.5 (0.7–4.2)	0.9
HIV/AIDS street outreach or mobile unit	82	16.9 (11.1–22.9)	3.0
Drug treatment program	7	0.6 (0.2–1.1)	0.2
Correctional facility	55	9.0 (5.3–12.7)	1.9
Family planning or obstetrics clinic	19	4.8 (2.1–7.4)	1.4
Community health center	149	39.0 (30.4–47.5)	4.3
Private doctor's office	27	6.7 (3.4–10.0)	1.7
Emergency room	19	4.8 (1.5–8.1)	1.7
Hospital (inpatient)	37	6.8 (3.8–9.9)	1.6
At home	3	0.8 (-0.2–1.8)	0.5
Other	33	8.2 (3.5–12.9)	2.4
Gonorrhea, Chlamydia, or Syphilis Test in the Past 12 Months			
Yes	32	5.4 (2.4–8.5)	1.6
No	559	94.6 (91.5–97.6)	1.6
HPV Vaccine Uptake			
Yes	50	8.3 (5.2–11.3)	1.6
No	541	91.7 (88.7–94.8)	1.6

Abbreviations: CI = confidence interval; SE = standard error; STI = sexually transmitted infection; HPV = human papillomavirus.

Table 3. Unadjusted and adjusted weighted and unweighted modified Poisson regression models assessing the relationship between healthcare utilization and sociodemographic characteristics in the study population.

	Healthcare Utilization in the Past 12 Months					
Characteristic	PR (95% CI)	*p*-Value	aPR (95% CI) [a]	Adjusted *p*-Value	aPR (95% CI) [b]	Adjusted *p*-Value
Age, Continuous	1.00 (1.00–1.01)	0.52	1.00 (1.00–1.01)	0.12	1.00 (1.00–1.01)	0.08
Sex						
Male (Ref)	1.00		1.00		1.00	
Female	1.24 (1.12–1.38)	<0.0001 ****	1.23 (1.13–1.34)	<0.0001 ****	1.11 (1.05–1.18)	0.0004 ***
Race/Ethnicity						
White (Ref)	1.00		1.00		1.00	
Black	1.13 (0.95–1.34)	0.17	1.13 (1.01–1.26)	0.04 *	0.97 (0.93–1.01)	0.13
Hispanic	1.09 (0.86–1.38)	0.49	1.10 (0.95–1.26)	0.20	0.95 (0.86–1.05)	0.32
Other	1.00 (0.47–2.15)	0.99	0.95 (0.44–2.05)	0.91	0.69 (0.41–1.15)	0.15
Education						
Less than HS diploma (Ref)	1.00		1.00		1.00	
HS diploma or equivalent	0.93 (0.74–1.17)	0.53	0.97 (0.83–1.14)	0.75	0.99 (0.93–1.06)	0.87
Some college or above	1.11 (0.90–1.38)	0.32	1.22 (1.04–1.43)	0.01 *	1.14 (1.07–1.21)	<0.0001 ****
Health Insurance Type						
No health insurance (Ref)	1.00		1.00		1.00	
Private/other plan	1.38 (1.21–1.58)	<0.0001 ****	1.31 (1.13–1.52)	0.0003 ***	1.29 (1.10–1.52)	0.002 **
Public plan	1.53 (1.41–1.66)	<0.0001 ****	1.51 (1.43–1.60)	<0.0001 ****	1.54 (1.45–1.64)	<0.0001 ****
Poverty						
Above poverty level (Ref)	1.00		1.00		1.00	
Below poverty level	1.02 (0.87–1.19)	0.82	1.13 (0.89–1.44)	0.33	0.99 (0.88–1.11)	0.90
Homelessness						
Never homeless (Ref)	1.00		1.00		1.00	
Currently homeless	0.85 (0.69–1.06)	0.16	0.87 (0.70–1.08)	0.21	0.97 (0.86–1.09)	0.54
Previously but not currently homeless	0.80 (0.73–0.88)	<0.0001 ****	0.76 (0.69–0.84)	<0.0001 ****	0.87 (0.79–0.96)	0.007 **
Incarcerated						
Never incarcerated (Ref)	1.00					
Incarcerated, but not within past 12 months	0.96 (0.88–1.05)	0.36	—	—	—	—
Incarcerated within past 12 months	0.91 (0.74–1.13)	0.39	—	—	—	—

[a] Model adjusted with RDS-weights; [b] model not adjusted with RDS-weights; abbreviations: PR = prevalence ratio; CI = confidence interval; aPR = adjusted prevalence ratio; Ref = referent group. Significance levels: * = $p < 0.05$, ** = $p < 0.01$, *** = $p < 0.001$, **** = $p < 0.0001$.

Table 4 shows the weighted unadjusted prevalence ratios and the weighted and unweighted adjusted prevalence ratios from modified Poisson regression models for having a usual source of healthcare and sociodemographic factors. There were 10 recruitment chains with a minimum cluster size of 1 and a maximum cluster size of 317. Although age, sex, race/ethnicity, educational attainment, poverty, and homelessness did not reach statistical significance in the bivariable models, age, sex, race/ethnicity, educational attainment, and poverty were retained in multivariable models due to a priori knowledge [5]. In the weighted multivariable models, reporting private or public health insurance coverage ($p < 0.0001$) was significantly associated with a higher prevalence of having a usual source of healthcare. By contrast, those with a history of homelessness but who were not currently homeless ($p = 0.005$), those with any incarceration history ($p = 0.0003$), and those who were incarcerated within the past 12 months ($p = 0.005$) were significantly associated with a lower prevalence of having a usual source of healthcare.

Table 4. Unadjusted and adjusted weighted and unweighted modified Poisson regression models assessing the relationship between usual source of healthcare and sociodemographic characteristics in the study population.

	Had a Usual Source of Healthcare					
Characteristic	**PR (95% CI)**	***p*-Value**	**aPR (95% CI) [a]**	**Adjusted *p*-Value**	**aPR (95% CI) [b]**	**Adjusted *p*-Value**
Age, Continuous	1.00 (1.00–1.01)	0.54	1.00 (0.99–1.00)	0.85	1.00 (0.99–1.00)	0.27
Sex						
Male (Ref)	1.00		1.00		1.00	
Female	1.13 (0.92–1.38)	0.26	0.99 (0.90–1.08)	0.76	1.04 (0.89–1.21)	0.62
Race/Ethnicity						
White (Ref)	1.00		1.00		1.00	
Black	1.08 (0.94–1.25)	0.29	0.97 (0.91–1.04)	0.37	0.94 (0.87–1.01)	0.10
Hispanic	1.11 (0.79–1.56)	0.54	0.97 (0.80–1.18)	0.76	1.00 (0.89–1.13)	0.94
Other	1.48 (0.88–2.49)	0.14	1.78 (0.78–4.03)	0.17	1.09 (0.82–1.44)	0.56
Education						
Less than HS diploma (Ref)	1.00		1.00		1.00	
HS diploma or equivalent	1.05 (0.88–1.26)	0.60	1.04 (0.94–1.15)	0.48	1.03 (0.96–1.10)	0.37
Some college or above	1.11 (0.89–1.39)	0.35	1.04 (0.83–1.30)	0.77	1.04 (0.96–1.11)	0.33
Health Insurance Type						
No health insurance (Ref)	1.00		1.00		1.00	
Private/other plan	2.89 (2.67–3.14)	<0.0001 ****	2.67 (2.21–3.21)	<0.0001 ****	2.16 (1.83–2.55)	<0.0001 ****
Public plan	2.54 (2.18–2.96)	<0.0001 ****	2.59 (2.24–3.00)	<0.0001 ****	2.24 (1.93–2.60)	<0.0001 ****
Poverty						
Above poverty level (Ref)	1.00		1.00		1.00	
Below poverty level	0.89 (0.64–1.23)	0.47	1.02 (0.86–1.22)	0.79	0.90 (0.82–0.99)	0.04 *
Homelessness						
Never homeless (Ref)	1.00		1.00		1.00	
Currently homeless	0.64 (0.47–0.87)	0.004 **	0.90 (0.80–1.01)	0.08	0.94 (0.84–1.06)	0.32
Previously but not currently homeless	0.76 (0.53–1.10)	0.15	0.89 (0.81–0.96)	0.005 **	0.93 (0.79–1.09)	0.37
Incarcerated						
Never incarcerated (Ref)	1.00		1.00		1.00	
Incarcerated, but not within past 12 months	0.77 (0.60–0.98)	0.03 *	0.69 (0.57–0.85)	0.0003 ***	0.73 (0.57–0.93)	0.01 *
Incarcerated within past 12 months	0.75 (0.63–0.90)	0.002 **	0.71 (0.55–0.90)	0.005 **	0.70 (0.48–1.04)	0.08

[a] Model adjusted with RDS-weights; [b] model not adjusted with RDS-weights; abbreviations: PR = prevalence ratio; CI = confidence interval; aPR = adjusted prevalence ratio; Ref = referent group. Significance levels: * = $p < 0.05$, ** = $p < 0.01$, *** = $p < 0.001$, **** = $p < 0.0001$.

4. Discussion

The findings from this study show a severe dearth of preventive healthcare utilization in this high-risk population. Almost half of the population reported having no usual source of healthcare, yet 68.6% reported having a healthcare encounter in the past year. We suspect that acute care facilities, such as emergency rooms, urgent care, and community health centers, may be utilized more often by these populations than doctor's offices, which is supported by the finding that higher-risk populations tend to report having no usual source of healthcare and no consistent location for healthcare needs [5]. Furthermore, less than half of the population had received an HIV test in the past 12 months, and 95% had not received any other STI testing in the past 12 months. A study conducted by Kates et al. suggests that most HIV testing is performed in the private setting [27]; thus, the low utilization of testing in our study may also be due to not having a usual source of healthcare.

In the adjusted regression analyses, we found that Black participants had a higher prevalence of recent healthcare utilization compared with White participants. This finding was not expected but may be due to a lack of heterogeneity, as most of the study participants were Black (78.3%). Our findings also suggest a positive association between the prevalence of recent healthcare utilization and being female, having at least some college education, and having health insurance. This is consistent with the literature, as females tend to access care more often than men [28]. This may especially be observed with regard to preventive care [29]. The literature also supports our finding that those with health insurance coverage have higher healthcare utilization, as those who are uninsured tend to use fewer preventive services [30], and those who are less educated tend to report worse general health [31–33]. We did not find a statistically significant association between having a recent healthcare encounter and poverty. This finding may be due to a lack of heterogeneity with regard to poverty, as over 83% of our study population lived below the poverty level.

The results showed that those who had any type of health insurance had a higher prevalence of having a usual source of healthcare. This is consistent with literature that suggests that those with health insurance tend to receive greater preventive healthcare coverage, more screening services, and more appropriate and timely utilization of these services [34]. Our finding that those who had been but were not currently homeless had a lower prevalence of having a usual source of healthcare is also consistent with literature that suggests that people with experiences of homelessness are often disengaged from primary services [35]. The finding that having any experience with incarceration resulted in a lower prevalence of having a usual source of healthcare is also consistent with the literature. The majority of our study population (68.3%) reported having some incarceration history; thus, there is an immense need to increase primary care access among those with a history of incarceration. The literature suggests that incarceration rates are higher among those of racial/ethnic minority groups and those with lower levels of education [36]. The high prevalence of incarceration history in our study population further elaborates the multilevel vulnerability of this population. Additional research is needed to effectively improve healthcare access for this population, specifically those with a history of incarceration.

The largest proportion of those who had a usual source of care reported the source as either a clinic or a community health center. Thus, there may be an opportunity to introduce other preventive sexual health services at these centers. Data from the National Association of Community Health Centers suggest that, on average, community health centers serve one in three low-income uninsured persons [37]. Additionally, those who frequent community healthcare centers are disproportionately members of racial/ethnic minority groups, such as Hispanic and Black populations [37]. Therefore, healthcare encounters at community health clinics may be the only place where preventive healthcare can occur. Further research is needed to better understand how to increase preventive healthcare, specifically HIV and other STI testing and HPV vaccination, among higher-risk populations, along with the gap that community health centers can help fill.

Limitations

This was a secondary analysis of a dataset that was not initially intended to examine healthcare utilization as a primary outcome. Thus, we may be missing other indicators of healthcare access and utilization, such as employment status, living in a rural community, lack of transportation, proximity to healthcare services, language barriers, and existing chronic conditions, as well as other contributing factors [38]. Additionally, there may be selection bias and other inherent biases because of the use of RDS methodology, which have been described elsewhere [25]. Our analyses are robust and account for the RDS sampling methodology; thus, we believe our results to be accurate estimates of the target population. The NHBS–HET cycle only captures data on male- or female-identifying persons; thus, other gender identities are not included, which may limit the generalizability of the results. In addition, the cross-sectional nature of the data limits the conclusions that can be drawn in relation to risk or causation [39]. Furthermore, the use of interview data increases the risk of information biases, such as recall bias and response bias. However, NHBS uses a CDC standardized questionnaire, which decreases this bias and increases the internal validity of this study [40]. The data should be interpreted with caution, as the attitudes that underlie the reported behaviors could not be ascertained. Notably, self-reported vaccination status has been shown to be racially biased; therefore, there may be some inherent bias with the use of self-reported vaccination as a marker or indicator of preventive healthcare utilization [41,42]. Lastly, the indicator used to estimate the HPV vaccine uptake in this study focuses on receiving one or more doses of the vaccine rather than vaccine completion.

5. Conclusions

In conclusion, preventive healthcare utilization, specifically HPV vaccine coverage and routine testing for HIV and other STIs, is extremely low in this high-risk, low-income population. Furthermore, almost half of the population reported not having a usual source of healthcare. Health insurance coverage, having experiences with homelessness, and having any history of incarceration were associated with whether a respondent reported having a usual source of healthcare, whereas sex, race/ethnicity, education, health insurance coverage, and having experiences with homelessness were associated with the time from the last healthcare encounter. Future efforts should be targeted at increasing preventive healthcare utilization among high-risk, low-income populations, specifically those with any history of incarceration and homelessness, as well as implementing more preventive sexual healthcare services in community health centers where these populations most frequently encounter healthcare.

Author Contributions: Conceptualization, T.L.A. and J.R.M.; methodology, T.L.A.; formal analysis, T.L.A.; resources, C.D.; data curation, T.L.A.; writing—original draft preparation, T.L.A. and J.R.M.; writing—review and editing, J.R.M., K.F., O.M., P.P.W. and C.D.; visualization, T.L.A.; supervision, O.M. and C.D.; validation, C.D.; project administration, funding acquisition, C.D. All authors have read and agreed to the published version of the manuscript.

Funding: This research received no external funding. CD was supported by NIH/NIAID grants R01AI116914 and R01AI150685. The APC was funded by NIH/NIAID grant R01AI150685.

Institutional Review Board Statement: The data used for this project was de-identified; thus, the identity of the human subjects cannot be readily ascertained directly or through identifiers, the investigator did not contact the subjects, and the investigator will not re-identify the subjects. Therefore, ethical review and approval were waived for this study.

Informed Consent Statement: Not applicable.

Data Availability Statement: The data used in this study are owned and governed by the Houston Health Department; thus, the data are not publicly available.

Acknowledgments: The data used for this study was obtained courtesy of the City of Houston Health Department. However, the findings and conclusions drawn in this project are solely the responsibility of the authors and do not necessarily represent the official position of the program funding agency, the U.S. Centers for Disease Control and Prevention, or the City of Houston Health Department.

Conflicts of Interest: The authors declare no conflict of interest.

References

1. Shivayogi, P. Vulnerable population and methods for their safeguard. *Perspect. Clin. Res.* **2013**, *4*, 53–57. [CrossRef] [PubMed]
2. Vulnerable Populations: Who are they? In: Prescription Drug Copays and Their Effect on Vulnerable Populations. *Am. J. Manag. Care* **2006**, *12*, s348–s352.
3. Waisel, D.B. Vulnerable populations in healthcare. *Curr. Opin. Anaesthesiol.* **2013**, *26*, 186–192. [CrossRef] [PubMed]
4. Ivanova, O.; Dræbel, T.; Tellier, S. Are Sexual and Reproductive Health Policies Designed for All? Vulnerable Groups in Policy Documents of Four European Countries and Their Involvement in Policy Development. *Int. J. Health Policy Manag.* **2015**, *4*, 663–671. [CrossRef] [PubMed]
5. National Academies of Sciences, Engineering, and Medicine; Health and Medicine Division; Board on Health Care Services; Committee on Health Care Utilization and Adults with Disabilities. *Health-Care Utilization as a Proxy in Disability Determination*; National Academies Press: Washington, DC, USA, 2018.
6. Joint United Nations Programme on HIV/AIDS. Global HIV & AIDS Statistics—Fact Sheet. UN-AIDS. 2021. Available online: https://www.unaids.org/en/resources/fact-sheet (accessed on 21 November 2021).
7. Shao, Y.; Williamson, C. The HIV-1 Epidemic: Low- to Middle-Income Countries. *Cold Spring Harb. Perspect. Med.* **2011**, 2, a007187. [CrossRef]
8. Aral, S.O.; Adimora, A.A.; Fenton, K.A. Understanding and responding to disparities in HIV and other sexually transmitted infections in African Americans. *Lancet* **2008**, *372*, 337–340. [CrossRef]
9. Centers for Disease Control and Prevention, HIV Surveillance Report. 2019. Available online: https://www.cdc.gov/hiv/library/reports/hiv-surveillance.html (accessed on 23 May 2021).
10. Moran, J.S.; Aral, S.O.; Jenkins, W.C.; Peterman, T.A.; Alexander, E.R. The impact of sexually transmitted diseases on minority populations. *Public Health Rep.* **1989**, *104*, 560.
11. Hogben, M.; Leichliter, J.S. Social Determinants and Sexually Transmitted Disease Disparities. *Sex. Transm. Dis.* **2008**, *35*, S13–S18. [CrossRef]
12. Centers for Disease Control and Prevention. Sexually Transmitted Diseases—STD Health Equity. Available online: https://www.cdc.gov/std/health-disparities/default.htm#:~{}:text=In%20communities%20with%20higher%20STD%20rates%2C%20sexually%20active,improve%20their%20health%20status%20and%20advance%20health%20equity (accessed on 2 March 2021).
13. Centers for Disease Control and Prevention. HPV-Associated Cancers Rates by Race and Ethnicity. 2020. Available online: https://www.cdc.gov/cancer/hpv/statistics/race.htm (accessed on 6 October 2021).
14. Meites, E.; Szilagyi, P.G.; Chesson, H.W.; Unger, E.R.; Romero, J.R.; Markowitz, L.E. Human Papillomavirus Vaccination for Adults: Updated Recommendations of the Advisory Committee on Immunization Practices. *Am. J. Transplant.* **2019**, *19*, 3202–3206. [CrossRef]
15. Office of Disease Prevention and Health Promotion. Healthy People 2030: Access to Health Services. Available online: https://health.gov/healthypeople/objectives-and-data/social-determinants-health/literature-summaries/access-health-services (accessed on 1 March 2021).
16. Centers for Disease Control and Prevention. National HIV Behavioral Surveillance System Round 6: Model Surveillance Protocol. 2020. Available online: www.cdc.gov/hiv/statistics/systems/nhbs/operations.html (accessed on 11 December 2021).
17. Centers for Disease Control and Prevention. National HIV Behavioral Surveillance System Protocol and Operations: NHBS Round 5 CRQ (2017–2019). 2020. Available online: https://www.cdc.gov/hiv/statistics/systems/nhbs/operations.html (accessed on 23 March 2022).
18. Heckathorn, D.D. Respondent-Driven Sampling: A New Approach to the Study of Hidden Populations. *Soc. Probl.* **1997**, *44*, 174–199. [CrossRef]
19. Kim, B.J.; Handcock, M.S. Population Size Estimation Using Multiple Respondent-Driven Sampling Surveys. *J. Surv. Stat. Methodol.* **2021**, *9*, 94–120. [CrossRef] [PubMed]
20. Richards, J.E.; Risser, J.M.; Padgett, P.M.; Rehman, H.U.; Wolverton, M.L.; Arafat, R.R. Condom use among high-risk heterosexual women with concurrent sexual partnerships, Houston, Texas, USA. *Int. J. Std Aids* **2008**, *19*, 768–771. [CrossRef] [PubMed]
21. Paz-Bailey, G.; Raymond, H.; Lansky, A.; Mermin, J. Using the National HIV Behavioral Surveillance System to Inform HIV Prevention Efforts in the United States. *AIDS Behav.* **2014**, *18*, 233–236. [CrossRef] [PubMed]
22. Sionean, C.; Le, B.C.; Hageman, K.; Oster, A.M.; Wejnert, C.; Hess, K.L.; Paz-Bailey, G.; NHBS Study Group. HIV Risk, prevention, and testing behaviors among hetero-sexuals at increased risk for HIV infection—National HIV Behavioral Surveillance System, 21 U.S. cities, 2010. *MMWR Surveill. Summ.* **2014**, *63*, 1–39.

23. Magnani, R.; Sabin, K.; Saidel, T.; Heckathorn, D. Review of sampling hard-to-reach and hidden populations for HIV surveillance. *Aids* **2005**, *19* (Suppl. S2), S67–S72. [CrossRef] [PubMed]
24. Handcock, M.S.; Fellows, I.E.; Gile, K.J. RDS Analyst: Software for the Analysis of Respondent-Driven Sampling Data. 2014. Available online: http://wiki.stat.ucla.edu/hpmrg/index.php/RDS_Analyst_Install (accessed on 2 February 2021).
25. Gile, K.J.; Handcock, M.S. 7. Respondent-Driven Sampling: An Assessment of Current Methodology. *Sociol. Methodol.* **2010**, *40*, 285–327. [CrossRef]
26. Zou, G. A Modified Poisson Regression Approach to Prospective Studies with Binary Data. *Am. J. Epidemiol.* **2004**, *159*, 702–706. [CrossRef]
27. Kates, J.; Levi, J. Insurance Coverage and Access to HIV Testing and Treatment: Considerations for Individuals at Risk for Infection and for Those with Undiagnosed Infection. *Clin. Infect. Dis.* **2007**, *45*, S255–S260. [CrossRef]
28. Bertakis, K.D.; Azari, R.; Helms, L.J.; Callahan, E.J.; Robbins, J.A. Gender differences in the utilization of health care services. *J. Fam. Pract.* **2000**, *49*, 147–152.
29. Redondo-Sendino, Á.; Guallar-Castillón, P.; Banegas, J.R.; Rodríguez-Artalejo, F. Gender differences in the utilization of health-care services among the older adult population of Spain. *BMC Public Health* **2006**, *6*, 155. [CrossRef]
30. Riley, W.J. Health disparities: Gaps in access, quality and affordability of medical care. *Trans. Am. Clin. Clim. Assoc.* **2012**, *123*, 167–174.
31. Zajacova, A.; Lawrence, E.M. The Relationship Between Education and Health: Reducing Disparities Through a Contextual Approach. *Annu. Rev. Public Health* **2018**, *39*, 273–289. [CrossRef] [PubMed]
32. Zajacova, A.; Hummer, R.A.; Rogers, R.G. Education and Health among U.S. Working-Age Adults: A Detailed Portrait across the Full Educational Attainment Spectrum. *Biodemography Soc. Biol.* **2012**, *58*, 40–61. [CrossRef] [PubMed]
33. Mirowsky, J.; Ross, C.E. Education and Self-Rated Health: Cumulative Advantage and Its Rising Importance. *Res. Aging.* **2008**, *30*, 93–122. [CrossRef]
34. Institute of Medicine (US) Committee on the Consequences of Uninsurance. *Care without Coverage: Too Little, Too Late*; National Academies Press: Washington, DC, USA, 2002. Available online: https://www.ncbi.nlm.nih.gov/books/NBK220639/ (accessed on 21 October 2021).
35. Davies, A.; Wood, L.J. Homeless health care: Meeting the challenges of providing primary care. *Med. J. Aust.* **2018**, *209*, 230–234. [CrossRef]
36. Dumont, D.M.; Brockmann, B.; Dickman, S.; Alexander, N.; Rich, J.D. Public Health and the Epidemic of Incarceration. *Annu. Rev. Public Health* **2012**, *33*, 325–339. [CrossRef]
37. National Association of Community Health Centers. Community Health Center Chartbook. 2020 January. Available online: https://www.nachc.org/wp-content/uploads/2020/01/Chartbook-2020-Final.pdf (accessed on 21 October 2021).
38. Millman, M. (Ed.) Access to Health Care in America. In *A Model for Monitoring Access*; National Academies Press, Institute of Medicine (US) Committee on Monitoring Access to Personal Health Care Services: Washington, DC, USA, 1993; Volume 2.
39. Levin, K.A. Study design III: Cross-sectional studies. *Evid.-Based Dent.* **2006**, *7*, 24–25. [CrossRef]
40. Cataldo, R.; Arancibia, M.; Stojanova, J.; Papuzinski, C. General concepts in biostatistics and clinical epidemiology: Observational studies with cross-sectional and ecological designs. *Medwave* **2019**, *19*, e7698. [CrossRef]
41. Spencer, J.C.; Calo, W.A.; Brewer, N.T. Disparities and reverse disparities in HPV vaccination: A systematic review and meta-analysis. *Prev. Med.* **2019**, *123*, 197–203. [CrossRef]
42. Vu, M.; Luu, M.; Haardörfer, R.; Berg, C.J.; Escoffery, C.; Bednarczyk, R.A. A multilevel analysis of factors influencing the inaccuracy of parental reports of adolescent HPV vaccination status. *Vaccine* **2019**, *37*, 869–876. [CrossRef]

International Journal of
Environmental Research and Public Health

MDPI

Article

Neighborhood Disadvantage and Poor Health: The Consequences of Race, Gender, and Age among Young Adults

C. André Christie-Mizell

Department of Sociology, Vanderbilt University, Nashville, TN 37325, USA; andre.christie-mizell@vanderbilt.edu

Abstract: The objective of this study is to examine the relationship between neighborhood disadvantage and poor self-rated health for a nationally representative sample of Blacks and Whites in young adulthood, 18 to 30 years old. Data were from 16 waves (1997–2013) of the National Longitudinal Survey of Youth 1997 cohort (N = 6820 individuals; observations = 58,901). Utilizing the stress process model and generalized estimating equations to account for the correlated nature of multiple responses over time, results show that neighborhood disadvantage increases the odds of poor health for all groups. This positive association is strongest in the most disadvantaged neighborhoods and is heightened as young adults age. There are also notable race and gender differences. For example, Blacks, who live in the most highly disadvantaged neighborhoods, seem to be somewhat shielded from the most deleterious effects of poor neighborhood conditions compared to their White counterparts. Despite greater proportions of Blacks residing in harsh neighborhood environments, Black men experience better health than all other groups, and the health of Black women is no worse compared to White men or women. Limitations and directions for future research are discussed.

Keywords: race; gender; age; young adulthood; neighborhood disadvantage; self-rated health

Citation: Christie-Mizell, C.A. Neighborhood Disadvantage and Poor Health: The Consequences of Race, Gender, and Age among Young Adults. *Int. J. Environ. Res. Public Health* **2022**, *19*, 8107. https://doi.org/10.3390/ijerph19138107

Academic Editor: Paul B. Tchounwou

Received: 1 June 2022
Accepted: 30 June 2022
Published: 1 July 2022

Publisher's Note: MDPI stays neutral with regard to jurisdictional claims in published maps and institutional affiliations.

1. Introduction

Research on health outcomes has firmly established that residents of disadvantaged neighborhoods (e.g., high crime rates, elevated poverty rates, and few employment opportunities) suffer worse health than their counterparts in more affluent communities [1–3]. Disadvantaged neighborhoods are characterized by high levels of poverty, physical dilapidation, a disproportionate number of female-headed households, high unemployment, and alarming rates of crime [2]. The social disorder inherent in disadvantaged neighborhoods inhibits health-promoting resources and behaviors, including economic stability, access to healthy foods, physical exercise, and psychological safety [2–4]. In poor communities, scholars observ higher rates of chronic conditions (e.g., obesity, asthma), depression, anxiety, sexually transmitted diseases, cigarette smoking, illicit drug use, and alcohol problems [1,5–7].

Recent data from the U.S. Census Bureau show that 24 million U.S. residents live in impoverished, disadvantaged neighborhoods [8]. These are neighborhoods in which one-fifth of all community members live below the federal poverty line [8,9]. Racial and ethnic minorities are more likely than Whites are to live in these areas. For example, 20.9% of Black Americans reside in disadvantaged neighborhoods compared to only 4.3% of their White counterparts [8–10]. Therefore, compared to Whites, Blacks are at greater risk for the negative health consequences associated with deprived neighborhood conditions. Moreover, poor neighborhoods threaten the health of women more than men [11,12]. Studies show that, in disadvantaged neighborhoods, women are at greater risk for a host of mental and physical health problems, and are more likely to experience violence and mortality [11–13]. Further, a constant feature of impoverished neighborhoods is the disproportionate numbers of mother-headed households, which are the poorest households in the U.S. [11].

The same research literature that pinpoints race and gender differences also implicates age as a factor in how neighborhoods are connected to the risk for poor health [14,15]. For instance, older adults may face more vulnerabilities to mental and physical health because of exposure to harsh neighborhood conditions over time [14–16]. On the other end of the age spectrum, there has been considerable attention to child outcomes. These studies generally find that the healthy development of children is challenged in disadvantaged neighborhoods due to less physically safe environments, family economic deprivation, high crime rates, and a lack of access to quality health care [17–20]. Despite the strength of these findings for the elderly and children, less is known about how the health effects of neighborhood conditions vary at other points in the life course.

In this study, I focus on the impact of neighborhood disadvantage on the self-rated health of young adults aged 18–30. As a subjective measure, self-rated health captures dimensions of both physical and mental health [21–23]. Numerous validation studies show that measures of self-rated health are reliable. Moreover, such measures are reliable regardless of race, ethnicity, gender, age, and country [24–29]. Young adulthood is a unique life stage in which individuals are taking on new roles (e.g., employment, marriage, and parenthood), individuating from families of origin, and developing an adult sense of self [30,31]. The processes associated with young adulthood are stress-inducing, and I examine whether race–gender status combined with neighborhood disadvantage puts some individuals at greater risk for poor health during this period. Beyond the focus on race–gender status and neighborhood conditions, I also investigate whether and how age matters among young adults. That is, I pay particular attention to whether the relationship between neighborhood disadvantage and health by race–gender status is the same, for example, for 18-year-olds compared to 25- and 30-year-olds.

The current study offers three innovations to the research literature. First, this exploration includes longitudinal data for a nationally representative sample of U.S. Blacks and Whites with enough variation to carefully explore race–gender differences. This work offers a level of generalizability not found in more localized samples. Second, this study focuses on young adulthood, a stage of the life course that has received less attention than older adulthood, adolescence, or childhood. While there is an expectation that young adults are relatively healthy compared to their older counterparts, whether and how poor neighborhood conditions are associated with less favorable health may add to our understanding of how certain groups accumulate health disadvantages in this part of the life course. Third, while young adulthood is often conceptualized as a single stage in the life course, this study takes seriously the need to better understand variations in how different groups age into young adulthood [32,33]. Expectation and outcomes for adulthood vary by race and gender [33]. For instance, Blacks have children at younger ages, while they marry at later ages, compared to Whites [32,34]. Therefore, this study provides understanding of whether and how the relationship between neighborhood disadvantage and health by race–gender status changes from 18 to 30 years old.

1.1. Background and Theory

This research is guided by elements of the stress process model [35,36]. According to this theoretical framework, the conditions associated with neighborhood disadvantage, including poverty, high unemployment, physical disarray, and elevated crime rates, are conceptualized as stressors, which impact health outcomes by challenging the individual's ability to adapt and cope [36,37]. These stressors create acute, immediate health challenges that, in turn, give way to chronic, longer-term health problems [35,36]. This process is referred to as stress proliferation, wherein primary stressors (e.g., few employment opportunities) spread to other areas of life and result in secondary stressors (e.g., lack of access to health care, untreated chronic conditions) [36,37]. In other words, neighborhood disadvantage has rippling effects that threaten health and maintain the disadvantage over time.

1.2. Neighborhoods, Race, Gender and Health

A key feature of the stress process is the recognition that experiences that impact health differ by race and gender across the life course [12]. With regard to neighborhood stressors, research on health clearly indicates that the stressors that are linked to health and well-being vary by racial minority status (e.g., minorities experience higher rates of impoverishment and unemployment) and gender (e.g., women are more likely to shoulder the burden of rearing children alone in the context of economic insecurity) [38]. This research indicates the importance of how race and gender intersect to impact health [39,40]. For instance, both Black and White women experience more health inequality compared to men; however, Black women generally have worse health than White women [41,42]. With regard to poor neighborhood conditions, these racialized gender differences emerge early in the life course and may be due to the greater likelihood that Black women endure life in more economically fragile communities, live in areas with inadequate access adequate health care, and remain in disadvantaged neighborhoods because of the lack of residential mobility [43,44]. Therefore, carefully assessing how race and gender jointly impact health outcomes is one important goal of this research.

1.3. Neighborhood Disadvantage and Health in Young Adulthood

In young adulthood, the major benchmarks for achieving adult status are the completion of education, launching stable employment and income, establishing residency independent of the family of origin, marrying, and entering parenthood [45–47]. While these transitions are not characteristics of all young people and may happen in varying order, they offer many opportunities to set goals, exercise choice, and direct one's life. All of these choices and transitions happen in the context of the neighborhoods in which the young adult lives [47]. Therefore, neighborhood disadvantage not only impacts the success of making the desired transitions, but also the psychological and physical well-being of young adults. To illustrate, if the individual resides in a high-crime community in which there are few employment or economic prospects, their health may suffer [48]. Unemployment is often accompanied by the inability to purchase health insurance and having limited means of transportation, which in turn challenges the ability to have access to quality health care [48,49]. Moreover, the likelihood to afford healthy foods, live in safe environments free of dilapidation, and enjoy spaces where exercise can occur is less in these disadvantaged neighborhoods [37,38,43]. Because racial minorities and women in young adulthood are more likely to live in neighborhoods with concentrated poverty, they are more likely to suffer the health and well-being consequences of community disadvantage than their White male counterparts are [39].

Gender socialization is another factor that may account for health differentials between young men and women. Gender ideals restrict both women and men, but in different ways. Women are constricted to ideals of femininity rooted in self-sacrifice and the nurturance of others, while men are encouraged to follow masculine notions in which they signal toughness, show a lack of emotional expression, and engage in questionable health behaviors (e.g., smoking and heavy drinking) [50–52]. Regardless of race, women are more likely to internalize stressors associated with neighborhood disadvantage [37]. Moreover, because socialization places them at the center of caring for family, especially minor children, the psychological and physical burdens connected to deprived neighborhood environments are more likely to wear on the health of women [37,38]. The weight of deprived neighborhood conditions may especially erode the health of Black women, who are not only more likely to live in poor communities, but also to be rearing their children as the sole breadwinner [53,54].

1.4. Summary and Hypotheses

The current study explores the relationship between neighborhood disadvantage and self-rated poor health for a nationally representative sample of Black and White young adults aged 18–30. Using representative longitudinal data, I investigate whether and how race–gender status matters for how poor neighborhood conditions impact health and whether age matters during young adulthood. Four hypotheses were developed for this study:

Hypothesis 1 (H1). *Neighborhood disadvantage is positively associated with poor health.*

Hypothesis 2a (H2a). *The size of the association between neighborhood disadvantage and poor health is greater for Black women compared to Black men.*

Hypothesis 2b (H2b). *The size of the association between neighborhood disadvantage and poor health is greater for White women compared to White men.*

Hypothesis 3 (H3). *Black women have the highest probability of poor health compared to all groups.*

Hypothesis 4 (H4). *Older age is associated with a larger association size between poor neighborhood conditions and poor health.*

2. Materials and Methods

2.1. Sample

I examine the relationship between neighborhood disadvantage and poor health using data from the National Longitudinal Study of Youth 1997 (NLSY97). The NLSY97 is a multiwave panel dataset of 8984 youths between the ages of 12 and 16 on 31 December 1996 [55]. The data include a wide range of measures ranging from health to family life to criminal justice involvement. Respondents were interviewed each year from 1997 to 2011, and biennially thereafter. For this study, I used data from 16 waves (1997–2013) of the NLSY97 and restricted the sample to those Black and White respondents who had at least two measures of the dependent variable, self-rated health. The analytic sample includes 2298 Blacks (1108 men and 1190 women) and 20,191 person-years, and 4522 Whites (2317 men and 2205 women) and 38,710 person-years.

All analyses below were weighted to maintain the national representation of the United States and correct for the oversampling of Black youth. To arrive at the final sample size, I conducted multiple imputations by chained equations for the less than 10% of respondents with missing data on our independent and control variables. Fifteen replicate datasets were imputed and analyzed, and results were pooled to arrive at the estimates presented below [56].

2.2. Measures

All variables in this study are time-varying and measured at each wave, with the exception of race and gender. Fair/poor self-rated health is the dependent variable. Respondents were asked to categorize their general health as excellent, very good, good, fair, or poor. I coded those who reported fair or poor health as 1 and compared them to all others. In the analyses and discussion below, this measure is referred to as "poor health".

My key independent variable is an index of neighborhood disadvantage, which includes three dimensions: (1) the percentage of poor female-headed houses, (2) the unemployment rate, and (3) serious crime rate per 100,000 (e.g., murder, forcible rape, robbery) [2]. These three dimensions were captured by county-level census data available through a contract with the Bureau of Labor Statistics, which manages the NLSY97 collection. Further, each component (e.g., unemployment rate) was centered at zero with a standard deviation of 1 and then summed to create a measure of neighborhood disadvantage that ranges from 0 (lower disadvantage) to 3 (higher disadvantage). One key independent and moderating variable is age, measured in years, and centered at 18 for the analyses below. Other moderator variables included dummy variables to indicate race (Black (1 = yes) and White (1 = yes)) and gender (female (1 = yes)).

Several relevant control variables were selected, including marriage (1 = yes), parenthood (1 = yes), and employment (1 = yes), compared to those who do not hold these roles. Other controls include whether the respondent had been arrested (1 = yes) and/or incarcerated (1 = yes). I also held constant education (1 = college degree or more) and household income (1 = top one-fifth of the household income distribution). Lastly, I controlled for community location, including whether the respondent lived in the southern region of the United States (1 = yes) and/or in an urban area (1 = yes).

2.3. Analytic Strategy

All analyses for this research were conducted using SAS 9.4 (SAS Institute, Cary, NC, USA). The first step in the analyses was to produce descriptive statistics for all study variables by race (Table 1). Second, I estimated two sets (i.e., one set for Blacks and the other for Whites) of subsample regression models. Generalized estimating equations were employed with exchangeable correlation structure and the logistic link function to handle the correlated nature of the repeated measures in the data [29]. In the first set of models, I established the impact of neighborhood disadvantage, age, and gender status by race (Table 2, Models 1A and 2A). In the second model, neighborhood disadvantage, age, and gender interactions were used to test whether the effect of neighborhood disadvantage varies by age and race–gender status (Table 2, Models 1B and 2B).

Table 1. Mean/proportions for all study variables by race [a]. National Longitudinal Survey of Youth 1997 (NLSY97), 1997–2013 [b].

	Blacks		Whites	
Variables [b]	**Mean/%**	**Std.**	**Mean/%**	**Std.**
Poor health	9.96%	—	6.29% *	—
Age (years)	22.55	3.06	22.47	3.04
Female (1 = yes)	51.80%	—	48.77% *	—
Neighborhood disadvantage	0.36	0.68	0.17 *	0.68
Employed (1 = yes)	59.96%	—	72.79% *	—
Married (1 = yes)	9.59%	—	19.04%	—
Parenthood (1 = yes)	41.67%	—	21.95% *	—
College degree or more (1 = yes)	6.76%	—	14.06% *	—
Family income (1 = top fifth)	9.43%	—	21.06%	—
Urban (1 = yes)	80.42%	—	69.02% *	—
South (1 = yes)	58.80%	—	29.67% *	—
Arrest history (1 = yes)	6.43%	—	4.79% *	—
Respondent's incarceration (1 = yes)	12.28%	—	7.84% *	—
N (person-years)	20,191		38,710	

[a] Reported sample sizes refer to number of person-years. Subsample *N*s comprised 2298 Blacks and 4522 Whites.
[b] Asterisks denote significant differences between Blacks and Whites at * $p < 0.001$.

Table 2. Generalized estimating equations for poor health by race. National Longitudinal Survey of Youth 1997 (NLSY97), 1997–2013.

	Blacks				Whites			
	Model 1A		Model 1B		Model 2A		Model 2B	
Variables [a]	**Odds Ratio**	**95% CI**	**Odds Ratio**	**95% CI**	**Odds Ratio**	**95% CI**	**Odds Ratio**	**95% CI**
Age (centered at 18)	1.04 ***	(1.02–1.05)	1.31	(0.87–1.98)	1.08 ***	(1.06–1.09)	0.85	(0.68–1.06)
Female (1 = yes)	1.83 ***	(1.70–1.97)	4.56 ***	(2.11–9.85)	1.46 ***	(1.34–1.57)	1.61 *	(1.52–1.72)
Neighborhood disadvantage (ND) [a]	1.13 ***	(1.04–1.23)	1.40 **	(1.12–1.75)	1.04 *	(1.02–1.07)	1.05 *	(1.03–1.07)
Control Variables								
Employed (1 = yes)	0.87 *	(0.77–0.98)	0.87 *	(0.77–0.98)	0.85 **	(0.77–0.94)	0.86 **	(0.77–0.95)
Married (1 = yes)	0.95	(0.84–1.07)	0.95	(0.84–1.07)	0.74 ***	(0.68–0.80)	0.74 ***	(0.68–0.80)
Parenthood (1 = yes)	1.38 ***	(1.28–1.48)	1.38 ***	(1.28–1.48)	1.38 ***	(1.28–1.49)	1.38 ***	(1.29–1.49)
College degree or more (1 = yes)	0.37 ***	(0.30–0.45)	0.37 ***	(0.30–0.45)	0.28 ***	(0.24–0.32)	0.28 ***	(0.24–0.32)
Family income (1 = top fifth)	0.74 ***	(0.65–0.85)	0.74 ***	(0.65–0.85)	0.56 ***	(0.51–0.61)	0.56 ***	(0.52–0.62)
Urban residence (1 = yes)	0.92	(0.84–1.01)	0.92	(0.84–1.01)	1.09 **	(1.02–1.16)	1.09 **	(1.02–1.16)
Southern residence (1 = yes)	0.80 ***	(0.75–0.86)	0.80 ***	(0.75–0.86)	1.08 *	(1.01–1.15)	1.08 *	(1.01–1.15)
Arrest history (1 = yes)	1.29 ***	(1.13–1.48)	1.29 ***	(1.13–1.48)	1.53 ***	(1.36–1.71)	1.54 ***	(1.37–1.72)
Respondent's incarceration (1 = yes)	1.24 ***	(1.11–1.38)	1.24 ***	(1.11–1.38)	1.80 ***	(1.64–1.97)	1.80 ***	(1.64–1.97)
Interactions								
Age × female	—	—	0.72 *	(0.53–0.98)	—	—	1.27 **	(1.16–1.40)
Age × ND	—	—	0.92	(0.81–1.06)	—	—	1.12 *	(1.02–1.27)
Female × ND	—	—	0.74 **	(0.60–0.91)	—	—	0.95	(0.78–1.17)
Age × female × ND	—	—	1.11	(0.94–1.32)	—	—	0.88 **	(0.82–0.93)
AIC	25,441.70		25,440.72		34,832.72		37,829.74	
−2 Log likelihood	−12,707.85		−12,704.36		−17,403.63		−17,397.73	

Note: N = 2298 Blacks with 20,191 observations, and 4522 Whites with 38,710 observations. [a] Neighborhood disadvantage ranges from 0 (lower disadvantage) to 3 (higher disadvantage).
* $p < 0.05$; ** $p < 0.01$; *** $p < 0.001$.

3. Results

Table 1 shows the means and percentages for all study variables. Consistent with other nationally representative data, a greater percentage of Blacks (9.96%) reported poor health compared to Whites (6.29%). There were no differences in age across the two groups, but in the subsamples, there was a greater percentage of Black women (51.80%) compared to White women (48.77%). Further, Blacks (0.36) reported higher levels of neighborhood disadvantage compared to Whites (0.17). Blacks also reported lower levels of employment (59.96% vs. 72.79%) and marriage (9.59% vs. 19.04%), but higher levels of parenthood (41.57% vs. 21.95%), than their White counterparts did. Moreover, in comparison to Whites, fewer Blacks had completed college degrees or higher (6.76% vs. 14.06%) and fewer fell into the top one-fifth in family income (9.43% vs. 21.06%). Moreover, greater percentages of Blacks than those of Whites lived in urban areas (80.42% vs. 69.02%) and the South (58.80% vs. 29.67%). Lastly, higher percentages of Blacks had an arrest history (6.43% vs. 4.79%) and reported having been incarcerated (12.28% vs. 7.84%) compared to Whites.

In Table 2, Models 1A and 2A show that the probability of poor health increases by odds of 4% and 8% with each year of age for Blacks and Whites, respectively. Further, Black women, compared to Black men, experience increased odds of 83% for poor health, while White women had increased odds of 46% compared to White men. Neighborhood disadvantage also increases the odds of poor health by 13% for Blacks and 4% for Whites. Additionally, employment, a college degree or more, and family income decreased the odds of poor health for both Blacks and Whites, while parenthood, a history of arrest, and incarceration increased the odds for both groups. For Blacks, southern residence decreased the odds of poor health. Among Whites, marriage decreased the odds of poor health, while urban residence and living in the South increased the odds of poor health.

In Table 2, Models 1B and 2B display the findings for how neighborhood disadvantage, age, and gender are jointly associated with the probability of poor health for Blacks and Whites. With the exception of the interactions added to these models, most covariates retain the same general effects as in Models 1A and 2A. For Blacks (Table 2, Model 1B), the interaction of age by female indicates that age results in greater decreased odds ($OR = 0.74$) for Black women compared to Black men. Further, the female by neighborhood disadvantage interaction indicates that poor neighborhood conditions are less nettlesome ($OR = 0.74$) for Black women than they are for Black men. However, these advantages for Black women are not outweighed by the increased odds associated with being female ($OR = 4.56$, $p < 0.001$), which indicates that Black women are still at greater risk for poor health in comparison to Black men.

For Whites (Table 2, Model 2B), White women experienced lower odds of poorer health as a result of the joint impact of age, gender, and neighborhood disadvantage (i.e., age × female × neighborhood disadvantage; $OR = 0.88$, $p < 0.01$) compared to White men. However, White women still had higher odds of poor health connected to aging (i.e., age × female; $OR = 1.27$, $p < 0.01$) and as a result of the increased odds being female ($OR = 1.61$, $p < 0.05$). The interaction findings are graphically displayed in Figure 1a,b.

In Figure 1a,b, neighborhood disadvantage is divided into low disadvantage (bottom one-third) and high disadvantage (top one-third) and includes age and race–gender status to allow both within and between race comparisons. Among those residents who live in communities with low neighborhood disadvantage (Figure 1a) at age 18, White men report the lowest probability of poor health followed by Black men who report the second lowest probability of poor health. At age 18, Black and White women have the highest probabilities of poor health, with Black women slightly higher as shown by the nearly overlapping error bars. At age 21, this pattern in low disadvantaged neighborhoods persists, with men having lower probabilities of poor health than those of women; however, by age 21, Black and White women do not differ significantly. As young adults mature to age 25, gender, not race, is the clearest driver of poor health. That is, Black and White men have equivalent probabilities of poor health, as do Black and White women. Nevertheless, by age 27, White women have the overall highest odds of poor health, followed by Black women. At age 30, White women still have poorer health than any other group. Black women do not differ significantly from White men, and Black men have the lowest overall probability of poor health.

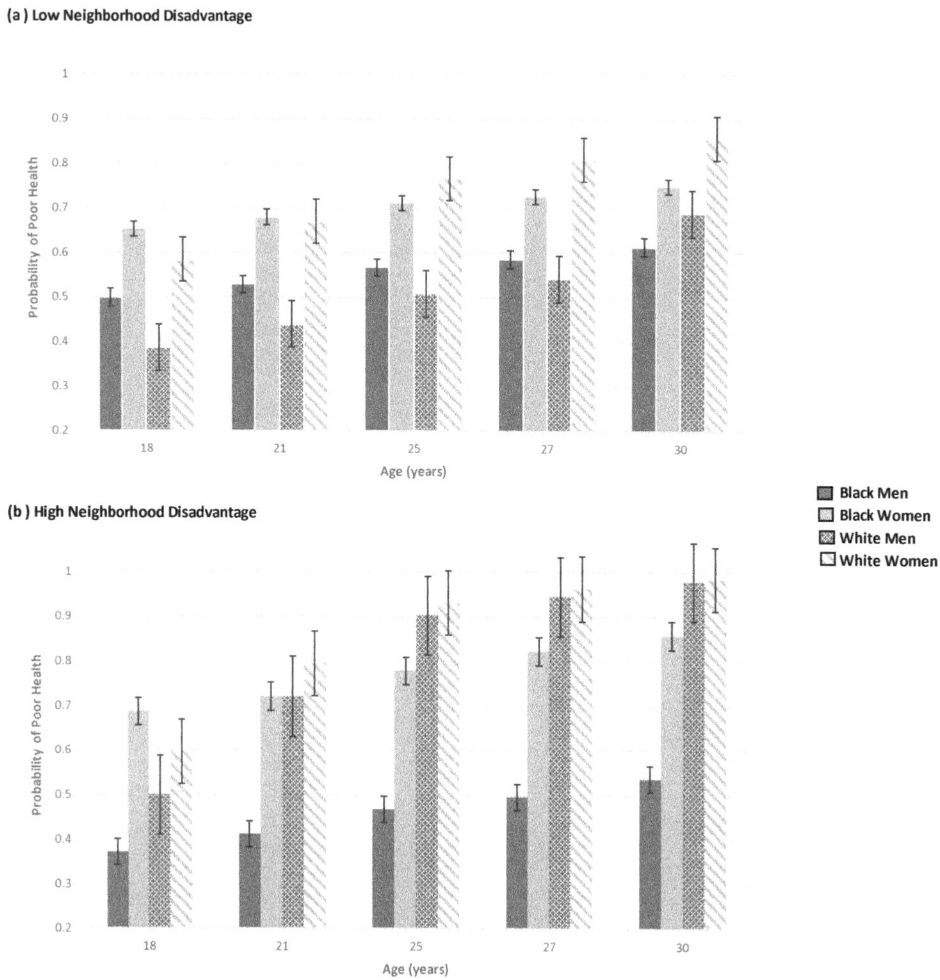

Figure 1. Relationship between poor health and race–gender status for those living in (**a**) low disadvantaged neighborhoods (bottom one-third) and (**b**) high disadvantaged neighborhoods (top one-third) at ages 18, 21, 25, 27, and 30.

Figure 1b displays the findings for poor health by age and race–gender status for young adults in in high disadvantaged neighborhoods. At age 18, Black men have the lowest probability of poor health, while Black and White women do not differ significantly. However, White men have a lower probability of poor health than Black women do, but do not differ from White women. At ages, 21, 25, 27, and 30, the pattern that emerges is that Black men remain at the lowest odds of poor health; however, Black women, White women, and White men do not differ significantly. Comparing Figure 1a,b, two things are worth noting. First, as might be expected, the odds of poor health are overall lower in the neighborhoods with low disadvantage. Second, in both high and low disadvantage, age is positively associated with poor health. That is, regardless of race–gender status, the general pattern is that all groups report higher odds of poor health as they age.

4. Discussion

In this study, I investigated the association between neighborhood disadvantage and poor health. Important to the assessment of this main relationship was whether and how race, gender, and age matter in young adulthood. In H1, I hypothesized that neighborhood disadvantage would be positively associated with poor health and found support for this hypothesis. As neighborhood disadvantage increases, so does the probability of poor health. Interestingly, the results also reveal several important, unexpected nuances. For example, while H2, which stated that neighborhood conditions would generate higher odds of poor health for women compared to men, was supported for Blacks, it was not supported for Whites. In both low and high disadvantaged neighborhoods, Black women have greater odds of poor health. Black men had the lowest odds of poor health in most disadvantaged neighborhoods compared to all other groups. However, among Whites, women only had higher odds of poor health in low disadvantage neighborhoods. In communities with high levels of disadvantage, White men did not differ from White women in the probability of poor health.

Further, I did not find support for H3, which stated that Black women would overall have the highest probability of poor health. In fact, in neighborhoods with low disadvantage, White women had the greatest odds of poor health, and in the most severely disadvantaged communities, there was no difference in the odds of poor health for Black and White women. H4 predicted that, as young adults age, the association between neighborhood disadvantage and poor health would grow. This hypothesis was supported for Whites, as shown by the significant interaction between age and neighborhood disadvantage. The indication is that, as Whites age across young adulthood, the impact of deprived neighborhood conditions worsens health. However, this "aging effect" is less severe for White women, as signified by the triple interaction (i.e., age × female × neighborhood disadvantage) in Table 2, Model 2B.

This research was fruitful in at least two ways. First, I verified the importance of neighborhood disadvantage for individuals in young adulthood. While people in this stage of the life course are generally healthy, this research shows that health during this period is impacted by neighborhood circumstances. Moreover, the severity of poor health increase significantly for individuals aged from 18 to 30 years old, especially in the most highly disadvantaged neighborhoods. The probability of poor health is much greater for most groups, and the more disadvantages and disorders are endured by neighborhood residents, except for Black males—a point to which I return below. Health is dependent on many factors, including environmental (e.g., physical dilapidation), psychosocial adjustment (e.g., low fear of crime), and socioeconomic resources (e.g., employment, transportation) [2,12,37]. Such resources are in short supply in poor neighborhoods and result in deprivation that render many of the developmental tasks (e.g., individuating from the family origin, completing education, and finding steady work) of young adulthood difficult, if not impossible [39,45]. In addition to having less access to economic resources such as employment and health care in disadvantaged neighborhoods, the failure to achieve markers of adulthood may cause additional stress that further puts health at risk.

Second, the results in this study support and add to our theoretical knowledge of how the neighborhood context is connected to health. In particular, the stress process model purports that stressors such as neighborhood disadvantage may vary by race and gender status [35,36]. In other words, on the basis of specific experience to group membership (e.g., Black women), stressors may have differential effects on health across groups. In the current study, I found a health paradox with respect to Black Americans, neighborhood disadvantage, and poor health. A health paradox occurs when one group is more highly exposed to a known health stressor (e.g., neighborhood disadvantage), but has health outcomes that are equivalent or better than those of groups with lower exposure to the same stressor [29,57]. That is, as I hypothesized, one might have anticipated that Black men and women, who experience neighborhood disadvantage at much higher rates than those of their White counterparts, would have comparatively poorer health. However, in the most disadvantaged neighborhoods, Black women experienced health outcomes equivalent to White men and women. Moreover, Black men experienced the lowest probability of poor health in communities with the highest levels of disadvantage.

Of course, this study is not the first to find a Black–White health paradox. To name a few areas, researchers interested in mental health, mortality, criminal justice involvement, and immigration have all found such health paradoxes [41,57–59]. The typical theoretical reasoning is that Blacks may have different coping strategies as a result of obstacles they face in their daily lives and owing to their history in U.S. (e.g., enslavement and exclusion), which has required a level of adaptation and adjustment not needed by other groups. In related work on health, Christie-Mizell and his colleagues [41] found a health paradox in which Black males do not suffer higher odds of poor health due to a history of arrests, even though they are more likely than White counterparts to be arrested or have other types of criminal justice involvement—stressors linked to poor health. They theorized beyond the initial encounter with the criminal justice system that Black men who have been arrested are far more likely than others to remain involved with the criminal justice system through restitution, probation, rehabilitation services (e.g., drug courts), and community service; see also [60,61]. As burdensome as this continued involvement may be for the individual, such supervision may promote health by curbing involvement in behaviors (e.g., alcohol and drug use) that harm health and may result further criminal justice involvement. They further posited that the fact that higher rates of arrest are unjustly foisted on Black men, these higher rates for may be viewed as a problem of the criminal justice system and thereby associated with less distress and stigma, which can harm health [41].

I similarly argue here regarding neighborhood disadvantage for the young adult Black men and women in this study. Because this group is more likely to live in disadvantaged neighborhoods, the stigma may also be less health-threatening than that for their White counterparts. Moreover, while Black and White individuals share the same developmental tasks in young adulthood, the patterns for accomplishing these tasks vary. For example, Blacks experience more unstable employment, later marriage, and earlier fertility than Whites do. Therefore, Black health may not be as compromised by neighborhood conditions that do not encourage the White middle-class normative developmental trajectories. Lastly, the greater likelihood that Blacks have intergenerationally lived in less desirable communities because of exclusion and segregation may shield health in ways not experienced by Whites. The intergenerational knowledge of how to cope and manage such environments may be more prevalent in disadvantaged communities that have had to find ways to survive. Nevertheless, the ability to cope in ways not experienced by Whites does not completely protect Blacks from neighborhood disadvantage. As shown in my analyses, poor neighborhood conditions are still significantly related to poorer health for Blacks, placing Black women among the race–gender groups with the highest levels of poor health in highly disadvantaged neighborhoods.

5. Conclusions

This research expands the knowledge of how neighborhood disadvantage is related to poor health for young adults. The findings reveal that even relatively healthy young people accrue health risks as they age through early adulthood. This risk is especially prominent in the most highly disadvantaged neighborhoods. Nevertheless, there are important differences by race and gender status that are worth noting. Blacks who live in the most highly disadvantaged neighborhoods seem to be somewhat shielded from the most deleterious effects of poor neighborhood conditions compared to their White counterparts. Despite greater proportions of Blacks residing in harsh neighborhood environments, Black men experience better health than all other groups, and the health of Black women is no worse than White men or women. These results provide and extend the stress process model's acknowledgement that individual and group experience molds how stressors and stress proliferation vary by important characteristics such as race and gender.

This study is limited in a few respects. First, although I measured neighborhood disadvantage over time, these data do not allow for us to know respondent perceptions of neighborhood conditions. Other research has found that both objective and subjective ratings of neighborhoods can reveal the nature and extent to which individuals have internalized the meanings of neighborhood conditions, thus clarifying the impact on health and well-being. Second, life course research indicates that the importance placed on social roles (e.g., employment, marriage, parenthood) is key to understanding health. The enactment of personally meaningful roles encourages health because individuals are more likely to adopt prosocial behavior, approach adversity with resilience, and develop effective coping strategies [2,35,37]. Therefore, data that include role expectations, aspirations, and meaning would be helpful in clarifying the impact of neighborhood disadvantage on health. Third, future research should further investigate the Black–White health paradox (i.e., higher residency in disadvantaged neighborhoods but better or equivalent health) and explore the mechanisms underlying this paradox and the extent to which it applies other, specific health measures (e.g., depression, anxiety, cardiovascular problems, insomnia). Lastly, I purposely restricted the current study to Black and White men and women, but other research should expand it to include other groups (e.g., Latinx, Asian, Native American) with an emphasis on how race and ethnicity intersect with gender to produce outcomes across groups.

Funding: This research received no external funding.

Institutional Review Board Statement: The data utilized in this study included deidentified survey data collected through the U.S. Bureau of Labor Statistics https://www.bls.gov/nls/ (accessed on 5 January 2022). The investigator has no way of reidentifying the subjects, and the research was deemed to be exempt by Vanderbilt University.

Informed Consent Statement: Not applicable.

Data Availability Statement: Data from this study are publicly available and can be retrieved through the U.S. Bureau of Labor Statistics at https://www.bls.gov/nls/nlsy97.htm (accessed 5 January 2022).

Conflicts of Interest: The author declares no conflict of interest.

References

1. Rodrigues, E.D.; César, C.C.; Xavier, C.C.; Caiaffa, T.W.; Proietti, A.F. Exploring neighborhood socioeconomic disparity in self-rated health: A multiple mediation analysis. *Prev. Med.* **2021**, *45*, 106443. [CrossRef] [PubMed]
2. Ross, C.E.; Mirowsky, J. Neighborhood disadvantage, disorder, and health. *J. Health Soc. Behav.* **2001**, *1*, 258–276. [CrossRef]
3. Tung, E.L.; Peek, M.E.; Rivas, M.A.; Yang, J.P.; Volerman, A. Association of neighborhood disadvantage with racial disparities in COVID-19 positivity in Chicago. *Health Affairs.* **2021**, *40*, 1784–1791. [CrossRef]
4. Cohen, D.A.; Mason, K.; Bedimo, A.; Scribner, R.; Basolo, V.; Farley, T.A. Neighborhood physical conditions and health. *Am. J. Public Health* **2003**, *93*, 467–471. [CrossRef] [PubMed]
5. Brown, A.F.; Ang, A.; Pebley, A.R. The relationship between neighborhood characteristics and self-rated health for adults with chronic conditions. *Am. J. Public Health* **2007**, *97*, 926–932. [CrossRef] [PubMed]
6. Green, K.M.; Matson, P.A.; Reboussin, B.A.; Milam, A.J.; Furr-Holden, C.D.M.; Rabinowitz, J.A.; Powell, T.W.; Ialongo, N.S. Individual and neighborhood factors associated with sexual behavior classes in an urban longitudinal sample. *Sex. Transm. Dis.* **2019**, *46*, 98–104. [CrossRef] [PubMed]
7. Hu, M.D.; Lawrence, K.G.; Bodkin, M.R.; Kwok, R.K.; Engel, L.S.; Sandler, D.P. Neighborhood deprivation, obesity, and diabetes in residents of the U.S. gulf coast. *Am. J. Epidemiol.* **2021**, *190*, 295–304. [CrossRef]
8. U.S. Census Bureau. American Community Survey 5-Year Data (2009–2020). 2022. Available online: https://www.census.gov/data/developers/data-sets/acs-5year.html (accessed on 1 February 2022).
9. Firebaugh, G.; Acciai, F. For blacks in America, the gap in neighborhood poverty has declined faster than segregation. *Proc. Natl. Acad. Sci. USA* **2016**, *113*, 13372–13377. [CrossRef]
10. National Equity Atlas. Neighborhood Poverty: All Neighborhoods Should be Communities of Opportunity. 2019. Available online: https://nationalequityatlas.org/indicators/Neighborhood_poverty# (accessed on 25 May 2022).
11. Baker, R.S.; O'Connell, H.A. Structural racism, family structure, and Black–White inequality: The differential impact of the legacy of slavery on poverty among single mother and married parent households. *J. Marriage Fam.* **2022**. [CrossRef]

12. Bassett, E.; Moore, S. Gender differences in the social pathways linking neighborhood disadvantage to depressive symptoms in adults. *PLoS ONE* **2013**, *8*, e76554. [CrossRef]
13. Stansfield, R.; Doherty, E. Neighborhood health, social structure and family violence. *Soc. Sci. Res.* **2019**, *81*, 12–22. [CrossRef] [PubMed]
14. Chamberlain, A.M.; St Sauver, J.L.; Finney Rutten, L.J.; Fan, C.; Jacobson, D.J.; Wilson, P.M.; Boyd, C.M.; Rocca, W.A. Associations of neighborhood socioeconomic disadvantage with chronic conditions by age, sex, race, and ethnicity in a population-based cohort. *Mayo Clin. Proc.* **2022**, *97*, 57–67. [CrossRef] [PubMed]
15. Riley, A.; Hawkley, L.C. Racial differences in the effects of neighborhood disadvantage on residential mobility in later life. *J. Gerontol. B Psychol. Sci. Soc. Sci.* **2016**, *71*, 1131–1140. [CrossRef] [PubMed]
16. Simons, R.L.; Lei, M.K.; Klopack, E.; Beach, S.R.H.; Gibbons, F.X.; Philibert, R.A. The effects of social adversity, discrimination, and health risk behaviors on the accelerated aging of African Americans: Further support for the weathering hypothesis. *Soc. Sci. Med.* **2021**, *282*, 113169. [CrossRef]
17. King, C.; Huang, X.; Dewan, N.A. Continuity and change in neighborhood disadvantage and adolescent depression and anxiety. *Health Place* **2022**, *73*, 102724. [CrossRef]
18. Pinchak, N.P.; Swisher, R.R. Neighborhoods, schools, and adolescent violence: Ecological relative deprivation, disadvantage saturation, or cumulative disadvantage? *J. Youth Adolesc.* **2022**, *51*, 261–277. [CrossRef]
19. Roubinov, D.S.; Hagan, M.J.; Boyce, W.T.; Adler, N.E.; Bush, N.R. Family Socioeconomic Status, Cortisol, and Physical Health in Early Childhood: The Role of Advantageous Neighborhood Characteristics. *Psychosom. Med.* **2018**, *80*, 492–501. [CrossRef]
20. Saitadze, I. The effects of neighborhood factors, maternal depression and parental emotional support on social—Behavioral outcomes of children involved in the child welfare system. *J. Public Child. Welf.* **2022**, *16*, 249–271. [CrossRef]
21. Christie-Mizell, C.A.; Leslie, E.T.A.; Hearne, B.N. Self-rated health, discrimination, and racial group identity: The consequences of ethnicity and nativity among black Americans. *J. Afr. Am. Stud.* **2017**, *21*, 643–664. [CrossRef]
22. DeSalvo, K.B.; Bloser, N.; Reynolds, K.; He, J.; Muntner, P. Mortality prediction with a single general self-rated health question. *J. Gen. Intern. Med.* **2006**, *21*, 267. [CrossRef]
23. Nakata, A.; Takahashi, M.; Otsuka, Y.; Swanson, N.G. Is self-rated health associated with blood immune markers in healthy individuals? *Int. J. Behav. Med.* **2010**, *17*, 234–242. [CrossRef] [PubMed]
24. Benjamins, M.R.; Hummer, R.A.; Eberstein, I.W.; Nam, C.B. Self-reported health and adult mortality risk: An analysis of cause-specific mortality. *Soc. Sci. Med.* **2004**, *59*, 1297–1306. [CrossRef]
25. Benyamini, Y.; Blumstein, T.; Lusky, A.; Modan, B. Gender differences in the self-rated health–mortality association: Is it poor self-rated health that predicts mortality or excellent self-rated health that predicts survival? *Gerontologist* **2003**, *43*, 396–405. [CrossRef] [PubMed]
26. Idler, E.; Leventhal, H.; Mclaughlin, J.; Leventhal, E. In sickness but not in health: Self-ratings, identity, and mortality. *J. Health Soc. Behav.* **2004**, *45*, 336–356. [CrossRef] [PubMed]
27. Miller, T.R.; Wolinsky, F.D. Self-rated health trajectories and mortality among older adults. *J. Gerontol. B Psychol. Sc.i Soc. Sci.* **2007**, *62*, S22–S27. [CrossRef]
28. Perlman, F.; Bobak, M. Determinants of self rated health and mortality in Russia—Are they the same? *Int. J. Equity Health* **2008**, *7*, 19. [CrossRef]
29. Boynton-Jarrett, R.; Ryan, L.M.; Berkman, L.F.; Wright, R.J. Cumulative violence exposure and self-rated health: Longitudinal study of adolescents in the United States. *Pediatrics* **2008**, *122*, 961–970. [CrossRef]
30. Pusch, S.; Mund, M.; Hagemeyer, B.; Finn, C. Personality development in emerging and young adulthood: A study of age differences. *Eur. J. Pers.* **2019**, *33*, 245–263. [CrossRef]
31. Wood, D.; Crapnell, T.; Lau, L.; Bennett, A.; Lotstein, D.; Ferris, M.; Kuo, A. Emerging adulthood as a critical stage in the life course. In *Handbook of Life Course Health Development*; Halfon, N., Forrest, C.B., Lerner, R.M., Faustman, E.M., Eds.; Springer: Cham, Switzerland, 2018.
32. Britton, M.L. Race/ethnicity, attitudes, and living with parents during young adulthood. *J. Marriage Fam.* **2013**, *75*, 995–1013. [CrossRef]
33. Cunningham, M.; Beutel, A.M.; Barber, J.S.; Thornton, A. Reciprocal relationships between attitudes about gender and social contexts during young adulthood. *Soc. Sci. Res.* **2005**, *34*, 862–892. [CrossRef]
34. Tillman, K.H.; Brewster, K.L.; Holway, G.V. Sexual and romantic relationships in young adulthood. *Ann. Rev. Soc.* **2019**, *45*, 133–153. [CrossRef]
35. Pearlin, L.I.; Menaghan, E.G.; Lieberman, M.A.; Mullan, J.T. The stress process. *J. Health Soc. Behav.* **1981**, *22*, 337. [CrossRef] [PubMed]
36. Pearlin, L.I.; Schieman, S.; Fazio, E.M.; Meersman, S.C. Stress, health, and the life course: Some conceptual perspectives. *J. Health Soc. Behav.* **2005**, *46*, 205–219. [CrossRef] [PubMed]
37. Christie-Mizell, C.A.; Erickson, R.J. Mothers and mastery: The consequences of perceived neighborhood disorder. *Soc. Psychol. Q.* **2007**, *70*, 340–365. [CrossRef]
38. Christie-Mizell, C.A.; Steelman, L.C.; Stewart, J. Seeing their surroundings: The effects of neighborhood setting and race on maternal distress. *Soc. Sci. Res.* **2003**, *32*, 402–428. [CrossRef]

39. López, N.; Gadsden, V.L. Health inequities, social determinants, and intersectionality. In *NAM Perspectives*; National Academy of Medicine: Washington, DC, USA, 2016. [CrossRef]
40. Malcome, M.L.D.; Fedock, G.; Garthe, R.C.; Golder, S.; Higgins, G.; Logan, T.K. Weathering probation and parole: The protective role of social support on black women's recent stressful events and depressive symptoms. *J. Black Psychol.* **2019**, *45*, 661–688. [CrossRef]
41. Christie-Mizell, C.A.; Talbert, R.D.; Frazier, C.G.; Rainock, M.R.; Jurinsky, J. Race-gender variation in the relationship between arrest history and poor health from adolescence to adulthood. *J. Nat. Med. Assoc.* **2022**. [CrossRef]
42. Franks, P.; Gold, M.R.; Fiscella, K. Sociodemographics, self-rated health, and mortality in the US. *Soc. Sci. Med.* **2003**, *56*, 2505–2514. [CrossRef]
43. Loh, V.H.Y.; Rachele, J.N.; Brown, W.J.; Ghani, F.; Turrell, G. Neighborhood disadvantage and physical function: The contributions of neighborhood-level perceptions of safety from crime and walking for recreation. *J. Phys. Act. Health* **2018**, *15*, 553–563. [CrossRef]
44. Zimmerman, G.M.; Messner, S.F. Neighborhood context and the gender gap in adolescent violent crime. *Am. Sociol. Rev.* **2010**, *75*, 958–980. [CrossRef]
45. Eliason, S.R.; Mortimer, J.T.; Vuolo, M. The Transition to Adulthood: Life Course Structures and Subjective Perceptions. *Soc. Psychol. Q.* **2015**, *78*, 205–227. [CrossRef] [PubMed]
46. Johnson, M.K.; Berg, J.A.; Sirotzki, T. Differentiation in self-perceived adulthood: Extending the confluence model of subjective age identity. *Soc. Psychol. Q* **2007**, *70*, 243–261. [CrossRef]
47. Shanahan, M.J. Pathways to adulthood in changing societies: Variability and mechanisms in life course perspective. *Ann. Rev. Soc.* **2000**, *26*, 667–692. [CrossRef]
48. Smith, D.A.; Akira, A.; Hudson, K.; Hudson, A.; Hudson, M.; Mitchell, M.; Crook, E. The effect of health insurance coverage and the doctor-patient relationship on health care utilization in high poverty neighborhoods. *Prev. Med. Rep.* **2017**, *7*, 158–161. [CrossRef] [PubMed]
49. Tsui, J.; Hirsch, J.A.; Bayer, F.J.; Quinn, J.W.; Cahill, J.; Siscovick, D.; Lovasi, G.S. Patterns in Geographic Access to Health Care Facilities Across Neighborhoods in the United States Based on Data From the National Establishment Time-Series Between 2000 and 2014. *JAMA Netw. Open* **2020**, *3*, e205105. [CrossRef]
50. Valdez, Z.; Golash-Boza, T. Towards an intersectionality of race and ethnicity. *Ethn. Racial. Stud.* **2017**, *40*, 2256–2261. [CrossRef]
51. Klostermann, S.; Connell, A.; Stormshak, E.A. Gender differences in the developmental links between conduct problems and depression across early adolescence. *J. Res. Adolesc.* **2016**, *26*, 76–89. [CrossRef]
52. Christie-Mizell, C.A.; Talbert, R.D.; Hope, A.R.; Frazier, C.G.; Hearne, B.N. Depression and African Americans in the first decade of midlife: The consequences of social roles and gender. *J. Nat. Med. Assoc.* **2019**, *111*, 285–295. [CrossRef]
53. Hill, T.D.; Needham, B.L. Rethinking gender and mental health: A critical analysis of three propositions. *Soc. Sci. Med.* **2013**, *92*, 83–91. [CrossRef]
54. Smith, D.T.; Mouzon, D.M.; Elliott, M. Reviewing the assumptions about men's mental health: An exploration of the gender binary. *Am. J. Mens Health* **2018**, *12*, 78–89. [CrossRef]
55. Moore, W.; Pedlow, S.; Krishnamurty, P.; Wolter, K. *National Longitudinal Sample of Youth 1997 (NSLY97): Technical Sampling Report*; National Opinion Research Center: Chicago, IL, USA, 2000.
56. McLeod, J.D.; Uemura, R.; Rohrman, S. Adolescent mental health, behavior problems, and academic achievement. *J. Health Soc. Behav.* **2012**, *53*, 482–497. [CrossRef] [PubMed]
57. Thomas Tobin, C.S.; Erving, C.L.; Hargrove, T.W.; Satcher, L.A. Is the Black-White mental health paradox consistent across age, gender, and psychiatric disorders? *Aging Ment. Health* **2022**, *26*, 196–204. [CrossRef] [PubMed]
58. Omenka, O.I.; Watson, D.P.; Hendrie, H.C. Understanding the healthcare experiences and needs of African immigrants in the United States: A scoping review. *BMC Public Health* **2020**, *20*, 27. [CrossRef] [PubMed]
59. Patterson, E.J. Incarcerating death: Mortality in U.S. state correctional facilities, 1985–1998. *Demography* **2010**, *47*, 587–607. [CrossRef] [PubMed]
60. Jeffers, J.L. Justice is not blind: Disproportionate incarceration rate of people of color. *Soc. Work Public Health* **2019**, *34*, 113–121. [CrossRef] [PubMed]
61. Fryer, D. Race, reform, & progressive prosecution. *J. Crim. Law Criminol.* **2020**, *110*, 769–802. [CrossRef]

International Journal of
Environmental Research and Public Health

MDPI

Article

Kinky Sex and Deliberate Partner Negotiations: Case Studies of Canadian Transgender Men Who Have Sex with Men, Their HIV Risks, Safer Sex Practices, and Prevention Needs

Renato M. Liboro [1,2,*], Charles Fehr [2] and George Da Silva [2]

1 Department of Psychology, University of Nevada, Las Vegas, NV 89154, USA
2 Centre for Addiction and Mental Health, Toronto, ON M5S 2S1, Canada
* Correspondence: renato.liboro@unlv.edu

Abstract: Growing research in the last two decades has begun to investigate the HIV risks and sexual health practices of transgender men, especially as a subpopulation of men who have sex with men (MSM) that likely shares certain HIV risks and sexual health practices with cisgender MSM, the sociodemographic group that continues to be at highest risk for HIV in many developed countries since the start of the epidemic. As part of our Community-Based Participatory Research project and larger strengths-based qualitative study that was dedicated to examine multiple factors that promote resilience to HIV utilizing the perspectives and lived experiences of middle-aged and older MSM, the case studies we present in this article feature the distinct insights and experiences of three HIV-negative transgender MSM from Downtown Toronto, Ontario, Canada, who participated in our one-on-one interviews. The three case studies provide not only an enlightening snapshot of some of the specific contexts, HIV risks, safer sex practices, and HIV prevention needs of transgender MSM, but also a unique opportunity to critically reflect on the potential implications of the insights and experiences that were shared by our participants, particularly for adapting and developing current and future HIV services and programs to maximally benefit transgender MSM.

Keywords: transgender men who have sex with men; resilience; HIV/AIDS; kinky sex; deliberate partner negotiations

Citation: Liboro, R.M.; Fehr, C.; Da Silva, G. Kinky Sex and Deliberate Partner Negotiations: Case Studies of Canadian Transgender Men Who Have Sex with Men, Their HIV Risks, Safer Sex Practices, and Prevention Needs. *Int. J. Environ. Res. Public Health* **2022**, *19*, 11382. https://doi.org/10.3390/ijerph191811382

Academic Editor: Carl A. Latkin

Received: 10 August 2022
Accepted: 7 September 2022
Published: 9 September 2022

1. Introduction

Transgender men, or trans men, have increasingly been situated and ingrained in communities and networks of gay, bisexual, and other men who have sex with men (MSM) [1–4], the communities and networks that in recent years have continued to consistently represent the highest proportion of all reported HIV diagnoses in Canada and the US since the start of the HIV epidemic in the early 1980s [5,6]. In the last two decades, international research has recognized that many trans men strongly identify with MSM communities and networks, and, often, have sexual encounters or activities with cisgender, or cis (i.e., non-trans), MSM (CMSM) [1,4,7–17]. Studies have documented that as many as two-thirds of trans men identify as gay, bisexual, queer, or MSM [15,18,19], and that many trans MSM (TMSM) have been reported having CMSM as sexual partners [1,2,15,16,20–25]. The studies have also documented that trans men who have joined MSM communities may be particularly sensitive to contextual norms around HIV infection [26]. For example, in MSM communities and contexts where an HIV-positive status is more likely to be perceived as normative [9,27–29], trans men may believe that seroconversion will likely increase their sense of belonging [4], and may even feel the need to conceal their HIV-negative status to avoid rejection from prospective HIV-positive sexual partners [26,30]. While in most of the MSM communities and contexts where an HIV-positive status is stigmatized [28,31,32], trans men may likely be more cautious with their sexual practices to avoid acquiring an HIV infection [26].

Globally, there has been a growing interest in HIV infection disease burden and risk among transgender individuals. However, it has become apparent that the majority of prior research that has been conducted has focused on transgender women, or trans women [11,26,33,34]. This is because the risk for HIV among trans men has largely been overshadowed by the HIV risk and prevalence among trans women [4], which has led to the early finding that the research related to HIV risk and behaviors among transgender people has been almost exclusively focused on trans women since the turn of the century [16]. Despite preliminary evidence that many trans men are at a high risk for HIV, a paucity of studies on trans men's sexual health and their HIV risks and prevention needs had been noted by many researchers [12,15,16,25,26,33], and has likely served as an impetus for conducting further research on the specific contexts, perspectives, and lived experiences of TMSM.

The prevalence rates of HIV infection and sexual risk behaviors among trans men have not been well understood because trans men have often been assumed to be primarily having sexual relations with cis women [9,12,16,23]. Due in part to this assumption, trans men have often been considered by healthcare professionals and researchers to be at low risk for HIV infection, especially in contrast to trans women [12,15]. The studies that have documented the HIV prevalence rates among trans men either have not indicated the gender of their participants' sexual partners, or have predominantly included trans men who have identified as heterosexual [16]. The few studies that have investigated the prevalence of HIV infections among trans men participants have reported rates between 0 to 3% [15–17,24,35–37]. Since only one documented small study has included confirmed HIV test results [24], and most other studies have been based on small convenience samples [1,15], definitive conclusions regarding the prevalence of HIV infections among trans men have not been drawn from these studies' data.

More recently, TMSM have been labeled as a key population at disproportionate risk for sexually transmitted infections, particularly Hepatitis C and HIV [1,12,38,39]. While the behavioral risk factors of TMSM have pointed to the high potential for HIV risk, recent research has indicated that the HIV prevalence among trans men has remained low [16,19,35,40], and consequently, there may still be time to intervene [24].

There have been important studies that have examined the HIV sexual risks, risk behaviors, and vulnerabilities of TMSM [1,4,16,20,41]. By 2010, the completed research with TMSM had largely been qualitative, focused on those who have been sexually active with CMSM, or descriptive of small convenience samples [15]. The qualitative studies have revealed that some TMSM engage in risk behaviors as they explore a new sexual identity, or integrate into a new community or sexual subculture, during or after gender transition. Some trans men have described a phase of post-transition shift in sexual attraction or post-transition sexual experimentation [15,41], which may involve intentional or incidental risk-taking behaviors [26,42].

Other research has shown that TMSM seem to share certain HIV-acquisition risk factors with their cis counterparts [1]. TMSM may be at risk for HIV infection when they have CMSM partners, or when they share needles for hormone or recreational drug injections [11]. TMSM have reported a variety of sexual risk behaviors, such as engaging in receptive anal and/or frontal genital sex with CMSM and inconsistent condom use [1,4,8,9,16,24,26,43]; compulsive sexual behaviors [35]; sex with anonymous or multiple partners [9,23,35]; sex with partners who were HIV-positive or of an unknown HIV status [4,9,35,37]; sex under the influence of alcohol or drugs [9,12,21,44]; and sex work [9,15,16,21,23,35]. Certain risk factors that have been identified to have a greater impact on TMSM compared to their cis counterparts include barriers to sexual negotiations with CMSM, such as unequal power dynamics; low self-esteem; and the need for gender identity affirmation [4,8,12,16,23]. TMSM have subsequently been included within the behavioral population of MSM, a well-established high risk population that has been disproportionately affected by HIV for the last four decades [23]. Additionally, research on buy-in of the use of pre-exposure prophylaxis (PrEP) among TMSM has shown that PrEP uptake among trans men has been limited, given the documented prevalent HIV risk behaviors among TMSM [11,22].

Despite the increasing number of studies involving TMSM and their sexual health in the last two decades, there are more research questions that prospectively still need to be explored [26]. Just as importantly, it is relevant to point out that many of the studies that have been conducted with TMSM since the turn of the century have focused primarily on their HIV risks and vulnerabilities [8,16,21,22,38], and very few have focused on their strengths, particularly their protective factors, strategies, and the sexual health practices that promote their resilience to HIV [16]. Broadly, there have been a growing number of studies in the past 20 years that have examined the resilience of transgender people [45–54], but none (as far as we could determine) have specifically examined the resilience of TMSM to HIV.

In this article, we present three case studies that highlight the findings of a Community-Based Participatory Research (CBPR) project and a larger qualitative study that we conducted to identify, determine, and examine the factors that promote the resilience of MSM to HIV, with a distinctive focus on the insights and lived experiences of TMSM. For the purposes of our CBPR project and case studies, our research team and community partners collaboratively established and focused the operational definition of resilience to HIV as the capacity of MSM to navigate, mitigate, avoid, address, and/or overcome the risks and adverse impacts of HIV in their lives. The three case studies we feature in this article provide not only an enlightening snapshot of some of the specific contexts, HIV risks, safer sex practices, and HIV prevention needs of transgender MSM, but also a unique opportunity to critically reflect on potential implications of the insights and lived experiences that were shared by our participants, particularly for adapting and developing current and future HIV services and programs to maximally benefit transgender MSM.

2. Materials and Methods

As part of a CBPR project and larger strengths-based qualitative study dedicated to exploring and investigating a variety of factors that promote resilience to HIV, based on the perspectives and lived experiences of racially and ethnically diverse, HIV-positive and HIV-negative, middle-aged and older MSM from Central and Southwestern Ontario, Canada, the case studies that we feature in this article were derived from a Big Data set that predominantly involved participants who identified as CMSM. The case studies we present in this article are focused on highlighting the insights and personal experiences of three HIV-negative TMSM who were all 40 years of age or older and were residing in Downtown Toronto, Ontario, Canada, at the time of their interviews.

In line with the guiding principles and tenets of CBPR [55], our larger qualitative study was conducted in close collaboration with our primary community partner, Realize, a community-based organization located in Toronto that addresses and responds to the diverse needs of older people at risk of or living with HIV. In partnership with Realize, our research team established a Community Advisory Board (CAB) to help determine the main aim, procedures, and conduct of our larger study. Our CAB was comprised of middle-aged and older MSM, as well as service providers from different regional not-for-profit lesbian, gay, bisexual, transgender, queer, intersex, and asexual (LGBTQIA+) agencies and AIDS service organizations (ASOs). The main aim, procedures, and conduct of our larger study were reviewed and approved by the Research Ethics Board (REB) of the Centre for Addiction and Mental Health (protocol reference number 032/2018), which is also located in Toronto. It is critical to note that middle-aged and older MSM were significantly involved in our community-engaged study, not only as the community-based agency service providers who assisted us considerably with our participant recruitment; members of our CAB; and study participants, but also as peer researchers (i.e., compensated members of our research team from the community whose identities, input, and lived/work experiences were pertinent and vital to achieving the research aim and agenda of our CBPR project, larger study, and the three case studies we feature in this article).

2.1. The Case Study Approach

Our choice to present and discuss the findings of the larger qualitative study of our CBPR project that was specific to TMSM as three illustrative case studies was a logical and judicious decision. A case study is a research approach that is utilized to produce an in depth, multi-faceted understanding of a complex issue in its real-life context [56]. As an established research design that is extensively used in a wide variety of disciplines, case studies can be described in various ways, the central tenet being the need to explore a phenomenon in depth and in its natural context. Each of the three case studies we describe in this article will provide an in depth look into some of the specific contexts, HIV risks, safer sex practices, and HIV prevention needs of TMSM, as well as an enlightening depiction of the insights and real-world experiences of our interview participants. Since the data in the case studies we present in this article were derived from only three participants, we exercised extra caution to help ensure our participants' confidentiality and privacy, particularly by expressly using pseudonyms and withholding very specific descriptions of the participants and their personal contexts to keep them anonymous, as recommended by the proponents of the case study approach [56,57].

2.2. Participants and Procedures

The participant recruitment plan we developed and implemented was based on the recommendations of multiple community stakeholders, which included representatives from our CAB. We recruited the participants using REB-approved flyers and recruitment messages posted on the websites, listservs, social media outlets, and physical premises of our numerous community collaborators and supporters, such as not-for-profit LGBTQIA+ agencies and ASOs across the province of Ontario. The individuals who expressed interest in participating in our interviews were screened and included in the larger study if they self-identified as MSM, were 40 years of age or older, and were living in Central or Southwestern Ontario, regardless of their HIV status, as long as they were willing to confidentially disclose their HIV status for the purposes of completing our study's participant sociodemographics. Our research team and community partners made a valiant effort to recruit a diverse range of participants in terms of their age, race, ethnicity, the geographical location of their residence, how they identified in particular as MSM (e.g., gay, bisexual, pansexual, queer, two-spirited, or simply as MSM), and gender identity. However, despite our best efforts, we were only able to recruit and include in our study three TMSM who met our specific inclusion criteria, all of whom we described and referred to in this article under the pseudonyms Aki, Bailey, and Cameron, and using the pronouns "they", "them", and "their", in accordance to their personal use of pronouns. All three participants have lived in Downtown Toronto for at least five years, and were very familiar with its LGBTQIA+ community and the health and social services it uses, particularly the services that have helped them to meet their own needs.

After receiving comprehensive information about our study, each of the three HIV-negative, middle-aged and older TMSM provided written consent prior to participating in our interviews. They were each interviewed by the first author and one of the two peer researchers in roughly one hour-long sessions. All of the sessions were digitally recorded and held at either the office of one of the interviewers or in a secure meeting room of a community-based organization of the participant's choosing. The interviews followed a semi-structured interview guide, which was developed and refined by our research team in collaboration with our CAB and community partners. The semi-structured interview guide utilized open-ended questions for the purpose of exploring distinct areas of research interest: (a) the lived experiences of the participants; (b) factors, strategies, or sexual health practices they employed that promoted their resilience to the clinical and social impacts of HIV; and (c) the reasons why they believed these factors, strategies, or practices promoted their resilience to HIV. Participants received compensation in the form of CAD25 cash for their time and participation. The peer researchers transcribed the interviews verbatim, and the first author reviewed each of the transcripts to confirm their accuracy prior to the thematic analysis of the case studies' data [58,59].

3. Case Studies

3.1. Aki

Aki is a 48 year old East Asian migrant who moved to Toronto several years prior to participating in our study. As a trans man who engaged in sex work for a few years, Aki's awareness of information on HIV risks and prevention interventions has been primarily based on the copious materials they studied from sexual health clinics that regularly provided brochures on safer sex practices.

At the very beginning of their interview, Aki reported experiencing persistent financial struggles, which began as early as the first year they migrated to Canada. They moved to Canada to escape discrimination and persecution from their country of origin, and without a lot of transferrable skills, subsequently experienced difficulty obtaining work in Toronto. Aki shared, "I didn't make a lot of money. Eventually, I ended up working on the streets. I did that for a few years to survive".

After several years of struggling financially, Aki was able to finally catch breaks with the help of community-based agencies and many referrals to social services. Aki developed a strong and genuine appreciation for the services and programs they were able to access in Toronto, specifically from international non-profit humanitarian organizations, LGBTQIA+ agencies, regional ASOs, large healthcare institutions, and several local multicultural and community health centers. Over the years, Aki then became slowly and heavily engaged with the LGBTQIA+ community of Toronto, where they were able to receive social support not only from the city's healthcare and social services, but also from queer and trans folks from the LGBTQIA+ community—social support that was essential to building their overall resilience.

When they were asked about their personal sexual experiences and practices during their interview, Aki talked to us about their initial difficulties finding the right spaces in the earlier years of their stay in Toronto, but then recalled how they gradually got into kinky sex, "It was a few years back when I began exploring kinky sex—bondage and discipline, dominance and submission, sadomasochism (BDSM), fetishes, role play, other stuff. Nowadays, it's the scene I feel most safe in terms of all types of risks". Aki claimed that it was a relatively easy choice for them to go kinky. For them, engaging in kinky sex would ensure that there was going to be an understanding between them and a prospective sexual partner first before any sexual exploits happened.

Aki then shared with us how they first discovered the role of private house sex parties in popularizing kinky sex, especially in communities they engaged in and enjoyed:

> "Before my access to the internet, I already went to different sexual communities. They played a more prominent role back then. Those communities have changed since my access to the internet. Sex parties and gatherings of sexually open people. Way back, there were just free-for-all orgies. Now, because of the internet, all the kinky people, those into BDSM and role playing, they gather and show up every Monday night, and they get to choose and go home with whomever they want after firmly setting expectations and ground rules".

Before discovering kinky sex at house parties, in the same way as many other MSM, Aki was engaged in spaces such as bathhouses, gay bars, and online apps to meet other men, and potentially initiate sexual encounters. However, they soon learned that they were not very comfortable with the different scenes in such spaces, especially because of the liberal use of alcohol and drugs in certain bars and bathhouses that could potentially increase physical and sexual health risks for them as a trans man. Aki reported:

> "I have seen a lot of cis gay men in bathhouses do heavy drugs. In the kinky sex I've been part of, there's maybe some drugs, but certainly not to the extreme

extent of how I've seen it been used in bathhouses. I can confidently say, it's not anywhere nearly as prevalent and concerning in the kinky sex parties I've joined".

At the kinky sex parties, Aki has progressively relied on deliberate partner negotiations to keep safe in terms of both their physical wellbeing and sexual health. Related to this, Aki expressed their great appreciation for Downtown Toronto and the MSM who live in it, "I have visited and travelled all over Canada since I moved here, and the most accessible house parties for kinky sex are definitely in Toronto". They also expressed how vital to their resilience the available healthcare and social services were in Toronto:

> "Toronto is the best city! I'm sure it is one of the best cities in the world. In terms of healthcare for queer and trans people, definitely. I learned about things here that I did not even know I needed for my sexual health".

3.2. *Bailey*

Bailey is a Canadian-born, 40 year old of Western European descent, who strictly speaking, prefers to remain a non-identarian, but would agree to self-identify as part of the MSM community, especially for the purpose of being included in our study. Bailey's considerable understanding of valuable aspects related to sexual health and HIV are derived from their extensive experiences being in a long-term serodiscordant relationship with an HIV-positive cis gay man.

Our interview with Bailey began with our open-ended question that asked how they were doing in general. Bailey explained how things could be better and shared with us how tight their finances were. Although they expressed that they were aware that many CMSM experienced economic difficulties because of underemployment and unemployment related to stigma and discrimination, they genuinely believed that transphobia, cisgenderism, and prejudice have had a greater negative impact on the job and financial security of many trans individuals in the 21st century. Bailey described the predicament they have been experiencing for years:

> "I am marginalized financially. There are not that many opportunities for trans people to make a decent income in large part because of stigma. Cis queer men, most don't worry about what passes under many employers' scrutiny. They take one look at me, and no. At this point, it's minute to minute, day to day. I'm managing poverty by finding research studies that I can participate in that will pay for my groceries. That's today. Other times in my life, I've been able to manage that differently".

When we asked them what they believed helped them thrive over the years, Bailey's response was almost immediate. They have long recognized the value of having a robust involvement in the LGBTQIA+ community that provides the support they need:

> "I've been extremely socially engaged. Learning [through social interaction] has been my biggest way of growing and finding supports. I am a bit of a sex radical and I've gone to many sex conferences. Gatherings with many different types of people, many different combinations. I've gained a ton of skills that I now recognize are almost completely impossible to replicate organically. These were skills I built to address short, medium, and long term issues [I have had as a trans person]".

In addition to appreciating the value of social engagement and support from friends to promoting their wellbeing, fortitude, and HIV resilience, another factor that Bailey also appreciated was the support of community-based agencies, organizations, and health and social services. In particular, they highly appreciated what the not-for-profit LGBTQIA+ agencies, ASOs, community health centers, and other Toronto health and social services brought to the table. Bailey discussed their strong connection to community resources:

> "One of the main reasons I'm alive is because I'm connected to community resources that will address specific issues that I have. Those are always changing.

So, [an LGBTQIA+ non-profit agency] feeds me twice a week. That's my source of food security. [A community health centre] is also where my family physician is, and my doctor helps me address my sexual health risks. I would not say that GPs have the capacity to deal with the kind of complexity that I'm living, but generally, they are a reliable source of support".

When our interview moved to the topics of sexual spaces, risks, encounters, and practices, Bailey began to talk about their experiences with going to bars and bathhouses several years back, as well as using apps to meet other MSM. Bailey was quick to point out that their experiences with these spaces were associated with an abundance of caution and quite short-lived because not only were they not as comfortable being in these spaces, but they also recognized that these spaces posed higher physical and sexual health risks for them as a trans man. They recounted some unpleasant experiences:

"I have been on apps, but apps can be dangerous for me as a trans man. I don't use them the same way that a cis gay man would. I make sure that I'm out on my profile as trans so that no one can ever claim that I did not tell them. That's one of the ways trans people get killed in sexual encounters. I work my way back from that reality. People still don't see what they don't want to see. People will get very angry with me if they later find out that I'm trans. They say things like, "You should have told me sooner". But I've already told them 3000 times. It's when it registers with them that it can become risky, or even violent".

Bailey then explained the strategies they employed to mitigate their personal risks:

"On my online profile, I have everything people need to know about why they should contact me if they want to have sex with me, and what kinds of sex I have. I make sure my profile is clear. I do not share face pics with somebody I have not met in person. So many people will only have sex with someone whom they have exchanged pictures with. For safety, I don't do that. I make it clear that no unsafe sex will happen. But we can have any kind of sex we want as long as it's safe. I assume everybody is HIV-positive, or I think people may be poz, but do not know it".

In the course of explaining how they have been able to keep safe during sexual encounters, Bailey started sharing with us their apparent preference for engaging in kinky sex. Since preliminary conversations are part and parcel of identifying and establishing the boundaries of the kinky sex that they were going to engage in with other MSM, Bailey emphasized the value of having a mutually expected and accepted safety step that was built into going kinky. They made the connection between kinky sex and the lowering of HIV risks clear for us in their interview:

"First of all, I have sex with people. But yes, I do have kinky sex with a lot of [cis gay] men. I think HIV is a disease that gives us all an opportunity to think communally. It is not a disease that is specific to only certain individuals, even though it does affect us very individually. [With HIV,] it's having that understanding that an exchange of bodily fluids can lead to negative impacts on your immune system. So you then realize, in kinky sex, pleasure does not always have to be about penetration".

Bailey provided more details on what went on during private house sex parties, and why they found good reasons to pursue kinky sex in such parties:

"One of the house sex parties that I go to is all kinky men who have sex with men. It's every month, and it's always different people from around the city. That is one of the places where I develop skills about that particular kind of sex. It's all very sexually rich. I see at least ten different men having sex once a month. One of my safety fallbacks in these house sex parties is that I'm having anonymous sex with people ... there's the unsafe side vs. the safe side. The unsafe side is that if some folks find out I'm trans, they can get very upset. The safe side is, if they don't want to have sex with me, there's a room full of other people they can have sex with and move on. Same goes for me. The stakes are also actually lower [in terms of HIV risks], even if there's a rejection factor involved".

According to Bailey, the more conversations prior to engaging in kinky sex were had, the safer it was for them. There is an openness to the conversations that eventually lead up to deliberate negotiations between prospective sexual partners, which may or may not work out. If the deliberate negotiations succeed, consent follows between partners, and initial trust is established. Bailey also narrated their kinky sex experiences related to deliberate negotiations:

"All my safer sex practices come from my kinky sex practices, which are all about consent and negotiations. Communication and heightening pleasure. I'm maintaining the wellbeing of all people involved. Being clear about which things can be protected and nurtured, and which things can't. My safer sex practices are due to philosophies and values [of kinky sex]. I'm never in a situation where I accidently don't have safer sex. For many of us [trans men], being kinky has been an important component of our survival".

There were other facets of kinky sex that were vital to the promotion of their HIV resilience. Based on their personal experiences, they were able to encounter more gender-affirming CMSM during their kinky sex exploits. According to Bailey:

"I've had a lot of socialization experiences during my sexual encounters. A lot of the [positive] acknowledgements of my gender in the wider social and sexual sphere have been really affirming, especially since I transitioned. Almost every [kinky sex] sexual interaction since I transitioned has been about gender-affirming relations".

During their sexual encounters in the earlier years at spaces such as bathhouses, bars, and online apps, where deliberate negotiations between prospective sexual partners were not as valued, prioritized, or even considered, Bailey noted that there were less opportunities to meet CMSM who made them feel accepted or gave them a sense of belonging in the MSM community. They shared that they were much more likely to experience a greater sense of belonging and/or an affirmation of their gender in the spaces where kinky sex was the norm.

Another vital facet of engaging in kinky sex that Bailey emphasized is their greater appreciation for the discipline to avoid the use of alcohol and drugs during deliberate negotiations and kinky sex in order to mitigate sexual health and HIV risks. Bailey explained this decision to avoid alcohol and drugs while initiating and then engaging in kinky sex:

"I guess one of the things I would have to say is that it goes back to the communication and clarity. I have not been a person who was having sex while high. I've used recreational drugs. But I don't have sex while doing it. That goes back to the kinky sex. Safe, sane, and consensual. You can't give consent if you are drunk or on drugs".

Beyond having provided the opportunity to meet, socially engage, and have sex with more trans-affirming CMSM, Bailey reported in their interview that Downtown Toronto was a prime location like no other place in Canada. They reported that in terms of accessing trans-competent health and social services, other cities could not match what Downtown Toronto offered, "I use every resource accessible to me. That's why I live in this postal code. It's the most resource rich area in the country. Outside of the Downtown core, most everything I need would be difficult to access".

Despite their laudable access to many health and social services, Bailey was keen to draw attention to the fact that, based on the HIV services and programs they have encountered and had the opportunity to evaluate with their long-term partner, most prevention interventions in the Ontario HIV sector were centered on the contexts, risks, practices, and needs of CMSM. Bailey expressed their frustration as they explained:

> "Unfortunately, in most community health centres and clinics, their attention is very much focused on cis gay men and their sexual health. So that's where all the efforts for STI and HIV prevention programming go. The type of sex I have, it doesn't always line up with traditional notions of condom use and the transmission of HIV. That has been a problem. I learned a lot of facts that I didn't know previously as I engaged more and more in kinky sex. When I sought out information about how we could protect ourselves, I found that all agencies just had a script. Here's how gay men have sex. Here's how we convey condom use as safer sex. Everything else, just goes away. That re-traumatizes trans men who have sex that does not line up exactly with sex of most cis gay men".

In addition to a lack of consideration for the specific contexts, risks, practices, and needs of TMSM, Bailey added that many healthcare practitioners and service providers made assumptions that could prove harmful to them as a trans man:

> "With me being trans, the assumption of many in healthcare was that my sexual partner and I both have penises that ejaculate, and all that top bottom shit that didn't apply to many of us at all. That's why PreP is bothering me. It's the new condom campaign. It still fucks up everything in my life ... it's traumatic for me to constantly hear the terms 'gay, bisexual, and MSM' in healthcare ... with my life constantly having to be subsumed under that MSM category, and yet, as a trans man [who has sex with men], still be largely excluded. People in healthcare need to understand that what they routinely offer in their HIV prevention programs for cis gay men don't always apply to trans men".

Bailey described that, in addition to the usual emphasis on the use of condoms and PrEP, there is a need to increase the focus on knowledge and skills for promoting deliberate partner negotiations and the benefits of engaging in kinky sex in HIV prevention interventions tailored for TMSM. According to Bailey:

> "As an example, I have yet to see much more healthcare or health services sites on the internet primarily focused on communication and negotiation skills, particularly in the context of trans men's sexual health and kinky sex. With regards to safer sex for trans men who have sexual experiences with other men, nobody is really talking about it".

3.3. Cameron

Cameron is a 53 year old French Canadian whose knowledge about sexual health practices and HIV risks and treatments comes mostly from several years of volunteering in Toronto LGBTQIA+ agencies and ASOs, and having very close friends who are MSM living with HIV.

Cameron began their interview by sharing with us how long they have been actively part of the LGBTQIA+ community of Toronto and their heartfelt gratitude for having several long-time friends from the community who have provided them with immense emotional and practical support over the years. According to Cameron:

> "In terms of friends, I have had a ton of support. I was always very engaged, and I was also privileged in the sense that I was able to navigate the [Ontario] healthcare system with the help of friends from the community. I knew [other trans] people who knew people so I could get good counselors, good doctors, and care and services I needed".

It has been this kind of consistent social engagement that has connected Cameron to bankable support systems within their chosen community. With respect to promoting their HIV resilience, Cameron expressed that community resources were vital to overcoming their specific challenges as a trans man and helping them thrive. Having spent so many years living in Toronto, Cameron has seen the city go through many changes, particularly in the Church and Wellesley area (i.e., "the village"), and how these changes have affected their community since the HIV epidemic began in the early 1980s. They explained how these changes have also personally affected them and the decisions they have made along the way. Cameron shared their experiences and the reasons why they have made certain calculated choices:

> "Back then, I did go to bathhouses, but I didn't really feel comfortable there. Being a trans man, I didn't get bottom surgery. So I was kind of uncomfortable about going to bathhouses. Nowadays, usually, a bar I go to is the Black Eagle. There's a monthly event called 'ruff house', not sure if you've heard about it. It's like a BDSM sex space at [a club that is no longer operational]. So it happens once a month, and that's a place where I can go where I can actually come out as trans, and it does not seem to be a problem in the kinky BDSM community. It seems to be less of a problem amongst cis men in that space, and I think, people there are a bit more open. I've also been online, like most everyone else. I've had some bad experiences of feeling objectified. Like, some people who don't even know me asked me really intrusive questions about my genitals. So you know, I just kind of rather meet in person and talk first".

Then, Cameron shared how later in life they eventually found private house sex parties, which have become crucial to keeping kinky sex and deliberate partner negotiations as enduring, viable, safer options, specifically for a trans man such as them:

> "I've tried very hard to avoid occasions where there will be spur-of-the-moment sex. That's why I prefer going to private [house] sex parties, where the circumstances are more controlled and contained . . . where there is an understanding among everyone in attendance. In terms of being with someone in private, it's where I can develop more communication and connections, and really, the conversations don't have to take that long!"

The deliberate partner negotiations may involve numerous aspects such as preferences, roles, and safety strategies, but almost always involve addressing sexual health, STI, and HIV risks, even if the negotiations are short and quick. Cameron described their experiences related to building trust through deliberate negotiations prior to kinky sex at private house sex parties:

> "In these private sex parties, there is more talk and developing trust. There's also the conscious elements of the power dynamic and power cycle, which makes it more exciting! Kinky sex is like a different flavor of sex, where we can embed more safeguards for trans folks like me".

When their sexual encounters were mutually satisfying, the experiences were not only safe, but they also became truly gender-affirming for Cameron. They reported, "I haven't had sex with trans men. I'm mostly attracted to cis men. When I suspect that they want to have sex with me, it seems like they think I'm hot. This is when I feel most accepted".

It was this kind of confidence and positivity that they developed when they experienced gender-affirmation from prospective kinky sex intimate partners at house parties, in addition to the increased feelings of safety and control they gained in the process. Although there were MSM who still drank alcohol and took drugs in private house sex parties, Cameron and the TMSMs who they knew who engaged in kinky sex intentionally remained alcohol- and drug-free in order to feel safe, stay in control and sober during deliberate negotiations, and clear headed to provide consent and build trust. Cameron shared how they felt they already had enough safety issues to contend with in the first place, and why it would be unwise for them to use alcohol or drugs that would decrease their ability to efficiently navigate deliberate negotiations prior to kinky sex, as well as provide or gain consent, "I've definitely seen it, especially in bathhouses. I don't participate in it. I'm not interested in drugs. I drink socially . . . that's about it. I already have enough safety concerns so I don't want to compound them with drug use during sex".

As we continued to discuss sexual exploits and access to safer options, Cameron, who was originally from the province of Quebec, explained why they were first attracted to the promise of living in Downtown Toronto, "Ultimately, I found [a city in the province of Quebec] was too small a community for me to be comfortable in, and not as accepting of trans folks like me. I wanted to meet guys, and overall, it had less open-minded men than Toronto". They shared details on how they eventually recognized just how ahead of the pack Toronto was in terms of accessible health and social services for trans men, and how important this was to them:

> "When I was in Quebec, it took me a really long time to find the right doctor. It was really hard to find any family physician who would take me in as a patient. Here in Toronto, it was easier to find a doctor, there's just so many ... trans-friendly doctors too. Seriously, I found a family physician within two weeks of moving here. But then, he later moved out of town. It didn't matter since I immediately found another doctor from the same clinic [at the gay village]. There are more health and support services for trans people here as well. Hands down, for trans people, Toronto is the place to be".

However, Cameron also described how disappointed they were to find out that most of the current HIV prevention interventions and campaigns they encountered were predominantly focused on the use of condoms and PrEP, which they acknowledged were very important, but noted to be geared more specifically to address concerns more pertinent to CMSM. Although they recognized that the vast majority of MSM in the province were cis, they also wanted to emphasize that prevention interventions focused on condoms and PrEP, that were targeted efforts to promote HIV resilience among CMSM, were not always as pertinent to them as TMSM. Cameron felt that if more MSM, especially CMSM, were made aware and informed of other sexual health practices, particularly those that line up with the practices of TMSM, then this would promote the resilience of TMSM to HIV. Additionally, they suggested that it would be essential for healthcare and service providers to learn more about the actual STI and HIV risks of TMSM. Cameron believed that many providers still thought that all trans men were at low risk for HIV and other STIs. Cameron reported:

> "Even though I was kept being told by people in health services that my risk for HIV was very low, I still tested for it every six months. I practiced safer sex with cis gay men, but I just felt better getting tested. So I got tested a lot!"

According to Cameron, what is harmful to TMSM is that many of the HIV services and programs, on one hand, treat TMSM as individuals with low sexual health risks that warrant little public health concern, and on the other hand, lump them together and combine them in the same category as CMSM, as if TMSM had no distinct sexual health practices and needs. They shared from their own experiences that even well-meaning healthcare and service providers did not have as much awareness that TMSM need to have HIV prevention interventions that are customized to their own sexual health risks and practices. Although the efforts to focus on promoting deliberate partner negotiations have over the years seemingly been almost sidelined in HIV services and programs in favor of a focus on promoting the use of condoms and/or PrEP with the HIV risks and sexual health practices of CMSM in mind, Cameron clearly believed that there is a need to seriously rethink and reconsider what will work best for HIV prevention interventions specifically customized for TMSM.

4. Discussion

In addition to the stereotypes, prejudice, stigma, and discrimination they have regularly faced from society as part of an umbrella HIV risk-category population, TMSM and CMSM have also historically shared other experiences and contexts worth noting. For instance, as we learned from the case studies, particularly from the experiences shared by Aki and Bailey, TMSM may also persistently face other HIV acquisition risk factors that commonly affect CMSM, such as financial struggles due to underemployment or unemployment. Several studies have documented the economic hardships experienced by many MSM (including TMSM), which inadvertently lead some MSM to engage in transactional sex work for survival [8,60–64]. Related to their capacity to promote their resilience to HIV, engaging in sex work has been found to increase the sexual health and HIV risks of MSM [15,16,35]. Other critical factors that significantly impact the capacity of both TMSM and CMSM to promote their HIV resilience are their perceived social support and accessible community resources that help them meet their most basic needs. In the case of TMSM, this reliance on and great appreciation of social engagement, social support, and accessible community resources were distinctly exemplified by the experiences and sentiments described in all three case studies. Several research studies have emphasized the benefits gained by MSM and trans individuals from having perceived social support from LGBTQIA+ friends [65–69], and strong connections with gender-affirming communities and sexual health care [46,47,51–53,65], especially those that prioritize the elimination of cisgenderism and transphobia [70]. They have also emphasized the need for such HIV services and programs to create sustainable opportunities to increase the financial security of TMSM, as well as develop more opportunities for TMSM to receive gender affirmation and social support from accessible community resources.

However, aside from the factors that TMSM have in common with CMSM that impact their capacity to promote their resilience to HIV, our three case studies illustrated that TMSM also have experiences, strategies, and sexual health practices that they favor or choose to exercise in order to lower their sexual health and HIV risks, which not as many CMSM seem to have or carry out as often (please see Table 1 for the thematic commonalities found among the three TMSM case study interviews). According to our participants, whereas many more CMSM reportedly frequent bathhouses and bars, as well as rely on online dating or hook-up apps to meet other MSM, as TMSM, they have personally had a stronger inclination to invest their efforts into seeking spaces that allow them to engage in kinky sex. This is because with kinky sex, there is the built-in protective strategy of going through deliberate negotiations between prospective sexual partners prior to engaging in sexual activity.

Table 1. Thematic commonalities found among the TMSM case study interviews.

Commonalities found among all Three TMSM Case Study Interviews:
Participants' appreciation for social engagement and support, and accessible community resources Deliberate partner negotiations seen as useful for fostering risk-mitigating strategies
Commonality found in the case study interviews with Aki and with Bailey:
Participants' experiences with financial struggles due to underemployment and unemployment
Commonalities found in the case study interviews with Bailey and with Cameron:
Participants' appreciation for gender-affirming sexual encounters Participants' strong preference to avoid alcohol to remain sober during sexual encounters Participants' strong preference to avoid drugs to remain clear-headed during sexual encounters Participants' concern for the predominant focus of HIV prevention intervention services and programs on the specific contexts of CMSM and the pressing need for more trans-focused and trans-competent health and social services

As a crucial point of clarification, when kinky sex was mentioned or discussed by the three TMSM participants in our case studies, they were referring to the catch-all term for a range of sexual practices that included BDSM, role play, fetishes, and other sexual practices that essentially involved consensual deliberate partner negotiations, as well as pleasurable experiences for all of the parties involved. Although it is beyond the scope of this article to present an elaborate discourse on kinky sex that explicitly discusses the complex relationship between kink and trans masculinity, it is important to acknowledge that there is published academic literature available that discusses this relationship in greater detail [71–73].

Based on the experiences of our three TMSM participants that were narrated in our case studies, deliberate partner negotiations prior to kinky sex foster clearer communication, establish explicit consent, and build trust, which are all important tactics that could be employed, in addition to the other risk-mitigating strategies that have been more traditionally perpetuated by CMSM-focused HIV services and programs such as the promotion of HIV status disclosure, condom use, and PrEP use [1,8,9,62]. In the last two decades, deliberate negotiations, clearer communication, explicit consent, and the forging of trust have gradually been entrenched and deeply embedded as part of evolving frameworks (i.e., safe, sane, and consensual (SSC); risk aware consensual kink (RACK); and caring, communication, consent, and caution (4cs)) that have informed and helped establish the culture and norms of BDSM, role playing, and other forms of kinky sex [74–76].

The practice of having deliberate negotiations between prospective or regular sexual partners prior to engaging in sexual activity to mitigate sexual health risks, specifically the risks of HIV transmission and acquisition, has been thoroughly researched, and even supported by HIV prevention intervention services and programs, for over four decades [77–80]. In particular, studies have examined the strategies, tactics, and challenges associated with using timely communication to obtain consent, often to engage in condomless anal intercourse, among MSM [77–80]. However, more recent research has shown that since the advent of PrEP, previous safer sex norms among MSM have arguably been disrupted as the centrality of condom use in HIV risk reduction has apparently decreased and new patterns of deliberate partner negotiations have consequently been introduced [81], likely including new patterns of deliberate partner negotiations involved prior to engaging in kinky sex.

Two facets of engaging in deliberate partner negotiations and kinky sex that our participants emphasized as crucial to promoting their HIV resilience were the significance of experiencing the validation of their gender identity from trans-affirming sexual partners and remaining sober during negotiations and sexual activities to ensure clear communication and explicit consent. Bailey and Cameron, in particular, detailed specific experiences and perspectives that underscored their personal appreciation for gender-affirming sexual encounters as well as their strong preferences to remain sober and clear headed during these sexual encounters. These two facets have already been previously explored and documented as research has already covered the benefits of receiving social gender affirmation during sexual interactions [45], and the complications brought about by alcohol and/or drug use during deliberate negotiations and sexual exploits that follow [77].

Among the many important messages that our participants conveyed in our case studies, a very salient point that they made concerned the need for having more accessible trans-focused and trans-competent care and services to promote their resilience to HIV. Despite their appreciation for being able to live and access many of their much-needed resources in Downtown Toronto, Bailey and Cameron discernibly expressed concern for the predominant focus of HIV prevention intervention services and programs they could access on the specific contexts of CMSM and the pressing need for more trans-focused and trans-competent health and social services. It has already been established that TMSM are at elevated risk of HIV, and therefore, they require access to HIV services and programs that are both tailored specifically for them [82], and preferably amenable to further adaptation [83]. In fact, TMSM have been found to have unique challenges related to accessing health services and the mitigation of HIV risks, ranging from obtaining optimal gender-affirmative care to negotiating safer sex with CMSM [8].

In terms of practical supports, free or low-cost HIV testing, condoms, and lubricants, as well as PrEP, are foundational HIV prevention strategies that are geared towards the needs of MSM, yet are often inaccessible to TMSM. In the global context of stigma and poor healthcare access, TMSM face additional barriers to HIV prevention services since many healthcare and social service providers are unaware of, unfamiliar with, or insensitive and unresponsive to their risks and needs [2,62]. Research has shown that TMSM have reported inadequate access to basic prevention services and that they have been less likely than CMSM to have access to HIV testing, condoms, lubricants, and PrEP [2,62]. This indicates the need to enhance access to basic HIV prevention services for TMSM, including MSM-specific services [2]. The barriers to such access have included both general and trans-specific difficulties in accessing sexual health services, a lack of trans health knowledge among testing providers, limited clinical capacity to meet HIV testing needs, and a perceived gap between trans-inclusive policies and their implementation in practice [1]. Many TMSM still lack adequate information about PrEP and have encountered significant barriers to accessing PrEP. They have also reported that many providers avoid important discussions regarding sexuality and contraception related to the contexts of TMSM [62].

Beyond drawing attention to the issue that TMSM have perceived additional barriers to gaining access to HIV prevention intervention services and programs compared to their cis counterparts, the lived experiences of our participants described in our case studies support the data from prior research that has highlighted the need to develop and provide HIV services and programs that would meet the unique needs of TMSM. Therefore, more detailed, specifically designed studies, services, and programs for TMSM are necessary to complete what we do not know about their sexual health needs, HIV risks, challenges, and strengths [8,24,83].

In the adaptation, tailoring, and creation of HIV prevention intervention services and programs for TMSM, the changes and improvements would first need to be explicitly designed to help prevent significant issues such as the exclusion of trans perspectives and preferences, as well as the promotion of gender dysphoria among TMSM, at the most fundamental levels. These changes and improvements would need to ensure the implementation of supportive language and pronoun use directed by the trans individuals; use of trans individuals' preferred body terminologies or general terms that do not gender the body in services and program pamphlets, resources, and discussions; promotion of supportive interpersonal engagements of service providers; and hiring more trans individuals on staff [84]. Integrating sexual health information "by and for" TMSM into health services, such as some of the information shared by our participants in the case studies we presented in this article; involving peer support from a more trans-affirming community; addressing the psychological wellbeing of TMSM; and increasing internet-delivered information for TMSM and their sexual partners, have been seen by TMSM as important aspects for improvement and innovation in future HIV prevention intervention design and delivery [25].

Trans men often encounter resistance and reluctance pertaining to their healthcare needs, and are routinely left out of representation not only in healthcare and research, but also in education [85]. Several researchers have indicated the dire need to raise awareness among, and provide appropriate education and training on the contexts, sexual health and HIV risks, and most useful and effective safer sex practices and prevention tactics (e.g., communication and negotiation skills) specific to TMSM, to not only the healthcare and service providers in the HIV sector, but also the CMSM, TMSM, and other trans individuals [14,15,25,84–88]. Some researchers have pointed to the lack of relevant HIV risk education and re-education in TMSM communities, especially around the lack of condom use and other practical evidence-based preventive strategies [14,15]; while other researchers have gone as far as advocating for promoting these awareness and training efforts to be incorporated into the post-secondary education curricula of future health professionals in order to ensure future gender sensitive and affirmative care in sexual health [87,88]. Collectively, these recommendations could potentially help rectify the lack of awareness and knowledge on, and neglect of the prevention contexts and preferences of TMSM in, HIV services and programs, which our participants called attention to in our case studies. These recommendations have also brought to light what we believe is the shared responsibility of TMSM, CMSM, their healthcare and service providers, and larger communities; the shared responsibility to redress the inattention to the HIV prevention needs of TMSM so that TMSM are not left out in the ongoing mission to end the HIV epidemic.

Ultimately, the HIV prevention intervention services must tailor their programs and efforts to focus on and address concerns more pertinent to TMSM and their MSM partners [8,16,24,83], such as promoting and generating more spaces that: (a) help improve the financial stability of TMSM; (b) allow for and facilitate deliberate partner negotiations and kinky sex; (c) promulgate clearer communication and the establishment of explicit consent; (d) endorse and encourage gender affirmation and validation; and (e) educate other MSM, providers, and the larger communities about the kinds of sex that TMSM engage in and the HIV prevention strategies, services, and programs that will be the most suitable and effective for them. It would also be critical for HIV services and programs to recognize that not only do they need to disaggregate trans women from MSM in the development and creation of HIV prevention strategies to mitigate HIV risks, as some researchers have suggested [31], but based on the perspectives and lived experiences of our participants that we described in our case studies, they also need to disaggregate TMSM from CMSM in the design and implementation of their HIV prevention efforts and care programs.

5. Conclusions

We have learned that as much as TMSM could greatly benefit from the MSM-focused HIV prevention interventions, they still require services and programs that promote spaces and sexual health practices that they believe would make them feel more validated and affirmed, healthier, and safer. Incorporating information in HIV services and programs that places greater emphasis on deliberate partner negotiations, such as those that are highly valued in the practice of kinky sex, is only one step towards explicitly supporting TMSM. They also need other MSM, their healthcare and service providers, and the larger LGBTQIA+ communities to become more aware, acquire more tailored education and training, and learn and care more about their preferences, needs, challenges, and strengths as TMSM, so that everyone could continue to help promote their resilience to HIV in solidarity.

In order to promote the spaces and sexual health practices that would help TMSM feel more validated and affirmed, healthier, and safer, future research projects could potentially conduct studies that would not only further investigate more of the resilience-building factors that could be incorporated into HIV services and programs specifically dedicated to the contexts and needs of TMSM, but also actively and collaboratively involve TMSM in their research efforts. In the future, the scholars working on this research agenda would need to prospectively identify and implement innovative ways to meaningfully involve TMSM in their studies, perhaps by considering community-based participatory research as well as strengths-based, capacity-building approaches that would include TMSM from the community as the key opinion leaders, community advisory board members, knowledge and cultural brokers, and/or peer researchers who are significantly invested in the work of forward-thinking research teams. These approaches could conceivably help obtain even more useful knowledge that was not garnered by our study, primarily due to the lack of involvement and direct input of TMSM in its research process and conduct.

Author Contributions: Conceptualization, R.M.L., C.F. and G.D.S.; Data curation, R.M.L., C.F. and G.D.S.; Formal analysis, R.M.L., C.F. and G.D.S.; Funding acquisition, R.M.L.; Investigation, R.M.L., C.F. and G.D.S.; Methodology, R.M.L., C.F. and G.D.S.; Project administration, R.M.L., C.F. and G.D.S.; Resources, R.M.L.; Supervision, R.M.L.; Validation, R.M.L., C.F. and G.D.S.; Visualization, R.M.L., C.F. and G.D.S.; Writing—original draft, R.M.L.; Writing—review & editing, R.M.L., C.F. and G.D.S. All authors have read and agreed to the published version of the manuscript.

Funding: This research was funded by the Canadian Institutes of Health Research Operating Grant—HIV/AIDS Community-Based Research Program (funding reference # 156917).

Institutional Review Board Statement: The study was conducted according to the guidelines of the Declaration of Helsinki, and approved by the Research Ethics Board of the Centre for Addiction and Mental Health (protocol reference number 032/2018).

Informed Consent Statement: Consent was obtained from all participants involved in the study.

Conflicts of Interest: The authors declare no conflict of interest.

References

1. Scheim, A.I.; Bauer, G.R.; Travers, R. HIV-related sexual risk among transgender men who are gay, bisexual, or have sex with men. *JAIDS J. Acquir. Immune Defic. Syndr.* **2017**, *74*, e89–e96. [CrossRef] [PubMed]
2. Scheim, A.I.; Santos, G.M.; Arreola, S.; Makofane, K.; Do, T.D.; Hebert, P.; Thomann, M.; Ayala, G. Inequities in access to HIV prevention services for transgender men: Results of a global survey of men who have sex with men. *J. Int. AIDS Soc.* **2016**, *19* (Suppl. 2), 20779. [CrossRef] [PubMed]
3. Williams, C.J.; Weinberg, M.S.; Rosenberger, J.G. Trans men: Embodiments, identities, and sexualities. *Sociol. Forum* **2013**, *28*, 719–741. [CrossRef]
4. Rowniak, S.; Chesla, C.; Rose, C.D.; Holzemer, W.L. Transmen: The HIV risk of gay identity. *AIDS Educ. Prev.* **2011**, *23*, 508–520. [CrossRef]
5. Centers for Disease Control and Prevention, HIV Surveillance Report, 2020. Volume 33, Published May 2022. Available online: https://www.cdc.gov/hiv/library/reports/hiv-surveillance.html (accessed on 6 June 2022).
6. Haddad, N.; Weeks, A.; Robert, A.; Totten, S. *HIV in Canada Surveillance Report*; Centre for Communicable Diseases and Infection Control, Public Health Agency of Canada: Ottawa, ON, Canada, 2019; Available online: https://www.canada.ca/en/public-health/services/reports-publications/canada-communicable-disease-report-ccdr/monthly-issue/2021-47/issue-1-january-2021/hiv-surveillance-report-2019.html (accessed on 6 June 2022).
7. Albury, K.; Dietzel, C.; Pym, T.; Vivienne, S.; Cook, T. Not your unicorn: Trans dating app users' negotiations of personal safety and sexual health. *Health Sociol. Rev.* **2021**, *30*, 72–86. [CrossRef]
8. Mayer, K.H.; Nelson, L.; Hightow-Weidman, L.; Mimiaga, M.J.; Mena, L.; Reisner, S.; Daskalakis, D.; A Safren, S.; Beyrer, C.; Sullivan, P.S. The persistent and evolving HIV epidemic in American men who have sex with men. *Lancet* **2021**, *397*, 1116–1126. [CrossRef]
9. Mujugira, A.; Kasiita, V.; Bagaya, M.; Nakyanzi, A.; Bambia, F.; Nampewo, O.; Kamusiime, B.; Mugisha, J.; Nalumansi, A.; Twesigye, C.C.; et al. "You are not a man": A multi-method study of trans stigma and risk of HIV and sexually transmitted infections among trans men in Uganda. *J. Int. AIDS Soc.* **2021**, *24*, e25860. [CrossRef]
10. Hickson, F.; Appenroth, M.; Koppe, U.; Schmidt, A.J.; Reid, D.; Weatherburn, P. Sexual and mental health inequalities across gender identity and sex-assigned-at-birth among men-who-have-sex-with-men in Europe: Findings from EMIS-2017. *Int. J. Environ. Res. Public Health* **2020**, *17*, 7379. [CrossRef]
11. Reisner, S.L.; Moore, C.S.; Asquith, A.; Pardee, D.J.; Sarvet, A.; Mayer, G.; Mayer, K.H. High risk and low uptake of pre-exposure prophylaxis to prevent HIV acquisition in a national online sample of transgender men who have sex with men in the United States. *J. Int. AIDS Soc.* **2019**, *22*, e25391. [CrossRef]
12. Reisner, S.L.; Hughto, J.M.W.; Pardee, D.J.; Kuhns, L.; Garofalo, R.; Mimiaga, M.J. LifeSkills for men (LS4M): Pilot evaluation of a gender-affirmative HIV and STI prevention intervention for young adult transgender men who have sex with men. *J. Urban Health.* **2016**, *93*, 189–205. [CrossRef]
13. Witzel, C.T.; Rodger, A.J.; Burns, F.M.; Rhodes, T.; Weatherburn, P. HIV self-testing among men who have sex with men (MSM) in the UK: A qualitative study of barriers and facilitators, intervention preferences and perceived impacts. *PLoS ONE* **2016**, *11*, e0162713. [CrossRef] [PubMed]
14. Jones, T.; De Bolger, A.D.P.; Dune, T.; Lykins, A.; Hawkes. *Female-to-Male (FtM) Transgender People's Experiences in Australia: A National Study*; Springer: Berlin/Heidelberg, Germany, 2015.
15. Bauer, G.; Redman, N.; Bradley, K.; Scheim, A.I. Sexual health of trans men who are gay, bisexual, or who have sex with men: Results from Ontario, Canada. *Int. J. Transgend.* **2013**, *14*, 66–74. [CrossRef] [PubMed]
16. Sevelius, J. "There's no pamphlet for the kind of sex I have": HIV-related risk factors and protective behaviors among transgender men who have sex with non-transgender men. *J. Assoc. Nurses AIDS Care* **2009**, *20*, 398–410. [CrossRef] [PubMed]
17. Herbst, J.H.; Jacobs, E.D.; Finlayson, T.J.; McKleroy, V.S.; Neumann, M.S.; Crepaz, N.; HIV/AIDS Prevention Research Synthesis Team. Estimating HIV prevalence and risk behaviors of transgender persons in the United States: A systematic review. *AIDS Behav.* **2008**, *12*, 1–17. [CrossRef]
18. Grant, J.M.; Mottet, L.A.; Tanis, J.; Harrison, J.; Herman, J.L.; Keisling, M. *Injustice at Every Turn: A Report of the National Transgender Discrimination Survey*; National Center for Transgender Equality and National Gay and Lesbian Task Force: Washington, DC, USA, 2011.
19. Iantaffi, A.; Bockting, W.O. Views from both sides of the bridge? Gender, sexual legitimacy, and transgender people's experiences of relationships. *Cult. Health Sex.* **2011**, *13*, 355–370. [CrossRef]
20. Reisner, S.L.; Moore, C.S.; Asquith, A.; Pardee, D.J.; Mayer, K.H. Gender non-affirmation from cisgender male partners: Development and validation of a brief stigma scale for HIV research with transgender men who have sex with men (trans MSM). *AIDS Behav.* **2020**, *24*, 331–343. [CrossRef]

21. Westmoreland, D.A.; Carrico, A.W.; Goodwin, R.D.; Pantalone, D.W.; Nash, D.; Grov, C. Higher and higher? Drug and alcohol use and misuse among HIV-vulnerable men, trans men, and trans women who have sex with men in the United States. *Subst. Use Misuse* **2021**, *56*, 111–122. [CrossRef]
22. Westmoreland, D.A.; D'Angelo, A.; Nash, D.; Grov, C. Individual and partner characteristics associated with intentions to use PrEP among partnered men, trans men, and trans women in sero-concordant and –discordant relationships in the United States. *AIDS Educ. Prev.* **2020**, *32*, 367–377. [CrossRef]
23. Rich, A.; Scott, K.; Johnston, C.; Blackwell, E.; Lachowsky, N.; Cui, Z.; Sereda, P.; Moore, D.; -Hogg, R.; Roth, E. Sexual HIV risk among gay, bisexual, and queer transgender men: Findings from interviews in Vancouver, Canada. *Cult. Health Sex.* **2017**, *19*, 1197–1209. [CrossRef]
24. Chen, S.; McFarland, W.; Thompson, H.M.; Raymond, H.F. Transmen in San Francisco: What do we know from HIV test site data? *AIDS Behav.* **2011**, *15*, 659–662. [CrossRef] [PubMed]
25. Reisner, S.L.; Perkovich, B.; Mimiaga, M.J. A mixed methods study of the sexual health needs of New England transmen who have sex with nontransgender men. *AIDS Patient Care STDS* **2010**, *24*, 501–513. [CrossRef] [PubMed]
26. Reisner, S.L.; Murchison, G.R. A global research synthesis of HIV and STI biobehavioural risks in female-to-male transgender adults. *Glob. Public Health.* **2016**, *11*, 866–878. [CrossRef] [PubMed]
27. Van Hout, M.C.; Crowley, D.; O'Dea, S.; Clarke, S. Chasing the rainbow: Pleasure, sex-based sociality and consumerism in navigating and exiting the Irish chemsex scene. *Cult. Health Sex.* **2019**, *21*, 1074–1086. [CrossRef]
28. Ahmed, A.; Weatherburn, P.; Reid, D.; Hickson, F.; Torres-Rueda, S.; Steinberg, P.; Bourne, A. Social norms related to combining drugs and sex ("chemsex") among gay men in South London. *Int. J. Drug Policy* **2016**, *38*, 29–35. [CrossRef] [PubMed]
29. Page, E.E.; Nelson, M. Hepatitis and sex. *Clin Med.* **2016**, *16*, 189–192. [CrossRef]
30. Rowniak, S.; Chesla, C. Coming out for a third time: Transmen, sexual orientation, and identity. *Arch. Sex. Behav.* **2012**, *42*, 449–461. [CrossRef]
31. Sevelius, J.; Keatley, J.; Calma, N.; Arnold, E. 'I am not a man': Trans-specific barriers and facilitators to PrEP acceptability among transgender women. *Glob. Public Health* **2016**, *11*, 1060–1075. [CrossRef]
32. Moyer, E.; Hardon, A. A disease unlike any other? Why HIV remains exceptional in the age of treatment. *Med Anthr.* **2014**, *33*, 263–269. [CrossRef]
33. Stephenson, R.; Riley, E.; Rogers, E.; Suarez, N.; Metheny, N.; Senda, J.; Saylor, K.M.; Bauermeister, J.A. The sexual health of transgender men: A scoping review. *J. Sex Res.* **2017**, *54*, 424–445. [CrossRef]
34. Baral, S.D.; Poteat, T.; Stromdahl, S.; Wirtz, A.L.; Guadamuz, T.E.; Beyrer, C. Worldwide burden of HIV in transgender women: A systematic review and meta-analysis. *Lancet Infect. Dis.* **2013**, *13*, 214–222. [CrossRef]
35. Bauer, G.R.; Travers, R.; Scanlon, K.; Coleman, T.A. High heterogeneity of HIV-related sexual risk among transgender people in Ontario, Canada: A province-wide, respondent-driven sampling survey. *BMC Public Health* **2012**, *12*, 292. [CrossRef]
36. Adams, A.; Lundie, M.; Marshall, Z.; Pires, R.; Scanlon, K.; Scheim, A.; Smith, T. *Getting Primed: Informing HIV Prevention with Gay/bi/Queer Trans Men in Ontario*; Ontario Gay Men's HIV Prevention Strategy; AIDS Bureau, Ontario Ministry of Health and Long-Term Care: Toronto, ON, Canada, 2008.
37. Schulden, J.D.; Song, B.; Barros, A.; Mares-Del Grasso, A.; Martin, C.W.; Ramirez, R.; Smith, L.C.; Wheeler, D.P.; Oster, A.M.; Sullivan, P.; et al. Rapid HIV Testing in Transgender Communities by Community-Based Organizations in Three Cities. *Public Health Rep.* **2008**, *123*, 101–114. [CrossRef] [PubMed]
38. Grov, C.; Westmoreland, D.A.; Carrico, A.W.; Nash, D. Are we on the precipice of a new epidemic? Risk for hepatitis C among HIV-negative men-, trans women-, and trans men- who have sex with men in the United States. *AIDS Care* **2020**, *32*, 74–82. [CrossRef] [PubMed]
39. World Health Organization [WHO]. *Consolidated Guidelines on HIV Prevention, Diagnosis, Treatment and Care for Key Populations*; WHO: Geneva, Switzerland, 2014; Available online: https://apps.who.int/iris/bitstream/handle/10665/128048/9789241507431_eng.pdf;jsessionid=0B20649F9E1CF62F328DFDD1E7995B2A?sequence=1 (accessed on 7 June 2022).
40. Centers for Disease Control and Prevention. HIV and Transgender People Fact Sheet; Published April 2022. 2022. Available online: https://www.cdc.gov/hiv/group/gender/transgender/index.html (accessed on 7 June 2022).
41. Bockting, W.; Benner, A.; Coleman, E. Gay and bisexual identity development among female-to-male transsexuals in North America: Emergence of a transgender sexuality. *Arch. Sex. Behav.* **2009**, *38*, 688–701. [CrossRef] [PubMed]
42. Clements, K.; Wilkinson, W.; Kitano, K.; Marx, R. HIV prevention and health service needs of the transgender community in San Francisco. In *Transgender and HIV*; Routledge: Oxfordshire, UK, 2014.
43. Nicholls, E.J.; Samba, P.; McCabe, L.; Gafos, M.; Philips, A.N.; Trevelion, R.; Rodger, A.J.; Burns, F.M.; Weatherburn, P.; Witzel, T.C. Experiences of and attitudes towards HIV testing for Asian, Black and Latin American men who have sex with men (MSM) in the SELPHI (HIV Self-Testing Public Health Intervention) randomized controlled trial in England and Wales: Implications for HIV self-testing. *BMC Public Health* **2022**, *22*, 809. [CrossRef]
44. Antebi-Gruszka, N.; Talan, A.J.; Reisner, S.L.; Rendina, H.J. Sociodemographic and behavioural factors associated with testing for HIV and STIs in a US nationwide sample of transgender men who have sex with men. *Sex. Transm. Infect.* **2020**, *96*, 422–427. [CrossRef]

45. Chakrapani, V.; Scheim, A.I.; Newman, P.A.; Shunmugam, M.; Rawat, S.; Baruah, D.; Bhatter, A.; Nelson, R.; Jaya, A.; Kaur, M. Affirming and negotiating gender in family and social spaces: Stigma, mental health and resilience among transmasculine people in India. *Cult. Health Sex.* **2021**, *24*, 951–967. [CrossRef]
46. Koech, J.M.; Sostre, J.P.; Lockett, G.M.; Gonzalez, K.A.; Abreu, R.L. Resisting by existing: Trans Latinx mental health, well-being, and resilience in the United States. In *Latinx Queer Psychology: Contributions to the Study of LGBTIQ+, Sexual and Gender Diversity Issues*; Chaparro, R.A., Prado, M.A., Eds.; Springer Nature: Cham, Switzerland, 2021; pp. 43–68. [CrossRef]
47. Hillier, A.; Kroehle, K.; Edwards, H.; Graves, G. Risk, resilience, resistance and situated agency of trans high school students. *J. LGBT Youth* **2020**, *17*, 384–407. [CrossRef]
48. Snooks, M.P.; McLaren, S. Resilience among trans and gender-diverse adults: The protective role of dispositional hope in the perceived burdensomeness-suicide relationship. *Psychol. Sex. Orientat. Gend. Divers.* **2021**, *8*, 57–67. [CrossRef]
49. McCann, E.; Brown, M. Discrimination and resilience and the needs of people who identify as transgender: A narrative review of quantitative research studies. *J. Clin. Nurs.* **2017**, *26*, 4080–4093. [CrossRef] [PubMed]
50. Başar, K.; Öz, G. Resilience in individuals with gender dysphoria: Association with perceived social support and discrimination. *Turk. J. Psychiatry* **2016**, *27*, 225–234. [CrossRef]
51. Bariola, E.; Lyons, A.; Leonard, W.; Pitts, M.; Badcock, P.; Couch, M. Demographic and Psychosocial Factors Associated With Psychological Distress and Resilience among Transgender Individuals. *Am. J. Public Health* **2015**, *105*, 2108–2116. [CrossRef] [PubMed]
52. Nicolazzo, Z. "Just Go in Looking Good": The Resilience, Resistance, and Kinship-Building of Trans COLLEGE Students. Ph.D. Thesis, Miami University Graduate School, Miami, FL, USA, 2015.
53. Singh, A.A.; Meng, S.E.; Hanson, A.W. "I Am My Own Gender": Resilience Strategies of Trans Youth. *J. Couns. Dev.* **2014**, *92*, 208–218. [CrossRef]
54. Chamberland, L.; Saewyc, E. Stigma, vulnerability, and resilience: The psychosocial health of sexual minority and gender diverse people in Canada. *Can. J. Community Ment. Health* **2012**, *30*, 7–11. [CrossRef]
55. Israel, B.A.; Schulz, A.J.; Parker, E.A.; Becker, A.B. Review of community-based research: Assessing partnership approaches to improve public health. *Annu. Rev. Public Health* **1998**, *19*, 173–202. [CrossRef]
56. Crowe, S.; Cresswell, K.; Robertson, A.; Huby, G.; Avery, A.; Sheik, A. The case study approach. *BMC Med. Res. Methodol.* **2011**, *11*, 100. [CrossRef]
57. Stake, R.E. *The Art of Case Study Research*; SAGE Publications, Ltd.: London, UK, 1995.
58. Mills, A.; Duperos, G.; Wiebe, E. Thematic analysis. In *Encyclopedia of Case Study Research*; Sage: Newcastle upon Tyne, UK, 2010.
59. Braun, V.; Clarke, V. Using thematic analysis in psychology. *Qual. Res. Psychol.* **2006**, *3*, 77–101. [CrossRef]
60. Javanbakht, M.; Ragsdale, A.; Shoptaw, S.; Gorbach, P.M. Transactional sex among men who have sex with men: Differences by substance use and HIV status. *J. Urban Health* **2019**, *96*, 429–441. [CrossRef]
61. Lenning, E.; Buist, C.L. Social, psychological and economic challenges faced by transgender individuals and their significant others: Gaining insight through personal narratives. *Cult. Health Sex.* **2013**, *15*, 44–57. [CrossRef]
62. Rowniak, S.; Ong-Flaherty, C.; Selix, N.; Kowell, N. Attitudes, beliefs, and barriers to PrEP among trans men. *AIDS Educ. Prev.* **2017**, *29*, 302–314. [CrossRef] [PubMed]
63. Baral, S.D.; Friedman, M.R.; Geibel, S.; Rebe, K.; Bozhinov, B.; Diouf, D.; Sabin, K.; Holland, C.E.; Chan, R.; Cáceres, C.F. Male sex workers: Practices, contexts, and vulnerabilities for HIV acquisition and transmission. *Lancet* **2014**, *385*, 260–273. [CrossRef]
64. Katsulis, Y.; Durfee, A. Prevalence and correlates of sexual risk among male and female sex workers in Tijuana, Mexico. *Glob. Public Health* **2012**, *7*, 367–383. [CrossRef] [PubMed]
65. Holt, M.; Broady, T.; Callander, D.; Pony, M.; Duck-Chong, L.; Cook, T.; Rosenberg, S. Sexual experience, relationships, and factors associated with sexual and romantic satisfaction in the first Australian trans and gender diverse sexual health survey. *Int. J. Transgender Health* **2022**, 1–11. [CrossRef]
66. Liboro, R.; Bell, S.; Ranuschio, B.; Barnes, L.; Despres, J.; Sedere, A.; Puno, T.; Shuper, P. Barriers and facilitators to promoting resilience to HIV/AIDS: A qualitative study on the lived experiences of HIV-positive, racial and ethnic minority, middle-aged and older men who have sex with men from Ontario, Canada. *Int. J. Environ. Res. Public Health.* **2021**, *18*, 8084. [CrossRef] [PubMed]
67. Liboro, R.; Ranuschio, B.; Bell, S.; Yates, T.C.; Barnes, L.; Fehr, C.; Da Silva, G.; Despres, J.; Ibañez-Carrasco, F.; Eaton, A.; et al. Mitigating risks and building resilience to HIV/AIDS: Perspectives of HIV-negative, middle-aged and older men who have sex with men. *Community Psychol. Glob. Perspect.* **2021**, *7*, 129–144.
68. Liboro, R.; Yates, T.C.; Fehr, C.; Da Silva, G.; Ibañez-Carrasco, F.; Eaton, A.D.; Pugh, D.; Ross, L.; Shuper, P. Community-level resources bolstering resilience to HIV/AIDS: Perspectives of middle-aged and older men who have sex with men living with HIV/AIDS. *Glob. J. Community Psychol. Pract.* **2021**, *12*, 1–26.
69. Grocott, L.R.; Schlechter, T.E.; Wilder, S.M.J.; O'Hair, C.M.; Gidycz, C.A.; Shorey, R.C. Social support as a buffer of the association between sexual assault and trauma symptoms among transgender and gender diverse individuals. *J. Interpers. Violence.* **2022**, 1–24. [CrossRef]
70. Rosenberg, S.; Callander, D.; Holt, M.; Duck-Chong, L.; Pony, M.; Cornelisse, V.; Baradaran, A.; Duncan, D.T.; Cook, T. Cisgenderism and transphobia in sexual health care and associations with testing for HIV and other sexually transmitted infections: Findings from the Australian trans and gender diverse sexual health survey. *PLoS ONE* **2021**, *16*, e0253589. [CrossRef]

71. Muzacz, A.K. Expressions of queer intimacy: BDSM and kink as means of self-actualization. *J. Humanist. Psychol.* **2021**, 1–21. [CrossRef]
72. Sprott, R.A.; Vivid, J.; Vilkin, E.; Swallow, L.; Lev, E.M.; Orejudos, J.; Schnittman, D. A queer boundary: How sex and BDSM interact for people who identify as kinky. *Sexualities* **2020**, *24*, 708–732. [CrossRef]
73. Galupo, M.P.; Henise, S.B.; Mercer, N.L. "The labels don't work very well": Transgender individuals' conceptualizations of sexual orientation and sexual identity. *Int. J. Transgenderism* **2016**, *17*, 93–104. [CrossRef]
74. Williams, D.J.; Thomas, J.N.; Prior, E.E.; Christensen, M.C. From "SSC" and "RACK" to the "4Cs": Introducing a new framework for negotiating BDSM participation. *Electron. J. Hum. Sex.* **2014**, *17*, 1–10. Available online: http://www.ejhs.org/volume17/BDSM.html. (accessed on 7 June 2022).
75. Nielsen, M.E.J.; Center, P.D. Safe, Sane, and Consensual—Consent and the Ethics of BDSM. *Int. J. Appl. Philos.* **2010**, *24*, 265–288. [CrossRef]
76. Langdridge, D.; Barker, M. (Eds.) *Safe, Sane and Consensual: Contemporary Perspectives on Sadomasochism*; Palgrave Macmillan: Hampshire, UK, 2007.
77. Ayer, A.; Perez-Brumer, A.; Segura, E.R.; Chavez-Gomez, S.; Fernandez, R.; Arroyo, C.; Barrantes, A.; Lake, J.E.; Cabello, R.; Clark, J.L. Let's talk about sex: The impact of partnership contexts on communication about HIV serostatus and condom use among men who have sex with men (MSM) and transgender women (TW) in Lima, Peru. *AIDS Behav.* **2021**, *25*, 2139–2153. [CrossRef] [PubMed]
78. Nakiganda, L.J.; Bell, S.; Grulich, A.; Serwadda, D.; Nakubulwa, R.; Poynten, I.M.; Bavinton, B.R. Understanding and managing HIV infection risk among men who have sex with men in rural Uganda: A qualitative study. *BMC Public Health* **2021**, *21*, 1309. [CrossRef] [PubMed]
79. Horvath, K.J.; Oakes, J.M.; Rosser, B.R. Sexual negotiation and HIV serodisclosure among men who have sex with men with their online and offline partners. *J. Urban Health* **2008**, *85*, 744–758. [CrossRef] [PubMed]
80. Carballo-Diéguez, A.; Miner, M.; Dolezal, C.; Rosser, B.R.S.; Jacoby, S. Sexual negotiation, HIV-status disclosure, and sexual risk behavior among Latino men who use the internet to seek sex with other men. *Arch. Sex. Behav.* **2006**, *35*, 473–481. [CrossRef]
81. Haire, B.; Murphy, D.; Maher, L.; Zablotska-Manos, I.; Vaccher, S.; Kaldor, J. What does PrEP mean for 'safe sex' norms? A qualitative study. *PLoS ONE* **2021**, *16*, e0255731. [CrossRef]
82. Scheim, A.I.; Travers, R. Barriers and facilitators to HIV and sexually transmitted infections testing for gay, bisexual, and other transgender men who have sex with men. *AIDS Care* **2017**, *29*, 990–995. [CrossRef]
83. Callander, D.; Newman, C.E.; Holt, M.; Rosenberg, S.; Duncan, D.T.; Pony, M.; Timmins, L.; Cornelisse, V.; Duck-Chong, L.; Wang, B.; et al. The complexities of categorizing gender: A hierarchical clustering analysis of data from the first Australian trans and gender diverse sexual health survey. *Transgender Health* **2021**, *6*, 74–81. [CrossRef]
84. Kerr, L.; Jones, T.; Fisher, C.M. Alleviating gender dysphoria: A qualitative study of perspectives of trans and gender diverse people. *J. Health Serv. Res. Policy* **2021**, *27*, 4–13. [CrossRef] [PubMed]
85. Norris, M.; Borneskog, C. The cisnormative blindspot explained: Healthcare experiences of trans men and non-binary persons and the accessibility to inclusive sexual and reproductive healthcare, an integrative review. *Sex. Reprod. Healthc.* **2022**, *32*, 100733. [CrossRef] [PubMed]
86. Scandurro, A.E.; Celemen, E.J.; Hoff, C.C. Sex and sexual agreement negotiation among trans women and trans men partnered with cis men. *J. Sex Res.* **2022**, 1–9. [CrossRef] [PubMed]
87. De Vries, E.; Kathard, H.; Müller, A. Debate: Why should gender-affirming health care be included in health science curricula? *BMC Med. Educ.* **2020**, *20*, 51. [CrossRef] [PubMed]
88. Callander, D.; Cook, T.; Cornelisse, V.; Pony, M.; Duncan, D.; Wiggins, J.; Vlahakis, E.; Duck-Chong, L.; Rosenberg, S.; Holt, M. O11.4 Trans and gender diverse people's experiences of sexual health care are associated with sexual health screening uptake. *Sex. Transm. Infect.* **2019**, *95*, A64. [CrossRef]

International Journal of
Environmental Research and Public Health

MDPI

Article

Former Incarceration, Time Served, and Perceived Oral Health among African American Women and Men

Ryan D. Talbert [1,*] and Emma D. Macy [2]

[1] Department of Sociology, University of Connecticut, Storrs, CT 06269, USA
[2] Department of Human Development and Family Sciences, University of Connecticut, Storrs, CT 06269, USA
* Correspondence: ryan.talbert@uconn.edu

Abstract: A large body of research has documented the far-reaching health consequences of mass incarceration in the United States. Yet, less scholarship has examined the relationship between former incarceration and oral health, a key reflection of health and disease occurring within the rest of the body. Using data extracted from the National Survey of American Life (n = 3343), this study examines associations among former incarceration status, duration of detention, and self-reported oral health among African American women and men. Results from gender-stratified ordered logistic models reveal that formerly incarcerated African American men and women experience significantly poorer oral health than their never incarcerated counterparts even after controlling for important social determinants of health. Furthermore, oral health is curvilinearly associated with the length of time that men are incarcerated such that odds of poor health decrease as detention duration increases up to approximately 15 years incarcerated. After 15 years of detainment, the odds of poor health tend to increase as duration increases. Findings extend research identifying gendered spillover health consequences of contact with the criminal legal system. Health professionals and policymakers should be conscious of incarceration as an important deleterious experience for the immediate and long-term condition of people's teeth, mouth, and gums.

Keywords: incarceration; prison term; oral health; African Americans; gender; teeth; gums

Citation: Talbert, R.D.; Macy, E.D. Former Incarceration, Time Served, and Perceived Oral Health among African American Women and Men. *Int. J. Environ. Res. Public Health* **2022**, *19*, 12906. https://doi.org/10.3390/ijerph191912906

Academic Editors: Celia C. Lo, William Ash-Houchen and Tyrone C. Cheng

Received: 9 September 2022
Accepted: 2 October 2022
Published: 8 October 2022

Despite decarceration efforts in recent decades, the United States remains a world leader in incarceration with an imprisonment rate of 358 per 100,000 residents [1,2]. Research has demonstrated that people ensnared in the sprawling US criminal legal system experience extensive social, psychological, and economic consequences [3]. Mass incarceration reflects the disproportionate incarceration of specific social groups and comparably high incarceration rates historically and internationally [4]. In 2020, Black men were incarcerated at a rate 5.7 times white men, and Black women were 1.7 times more likely than white women to experience incarceration [1]. A large and growing body of literature documents the impacts of mass incarceration on US health disparities. Studies show that mass incarceration is a contributor to higher mortality, worse mental health patterns, and increased rates of communicable and chronic disease [5–13]. Despite the breadth of the literature, few studies examined whether incarceration is associated with oral health, which encompasses the condition of people's teeth, mouth, and gums. This omission is notable considering that oral health is an integral part of one's overall health status and operates as a mirror of health and disease occurring within the rest of the body [14–16]. This study extends the literature by examining the association among former incarceration, duration of detention, and oral health among African American women and men.

Incarceration reflects confinement in a penal facility including federal or state prisons, or county or city jails. Experiencing incarceration is likely to deteriorate oral health for several reasons. First, despite incarcerated Americans being guaranteed the right to healthcare according to the Eighth Amendment of the US Constitution, penal healthcare systems more often provide reactive medical care (e.g., responding to health emergencies) rather than preventative health services (e.g., health screening exams) [8,17–19]. Hence, the subpar quality of healthcare services for those incarcerated may lead to poorer oral health while incarcerated and after release. Second, threats to safety, meals with insufficient nutritious value, and lack of quality oral hygiene products while incarcerated likely contribute to worsening oral health, and these patterns may worsen the longer a person is confined [20,21]. Third, following release, formerly incarcerated adults face challenges in accessing and receiving oral healthcare services due to a lack of transportation, health insurance, or sufficient medication to manage health conditions that have oral health ramifications [16,22,23]. Hence, comparing adults with and without former incarceration status is important for understanding oral health disparities given that reentry into society necessitates navigating the US healthcare system (e.g., obtaining insurance, locating providers, and scheduling appointments).

The present study offers three contributions to the research literature. First, this study focuses on variation in self-reported oral health status among African American adults. While a preponderance of studies found that incarceration is associated with poorer health, [5–8] fewer studies examined whether this pattern holds for oral health, a key marker of overall health status [14–16]. Furthermore, Black Americans typically experience poorer oral health than people of other ethnoracial backgrounds [24]. However, we know less of whether disproportionate exposure to incarceration for Black Americans is a contributing factor to persistently poorer oral health patterns. Identifying the significance of incarceration for oral health is important considering that research identifies innumerable immediate and long-term consequences in other domains (e.g., labor market, housing, and education) [25,26]. By extending research documenting the spillover consequences of contact with the legal system, this study aims to inform health professionals of incarceration as a potentially important deleterious experience for oral health.

Second, this study examines two indicators of former incarceration status including whether one has ever been detained in a prison or jail, as well as the duration of one's detention. Studies examining associations between incarceration and health typically focus on single indicators of incarceration status (i.e., yes or no) to the neglect of additional measures that may add supplementary information about one's experience (e.g., years served) [5,6]. Research shows that any incarceration experience is associated with worse health consequences than the length that one is incarcerated [7,27]. However, the literature has sparsely tested whether these findings hold for oral health. Therefore, examining incarceration experience and detention duration offers an important contribution to the literature. Third, this study identifies associations between incarceration and oral health among men and women separately. To this end, some studies found that women experience worse health consequences from incarceration than men, and we interrogate this possibility for oral health.

1. Background and Theory

1.1. Mass Incarceration and Health Disparities

Two percent of all Black men in the United States are incarcerated [1]. Because the criminal legal system in the US is so vast, it shapes innumerable social domains including health. Research documents the profoundly negative effects of mass incarceration for health disparities [5–10,13,28–30]. Moreover, after release, incarceration affects the long-term health of those once ensnared in the system due to greater financial strain, the difficulties of reentering society, and the stigma attached to a criminal record [5,6]. Despite the voluminous literature documenting the ill-health effects of incarceration, we know less about the association between incarceration and oral health. Among the few studies closely related to the topic, findings show that incarcerated adults face greater struggles accessing oral care [20]. In other words, there is reason to anticipate that former incarceration is associated with poorer oral health compared to similarly positioned people without incarceration experience.

1.2. Incarcerated Populations and Oral Health

The oral health literature typically does not incorporate incarcerated populations, which has led to a relatively small boy of literature on incarceration and oral health. Of the studies inclusive of the carceral world, incarcerated people generally experience poorer oral health than nonincarcerated people [31,32]. One contributing factor is that those who are imprisoned struggle accessing quality healthcare, which includes oral healthcare [18,20,33]. Research shows there is a general lack of dental care and support in penal facilities for currently incarcerated people [31,34–37]. Unclear US federal and state guidelines on dental policy and procedures for prisons lead to a lack of services for incarcerated people [13]. As a consequence, the prevalence of treatable and preventable diseases such as periodontitis is high among those who are incarcerated and continues to be a challenge for those who need care [38,39]. Furthermore, among inmates, at least one study has found that longer detention durations are associated with progressively decaying dental health [34]. This finding is notable considering studies typically identify that experiencing incarceration of any amount of time is worse for health than the length of incarceration [7,27]. Ultimately, data limitations make it difficult to assess oral health for people who have experienced incarceration in the United States, which highlights the importance of the present study's foci.

Oral Health among Incarcerated Black Men. Incarcerated Black Americans face additional structural barriers to maintaining oral health and accessing treatment beyond the barrier that incarceration generates [34,40]. In other words, racial disparities in oral health occur not only in the general public to the disadvantage of Black populations, but also within the prison system. A consistent finding in the few studies that have documented racial disparities in oral health is that Black inmates are more likely than their white counterparts to have decaying teeth [34,41]. The present study builds on these insights to identify whether former incarceration status factors into variation in oral health among African American men and women specifically.

Oral Health among Incarcerated Black Women. Among incarcerated populations, evidence shows that women's healthcare needs including oral healthcare are typically more underserved than men [42]. In addition, incarcerated women from racially marginalized backgrounds more often experience oral pain than their white counterparts [40]. Said differently, incarcerated women are generally less likely to have their healthcare needs met, and this gender disadvantage is worse for women of color [43]. Poorer access to treatment and worse quality of care on average leads incarcerated women to hold more negative views of the treatment they receive while in prison [33,42]. Lack of proper oral healthcare has immediate and long-term ramifications. One study conducted outside of the US found that incarcerated women's perception of their oral health was strongly associated with their quality of life including perceived physical discomfort, psychological disability, and social disadvantage [40]. Thus, research demonstrates the struggles that many incarcerated women face with receiving proper dental healthcare, and studies document the importance of care for maintaining oral health for a person's quality of life.

1.3. Predictors of Post-Release Oral Health

Maintaining oral health and hygiene encompasses routine dental visits, transportation access to care, and having health insurance plans that cover dental health [22,44]. Moreover, despite the importance of wellness checks, disparities in access to care exist with considerable health consequences. Unfortunately, dental care creates one of the highest financial barriers in comparison to other healthcare services, and insurance plans sometimes do not cover dental health [45]. For formerly incarcerated people, the lack of publicly funded programs to assist with covering the cost of dental care creates challenges in accessing and financing care [45]. Routine dental visits often involve 6 month wellness checks, which studies show are clinically beneficial for people [46]. According to a meta-analysis, less frequent dental visits are associated with an increase in dental decay and tooth loss, as well as a lower perceived quality of life [46]. Regular oral wellness checks are important for identifying, treating, and managing some chronic diseases. For instance, evidence suggests that the tumor size and growth of many oral cancers increase with a decrease in dental visits [46]. Regardless of incarceration status, white Americans are on average more likely to receive preventative dental care, while less than half of Black Americans visit a dentist at least annually [47]. Consequently, inequitable access to care for Black Americans is compounded in the event that a person is formerly incarcerated.

Once a person is no longer incarcerated, reintegration into society remains challenging given the stigma associated with imprisonment and a criminal record [40]. Even if a person successfully navigates the healthcare system to schedule an appointment and visit a healthcare provider, almost half of people who have been incarcerated report experiencing discrimination from healthcare workers [48]. Thus, incarceration can cause long-term negative impacts on oral health via the stigma and discrimination one experiences in the healthcare system. Ultimately, formerly incarcerated adults are expected to have poorer oral health than their never incarcerated counterparts.

2. Summary and Hypotheses

The present study examines the association between incarceration experience and self-reported oral health among African American men and women. On the basis of the background research and tenets of our conceptual framework, formerly incarcerated people face extended challenges in accessing quality dental healthcare. Hence, *Hypotheses 1a,b* anticipate that (*a*) women and (*b*) men with a history of incarceration will have worse oral health than their never incarcerated counterparts. While foregoing studies typically show that any incarceration experience is worse for health than the amount of time one is incarcerated, some studies identified that oral health worsens as detention duration increases. Thus, *Hypotheses 2a,b* anticipate that longer durations of incarceration will be associated with poorer oral health among (*a*) women and (*b*) men.

2.1. *Data and Methods*

2.1.1. Data

Survey data for this study were extracted from the National Survey of American Life (NSAL), a nationally representative household probability survey collected between 2001 and 2003. The NSAL included 3570 non-Hispanic Blacks, 1438 non-Hispanic Black Caribbeans, 891 non-Hispanic Whites, and 183 Hispanics. The survey emphasized the nature of race and ethnicity within the US Black population by interviewing national samples of African American (n = 3570) and Caribbean (n = 1623) immigrant and older generation populations [49,50]. Full details about the sample and survey were published elsewhere [49,50]. Most interviews were conducted face-to-face in English. The NSAL data are well positioned to address the present study's aims for at least three reasons. First, the NSAL is one of few surveys to include questions on former incarceration, detention duration, and perceived oral health at the height of mass incarceration in the US. Second, the NSAL includes a nationally representative sample of African Americans. The representative and adequate sample allows for meaningfully examining variation in oral health among African American men and women separately [51–53]. Third, the data represent one of the most comprehensive social surveys of US-residing people of African descent ever conducted [50,54]. Thus, the data align well with the present foci.

2.1.2. Dependent Variable

Perceived Oral Health Status. The dependent variable, self-rated oral health, is a commonly used subjective global assessment of oral health status. We use this measure for three reasons. First, the measure aligns with tooth loss, oral pain and discomfort, and dentists' professional ratings of oral health [55–57]. Thus, the measure provides a valid, reliable, and cost-efficient way to assess oral health [58–60]. Second, the measure is a strong predictor of other health measures including hypertension, diabetes, and obesity [56,61]. Third, the item we use is commonly used in the research literature and has been validated for study population [62–64]. Self-rated oral health derives from answers to the following question: "How would you rate the overall condition of your teeth, gums, and mouth at the present time?" Answers were coded into five categories such that poor = 1, fair = 2, good = 3, very good = 4, and excellent = 5.

2.1.3. Independent Variables

Formerly Incarcerated. Formerly incarcerated identifies whether a person has ever spent time in a jail or prison (yes = 1).

Years Spent Incarcerated. Incarceration duration reflects the length of time in total years that a person experienced incarcerated in the past. We utilized a squared term in multivariable models given that the measure is overdispersed for women and men.

2.1.4. Covariates

The present study incorporates several measures important to research on criminal legal contact and health including age, education, employment, marital status, and health insurance status and type [28,29,65,66]. Age measures years since birth. Education measures completed years of schooling. Employment measures whether people are currently working (yes = 1). Health insurance coverage includes whether a person has no insurance (yes = 1), federally funded insurance (yes = 1), or employee sponsored insurance (yes = 1). No insurance served as the reference group in multivariable models. We created three marital status categories: married/cohabiting, formerly married (i.e., divorced, widowed, or separated), and never married. Married/cohabiting served as the reference group in multivariable models.

2.1.5. Methods

We began our analytic strategy by estimating descriptive statistics for African American adults for all study variables. Because we were interested in heterogeneity among the two groups, we stratified all analyses by gender. This study utilized ordered logistic regression models to examine self-rated oral health given its Likert scale construction [67,68]. We estimated four total models. The first models for women and men estimate the association between former incarceration status and oral health while controlling for covariates (i.e., Models 1 and 3). The second models for each gender group estimate the association between duration of incarceration and self-reported oral health among people who have any history of incarceration (i.e., Models 2 and 4). Results from regression models are presented using exponentiated coefficients for ease of interpretation (i.e., odds ratios). All statistics presented are corrected for the complex sampling design of the National Survey of American Life. Reference groups for multicategory measures are indicated using the abbreviation ref. Bayesian Information Criterion (BIC) statistics are calculated for each model.

3. Results

3.1. Descriptive Statistics

Descriptive statistics are presented in Table 1. On average, women rated their oral health as poorer than men (women mean = 3.08, sd = 1.21; men mean = 3.18, sd = 0.98; $p < 0.05$). Age ranged from 18 to 93 (women *mean* = 42.64, *sd* = 17.52; men *mean* = 41.58, *sd* = 14.12; $p < 0.05$). Women averaged 12.48 (*sd* = 2.59) years of education, and men averaged 12.50 (*sd* = 2.21). Approximately 73% of men were employed, which was significantly higher than the 64% of women that were employed ($p < 0.05$). The percentage of women who had federal program insurance (26%) was significantly higher than the percentage of men who did (15%; $p < 0.05$). The percentage of men who had employee-based insurance (62%) was significantly higher than the percentage of women who did (53%; $p < 0.05$). African American men were more likely to fall into the married/cohabiting category (50%; $p < 0.05$), while women were more likely to occupy the formerly married group (32%; $p < 0.05$).

Table 1. Descriptive statistics for African American women and men in the National Survey of American Life, 2003.

	African American Women		African American Men	
Variables	Mean/%	SD	Mean/%	SD
Oral Health Status				
Self-rated oral health * (*range* 1–5, 5 = excellent)	3.08	(1.21)	3.18	(0.98)
Incarceration Experience				
Formerly incarcerated *	6.33%	—	21.05%	—
Years spent incarcerated * [a] (*range* 0–30.34)	1.81	(3.50)	2.35	(4.11)
Covariates				
Age (in years; *range* 18–93)	42.64	(17.52)	41.58	(14.12)
Education (in years; *range* 4–17)	12.48	(2.59)	12.50	(2.21)
Employed (yes = 1) *	63.68%	—	72.67%	—
No insurance (yes = 1)	20.02%	—	23.01%	—
Federal program insurance * (yes = 1)	26.20%	—	15.18%	—
Employee sponsored insurance * (yes = 1)	52.78%	—	61.81%	—
Married/cohabiting (yes = 1) *	35.88%	—	50.30%	—
Formerly married * (yes = 1)	32.25 %	—	19.14%	—
Never married (yes = 1)	31.86%	—	30.56%	—
Sample size	2144		1166	

Note: Analyses are corrected for the sampling design. Means and percentages (%) are presented with standard deviations in parentheses (*SD*). * Means/proportions different at $p < 0.05$. [a] Only among people who have experienced incarceration.

3.2. Incarceration, Duration, and Dental Health

Results from ordered logistic regression models estimating oral health for African American women and men in the National Survey of American Life are presented in Table 2. Model 1 estimates self-rated oral health based on former incarceration status and covariates. Results show that formerly incarcerated women on average report poorer oral health by a factor of 0.65 ($se = 0.10$; $p < 0.01$). Older women also reported poorer oral health on average than younger women ($OR = 0.98$, $se = 0.01$; $p < 0.001$). Additionally, a year increase in education was associated with an improvement in oral health by a factor of 1.09 ($se = 0.02$; $p < 0.001$). On average, women with employment-based health insurance typically had better oral health than those with no insurance ($OR = 1.32$, $se = 0.14$; $p < 0.05$), and women who were formerly married had worse health than married/cohabiting women ($OR = 0.81$, $se = 0.08$; $p < 0.05$).

To present the association visually, Figure 1 graphs fully adjusted predictions of self-reported oral health for African American women across former incarceration status. Figure 1 shows that formerly incarcerated women are significantly more likely to rate their oral health as poor (12% probability versus 8%; $p < 0.05$) or fair (28% probability versus 22%; $p < 0.05$), and significantly less likely to report their oral health as very good (22% probability versus 27%; $p < 0.05$) or excellent (8% probability versus 11%; $p < 0.05$). In other words, former incarceration is associated with worse perceived oral health among women. In addition, Model 2 presented in Table 2 focuses on African American women with a history of incarceration to identify the association between duration of detention and oral health. Results show no significant associations among years spent incarcerated, the squared term, and self-reported oral health.

Table 2. Ordered logistic regression models predicting oral health for African American women and men in the National Survey of American Life, 2003.

	Self-Rated Oral Health (*Range* 1–5, 5 = *Excellent*)							
	African American Women				African American Men			
	Model 1		Model 2		Model 3		Model 4	
Variables	OR	SE	OR	SE	OR	SE	OR	SE
Incarceration Experience								
Formerly incarcerated (yes = 1)	0.65 **	(0.10)	—	—	0.74 *	(0.09)	—	—
Years spent Incarcerated	—	—	0.93	(0.09)	—	—	1.16 **	(0.06)
Years spent Incarcerated	—	—	1.00	(0.00)	—	—	0.99 *	(0.00)
Covariates								
Age (in years)	0.98 ***	(0.01)	0.94 *	(0.02)	0.98 ***	(0.01)	0.98	(0.01)
Education (in years)	1.09 ***	(0.02)	1.12 *	(0.02)	1.09 **	(0.04)	1.21 *	(0.10)
Employed (yes = 1)	1.01	(0.14)	0.93	(0.57)	1.53 *	(0.25)	2.28 *	(0.85)
Federal program Insurance (ref = no insurance)	0.79	(0.10)	0.83	(0.51)	0.97	(0.18)	1.22	(0.45)
Employee sponsored insurance (ref = no insurance)	1.32 *	(0.14)	1.43	(0.74)	1.05	(0.17)	1.28	(0.44)
Formerly married (ref = married/cohabiting)	0.81 *	(0.08)	1.13	(0.52)	0.78	(0.12)	0.52 *	(0.17)
Never married (ref = married/cohabiting)	1.13	(0.12)	1.59	(0.57)	1.13	(0.16)	1.46	(0.42)
Sample size	2144		127		1166		252	
BIC	4396.310		318.592		3333.870		773.058	
McFadden Pseudo R^2	0.031		0.080		0.031		0.060	

Note: Analyses are corrected for the sampling design. Odds ratios (*OR*) are presented with rounded standard errors (*SE*) in parentheses for African American women and men. Reference groups for multicategory measures are indicated using the abbreviation ref. Models 2 and 4 only include adults who have ever been incarcerated. BIC indicates the Bayesian Information Criterion. * $p < 0.05$; ** $p < 0.01$; *** $p < 0.001$ (two-tailed tests).

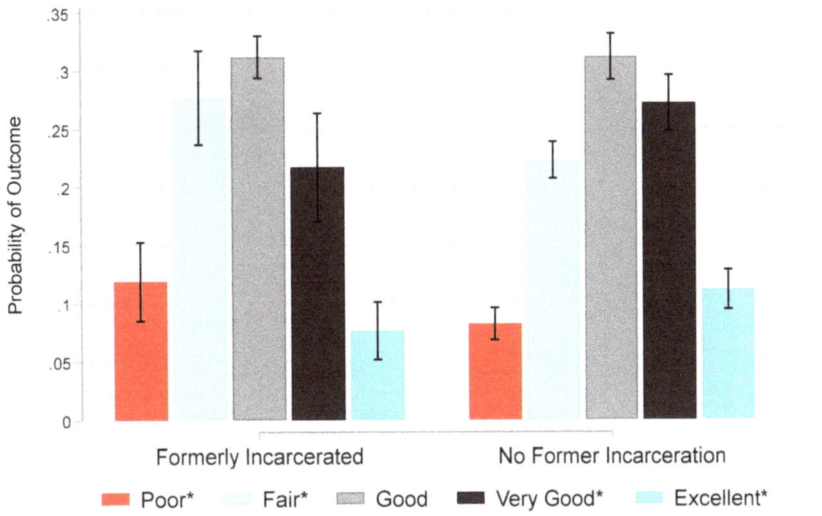

Figure 1. Predictions of Oral Health among African American Women in the National Survey of American Life, 2003. *Note*: Fully-adjusted estimates generated from Model 1 in Table 2 (n = 2144). Probabilities of poor and fair health are significantly higher for formerly incarcerated women. Probabilities of very good and excellent health are significantly lower for formerly incarcerated women. * Probabilities of an outcome are significantly different for formerly and never incarcerated women at $p < 0.05$.

Model 3 shows results for African American men (Table 2). Formerly incarcerated men on average rate their oral health worse by a factor of 0.74 ($se = 0.09$; $p < 0.05$). Older men

($OR = 0.98$, $se = 0.01$; $p < 0.001$) and less educated men ($OR = 1.09$, $se = 0.04$; $p < 0.01$) typically experience poorer oral health than younger and more educated men. Moreover, employed men have better oral health than their unemployed counterparts on average ($OR = 1.53$, $se = 0.25$; $p < 0.05$). Figure 2 graphs fully adjusted predictions of oral health for African American men by former incarceration status. On average, formerly incarcerated men are more likely to report their oral health as poor, fair, or good than their never incarcerated counterparts, and less likely to report their oral health as very good or excellent (all at $p < 0.05$). Formerly incarcerated men are 9% likely to have poor oral health, 24% likely to have fair health, and 32% likely to have good health. Contrarily, never incarcerated men have a 30% probability of very good oral health and an 11% probability of excellent health.

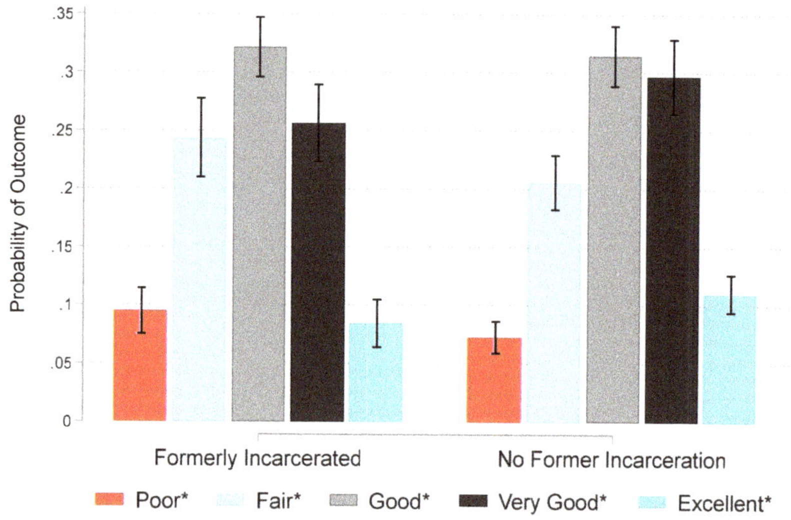

Figure 2. Predictions of Oral Health among African American Men in the National Survey of American Life, 2003. *Note*: Fully-adjusted estimates generated from Model 3 in Table 2 (n = 1166). Probabilities of poor, fair, and good health are significantly higher for formerly incarcerated men. Probabilities of very good and excellent health are significantly lower for formerly incarcerated men. * Probabilities of an outcome are significantly different for formerly and never incarcerated men at $p < 0.05$.

Model 4 in Table 2 incorporates years incarcerated and its squared term for African American men with a history of incarceration. Results show that an increase of 1 year incarcerated is associated with higher odds of reporting better oral health by a factor of 1.16 ($se = 0.06$; $p < 0.05$). However, the squared term indicates that the odds change directions such that oral health tends to deteriorate for those with the longest durations ($OR = 0.99$, $se = 0.00$; $p < 0.01$). To make sense of these patterns, Figure 3 shows the adjusted predictions for self-reported oral health for formerly incarcerated African American men across years of incarceration. Two notable patterns emerge. First, the slopes estimating probabilities of each of the five reported health options across years of incarceration are all statistically different from zero, which statistically verifies that each of the lines is curvilinear. Said differently, the association between years incarcerated and oral health changes across years of incarceration. Second, the probabilities of reporting poor, fair, or good health tend to decrease across years incarcerated until approximately 15 years at which point the graph indicates that probabilities increase for these outcomes. By contrast, probabilities of very good or excellent health increase across time up until about 15 years at which point the oral health tends to worsen.

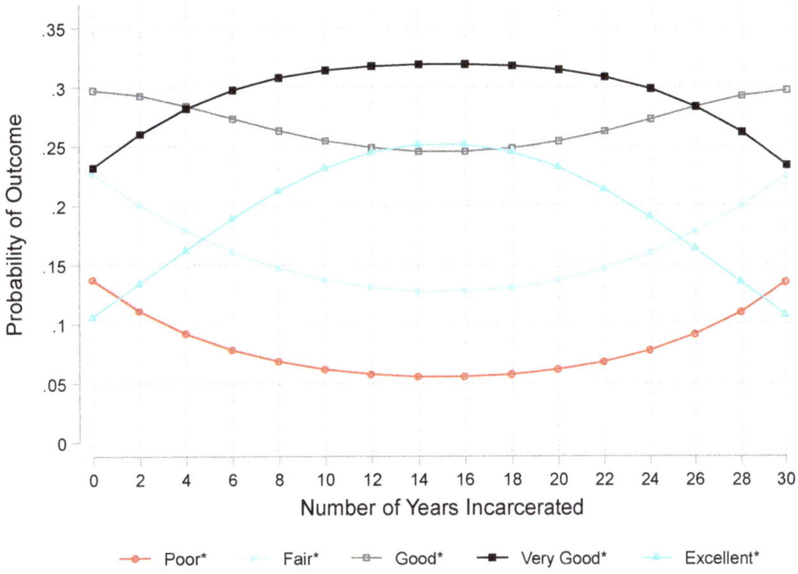

Figure 3. Predictions of Oral Health by Number of Years Incarcerated among Formerly Incarcerated African American Men in the National Survey of American Life, 2003. *Note*: Fully-adjusted estimates generated from Model 4 in Table 2 (n = 252). * Probabilities of an outcome across years incarcerated are significantly different for zero at $p < 0.05$ indicating curvilinear associations.

4. Discussion

This study examined the association between incarceration and oral health. On the basis of background research and tenets of our conceptual framework, we first expected that formerly incarcerated African American (*a*) women and (*b*) men would have poorer oral health than their never incarcerated counterparts (*Hypotheses 1a,b*). Results shown in Table 2 and Figures 1 and 2 support Hypotheses 1a,b such that formerly incarcerated women and men on average rate their oral health as poorer than their never incarcerated counterparts. Moreover, we anticipated that longer timespans of incarceration would be associated with poorer oral health for (*a*) women and (*b*) men (*Hypotheses 2a,b*). Results in Table 2 and Figure 3 did not offer support for Hypotheses 2a,b. We found evidence for a curvilinear association between detention duration and oral health such that odds of having poor oral health decrease across time up to approximately 15 years incarcerated after which time each additional year a person spends incarcerated is associated with progressively poorer oral health (Figure 3).

We found that incarceration is associated with worse oral health for African American men and women. The literature offers explanations for these patterns. Following release, formerly incarcerated adults may face challenges in accessing and receiving oral healthcare services due to a lack of transportation, health insurance, or sufficient medication to manage health conditions [16,22,23]. In fact, transportation remains one of the main barriers to acquiring proper dental care for older adults [44]. Lack of transportation impedes regular dental visits, which are vital to proper dental health [46]. Moreover, formerly incarcerated people may lack dental insurance, and dental care creates one of the highest financial barriers in comparison to other healthcare services [45]. The lack of publicly funded programs offers people little recourse to access oral healthcare in the absence of dental insurance and expendable income. Furthermore, in cases where people successfully obtain insurance that covers dental healthcare, one will still need to navigate the system to locate a provider and schedule an appointment. Additionally, formerly incarcerated people are also typically released without sufficient medication to manage health conditions [16,22]. Not having medications to manage chronic health conditions can worsen oral health.

The length of incarceration was curvilinearly associated with oral health among African American men such that spending some time incarcerated is associated with better oral health than those that spend very little time incarcerated. Findings from this research add to a line of studies identifying complex results on the association between criminal legal contact and health specifically among Black men. Some studies found that, while incarceration tends to worsen health for most race–gender groups, Black men do not as often experience the health-worsening effects of incarceration or other forms of criminal legal contact (e.g., arrest) [6,10–12]. Scholars posit that incarceration may not always significantly harm Black men's health due to incarceration shielding them from car crashes, lethal violence, and inaccessible healthcare services given that insurance in the US is often tied to one's employer [6,11,12]. However, we also found there was a turning point such that the greatest number of years incarcerated is associated with poorer oral health. We propose several explanations for these findings. First, however limited, these men have access to some degree of healthcare services. Some substandard healthcare while incarcerated is likely better for oral health than having no healthcare while not incarcerated. Second, prolonged exposure to threats to safety, meals with insufficient nutritious value, and lack of quality oral hygiene products may worsen oral health after a period of successfully navigating these conditions and strains [20,21]. Third, once released, reintegration into society may present more challenges the longer that one is incarcerated [40]. In other words, the stigma attached to former incarceration may be greater for those with the longest detention durations, and the stigma may manifest in substandard and discriminatory treatment by medical professionals [48].

The present study contributes to existing research but is limited in multiple ways. First, it is likely that incarceration exacerbates preexisting health disparities such that those who become incarcerated are often a population already disadvantaged on the basis of race/ethnicity and socioeconomic status [26]. Future research would benefit from testing the effect of incarceration on oral health while accounting for oral health status prior to incarceration. Doing so would allow a fuller test of incarceration's longitudinal oral health effects. Second, the data used in this study are a unique and well-positioned source of information to address our research questions. However, the datedness of the data means that future work may build on these findings to ascertain incarceration status, ethnoracial identification, and oral health among a more recent sample of African American adults. Future work may also benefit from use of digital technologies to ascertain health status and to ensure healthcare services are successful [69]. Third, we utilized a common measure of perceived oral health status [62–64]. Nonetheless, future studies would benefit from examining additional indicators of oral health status including the presence of oral disease, tooth loss, or functional limitations. Including these additional measures may offer a more comprehensive assessment of the oral health impacts of incarceration.

5. Conclusions

Despite decarceration efforts, the US remains a world leader in incarceration. The present study found that former incarceration is associated with poorer perceived oral health among African American women and men. In doing so, this study adds to research identifying the criminal legal system as having spillover consequences for racial health disparities. While oral health is typically isolated from consideration of a person's overall health status, oral health reflects health and disease occurring within the rest of one's body. To this end, medical professionals and policymakers should be aware of incarceration as a consequential experience for the condition of people's teeth, mouth, and gums. Moreover, healthcare services available within prison systems should include regular oral health examinations, screening test for dental caries, and routine cleanings. Oral health remains integral to overall health, and it would benefit formerly incarcerated men and women to have had regular access to oral healthcare while they were incarcerated. Furthermore, to ensure equitable access to good oral health and healthcare, it remains imperative for federal and US state governments to divest from punitive criminal justice policies that disproportionately incarcerate African American men and women for longer durations often in overcrowded and underserved facilities.

Author Contributions: Conceptualization, R.D.T.; methodology, R.D.T.; software, R.D.T.; formal analysis, R.D.T.; investigation, R.D.T.; resources, R.D.T.; data curation, R.D.T.; writing—original draft preparation, R.D.T. and E.D.M.; writing—review and editing, R.D.T. and E.D.M.; visualization, R.D.T.; supervision, R.D.T.; project administration, R.D.T.; funding acquisition, R.D.T. All authors have read and agreed to the published version of the manuscript.

Funding: This research was generously funded by the College of Liberal Arts and Sciences at the University of Connecticut, grant number 2541100.

Institutional Review Board Statement: This study utilized access to the restricted version of the National Survey of American Life and was approved by the Institutional Review Board of the University of Connecticut (protocol number H20-0132, approved on 13 November 2020).

Informed Consent Statement: Not Applicable.

Data Availability Statement: The data utilized in this study have special restrictions and are not publicly available. To obtain these data, researchers must agree to the terms and conditions of a Restricted Data Use Agreement in accordance with existing Inter-university Consortium for Political and Social Research servicing policies (https://www.icpsr.umich.edu/web/ICPSR/studies/20240, accessed on 1 October 2022).

Conflicts of Interest: The authors declare no conflict of interest.

References

1. Carson, E.A. *Prisoners in 2020—Statistical Tables*; NCJ 302776; U.S. Department of Justice: Washington, DC, USA, 2021; pp. 1–50.
2. Fair, H.; Walmsley, R. *World Prison Population List*; Institute for Crime & Justice Policy Research: London, UK, 2021; pp. 1–18.
3. Lee, H.; Wildeman, C. Assessing Mass Incarceration's Effects on Families. *Science* **2021**, *374*, 277–281. [CrossRef] [PubMed]
4. Garland, D. (Ed.) *Mass Imprisonment: Social Causes and Consequences*; SAGE Publications Ltd.: Thousand Oaks, CA, USA, 2001.
5. Wildeman, C.; Lee, H. Women's Health in the Era of Mass Incarceration. *Annu. Rev. Sociol.* **2021**, *47*, 563–565. [CrossRef]
6. Wildeman, C.; Wang, E.A. Mass Incarceration, Public Health, and Widening Inequality in the USA. *Lancet* **2017**, *389*, 1464–1474. [CrossRef]
7. Massoglia, M. Incarceration as Exposure: The Prison, Infectious Disease, and Other Stress-Related Illnesses. *J. Health Soc. Behav.* **2008**, *49*, 56–71. [CrossRef]
8. Puglisi, L.B.; Wang, E.A. Health Care for People Who Are Incarcerated. *Nat. Rev. Dis. Primers* **2021**, *7*, 50. [CrossRef]
9. Kalinowski, J.; Talbert, R.D.; Woods, B.; Langford, A.; Cole, H.; Barcelona, V.; Crusto, C.; Taylor, J.Y. Police Discrimination and Depressive Symptoms in African American Women: The Intergenerational Impact of Genetic and Psychological Factors on Blood Pressure Study. *Health Equity* **2022**, *6*, 527–532. [CrossRef]
10. Talbert, R.D. Lethal Police Encounters and Cardiovascular Health among Black Americans. *J. Racial Ethn. Health Disparities* **2022**. [CrossRef]
11. Christie-Mizell, C.A.; Talbert, R.D.; Frazier, C.G.; Rainock, M.R.; Jurinsky, J. Race-Gender Variation in the Relationship between Arrest History and Poor Health from Adolescence to Adulthood. *J. Natl. Med. Assoc.* **2022**, *114*, 353–362. [CrossRef]
12. Patterson, E.J. Incarcerating Death: Mortality in U.S. State Correctional Facilities, 1985–1998. *Demography* **2010**, *47*, 587–607. [CrossRef]
13. Camplain, R.; Lininger, M.R.; Baldwin, J.A.; Trotter, R.T. Cardiovascular Risk Factors among Individuals Incarcerated in an Arizona County Jail. *Int. J. Environ. Res. Public Health* **2021**, *18*, 7007. [CrossRef]
14. Institute of Medicine of the National Academies (IOM). *Advancing Oral Health in America*; The National Academies Press: Washington, DC, USA, 2011; pp. 1–248.
15. Kleinberger, J.A.; Strickhouser, S.M. Missing Teeth: Reviewing the Sociology of Oral Health and Healthcare. *Sociol. Compass* **2014**, *8*, 1296–1314. [CrossRef]
16. Centers for Disease Control and Prevention (CDC). *Disparities in Oral Health*; Division of Oral Health, National Center for Chronic Disease Prevention and Health Promotion: Atlanta, GA, USA, 2021.
17. *US 97*; Estelle v. Gamble. Supreme Court of the United States: Washington, DC, USA, 1976; Volume 429, p. 103.
18. Zaitzow, B.H.; Willis, A.K. Behind the Wall of Indifference: Prisoner Voices about the Realities of Prison Health Care. *Laws* **2021**, *10*, 11. [CrossRef]
19. Isailă, O.-M.; Hostiuc, S. Malpractice Claims and Ethical Issues in Prison Health Care Related to Consent and Confidentiality. *Healthcare* **2022**, *10*, 1290. [CrossRef] [PubMed]
20. Johnson, V.; Brondani, M.; von Bergmann, H.; Grossman, S.; Donnelly, L. Dental Service and Resource Needs during COVID-19 among Underserved Populations. *JDR Clin. Transl. Res.* **2022**, *7*, 315–325. [CrossRef] [PubMed]

21. Kosendiak, A.; Stanikowski, P.; Domagała, D.; Gustaw, W.; Bronkowska, M. Dietary Habits, Diet Quality, Nutrition Knowledge, and Associations with Physical Activity in Polish Prisoners: A Pilot Study. *Int. J. Environ. Res. Public Health* **2022**, *19*, 1422. [CrossRef] [PubMed]
22. Northridge, M.E.; Kumar, A.; Kaur, R. Disparities in Access to Oral Health Care. *Annu. Rev. Public Health* **2020**, *41*, 513–535. [CrossRef]
23. Pękala-Wojciechowska, A.; Kacprzak, A.; Pękala, K.; Chomczyńska, M.; Chomczyński, P.; Marczak, M.; Kozłowski, R.; Timler, D.; Lipert, A.; Ogonowska, A.; et al. Mental and Physical Health Problems as Conditions of Ex-Prisoner Re-Entry. *Int. J. Environ. Res. Public Health* **2021**, *18*, 7642. [CrossRef]
24. Hudson, K.; Stockard, J.; Ramberg, Z. The Impact of Socioeconomic Status and Race-Ethnicity on Dental Health. *Sociol. Perspect.* **2007**, *50*, 7–25. [CrossRef]
25. Patterson, E.J.; Wildeman, C. Mass Imprisonment and the Life Course Revisited: Cumulative Years Spent Imprisoned and Marked for Working-Age Black and White Men. *Soc. Sci. Res.* **2015**, *53*, 325–337. [CrossRef]
26. Hinton, E.; Cook, D. The Mass Criminalization of Black Americans: A Historical Overview. *Annu. Rev. Criminol.* **2021**, *4*, 261–286. [CrossRef]
27. Schnittker, J.; John, A. Enduring Stigma: The Long-Term Effects of Incarceration on Health. *J. Health Soc. Behav.* **2007**, *48*, 115–130. [CrossRef] [PubMed]
28. Patterson, E.J.; Talbert, R.D.; Brown, T.N. Familial Incarceration, Social Role Combinations, and Mental Health among African American Women. *J. Marriage Fam.* **2021**, *83*, 86–101. [CrossRef]
29. Brown, T.N.; Bell, M.L.; Patterson, E.J. Imprisoned by Empathy: Familial Incarceration and Psychological Distress among African American Men in the National Survey of American Life. *J. Health Soc. Behav.* **2016**, *57*, 240–256. [CrossRef] [PubMed]
30. Trotter, R.T.; Lininger, M.R.; Camplain, R.; Fofanov, V.Y.; Camplain, C.; Baldwin, J.A. A Survey of Health Disparities, Social Determinants of Health, and Converging Morbidities in a County Jail: A Cultural-Ecological Assessment of Health Conditions in Jail Populations. *Int. J. Environ. Res. Public Health* **2018**, *15*, 2500. [CrossRef] [PubMed]
31. Testa, A.; Fahmy, C. Oral Health Status and Oral Health Care Use among Formerly Incarcerated People. *J. Am. Dent. Assoc.* **2020**, *151*, 164–173. [CrossRef] [PubMed]
32. Freeman, R.; Richards, D. Factors Associated with Accessing Prison Dental Services in Scotland: A Cross-Sectional Study. *Dent. J.* **2019**, *7*, 12. [CrossRef]
33. Rogalska, A.; Barański, K.; Rachwaniec-Szczecińska, Ż.; Holecki, T.; Bąk-Sosnowska, M. Assessment of Satisfaction with Health Services among Prisoners—Descriptive Study. *Healthcare* **2022**, *10*, 548. [CrossRef]
34. Douds, A.S.; Ahlin, E.M.; Kavanaugh, P.R.; Olaghere, A. Decayed Prospects: A Qualitative Study of Prison Dental Care and Its Impact on Former Prisoners. *Crim. Justice Rev.* **2016**, *41*, 21–40. [CrossRef]
35. Trotter II, R.T.; Camplain, R.; Eaves, E.R.; Fofanov, V.Y.; Dmitrieva, N.O.; Hepp, C.M.; Warren, M.; Barrios, B.A.; Pagel, N.; Mayer, A.; et al. Health Disparities and Converging Epidemics in Jail Populations: Protocol for a Mixed-Methods Study. *JMIR Res. Protoc.* **2018**, *7*, e10337. [CrossRef]
36. Bolcato, M.; Fiore, V.; Casella, F.; Babudieri, S.; Lucania, L.; Di Mizio, G. Health in Prison: Does Penitentiary Medicine in Italy Still Exist? *Healthcare* **2021**, *9*, 1511. [CrossRef]
37. Barragan, M.; Gonzalez, G.; Strong, J.D.; Augustine, D.; Chesnut, K.; Reiter, K.; Pifer, N.A. Triaged Out of Care: How Carceral Logics Complicate a 'Course of Care' in Solitary Confinement. *Healthcare* **2022**, *10*, 289. [CrossRef] [PubMed]
38. Dayakar, M.M.; Shivprasad, D.; Pai, P.G. Assessment of Periodontal Health Status among Prison Inmates: A Cross-Sectional Survey. *J. Indian Soc. Periodontol.* **2014**, *18*, 74. [CrossRef]
39. Cavalcanti, A.L.; Rodrigues, I.S.A.; De Melo Silveira, I.T.; De Oliveira, T.B.S.; De Almeida Pinto, M.S.; Xavier, A.F.C.; De Castro, R.D.; Padilha, W.W.N. Dental Caries Experience and Use of Dental Services among Brazilian Prisoners. *Int. J. Environ. Res. Public Health* **2014**, *11*, 12118. [CrossRef]
40. Moraes, L.R.; Duarte de Aquino, L.C.; Cruz, D.T.D.; Leite, I.C.G. Self-Perceived Impact of Oral Health on the Quality of Life of Women Deprived of Their Liberty. *Int. J. Dent.* **2021**, *2021*, e5520652. [CrossRef] [PubMed]
41. Mixson, J.M.; Eplee, H.C.; Fell, P.H.; Jones, J.J.; Rico, M. Oral Health Status of a Federal Prison Population. *J. Public Health Dent.* **1990**, *50*, 257–261. [CrossRef] [PubMed]
42. Young, D.S. Women's Perceptions of Health Care in Prison. *Health Care Women Int.* **2000**, *21*, 219–234. [CrossRef]
43. Norris, W.K.; Allison, M.K.; Fradley, M.F.; Zielinski, M.J. 'You'Re Setting a Lot of People up for Failure': What Formerly Incarcerated Women Would Tell Healthcare Decision Makers. *Health Justice* **2022**, *10*, 4. [CrossRef] [PubMed]
44. Davis, D.L.; Reisine, S. Barriers to Dental Care for Older Minority Adults: Barriers to Dental Care. *Spec. Care Dentist.* **2015**, *35*, 182–189. [CrossRef] [PubMed]
45. Vujicic, M.; Buchmueller, T.; Klein, R. Dental Care Presents The Highest Level Of Financial Barriers, Compared To Other Types Of Health Care Services. *Health Aff.* **2016**, *35*, 2176–2182. [CrossRef] [PubMed]
46. Davenport, C.; Elley, K.; Salas, C.; Taylor-Weetman, C.L.; Fry-Smith, A.; Bryan, S.; Taylor, R. The Clinical Effectiveness and Cost-Effectiveness of Routine Dental Checks: A Systematic Review and Economic Evaluation. *Health Technol. Assess* **2003**, *7*, 1–3. [CrossRef] [PubMed]
47. Treadwell, H.M.; Formicola, A.J. Improving the Oral Health of Prisoners to Improve Overall Health and Well-Being. *Am. J. Public Health* **2008**, *98* (Suppl. 1), S171–S172. [CrossRef] [PubMed]

48. Frank, J.W.; Wang, E.A.; Nunez-Smith, M.; Lee, H.; Comfort, M. Discrimination Based on Criminal Record and Healthcare Utilization among Men Recently Released from Prison: A Descriptive Study. *Health Justice* **2014**, *2*, 6. [CrossRef]
49. Heeringa, S.G.; Wagner, J.; Torres, M.; Duan, N.; Adams, T.; Berglund, P. Sample Designs and Sampling Methods for the Collaborative Psychiatric Epidemiology Studies (CPES). *Int. J. Methods Psychiatr. Res.* **2004**, *13*, 221–240. [CrossRef] [PubMed]
50. Jackson, J.S.; Torres, M.; Caldwell, C.H.; Neighbors, H.W.; Nesse, R.M.; Taylor, R.J.; Trierweiler, S.J.; Williams, D.R. The National Survey of American Life: A Study of Racial, Ethnic and Cultural Influences on Mental Disorders and Mental Health. *Int. J. Methods Psychiatr. Res.* **2004**, *13*, 196–207. [CrossRef] [PubMed]
51. Muruthi, J.R.; Muruthi, B.A.; Thompson Cañas, R.E.; Romero, L.; Taiwo, A.; Ehlinger, P.P. Daily Discrimination, Church Support, Personal Mastery, and Psychological Distress in Black People in the United States. *Ethn. Health* **2022**, 1–19. [CrossRef]
52. Whaley, A.L. Ethnicity, Nativity, and the Effects of Stereotypes on Cardiovascular Health among People of African Ancestry in the United States: Internal versus External Sources of Racism. *Ethn. Health* **2022**, *27*, 1010–1030. [CrossRef] [PubMed]
53. Smith, N.C.; Nicholson, H.L. Perceived Discrimination and Mental Health among African American and Caribbean Black Adolescents: Ethnic Differences in Processes and Effects. *Ethn. Health* **2022**, *27*, 687–704. [CrossRef]
54. Irby-Shasanmi, A.; Erving, C.L. Do Discrimination and Negative Interactions with Family Explain the Relationship between Interracial Relationship Status and Mental Disorder? *Socius* **2022**, *8*, 23780231221124852. [CrossRef]
55. Chatzopoulos, G.S.; Cisneros, A.; Sanchez, M.; Lunos, S.; Wolff, L.F. Validity of Self-Reported Periodontal Measures, Demographic Characteristics, and Systemic Medical Conditions. *J. Periodontol.* **2018**, *89*, 924–932. [CrossRef]
56. Cozier, Y.C.; Heaton, B.; Bethea, T.N.; Freudenheim, J.L.; Garcia, R.I.; Rosenberg, L. Predictors of Self-Reported Oral Health in the Black Women's Health Study. *J. Public Health Dent.* **2020**, *80*, 70–78. [CrossRef]
57. Thomson, W.M.; Mejia, G.C.; Broadbent, J.M.; Poulton, R. Construct Validity of Locker's Global Oral Health Item. *J. Dent. Res.* **2012**, *91*, 1038–1042. [CrossRef] [PubMed]
58. Heaton, B.; Gordon, N.B.; Garcia, R.I.; Rosenberg, L.; Rich, S.; Fox, M.P.; Cozier, Y.C. A Clinical Validation of Self-Reported Periodontitis Among Participants in the Black Women's Health Study. *J. Periodontol.* **2017**, *88*, 582–592. [CrossRef] [PubMed]
59. Joshipura, K.J.; Pitiphat, W.; Douglass, C.W. Validation of Self-Reported Periodontal Measures Among Health Professionals. *J. Public Health Dent.* **2002**, *62*, 115–121. [CrossRef]
60. Pitiphat, W.; Garcia, R.I.; Douglass, C.W.; Joshipura, K.J. Validation of Self-Reported Oral Health Measures. *J. Public Health Dent.* **2002**, *62*, 122–128. [CrossRef] [PubMed]
61. Aldossri, M.; Saarela, O.; Rosella, L.; Quiñonez, C. Suboptimal Oral Health and the Risk of Cardiovascular Disease in the Presence of Competing Death: A Data Linkage Analysis. *Can. J. Public Health* **2022**. [CrossRef]
62. Assari, S. Socioeconomic Status and Self-Rated Oral Health; Diminished Return among Hispanic Whites. *Dent. J.* **2018**, *6*, 11. [CrossRef]
63. Williams, M.T.; Taylor, R.J.; George, J.R.; Schlaudt, V.A.; Ifatunji, M.A.; Chatters, L.M. Correlates of Obsessive-Compulsive Symptoms among Black Caribbean Americans. *Int. J. Ment. Health* **2021**, *50*, 53–77. [CrossRef]
64. Williams, M.T.; Taylor, R.J.; Himle, J.A.; Chatters, L.M. Demographic and Health-Related Correlates of Obsessive-Compulsive Symptoms among African Americans. *J. Obs. -Compuls. Relat. Disord.* **2017**, *14*, 119–126. [CrossRef] [PubMed]
65. Lee, R.D.; Fang, X.; Luo, F. The Impact of Parental Incarceration on the Physical and Mental Health of Young Adults. *Pediatrics* **2013**, *131*, e1188–e1195. [CrossRef]
66. Wildeman, C.; Schnittker, J.; Turney, K. Despair by Association? The Mental Health of Mothers with Children by Recently Incarcerated Fathers. *Am. Sociol. Rev.* **2012**, *77*, 216–243. [CrossRef]
67. Long, J.S.; Freese, J. *Regression Models for Categorical Dependent Variables Using Stata*; Stata Press: College Station, TX, USA, 2014.
68. Williams, R. Using the Margins Command to Estimate and Interpret Adjusted Predictions and Marginal Effects. *Stata J.* **2012**, *12*, 308–331. [CrossRef]
69. Rantanen, T.; Järveläinen, E.; Leppälahti, T. Prisoners as Users of Digital Health Care and Social Welfare Services: A Finnish Attitude Survey. *Int. J. Environ. Res. Public Health* **2021**, *18*, 5528. [CrossRef] [PubMed]

International Journal of
Environmental Research and Public Health

MDPI

Article

Online Dating and Mental Health among Young Sexual Minority Black Men: Is Ethnic Identity Protective in the Face of Sexual Racism?

Ryan M. Wade * and Matthew M. Pear

School of Social Work, University of Illinois Urbana-Champaign, Champaign, IL 61820, USA
* Correspondence: wlryan@illinois.edu

Abstract: Racialized Sexual Discrimination (RSD), also known as 'sexual racism,' is pervasive within online dating venues. RSD is associated with poor mental health outcomes among young sexual minority Black men (YSMBM), and there is limited research on factors that may mitigate this association. Ethnic identity has been identified as a potential protective factor for racial/ethnic minorities who encounter racialized stressors, though some evidence suggests that ethnic identity may also intensify the negative effects of racial discrimination. Using data from a cross-sectional web-survey of YSMBM (n = 690), a series of linear regression models were estimated to examine the moderating effect of ethnic identity search and ethnic identity commitment on the relationship between RSD and depressive symptoms/feeling of self-worth. Results indicated that having moderate-to-high scores on commitment attenuated the association between being physically objectified by White men and higher depressive symptoms. However, having high scores on commitment intensified the association between being rejected by Black men and lower feelings of self-worth. Stronger identity commitment may be protective against objectification from White men, though it may also exacerbate negative outcomes related to in-group discrimination. These findings may have important implications for the development of individual and group-level interventions addressing ethnic identity among YSMBM.

Keywords: sexual racism; ethnic identity; gay/bisexual men; mobile apps; mental health

Citation: Wade, R.M.; Pear, M.M. Online Dating and Mental Health among Young Sexual Minority Black Men: Is Ethnic Identity Protective in the Face of Sexual Racism?. *Int. J. Environ. Res. Public Health* **2022**, *19*, 14263. https://doi.org/10.3390/ijerph192114263

Academic Editors: Paul B. Tchounwou and Cheng-Fang Yen

Received: 27 August 2022
Accepted: 27 October 2022
Published: 1 November 2022

1. Introduction

Online intimate partner-seeking is now widespread among Americans, especially among sexual minority adolescents and young adults. Young sexual minority populations use dating apps and websites at higher rates than their older and heterosexual counterparts, and use of such platforms has been increasing over the past decade [1,2]. Sexual minority men of color face frequent discrimination on these dating apps and websites, a phenomenon referred to as Racialized Sexual Discrimination (RSD) [3,4]. RSD is a multidimensional construct that encompasses a variety of racially mediated discriminatory experiences—such as overt and covert rejection on the basis of race, and the positioning of White men as superior or more desirable than other racial/ethnic minority groups—all of which have been well-documented in the literature [4–9]. Users may express their sexual "preferences" based on race directly on their profiles (e.g., writing "White men only;' "not into Black guys, etc.); users may also systematically ignore messages from men of color, or explicitly reject men of color on the basis of their racial/ethnic minority background. Erotic objectification is also commonly reported on these platforms and is another key dimension of RSD. Patterns of objectification are largely driven by racial stereotypes that are deeply ingrained in American and many other Western cultures. For Black men, these stereotypes often cast them as having large penises, as well as being physically imposing, dominant, and aggressive [10–15].

The phenomenon of RSD is situated within a broader literature of sexual racism. Sexual racism has been described as the systemic ways in which individuals and society establish a racial hierarchy of desire—wherein White identity/Eurocentric features are considered ideal, interracial intimacy is less socially accepted, and the erotic capital of racial/ethnic minorities are altogether diminished, or wholly afforded through racial fetishization [16–18]. As a contemporary online phenomenon, RSD has been receiving growing attention in the social science and health literature [19–23]. Recently, researchers have demonstrated links between RSD and negative health outcomes, such as anxiety and psychological distress—as well as lower self-esteem and well-being among sexual minority men of color [24–29]. In a series of recent studies, we developed the first psychometrically evaluated scale of RSD and examined the association between RSD and psychological well-being among young sexual minority Black men (YSMBM) [30,31]. We found that encountering same-race rejection and White superiority when seeking intimate partners online was associated with higher depressive symptoms among YSMBM. We also found that encountering objectification from White men was associated with both higher depressive symptoms and lower feelings of self-worth among the study sample. Altogether, the emerging literature on RSD has provided evidence that this unique and understudied phenomenon may negatively impact the health of sexual minority men of color.

1.1. Theoretical Underpinnings of Identity, Discrimination, and Health

Much of our work on RSD has been grounded in Meyer's Minority Stress Theory (MST), which provides an apt framework for understanding how RSD contributes to adverse health outcomes among sexual minority populations [32]. MST explicates the mechanisms through which distal and proximal identity-related stressors lead to poor mental health outcomes among marginalized populations, drawing special attention to the role of identity in the experience of stress—such as race- or sexuality-based discrimination. Meyer posits that characteristics of an individual's minoritized identity—such as the extent to which an individual identifies with their minority status (salience) and their evaluation of that identity (valence)—modulates the experience of identity-related stress and subsequent health outcomes. However, there is limited research focusing specifically on ethnic identity among YSMBM, and how ethnic identity operates in the context of race-related stress within this population.

There are a number of theories addressing ethnic identity that may complement MST and provide important nuance in investigating RSD among sexual minority men of color. Building upon Erickson's and Marcia's seminal work on adolescent identity development [33–35], Phinney pioneered one of the most well recognized frameworks of ethnic identity [36,37], culminating in the creation of the widely used Multi-Ethnic Identity Measure (MEIM). In subsequent psychometric and construct validity work, Phinney established two key components of ethnic identity: identity search/exploration and identity commitment. Identity search/exploration refers to the effort that individuals expend in learning about, and making meaning of, their ethnic group membership. Identity commitment refers to individuals' sense of belonging to their ethnic group, as well as how they appraise the relative value of belonging to their ethnic group.

Both Phinney and other scholars have suggested that higher levels of identity commitment may confer protective benefits and partially mitigate the effects of racial discrimination [36,38–40]. Having a robust and assured sense of self, as well as finding strength and solidarity through one's group membership, is thought to deflect threats to an individual's self-concept—thereby preventing identity-based attacks (i.e., racial discrimination) from negatively impacting psychosocial functioning [36,41,42]. Identity search/exploration, however, has been hypothesized to operate differently in the context of discrimination among some scholars. While not strictly negatively valenced, identity search/exploration is thought to represent a lack of clarity or full integration of one's sense of ethnic identity (hence the need to explore). This uncertainty may make an individual more vulnerable to racial discrimination or prejudice, thereby acting as an exacerbating characteristic in the context of identity-related stress [39,40,43]. Though these two aspects of ethnic identity are conceptually distinct, researchers have mostly examined identity search and commitment in tandem (i.e., a composite measure is most often used), and the researchers who have disaggregated these two constructs have largely only focused on Latino and Asian men in their study samples [39,44–46]. Moreover, there is considerably less research examining ethnic identity among sexual minority populations in general, and among YSMBM in particular [47]. The ways in which ethnic identity functions as a protective or exacerbating characteristic in the context of race-related stress is ultimately an ongoing empirical question, especially among populations that have historically been underexamined—and in the context of understudied racialized stressors, such as RSD.

1.2. Empirical Findings on the Moderating Role of Ethnic Identity

There is an extensive body of empirical literature on ethnic identity in general, with most researchers reporting that stronger ethnic identity is associated with positive psychosocial outcomes among Black Americans and other racial/ethnic minority groups [47–52]. However, researchers have reported far more nuanced findings with respect to how identity search and commitment operates in the context of race-related stress. Among a sample of Latino adults, Torres et al. reported that ethnic identity exploration exacerbated the association between public, work-related, and academic-related discrimination and psychological distress [46]. In contrast, ethnic identity commitment attenuated the association between covert discrimination and negative mental health outcomes. Torres and Ong reported near identical findings in a comparable study, in which they investigated the association between daily discrimination and next-day depression among Latino adults [39]. Identity exploration again exacerbated the association between discrimination and depression, whereas identity commitment acted as a buffer. These findings coincide with theories of ethnic identity that position commitment as a protective characteristic and exploration as an exacerbating characteristic in the context of race-related stress.

In a study of online discrimination and well-being, Tynes et al. reported that that ethnic identity buffered the association between online discrimination and anxiety symptoms among Black adolescents, but did not significantly alter the association between online discrimination and depressive symptoms [53]. Romero and Roberts similarly reported that high levels of identity commitment buffered the effects of discrimination on Latino adolescents' self-esteem, and they also found that low levels of identity commitment exacerbated this association [54]. Other researchers have also found that ethnic identity serves as a protective factor in the context of racial discrimination and adverse psychosocial health outcomes, though these researchers used ethnic identity as a composite measure [51,55]. In such cases, it is difficult to determine whether these associations are driven by both commitment and exploration, or one over the other. In all cases, however, researchers have not expressly focused on the experiences of sexual minority populations of color. This points to a significant gap in our understanding given the added complexity of intersectional identity, and the elevated risk associated with holding multiple oppressed identities [56,57].

1.3. Does Ethnic Identity Buffer or Exacerbate the Impact of RSD?

There are two key benefits of examining ethnic identity as a moderator between RSD and health. First, the theoretical and empirical literature has indicated that not all characteristics of ethnic identity are uniformly protective—and in some instances, certain aspects of ethnic identity may actually worsen the negative effects of discrimination [39,40,43,58,59]. Understanding which aspects of identity are protective—and which are not—may be crucial in developing culturally tailored interventions that address discrimination and psychological well-being. Second, ethnic identity has been minimally investigated among YSMBM in general, and in the context of RSD specifically. The very personal and often vulnerable nature of intimate partner-seeking makes RSD a unique racialized stressor. That RSD is defined as an online-specific phenomenon also makes it unique—given that discrimination is typically more brazen, prejudices more overt, and rejection more frequent–in high density, quasi-anonymous settings such as online venues [60–64]. The novel RSD scale used in this study captures a broad scope of these experiences and distinguishes between expressions of discrimination to a greater degree than most measures of discrimination [30]. Its distinction between race of perpetrator (same-race and White perpetration of RSD) is especially useful, as there is a noteworthy deficit of research that accounts for differences between in-group and out-group discrimination in the context of RSD. Examination of same-race perpetration of RSD is rare in general, though we have found that YSMBM report complex attitudes toward same-race perpetration of RSD in previous work [65].

Given the importance of ethnic identity in the context of race-related stress, the current study aims to examine the ways in which ethnic identity might serve to modify the relationship between RSD and psychological well-being among YSMBM. In accordance with prior theoretical and empirical work, we hypothesized that (**Hypothesis 1; H1**) higher scores on RSD would be associated with poorer psychological well-being among the study sample; (**Hypothesis 2; H2**) higher scores on ethnic identity search would exacerbate the association between RSD and well-being; and (**Hypothesis 3; H3**) higher scores on ethnic identity commitment would attenuate the association between RSD and well-being.

2. Materials and Methods

2.1. Participants

Eligibility Criteria. In order to be eligible for the study, participants had to meet the following criteria: (1) identify as a man; (2) be assigned male sex at birth; (3) identify primarily as Black, African American, or with any other racial/ethnic identity across the African diaspora (e.g., Afro-Caribbean, African, etc.); (4) be between the ages of 18 and 29 inclusive; (5) identify as gay, bisexual, queer, same-gender-loving, or another non-heterosexual identity, or report having had any sexual contact with a man in the last 3 months; (6) report having used a website or mobile app to find male partners for sexual activity in the last 3 months; and (7) reside in the United States.

2.2. Recruitment

A non-probability convenience sample of YSMBM were recruited using best practices for online survey sampling [66,67] between July 2017 and January 2018. Participants were primarily recruited through Facebook and Scruff, a mobile app for gay and bisexual men to meet one another for sex or dating. Prospective participants viewed advertisements for the study and clicked on a link embedded in the advertisement that directed them to the study webpage. Advertisements on Facebook were only made viewable to men in the targeted age range who lived in the United States. Facebook ads were further tailored to target individuals who (1) indicated that they were "interested in" men, or who omitted information on the gender in which they were interested; (2) indicated interest in various LGBTQ-related pages on Facebook; (3) matched Facebook's behavior algorithms for U.S. African American Multicultural Affinity; or (4) indicated interest in various pages related to popular Black culture.

2.3. Procedure

Prospective participants were directed to a survey hosted on Qualtrics upon clicking on the study advertisement. Participants were presented with a set of screening questions to determine their eligibility. Those who met the eligibility criteria were directed to a consent page, which contained detailed study information (i.e., purpose of the research, description of participant involvement, risk/discomforts; benefits; confidentiality, etc.). Those consenting to participate proceeded to the full survey which lasted 30 to 45 min. Participants were not compensated for taking the survey. While completing the survey, participants were permitted to save their answers and return to the survey at a later time if they were not able to complete it in a single sitting. Study data were kept in an encrypted and firewall-protected server, and the Institutional Review Board at the University of Michigan all study procedures.

2.4. Measures

Outcome Variables. The two dependent variables used in this study include Depressive Symptoms and Feelings of Self-Worth.

Depressive Symptoms. We measured depressive symptoms using the Center for Epidemiologic Studies Depression scale [68,69]. Participants were presented with a series of statements (e.g., 'I thought my life had been a failure') and were asked to indicate how often they have experienced each one. Each item was measured on a 4-point Likert scale ranging from 0 (Rarely or none of the time) to 3 (Most or all of the time). The mean of 20 items was computed to generate an overall CES-D score. Four items on the scale were reverse coded so that all responses were in directional alignment; higher scores indicate higher self-reported levels of depressive symptoms in the past week. The Cronbach's alpha value for depressive symptoms demonstrated excellent reliability ($\alpha = 0.920$).

Feelings of Self-Worth. We measured self-worth using the Feelings of Self-Worth Measure [70]. Participants were asked to indicate the degree to which they agree with a series of statements (e.g., 'I feel good about myself right now'). Each item was measured on a 9-point Likert scale ranging from 0 (Not at all) to 8 (Extremely). The mean of 14 items was computed to generate a self-worth score. Seven items on the scale were reverse coded so that all responses were in directional alignment; higher scores indicate higher self-reported feelings of self-worth. The Cronbach's alpha value for feelings of self-worth demonstrated excellent reliability ($\alpha = 0.950$).

Moderator Variables. We measured two dimensions of ethnic identity using the Multiethnic Identity Measure (MEIM) [37]. Participants were asked to indicate the degree to which they agreed with a series of statements (e.g., 'In order to learn more about my ethnic background, I have often talked to other people about my ethnic group;' 'I feel a strong attachment towards my own ethnic group'). Each item was measured on a 4-point Likert scale ranging from 1 (Strongly disagree) to 4 (Strongly agree). For the first subscale, the mean of 5 items was computed to generate an ethnic identity search (EIS) score. For the second subscale, the mean of 7 items was computed to generate an ethnic identity commitment (EIC) score. Higher scores indicate higher self-reported ethnic identity for each subscale. The Cronbach's alpha value for EIS ($\alpha = 0.780$) and EIC ($\alpha = 0.907$) demonstrated acceptable to excellent reliability.

Covariates. The covariates in this study include self-perceived sexual attractiveness, perceived rejection, mobile app/website use for partner seeking, and four sociodemographic variables (age, relationship status, HIV status, and educational attainment). Sexual orientation is reported for descriptive purposes only.

Self-Perceived Sexual Attractiveness. We measured Self-Perceived Sexual Attractiveness (SPSA) using the SPSA scale [71]. Participants were asked to indicate the degree to which they agreed with a series of statements (e.g., 'I believe I can elicit sexual desire in other people'). Each item was measured on a 7-point Likert scale ranging from 1 (Strongly disagree) to 7 (Strongly agree). The mean of 6 items was computed to generate an SPSA score. Higher scores indicate higher self-reported levels of SPSA. The Cronbach's alpha value for SPSA demonstrated excellent reliability ($\alpha = 0.951$).

Perceived Rejection. We measured sensitivity to rejection using the Perceived Rejection Scale [72]. Participants were asked to indicate the degree to which a series of statements was true at the immediate moment (e.g., 'I am accepted by others'). Each item was measured on a 5-point Likert scale ranging from 0 (Not at all) to 4 (Extremely). The mean of 4 items was computed to generate a perceived rejection score. Two items on the scale were reverse coded so that all responses were in directional alignment; higher scores indicate higher self-reported levels of perceived rejection. The Cronbach's alpha value for perceived rejection demonstrated acceptable reliability ($\alpha = 0.761$).

Sociodemographics. Participants were instructed to enter their numerical age. Participants could indicate a response of 'yes' or 'no' when asked if they were single and when asked if they have ever tested positive for HIV. Frequency of mobile app/website use to find partners was measured using a 6-point Likert scale containing the following values:

1 = 'Once a month or less;' 2 = '2–3 times a month;' 3 = 'About once a week;' 4 = '2–6 times a week;' 5 = 'About once a day;' 6 = 'More than once a day.' Educational attainment was measured using a 5-point Likert scale containing the following values: 1 = 'Less than high school;' 2 = 'High school graduate;' 3 = 'Some college;' 4 = 'College graduate;' 5 = 'Post College.' Finally, participants could select one of 11 sexual orientation categories (e.g., Gay, Bisexual, Queer, etc.)

Independent Variables. Data were collected on participants' self-reported experiences of sexual racism using the Racialized Sexual Discrimination Scale (RSDS) [30]. Each experience on the scale has two corresponding items: one that captures the effect (i.e., to what degree the experience has a negative effect on the participant) and the frequency (i.e., how often a participant encounters the experience). Experiences described on the scale could occur in one of two contexts: partner browsing (i.e., viewing user profiles on mobile apps/websites) and partner negotiation (i.e., written communication between users on mobile apps/websites). Items within the partner browsing context were measured on a 5-point Likert scale ranging from 0 (Strongly disagree) to 4 (Strongly agree). Items within the partner negotiation context were measured on a 6-point Likert scale ranging from 0 (I have not contacted this group) to 5 (Strongly agree).

The effect and frequency scores for each item within the partner browsing context were multiplied to develop an impact score, ranging from 0 to 16. This impact score was divided by 16 and multiplied by 100 to result in a final impact score for each partner browsing item, ranging from 0 to 100. Likewise, the effect and frequency scores for each item within the partner negotiation context were multiplied to develop an impact score, ranging from 0 to 25. For ease of interpretation, this impact score was divided by 25 and multiplied by 100 to result in a final impact score for each partner negotiation item, ranging from 0 to 100. Subsequently, all partner browsing and partner negotiation item impact scores ranged from 0 to 100, where higher scores indicate higher overall impact of RSD.

White Superiority, White Physical Objectification, and Same-Race Rejection. The White superiority subscale score was computed using the mean of 8 impact items (e.g., 'When White people clearly state that they want to meet other White people, I have a negative reaction'). The White physical objectification subscale score was computed using the mean of 2 impact items (e.g., 'How often do White people express a desire for a specific physical trait related to your race/ethnicity?'). The same-race rejection subscale score was computed using the mean of 2 impact items (e.g., 'How often are your messages ignored by people of your own race/ethnicity?). The Cronbach's alpha value for White superiority ($\alpha = 0.833$), White physical objectification ($\alpha = 0.857$), and same-race rejection ($\alpha = 0.851$) demonstrated strong reliability.

2.5. Data Analytic Strategy

A total of 2188 eligible and consenting participants were recruited for the study. Participants with missing data were excluded, resulting in a final analytic sample of 690 participants. Descriptive statistics were computed for the study sample, including mean scores, frequency counts, and percentages for demographic characteristics and study variables. Moderation analyses were conducted using the PROCESS Macro in SPSS [73]. The moderating effect of EIS and EIC on the association between five RSD subscales and two indicators of psychological health (depression and self-worth) was examined. Participants' sociodemographic characteristics (age, education level, HIV-status, relationship status) and relevant behavioral/psychosocial characteristics (frequency of app/website use for partner seeking, sensitivity to rejection, and self-perceived sexual attractiveness) were modeled as covariates. In total, twelve hierarchical linear regression models were estimated (three for depression and EIS, three for depression and EIC; three for self-worth and EIS, and three for self-worth and EIC). Using the PROCESS analysis output, A simple slope graph was plotted to visualize the conditional effects for all significant interactions.

3. Results

3.1. Sample Description

The median survey completion time was 33.93 min. The mean age of the sample was 24.47 years (*SD* = 3.18), and most study participants (85.9%) were single. The majority of participants identified as gay (71.2%) or bisexual (16.1%), and a little more than one-eighth of the sample (14.5%) reported being HIV-positive. Nearly one-third of the sample (30.3%) had completed a college degree and more than one-eighth of the sample (15.7%) had received a post-graduate education. Slightly more than two-fifths of the sample (42.6%) had received some college education and only one participant had not completed high school. Participants varied in their app usage, with approximately a quarter of participants (26.1%) reporting a minimum of once-a-day usage, and nearly half of participants (45.6%) reporting less than once-a-week usage. Participants reported moderate levels of self-worth (*M* = 5.56) and low-to-moderate depressive symptoms (*M* = 1.05). Participants also reported low-to-moderate perceived rejection (*M* = 1.49) and moderate to high self-perceived sexual attractiveness (*M* = 5.06). Participants reported overall high ethnic identity search (*M* = 3.08) and commitment (*M* = 3.28) scores on the MEIM (see Table 1).

Table 1. Descriptive Statistics for Study Sample.

Categorical Variables	*n* (*M*)	% (*SD*)			
Sexual Orientation					
Gay	491	71.2%			
Bisexual	111	16.1%			
Other	90	12.7%			
Education					
Less than high school	1	0.1%			
High school graduate	78	11.3%			
Some college	294	42.6%			
College graduate	209	30.3%			
Post college	108	15.7%			
App Use					
Once a month or less	183	26.5%			
2–3 times a month	132	19.1%			
About once a week	74	10.7%			
2–6 times a week	121	17.5%			
About once a day	64	9.3%			
More than once a day	116	16.8%			
Relationship Status (single)	593	85.9%			
HIV Status (positive)	100	14.5%			
Continuous Variables	*M*	*SD*	**Min**	**Max**	α
Age	24.47	3.18	18	29	—
Perceived Rejection	1.49	0.81	0	4	0.761
Perceived Attractiveness	5.06	1.62	1	7	0.951
Moderator Variables					
EI Commitment	3.28	0.63	1	4	0.907
EI Search	3.08	0.64	1	4	0.780
Dependent Variables					
Depressive Symptoms	1.05	0.63	0	2.90	0.920
Feelings of Self-Worth	5.56	1.87	0	8	0.950
RSD Subscales					
White Superiority	32.03	18.42	0	87.5	0.833
Same-Race Rejection	26.55	16.71	0	100	0.851
White Physical Obj.	39.13	27.69	0	100	0.857

3.2. Regression Analyses

3.2.1. White Superiority

Higher scores on White superiority were associated with higher depressive symptoms in both the EIS ($b = 0.003$, $p < 0.01$, 95% CI [0.001, 0.006]) and EIC models ($b = 0.004$, $p < 0.01$, 95% CI [0.001, 0.006]). Higher scores on EIC were associated with lower depressive symptoms ($b = -0.104$, $p < 0.01$, 95% CI [−0.172, −0.037]) and higher feelings of self-worth ($b = 0.462$, $p < 0.001$, 95% CI [0.272, 0.652]). No significant interaction effects were observed between White superiority and ethnic identity. All four White superiority models were significant ($p < 0.001$) and explained 26–36% of the variance in depressive symptoms and self-worth (see Table 2).

3.2.2. Same-Race Rejection

Higher scores on same-race rejection were associated with higher depressive symptoms in both the EIS ($b = 0.005$, $p < 0.001$, 95% CI [0.003, 0.008]) and EIC models ($b = 0.006$, $p < 0.01$, 95% CI [0.003, 0.008]). Higher scores on EIC were associated with lower depressive symptoms ($b = -0.106$, $p < 0.01$, 95% CI [−0.173, −0.038]) and higher feelings of self-worth ($b = 0.472$, $p < 0.001$, 95% CI [0.283, 0.661]). A significant interaction effect was observed in the self-worth and EIC model ($b = -0.013$, $p < 0.01$, 95% CI [−0.023, −0.003]), with results indicating that EIC exacerbated the association between same-race rejection and feelings of self-worth. Figure 1 displays the conditional effects of same-race rejection on self-worth at low, moderate, and high levels of EIC. Participants who reported high levels of EIC ($b = -0.015$, $p < 0.01$, 95% CI [−0.025, −0.004]) scored significantly lower on feelings of self-worth. Moderate and low levels of EIC did not significantly modify this association. All four same-race rejection models were significant ($p < 0.001$) and explained 26–37% of the variance in depressive symptoms and self-worth (see Table 3).

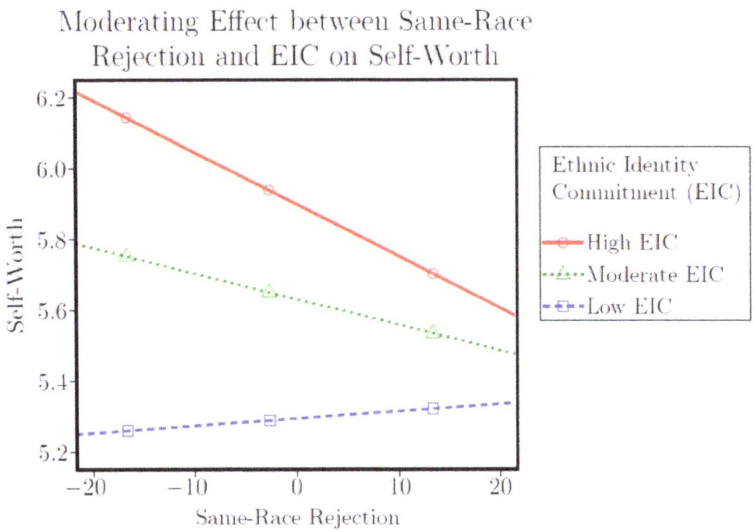

Figure 1. Effect of Same-Race Rejection X EIC on Self-Worth.

Table 2. White Superiority and Ethnic Identity on Depression and Self-Worth.

	Depression & EIS				Self-Worth & EIS				Depression & EIC				Self-Worth & EIC			
	b	*SE*	LL	UL	*b*	*SE*	LL	UL	*b*	*SE*	LL	UL	*b*	*SE*	LL	UL
(Constant)	1.677 ***	0.238	1.210	2.144	3.270 ***	0.673	1.949	4.591	1.672 ***	0.236	1.208	2.136	3.267 ***	0.663	1.966	4.568
Covariates																
Age	−0.025 ***	0.008	−0.010	−0.011	0.059 **	0.021	0.017	0.101	−0.026 ***	0.007	−0.040	−0.011	0.059 **	0.021	0.018	0.099
Education	−0.023	0.027	−0.075	0.029	0.003	0.075	−0.144	0.150	−0.019	0.026	−0.070	0.032	−0.002	0.073	−0.146	0.141
HIV+	0.015	0.060	−0.103	0.133	−0.198	0.170	−0.532	0.136	−0.009	0.060	−0.127	0.109	−0.108	0.169	−0.440	0.223
App Use	0.016	0.012	−0.006	0.039	−0.052	0.033	−0.117	0.012	0.015	0.012	−0.008	0.037	−0.045	0.032	−0.109	0.018
Single	−0.054	0.061	−0.174	0.065	0.068	0.171	−0.268	0.405	−0.047	0.060	−0.165	0.072	0.049	0.170	−0.284	0.382
PR	0.256 ***	0.030	0.198	0.315	−0.576 ***	0.085	−0.741	−0.410	0.253 ***	0.030	0.194	0.311	−0.555 ***	0.083	−0.719	−0.391
SPSA	−0.070 ***	0.015	−0.100	−0.041	0.436 ***	0.042	0.353	0.519	−0.062 ***	0.015	−0.091	−0.032	0.404 ***	0.042	0.321	0.486
Predictors																
WS	0.003 **	0.002	0.001	0.006	−0.004	0.004	−0.011	0.003	0.004 **	0.001	0.001	0.006	−0.004	0.003	−0.011	0.002
EIS	−0.030	0.034	−0.098	0.037	0.182	0.097	−0.009	0.373								
EIC									−0.104 **	0.035	−0.172	−0.037	0.462 ***	0.097	0.272	0.652
Interactions																
WS × EIS	−0.003	0.002	−0.006	0.000	0.005	0.005	−0.005	0.015								
WS × EIC									−0.002	0.002	−0.005	−0.001	0.002	0.005	−0.007	0.010
Model fit	R^2 = 0.263, MSE = 0.295 *F* (10,679) = 24.225 *** R^2 change = 0.0033 *F* (1679) = 3.074				R^2 = 0.337, MSE = 2.361 *F* (10,679) = 34.589 *** R^2 change = 0.0011 *F* (1679) = 1.102				R^2 = 0.270, MSE = 0.292 *F* (10,679) = 25.137 *** R^2 change = 0.0015 *F* (1679) = 1.442				R^2 = 0.355, MSE = 2.298 *F* (10,679) = 37.384 *** R^2 change = 0.0001 *F* (1679) = 0.112			

Notes. *b* = unstandardized regression coefficients, *SE* = standard error, LL = low limit, UL = upper limit, PR = Perceived Rejection, SPSA = Self-Perceived Sexual Attractiveness, WS = White Superiority, EIS = Ethnic Identity Search, EIC = Ethnic Identity Commitment. Referent groups are being in a relationship (Single); negative HIV status (HIV+). ** $p < 0.01$; *** $p < 0.001$.

Table 3. Same-Race Rejection and Ethnic Identity on Depression and Self-Worth.

	Depression & EIS				Self-Worth & EIS				Depression & EIC				Self-Worth & EIC			
	b	*SE*	LL	UL	*b*	*SE*	LL	UL	*b*	*SE*	LL	UL	*b*	*SE*	LL	UL
(Constant)	1.604 ***	0.237	1.138	2.071	3.345 ***	0.675	2.020	4.670	1.599 ***	0.235	1.137	2.061	3.420 ***	0.661	2.122	4.719
Covariates																
Age	−0.026 ***	0.008	−0.040	−0.011	0.059 **	0.021	0.018	0.101	−0.025 ***	0.007	−0.040	−0.010	0.054 **	0.021	0.013	0.095
Education	−0.013	0.026	−0.065	0.038	−0.008	0.075	−0.155	0.138	−0.014	0.026	−0.064	0.037	0.005	0.073	−0.138	0.147
HIV+	0.037	0.060	−0.081	0.155	−0.216	0.170	−0.551	0.118	0.016	0.060	−0.101	0.134	−0.135	0.168	−0.465	0.195
App Use	0.017	0.012	0.005	0.040	−0.055	0.033	−0.120	0.009	0.015	0.011	−0.008	0.037	−0.046	0.032	−0.110	0.017
Single	−0.039	0.061	−0.158	0.080	0.062	0.173	−0.277	0.400	−0.037	0.060	−0.155	0.082	0.058	0.169	−0.274	0.390
PR	0.245 ***	0.030	0.185	0.304	−0.575 ***	0.086	−0.743	−0.406	0.240 ***	0.030	0.181	0.299	−0.557 ***	0.084	−0.722	−0.392
SPSA	−0.070 ***	0.015	−0.099	−0.042	0.439 ***	0.042	0.357	0.521	−0.062 ***	0.015	−0.091	−0.033	0.402 ***	0.042	0.320	0.484
Predictors																
SRR	0.005 ***	0.001	0.003	0.008	−0.004	0.004	−0.011	0.004	0.006 ***	0.001	0.003	0.008	−0.005	0.004	−0.013	0.002
EIS	−0.021	0.034	−0.087	0.044	0.159	0.095	−0.028	0.346								
EIC									−0.106 **	0.034	−0.173	−0.038	0.472 ***	0.096	0.283	0.661
Interactions																
SRR × EIS	0.001	0.002	−0.003	−0.004	−0.000	0.005	−0.011	−0.010								
SRR × EIC									0.003	0.002	−0.001	0.006	−0.013 **	0.005	−0.023	−0.003
Model fit	R^2 = 0.269, MSE = 0.293 F (10,679) = 24.995 *** R^2 change = 0.0001 F (1679) = 0.132				R^2 = 0.336, MSE = 2.365 F (10,679) = 34.401 *** R^2 change = 0.0000 F (1679) = 0.004				R^2 = 0.280, MSE = 0.288 F (10,679) = 26.458 *** R^2 change = 0.0024 F (1679) = 2.310				R^2 = 0.361, MSE = 2.276 F (10,679) = 38.424 *** R^2 change = 0.0067 F (1679) = 7.093 **			

Notes. *b* = unstandardized regression coefficients, *SE* = standard error, LL = low limit, UL = upper limit, PR = Perceived Rejection, SPSA = Self-Perceived Sexual Attractiveness, SRR = Same-Race Rejection, EIS = Ethnic Identity Search, EIC = Ethnic Identity Commitment. Referent groups are being in a relationship (Single); negative HIV status (HIV+). ** $p < 0.01$; *** $p < 0.001$.

3.2.3. White Physical Objectification

Higher scores on White physical objectification were associated with higher depressive symptoms in both the EIS ($b = 0.003$, $p < 0.001$, 95% CI [0.001, 0.005]) and EIC models ($b = 0.003$, $p < 0.001$, 95% CI [0.002, 0.005]). Higher scores on White physical objectification were also associated with lower feelings of self-worth in both the EIS ($b = -0.005$, $p < 0.05$, 95% CI [−0.009, −0.000]) and EIC models ($b = -0.006$, $p < 0.05$, 95% CI [−0.010, −0.001]). Higher scores on EIC were associated with lower depressive symptoms ($b = -0.120$, $p < 0.001$, 95% CI [−0.189, −0.052]) and higher feelings of self-worth ($b = 0.493$, $p < 0.001$, 95% CI [0.301, 0.685]). A significant interaction effect was observed in the depression and EIC model ($b = -0.002$, $p < 0.05$, 95% CI [−0.005, 0.000]), with results indicating that EIC attenuated the association between White physical objectification and depressive symptoms. Figure 2 displays the conditional effects of White physical objectification on depressive symptoms at low, moderate, and high levels of EIC. Participants who reported moderate ($b = 0.003$, $p < 0.001$, 95% CI [0.001, 0.004]) and high ($b = 0.005$, $p < 0.001$, 95% CI [0.002, 0.007]) levels of EIC scored significantly lower on depressive symptoms. Low levels of EIC did not significantly modify this association. All four White physical objectification models were significant ($p < 0.001$) and explained 26–36% of the variance in depressive symptoms and self-worth (see Table 4).

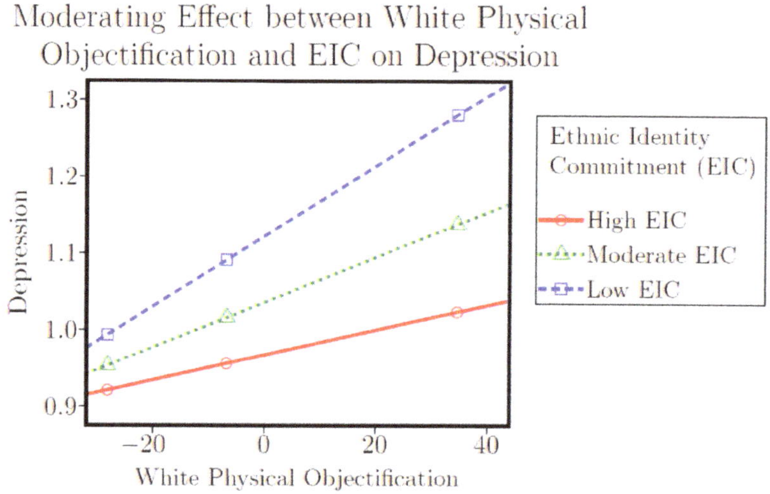

Figure 2. Effect of White Physical Objectification X EIC on Depression.

3.2.4. Covariates

Age, perceived rejection, and self-perceived sexual attractiveness were significant across all twelve regression models. No other covariates emerged as significant. Across all models, age was associated with lower depressive symptoms ($p < 0.001$) and higher feelings of self-worth ($p < 0.01$); perceived rejection was associated with higher depressive symptoms ($p < 0.001$) and lower feelings of self-worth ($p < 0.001$); and self-perceived sexual attractiveness was associated with lower depressive symptoms ($p < 0.001$) and higher feelings of self-worth ($p < 0.001$).

Table 4. White Physical Objectification and Ethnic Identity on Depression and Self-Worth.

	Depression & EIS				Self-Worth & EIS				Depression & EIC				Self-Worth & EIC			
	b	*SE*	LL	UL	*b*	*SE*	LL	UL	*b*	*SE*	LL	UL	*b*	*SE*	LL	UL
(Constant)	1.720 ***	0.238	1.253	2.187	3.225 ***	0.674	1.902	4.548	1.734 ***	0.236	1.271	2.197	3.210 ***	0.663	1.908	4.511
Covariates																
Age	−0.027 ***	0.008	−0.041	−0.012	0.060 **	0.021	0.018	0.102	−0.026 ***	0.007	−0.041	−0.012	0.058 **	0.021	0.018	0.099
Education	−0.023	0.026	−0.074	0.029	0.002	0.075	−0.144	0.148	−0.023	0.026	−0.074	0.028	0.003	0.073	−0.140	0.146
HIV+	0.026	0.060	−0.091	0.144	−0.210	0.170	−0.543	0.123	0.001	0.060	−0.116	0.119	−0.120	0.168	−0.450	0.210
App Use	0.015	0.012	−0.007	0.038	−0.049	0.033	−0.114	0.015	00.13	0.012	−0.010	0.035	−0.040	0.032	−0.104	0.023
Single	−0.074	0.060	−0.193	0.044	0.091	0.171	−0.250	0.427	−0.066	0.060	−0.183	0.052	0.070	0.168	−0.261	0.400
PR	0.262 ***	0.029	0.205	0.320	−0.576 ***	0.083	−0.739	−0.412	0.255 ***	0.029	0.197	0.312	−0.547 ***	0.032	−0.708	−0.385
SPSA	−0.079 ***	0.015	−0.103	−0.045	0.439 ***	0.042	0.358	0.521	−0.065 ***	0.015	−0.095	−0.036	0.406 ***	0.042	0.325	0.488
Predictors																
WO	0.003 ***	0.001	0.001	0.005	−0.005 *	0.002	−0.009	−0.000	0.003 ***	0.001	0.002	0.005	−0.006 *	0.002	−0.010	−0.001
EIS	−0.037	0.034	−0.105	0.030	0.198 *	0.097	0.007	0.388								
EIC									−0.120 ***	0.035	−0.189	−0.052	0.493 ***	0.098	0.301	0.685
Interactions																
WO × EIS	−0.002	0.001	−0.005	0.000	0.002	0.003	−0.005	0.008								
WO × EIC									−0.002 *	0.001	−0.005	0.000	0.000	0.003	−0.006	0.007
Model fit	R^2 = 0.269, MSE = 0.293 *F* (10,679) = 24.929 *** R^2 change = 0.0041 *F* (1679) = 3.801				R^2 = 0.340, MSE = 2.354 *F* (10,679) = 34.916 *** R^2 change = 0.0003 *F* (1679) = 0.298				R^2 = 0.280, MSE = 0.289 *F* (10,679) = 26.379 *** R^2 change = 0.0042 *F* (1679) = 4.006 *				R^2 = 0.360, MSE = 2.282 *F* (10,679) = 38.132 *** R^2 change = 0.0000 *F* (1679) = 0.003			

Notes. *b* = unstandardized regression coefficients, *SE* = standard error, LL = low limit, UL = upper limit, PR = Perceived Rejection, SPSA = Self-Perceived Sexual Attractiveness, WO = White Objectification, EIS = Ethnic Identity Search, EIC = Ethnic Identity Commitment. Referent groups are being in a relationship (Single); negative HIV status (HIV+). * $p < 0.05$; ** $p < 0.01$; *** $p < 0.001$.

4. Discussion

This study aimed to examine ethnic identity as a moderator of the association between RSD and psychological well-being among a large sample of YSMBM. Researchers have provided substantial evidence for the protective qualities of ethnic identity, but some researchers have also reported that certain aspects of ethnic identity may exacerbate the effects of certain racialized stressors [39,40,43,58,59]. We estimated twelve hierarchical linear regression models in total, using three RSD subscales, two psychological well-being outcomes, and two subscales of ethnic identity. We hypothesized that ethnic identity commitment would attenuate the association between RSD and well-being, while ethnic identity exploration would exacerbate the association between RSD and well-being.

4.1. Main Effects

All study covariates performed identically to previous main effects analyses examining the relationship between RSD and psychological well-being. We discuss the implications of these associations at length in prior published work [31]. In addition, all three RSD subscales were associated with poorer psychological well-being (**H1**), consistent with our prior work, as well as other scholars' work examining sexual racism among sexual minority men of color [24–29].

Participants reported overall moderate to high scores on both ethnic identity subscales. This coincides with extensive research showing that Black sexual minority individuals tend to identify strongly with their racial/ethnic identity [56,74]. The identity commitment subscale was significantly associated with higher feelings of self-worth and lower depressive symptoms in all twelve models. The identity search subscale, however, was significantly associated with higher feelings of self-worth, but only in the White physical objectification model; it failed to achieve significance in the other eleven models. These findings are consistent with prior research indicating that the sense of belonging, pride, and commitment towards one's ethnic background appears to be health promotive for Black Americans [47,49,51]. By comparison, the fewer significant findings for identity search suggest that this particular aspect of ethnic identity is not as strongly associated with positive psychological well-being, which has been reported in prior research [39,46]. While other researchers have indicated that identity search may, in fact, be associated with less psychological distress, many of these studies have only investigated identity search in a composite measure combined with other aspects of identity, and/or have only noted these associations among participants who do not identify as Black [45,75–79]. For YSMBM, our findings indicate that ethnic identity search may have limited bearing on depressive symptoms or feelings of self-worth in the context of RSD.

4.2. Moderation Effects

Contrary to our hypothesis (**H2**), higher scores on identity search did not significantly exacerbate the association between RSD and psychological well-being in any model. Although our findings do not support the prior theoretical and empirical work in which we grounded our hypothesis [39,40,43,80], it is nevertheless encouraging that a factor thought to exacerbate racial stress may be inconsequential among YSMBM—at least with respect to the health outcomes under investigation. As previously discussed, ethnic identity search is not inherently negative, though the rationale behind predicting an exacerbation effect is well situated when *uncertainty* is thought to be the underlying component of exploration. Scholars have noted, however, that certain aspects of identity that have a more definitive positive valence (e.g., identity commitment), are not only highly correlated with identity search, but may have a reciprocal relationship with identity search [81]. For example, having a firm commitment to one's ethnic identity may encourage individuals to explore more about their ethnic group heritage; conversely, through the process of exploring one's background, individuals may arrive at a stronger sense of commitment. These two closely related aspects of identity are part of the reason why the MEIM is so often used as a composite measure in ethnic identity research. When disaggregated, however, researchers are able to parse out the effects of these two related but distinct constructs. In the process, it has come to light that identity search may not necessarily have the same protective qualities as identity commitment, and may in fact exacerbate a stressor—or, in our case, exert no influence at all. Altogether, our findings offer additional clarity on how ethnic identity search operates in the context of RSD as experienced by YSMBM.

In contrast to our null findings for identity search, our results do suggest that identity commitment may significantly modify the relationship between RSD and psychological well-being. Moderate to high levels of commitment buffered the association between White physical objectification and depressive symptoms among the study sample, thus partially supporting one of our central hypothesis (**H3**). This is consistent with prior research illustrating that ethnic identity may serve as a potential safeguard against racialized stress [38–40,46,51,54,55], and may therefore be of interest to mental health scholars/practitioners who work with YSMBM. Being physically objectified by White men is not only one of the most dominant themes in the broader discourse on sexual racism [14,15,82–84], but this subscale also had the largest effect size of any RSD subscale in our original main effects analysis [31]. Thus, identifying and strengthening factors that may mitigate the adverse effects of White physical objectification may be a priority area for sexual racism researchers and interventionists.

Although the buffering hypothesis received partial support, our moderation results did reveal an unexpected finding: identity commitment exacerbated the association between same-race rejection and lower feelings of self-worth, rendering this interaction significant for participants who reported high levels of commitment. Though contrary to our hypothesis, this does coincide with some literature indicating that certain aspects of ethnic identity (e.g., centrality of identity, affective identity pride) may exacerbate the effects of racial discrimination [85–87]. Moreover, prior scholarship has predominantly focused on the protective qualities of ethnic identity commitment using measures of discrimination that do not distinguish between in-group and out-group discrimination [55,88–90]. The role of ethnic identity in response to in-group discrimination is likely more complex, and, to our knowledge, has not been investigated quantitatively among YSMBM, nor within the context of intimate partner seeking in general. In our earlier qualitative work, YSMBM expressed complicated feelings with respect to being rejected by members of their same race or from other racial/ethnic minority men, ranging from bewilderment to despondency and disbelief [65]. It is possible that YSMBM who experience a strong sense of ethnic identity may put greater stock into being accepted by other Black men, or generally expect that Black men would be more likely to desire them as a partner; thus, they may be more negatively impacted by experiencing rejection from them. In contrast, YSMBM with a lower sense of commitment to their ethnic identity may place less value on being selected as a mate by other Black men, and are therefore less significantly impacted if/when they experience rejection from them. Ultimately, a key takeaway from these findings is that certain aspects of identity—even those that are conceptualized as inherently positive—may not behave in a uniform manner in the presence of discrimination. The ways in which identity serves to buffer or exacerbate the effects of identity-related stress may be contingent upon the specific nature of the stressor, as well the source of that stress.

4.3. Implications

These findings contribute to a growing body of research into the associations between ethnic identity and well-being among sexual minority people of color [56,91], and may have important implications for individual and group-level interventions. It may be critical for clinicians who work with YSMBM to engage, affirm, and leverage ethnic belonging in facing objectification and other forms of discrimination from White men. Clinical approaches based on cognitive behavioral therapy (CBT) may be particularly helpful in enabling YSMBM to leverage their sense of ethnic belonging when coping with RSD. Many researchers have adapted CBT for Black clients and for sexual minority clients, and it has proven effective in helping clients cope with discrimination [92–96]. However, research on CBT as an intervention for discrimination among sexual minority people of color is in its infancy. In a recent pilot test, Jackson et al. tested a CBT-informed group therapy intervention for coping with intersectional stigmas among Black and Latino sexual minority men [93]. Most participants reported improvements in mental health symptoms—including anxiety, depression, and suicidality—and many reported decreased identity-related stress. Such interventions may be applied in clinical settings to address experiences of RSD, and may also integrate ethnic identity as a component of the treatment process.

YSMBM with high ethnic identity commitment may require support in grappling with same-race rejection while maintaining the overall benefits of ethnic identity commitment. Critical consciousness interventions, which support participants in understanding and opposing oppressive forces, may help them to understand interpersonal discrimination in terms of broader structures of White supremacy. Various researchers have advocated for critical consciousness interventions in addressing racism and other forms of oppression [97,98]. In a recent study, Goodkind et al. evaluated a critical consciousness program for Black girls in high school. The program was designed to enhance participants' well-being, as well as their capacity to engage in critical reflection related to race- and gender-related stress [99]. The researchers found that participants were more likely to reframe racist encounters as an injustice rather than internalizing these experiences, and participants were also motivated to organize amongst themselves to address racially mediated mistreatment. Critical consciousness programs such as these could address RSD through analysis of the objectification of Black men in popular media, or exploration of same-race discrimination as a facet of White supremacy throughout American history. Successful critical consciousness interventions focused on RSD may, in turn, enhance YSMBM's self-efficacy to confront, resist, or subvert patterns of discrimination perpetuated in online settings through individual or collective action.

Critical consciousness interventions are not limited to those who are subject to oppression, but may also be fostered among health professionals and clinical practitioners. A robust cultivation of critical consciousness on the part of clinicians may enable them to more effectively engage with YSMBM, and help them navigate complex intersectional stressors that they encounter in intimate partner-seeking contexts [100]. Moreover, cultural competency and cultural humility training remains imperative for practitioners, particularly those who do not hold sexual or racial/ethnic minority identities [101,102]. Altogether, effective clinical interventions that engage with RSD and ethnic identity call for a high degree of critical awareness, sensitivity, and reflexivity on the part of providers.

5. Strengths and Limitations

To our knowledge, this is the first study to examine ethnic identity as a moderator of the association between RSD and psychological well-being among YSMBM. It is also among the first to examine the association between ethnic identity and feelings of self-worth and depressive symptoms in any sexual minority population. Our disaggregation of the search and commitment subscales of the MEIM adds further clarity to the ethnic identity literature, as the majority of studies using the MEIM use the scale as a composite measure [40]. The study's large national sample and the breadth of the RSD scale in measuring various forms of discrimination were also significant strengths. Notably, the RSD scale used in this study distinguishes between expressions of discrimination to a greater degree than most measures of discrimination. This distinction between race of perpetrator is rare in research on RSD, and thus constitutes a unique contribution to the field.

This study, however, is not without its limitations. The study's cross-sectional design and lack of representative sample limits generalizability, as well as our capacity to make causal inferences about the relationships between ethnic identity, RSD, and well-being among YSMBM. The study is further limited by its all-Black sample and by its focus on RSD as perpetrated by Black or White users online; thus, the findings cannot generalize to other racial/ethnic groups, nor can they provide insights into RSD as perpetuated by racial/ethnic groups other than Black or White men. The MEIM is also not without critique. The scale has been subject to revisions, including both expanding and shortening the 12-item version used in this study, and researchers have also reported slightly different factor solutions for the scale among different populations [81,103]. Moreover, competing theoretical frameworks of ethnic identity (e.g., social identity theory, self-categorization theory) and their corresponding measures could produce different results than reported here. To arrive a more robust understanding of ethnic identity and its role in the context of RSD, it will be important to consider different identity measures and apply different theoretical frameworks in future work.

6. Directions for Future Research

Although the health and social science literature on RSD has been largely qualitative, there are still many important questions about RSD that call for qualitative or mixed methodological approaches. Most qualitative research on RSD among sexual minority men has focused on the experience of discrimination, but only a handful of studies have focused on strengths for coping with RSD, including identity-based strengths [11,13,22]. Carefully designed qualitative studies will enable researchers to ascertain the types of strategies that sexual minority men of color are leveraging to mitigate the adverse effects of RSD, as well as identify other intrapersonal characteristics that may be protective in the context of RSD. Such studies may add important nuance to existing quantitative findings, inform future quantitative studies, and provide a foundation for intervention research and clinical application.

A closer examination of same-race rejection may be especially important for sexual racism researchers, particularly in light of our unexpected findings. Although commitment to one's ethnic identity exacerbates the effect of same-race rejection, its overall effect is positive, and YSMBM struggling in the face of same-race rejection are not likely to benefit from lessening their commitment. Given the complexity inherent in navigating this experience, it may be more beneficial to focus on the motivations of YSMBM who are inclined to reject members of their same race. As with other forms of internalized racism, perpetrators of same-race rejection are devalued by the same system of White supremacy in which they participate. However, only a small amount of research on RSD examines same-race discrimination [104–106]. Research on both in-group and out-group perpetrators of sexual racism has usually focused on refuting their actions or examining their pathology rather than on interventions that might change their actions and ideologies [5,13,107–109]. However, intervention research aiming to address general internalized racism has shown promise. In a recent pilot study, Banks et al. examined an acceptance commitment therapy (ACT) intervention designed to address internalized racism among Black women. They found decreases in internalized oppression, internalized shame, and negative psychological symptoms [110]. Similar interventions may be applicable to YSMBM, and researchers may wish to examine the degree to which such interventions reduce instances of same-race rejection in intimate partner-seeking contexts.

Future research should also examine ethnic identity, RSD, and health among other sexual minority men of color. Patterns of RSD may manifest differentially across different racial/ethnic groups (e.g., certain stereotypes and sexual scripts are ascribed to certain groups and not others), and some groups may respond differently to RSD than others. For some racial/ethnic minority groups, generational status—or recency of immigration—should also be examined in the context of RSD. Generational status may have some bearing on both self-reported ethnic identification and exposure to RSD over time [85,111,112]. Moreover, there is a large and complex literature base examining how acculturation and acculturative stress relate to experiences of discrimination and psychosocial functioning among Asian and Latino populations, and these processes may be distinct from the experiences of Black Americans [113–116]. Studies should also be conducted in other regional contexts, as racial hierarchies in other parts of the world are distinct from those in the United States [20,107].

Using intersectional identity measures (e.g., a measure of both racial/ethnic and sexual orientation identity in tandem) will also add important nuance to work of this nature moving forward. There is a marked deficit of intersectional measures for sexual and gender minority populations, but scholars have long highlighted the importance of examining overlapping identities instead of focusing on singular markers of identity [56,117–119]. An intersectional analysis will enable researchers to quantitatively model how specific intersecting identity statuses operate in the context of RSD—a key distinction when examining sexual minority men of color across multiple racial/ethnic groups. It will also be important to examine factors other than identity that may exert influence over the relationship between RSD and psychological well-being. Social support, for example, is widely regarded as a critical protective asset in the health literature [120–122]. However, there is limited research that explores how sexual minority men of color respond to instances of RSD, and/or if they seek out support networks to help process these experiences [4,6,25,123,124]. Understanding how social support operates in the context of RSD—both in terms of the presence and/or absence of support networks, as well as the active leveraging of support—may provide important avenues for intervention.

7. Conclusions

Overall, this study provides valuable insight into the relationship between ethnic identity, RSD, and psychological well-being. Moving forward, researchers should continue to account for factors that may further elucidate these relationships. They should also explore multi-pronged strategies to disrupt harmful behavior perpetrated online. RSD, like any form of racialist discrimination, is neither natural nor inevitable, and combatting racialist ideologies at their root remains critical to advance health equity for marginalized populations.

Author Contributions: Conceptualization, Methodology, Validation, Formal Analysis, Investigation, Data Curation, Supervision, and Project Administration, R.M.W.; Visualization, Resources, Writing (Original Draft Preparation), and Writing (Review and Editing), R.M.W. and M.M.P. All authors have read and agreed to the published version of the manuscript.

Funding: This research received no external funding.

Institutional Review Board Statement: The study was conducted according to the guidelines of the Declaration of Helsinki, and approved by the Institutional Review Board of University of Michigan (protocol code HUM00128829; May 2017).

Informed Consent Statement: Prior to any data collection, verbal and written informed consent were obtained from each participant.

Data Availability Statement: The data presented in this study are available on request from the corresponding author.

Conflicts of Interest: The authors declare no conflict of interest.

References

1. Anderson, M.; Vogels, E.A.; Turner, E. The Virtues and Downsides of Online Dating. Available online: https://www.pewresearch.org/internet/2020/02/06/the-virtues-and-downsides-of-online-dating/ (accessed on 9 July 2022).
2. Paz-Bailey, G.; Hoots, B.E.; Xia, M.; Finlayson, T.; Prejean, J.; Purcell, D.W. Trends in internet use among men who have sex with men in the United States. *J. Acquir. Immune Defic. Syndr.* **2017**, *75*, S288–S295. [CrossRef] [PubMed]
3. Gleason, N.; Serrano, P.A.; Muñoz, A.; French, A.L.; Hosek, S.G. Experiences of Online Racialized Sexual Discrimination among Sexual and Gender Minorities in the United States: Online Survey Data from Keeping It LITE. *J. Sex Res.* 2022, 1–6, *ahead of print*. [CrossRef]
4. Wade, R.M.; Harper, G.W. Racialized Sexual Discrimination (RSD) in the Age of Online Sexual Networking: Are Young Black Gay/Bisexual Men (YBGBM) at Elevated Risk for Adverse Psychological Health? *Am. J. Community Psychol.* **2019**, *65*, 504–523. [CrossRef] [PubMed]
5. Cascalheira, C.J.; Smith, B.A. Hierarchy of Desire: Partner Preferences and Social Identities of Men Who Have Sex with Men on Geosocial Networks. *Sex. Cult.* **2020**, *24*, 630–648. [CrossRef]

6. Han, C.-S.; Proctor, K.; Choi, K.-H. I Know a Lot of Gay Asian Men Who Are Actually Tops: Managing and Negotiating Gay Racial Stigma. *Sex. Cult.* **2014**, *18*, 219–234. [CrossRef]
7. Robinson, B.A. "Personal Preference" as the New Racism: Gay Desire and Racial Cleansing in Cyberspace. *Sociol. Race Ethn.* **2015**, *1*, 317–330. [CrossRef]
8. Robinson, R.K. Structural Dimensions of Romantic Preferences. *Fordam Law Rev.* **2008**, *76*, 2787–2819.
9. Rosengren, A.L.; Menza, T.W.; Legrand, S.; Muessig, K.E.; Bauermeister, J.; Hightow-Weidman, L.B. Stigma and Mobile App Use among Young Black Men Who Have Sex with Men. *AIDS Educ. Prev.* **2019**, *31*, 523–537. [CrossRef]
10. Calabrese, S.K.; Rosenberger, J.G.; Schick, V.R.; Novak, D.S. Pleasure, Affection, and Love Among Black Men Who Have Sex with Men (MSM) versus MSM of Other Races: Countering Dehumanizing Stereotypes via Cross-Race Comparisons of Reported Sexual Experience at Last Sexual Event. *Arch. Sex. Behav.* **2015**, *44*, 2001–2014. [CrossRef]
11. Hammack, P.L.; Grecco, B.; Wilson, B.D.M.; Meyer, I.H. "White, Tall, Top, Masculine, Muscular": Narratives of Intracommunity Stigma in Young Sexual Minority Men's Experience on Mobile Apps. *Arch. Sex. Behav.* **2021**, *51*, 2413–2428. [CrossRef]
12. Husbands, W.; Makoroka, L.; Walcott, R.; Adam, B.; George, C.; Remis, R.S.; Rourke, S.B. Black gay men as sexual subjects: Race, racialisation and the social relations of sex among Black gay men in Toronto. *Cult. Health Sex.* **2013**, *15*, 434–449. [CrossRef]
13. Stacey, L.; Forbes, T.D. Feeling Like a Fetish: Racialized Feelings, Fetishization, and the Contours of Sexual Racism on Gay Dating Apps. *J. Sex Res.* **2021**, *59*, 372–384. [CrossRef] [PubMed]
14. Teunis, N. Sexual objectification and the construction of whiteness in the gay male community. *Cult. Health Sex.* **2007**, *9*, 263–275. [CrossRef] [PubMed]
15. Wilson, P.A.; Valera, P.; Ventuneac, A.; Balan, I.; Rowe, M.; Carballo-Diéguez, A. Race-Based Sexual Stereotyping and Sexual Partnering Among Men Who Use the Internet to Identify Other Men for Bareback Sex. *J. Sex Res.* **2009**, *46*, 399–413. [CrossRef] [PubMed]
16. Bedi, S. Sexual Racism: Intimacy as a Matter of Justice. *J. Politi.* **2015**, *77*, 998–1011. [CrossRef]
17. Han, C.W. *Racial Erotics: Gay Men of Color, Sexual Racism, and the Politics of Desire*; University of Washington Press: Seattle, WA, USA, 2021. ISBN 978-0-295-74910-5.
18. Stember, C.H. *Sexual Racism: The Emotional Barrier to an Integrated Society*; Elsevier: New York, NY, USA, 1976. ISBN 978-0-444-99034-1.
19. Abbate, C. Racialized Sexual Discrimination: A Moral Right or Morally Wrong? In *The Palgrave Handbook of Sexual Ethics*; Boonin, D., Ed.; Springer International Publishing: Cham, Switzerland, 2022; pp. 421–436. ISBN 978-3-030-87786-6.
20. Callander, D.; Holt, M.; Newman, C. Just a preference: Racialised language in the sex-seeking profiles of gay and bisexual men. *Cult. Health Sex.* **2012**, *14*, 1049–1063. [CrossRef] [PubMed]
21. Callander, D.; Newman, C.E.; Holt, M. Is Sexual Racism Really Racism? Distinguishing Attitudes Toward Sexual Racism and Generic Racism Among Gay and Bisexual Men. *Arch. Sex. Behav.* **2015**, *44*, 1991–2000. [CrossRef] [PubMed]
22. Callander, D.; Holt, M.; Newman, C.E. 'Not everyone's gonna like me': Accounting for race and racism in sex and dating web services for gay and bisexual men. *Ethnicities* **2016**, *16*, 3–21. [CrossRef]
23. Han, C.-S.; Ayala, G.; Paul, J.P.; Boylan, R.; Gregorich, S.E.; Choi, K.-H. Stress and Coping with Racism and Their Role in Sexual Risk for HIV Among African American, Asian/Pacific Islander, and Latino Men Who Have Sex with Men. *Arch. Sex. Behav.* **2015**, *44*, 411–420. [CrossRef]
24. Brennan, D.J.; Asakura, K.; George, C.; Newman, P.A.; Giwa, S.; Hart, T.; Souleymanov, R.; Betancourt, G. "Never reflected anywhere": Body image among ethnoracialized gay and bisexual men. *Body Image* **2013**, *10*, 389–398. [CrossRef]
25. English, D.; Hickson, D.A.; Callander, D.; Goodman, M.S.; Duncan, D.T. Racial Discrimination, Sexual Partner Race/Ethnicity, and Depressive Symptoms Among Black Sexual Minority Men. *Arch. Sex. Behav.* **2020**, *49*, 1799–1809. [CrossRef]
26. Hidalgo, M.A.; Layland, E.; Kubicek, K.; Kipke, M. Sexual Racism, Psychological Symptoms, and Mindfulness Among Ethnically/Racially Diverse Young Men Who Have Sex with Men: A Moderation Analysis. *Mindfulness* **2020**, *11*, 452–461. [CrossRef] [PubMed]
27. Meanley, S.; Bruce, O.; Hidalgo, M.A.; Bauermeister, J.A. When young adult men who have sex with men seek partners online: Online discrimination and implications for mental health. *Psychol. Sex. Orientat. Gend. Divers.* **2020**, *7*, 418–432. [CrossRef]
28. Paul, J.P.; Ayala, G.; Choi, K.-H. Internet Sex Ads for MSM and Partner Selection Criteria: The Potency of Race/Ethnicity Online. *J. Sex Res.* **2010**, *47*, 528–538. [CrossRef] [PubMed]
29. Thai, M. Sexual Racism Is Associated with Lower Self-Esteem and Life Satisfaction in Men Who Have Sex with Men. *Arch. Sex. Behav.* **2020**, *49*, 347–353. [CrossRef]
30. Wade, R.M.; Harper, G.W. Racialized Sexual Discrimination (RSD) in Online Sexual Networking: Moving from Discourse to Measurement. *J. Sex Res.* **2021**, *58*, 795–807. [CrossRef]
31. Wade, R.M.; Bouris, A.M.; Neilands, T.B.; Harper, G.W. Racialized Sexual Discrimination (RSD) and Psychological Wellbeing among Young Sexual Minority Black Men (YSMBM) Who Seek Intimate Partners Online. *Sex. Res. Soc. Policy* **2022**, *19*, 1341–1356. [CrossRef]
32. Meyer, I.H. Prejudice, social stress, and mental health in lesbian, gay, and bisexual populations: Conceptual issues and research evidence. *Psychol. Bull.* **2003**, *129*, 674–697. [CrossRef]
33. Marcia, J.E. Development and validation of ego-identity status. *J. Pers. Soc. Psychol.* **1966**, *3*, 551–558. [CrossRef]
34. Marcia, J.E. Identity in Adolescence. Foundational Article. In *Handbook of Adolescent Psychology*; Wiley: Singapore, 1980; pp. 159–187.

35. Erickson, J.M.; Slayton, A.M.; Petersen, J.G.; Hyams, H.M.; Howard, L.J.; Sharp, S.; Sagarin, B.J. Challenge at the Intersection of Race and Kink: Racial Discrimination, Fetishization, and Inclusivity Within the BDSM (Bondage-Discipline, Dominance-Submission, and Sadism-Masochism) Community. *Arch. Sex. Behav.* **2022**, *51*, 1063–1074. [CrossRef]
36. Phinney, J.S. Ethnic identity in adolescents and adults: Review of research. *Psychol. Bull.* **1990**, *108*, 499–514. [CrossRef]
37. Phinney, J.S. The Multigroup Ethnic Identity Measure: A New Scale for Use with Diverse Groups. *J. Adolesc. Res.* **1992**, *7*, 156–176. [CrossRef]
38. Rivas-Drake, D.; Seaton, E.K.; Markstrom, C.; Quintana, S.; Syed, M.; Lee, R.M.; Schwartz, S.J.; Umana-Taylor, A.; French, S.; Yip, T.; et al. Ethnic and Racial Identity in Adolescence: Implications for Psychosocial, Academic, and Health Outcomes. *Child Dev.* **2014**, *85*, 40–57. [CrossRef] [PubMed]
39. Torres, L.; Ong, A.D. A daily diary investigation of latino ethnic identity, discrimination, and depression. *Cult. Divers. Ethn. Minor. Psychol.* **2010**, *16*, 561–568. [CrossRef]
40. Yip, T.; Wang, Y.; Mootoo, C.; Mirpuri, S. Moderating the association between discrimination and adjustment: A meta-analysis of ethnic/racial identity. *Dev. Psychol.* **2019**, *55*, 1274–1298. [CrossRef]
41. Tajfel, H. *Human Groups and Social Categories: Studies in Social Psychology*; Cambridge University Press: Cambridge, UK, 1981. ISBN 978-0-521-22839-8.
42. Tajfel, H.; Turner, J. An Integrative Theory of Intergroup Conflict. In *The Social Psychology of Intergroup Relations*; Austin, W., Worchel, S., Eds.; Key Readings in Social Psychology; Brooks/Cole: Monterey, CA, USA, 1979; pp. 33–47. ISBN 978-0-86377-678-6.
43. Greene, M.L.; Way, N.; Pahl, K. Trajectories of perceived adult and peer discrimination among Black, Latino, and Asian American adolescents: Patterns and psychological correlates. *Dev. Psychol.* **2006**, *42*, 218–236. [CrossRef]
44. Lee, J.P.; Lee, R.M.; Hu, A.W.; Kim, O.M. Ethnic identity as a moderator against discrimination for transracially and transnationally adopted Korean American adolescents. *Asian Am. J. Psychol.* **2015**, *6*, 154–163. [CrossRef]
45. Stein, G.L.; Kiang, L.; Supple, A.J.; Gonzalez, L.M. Ethnic identity as a protective factor in the lives of Asian American adolescents. *Asian Am. J. Psychol.* **2014**, *5*, 206–213. [CrossRef]
46. Torres, L.; Yznaga, S.D.; Moore, K.M. Discrimination and Latino psychological distress: The moderating role of ethnic identity exploration and commitment. *Am. J. Orthopsychiatry* **2011**, *81*, 526–534. [CrossRef] [PubMed]
47. Lewin, A.; Mitchell, S.J.; Rasmussen, A.; Sanders-Phillips, K.; Joseph, J.G. Do Human and Social Capital Protect Young African American Mothers from Depression Associated with Ethnic Discrimination and Violence Exposure? *J. Black Psychol.* **2011**, *37*, 286–310. [CrossRef]
48. Mossakowski, K.N. Coping with Perceived Discrimination: Does Ethnic Identity Protect Mental Health? *J. Health Soc. Behav.* **2003**, *44*, 318–331. [CrossRef]
49. Smith, T.B.; Trimble, J.E. Ethnic Identity and Well-Being of People of Color: An Updated Meta-Analysis. In *Foundations of Multicultural Psychology: Research to Inform Effective Practice*; American Psychological Association: Washington, DC, USA, 2016; pp. 181–205. ISBN 978-1-4338-2057-1.
50. Umaña-Taylor, A.J.; Diversi, M.; Fine, M.A. Ethnic Identity and Self-Esteem of Latino Adolescents: Distinctions among the Latino Populations. *J. Adolesc. Res.* **2002**, *17*, 303–327. [CrossRef]
51. Vera, E.M.; Vacek, K.; Coyle, L.D.; Stinson, J.; Mull, M.; Doud, K.; Buchheit, C.; Gorman, C.; Hewitt, A.; Keene, C.; et al. An Examination of Culturally Relevant Stressors, Coping, Ethnic Identity, and Subjective Well-Being in Urban, Ethnic Minority Adolescents. *Prof. Sch. Couns.* **2011**, *15*, 55–56. [CrossRef]
52. Yoo, H.C.; Lee, R.M. Ethnic Identity and Approach-Type Coping as Moderators of the Racial Discrimination/Well-Being Relation in Asian Americans. *J. Couns. Psychol.* **2005**, *52*, 497–506. [CrossRef]
53. Tynes, B.M.; Umaña-Taylor, A.J.; Rose, C.A.; Lin, J.; Anderson, C.J. Online racial discrimination and the protective function of ethnic identity and self-esteem for African American adolescents. *Dev. Psychol.* **2012**, *48*, 343–355. [CrossRef]
54. Romero, A.J.; Roberts, R.E. The Impact of Multiple Dimensions of Ethnic Identity on Discrimination and Adolescents' Self-Estees. *J. Appl. Soc. Psychol.* **2003**, *33*, 2288–2305. [CrossRef]
55. Anglin, D.M.; Lui, F.; Espinosa, A.; Tikhonov, A.; Ellman, L. Ethnic identity, racial discrimination and attenuated psychotic symptoms in an urban population of emerging adults. *Early Interv. Psychiatry* **2018**, *12*, 380–390. [CrossRef] [PubMed]
56. Bowleg, L. "Once You've Blended the Cake, You Can't Take the Parts Back to the Main Ingredients": Black Gay and Bisexual Men's Descriptions and Experiences of Intersectionality. *Sex Roles* **2013**, *68*, 754–767. [CrossRef]
57. Quinn, K.G. Applying an intersectional framework to understand syndemic conditions among young Black gay, bisexual, and other men who have sex with men. *Soc. Sci. Med.* **2022**, *295*, 112779. [CrossRef]
58. Lee, R.M. Resilience Against Discrimination: Ethnic Identity and Other-Group Orientation as Protective Factors for Korean Americans. *J. Couns. Psychol.* **2005**, *52*, 36–44. [CrossRef]
59. Turner, J.C.; Hogg, M.A.; Oakes, P.J.; Reicher, S.D.; Wetherell, M.S. *Rediscovering the Social Group: A Self-Categorization Theory*; Basil Blackwell: Oxford, UK, 1987; p. 239. ISBN 978-0-631-14806-7.
60. Barlett, C.P. Anonymously hurting others online: The effect of anonymity on cyberbullying frequency. *Psychol. Popul. Media* **2015**, *4*, 70–79. [CrossRef]
61. Conner, C.T. The Gay Gayze: Expressions of Inequality on Grindr. *Sociol. Q.* **2019**, *60*, 397–419. [CrossRef]

62. Lauckner, C.; Truszczynski, N.; Lambert, D.; Kottamasu, V.; Meherally, S.; Schipani-McLaughlin, A.M.; Taylor, E.; Hansen, N. "Catfishing," cyberbullying, and coercion: An exploration of the risks associated with dating app use among rural sexual minority males. *J. Gay Lesbian Ment. Health* **2019**, *23*, 289–306. [CrossRef]
63. Moore, M.J.; Nakano, T.; Enomoto, A.; Suda, T. Anonymity and roles associated with aggressive posts in an online forum. *Comput. Hum. Behav.* **2012**, *28*, 861–867. [CrossRef]
64. Mowlabocus, S. A Kindr Grindr: Moderating Race (Ism) in Techno-Spaces of Desire. In *Queer Sites in Global Contexts*; Ramos, R., Mowlabocus, S., Eds.; Routledge: New York, NY, USA, 2020; pp. 33–47. ISBN 978-1-00-300233-8.
65. Wade, R.M.; Harper, G.W. Toward a multidimensional construct of racialized sexual discrimination (RSD): Implications for scale development. *Psychol. Sex. Orientat. Gend. Divers.* **2021**, *8*, 401–406. [CrossRef]
66. Bauermeister, J.A.; Pingel, E.; Zimmerman, M.; Couper, M.; Carballo-Diéguez, A.; Strecher, V.J. Data Quality in HIV/AIDS Web-Based Surveys: Handling Invalid and Suspicious Data. *Field Methods* **2012**, *24*, 272–291. [CrossRef]
67. Fricker, R.D. Sampling Methods for Web and E-Mail Surveys. In *The SAGE Handbook of Online Research Methods*; Fielding, N., Lee, R.M., Blank, G., Eds.; Sage: Thousand Oaks, CA, USA, 2008; pp. 195–216.
68. Radloff, L.S. The CES-D Scale: A Self-Report Depression Scale for Research in the General Population. *Appl. Psychol. Meas.* **1977**, *1*, 385–401. [CrossRef]
69. Roberts, R.E. Reliability of the CES-D scale in different ethnic contexts. *Psychiatry Res.* **1980**, *2*, 125–134. [CrossRef]
70. Critcher, C.R.; Dunning, D. Self-Affirmations Provide a Broader Perspective on Self-Threat. *Pers. Soc. Psychol. Bull.* **2015**, *41*, 3–18. [CrossRef]
71. Amos, N.; McCabe, M.P. Conceptualizing and measuring perceptions of sexual attractiveness: Are there differences across gender and sexual orientation? *Pers. Individ. Differ.* **2015**, *76*, 111–122. [CrossRef]
72. Berenson, K.R.; Downey, G.; Rafaeli, E.; Coifman, K.G.; Paquin, N.L. The rejection–rage contingency in borderline personality disorder. *J. Abnorm. Psychol.* **2011**, *120*, 681–690. [CrossRef]
73. Hayes, A.F. *Introduction to Mediation, Moderation, and Conditional Process Analysis: A Regression-Based Approach*, 2nd ed.; Guilford Publications: New York, NY, USA, 2017. ISBN 978-1-4625-3466-1.
74. McQueeney, K. "We are God's Children, Y'All:" Race, Gender, and Sexuality in Lesbian- and Gay-Affirming Congregations. *Soc. Probl.* **2009**, *56*, 151–173. [CrossRef]
75. Bracey, J.R.; Bámaca, M.Y.; Umaña-Taylor, A.J. Examining Ethnic Identity and Self-Esteem Among Biracial and Monoracial Adolescents. *J. Youth Adolesc.* **2004**, *33*, 123–132. [CrossRef]
76. Jones, M.D.; Galliher, R.V. Ethnic Identity and Psychosocial Functioning in Navajo Adolescents. *J. Res. Adolesc.* **2007**, *17*, 683–696. [CrossRef]
77. Phinney, J.S.; Cantu, C.L.; Kurtz, D.A. Ethnic and American Identity as Predictors of Self-Esteem Among African American, Latino, and White Adolescents. *J. Youth Adolesc.* **1997**, *26*, 165–185. [CrossRef]
78. Turnage, B.F. Influences on Adolescent African American Females' Global Self-Esteem. *J. Ethn. Cult. Divers. Soc. Work* **2005**, *13*, 27–45. [CrossRef]
79. Umaña-Taylor, A.J.; Updegraff, K.A. Latino adolescents' mental health: Exploring the interrelations among discrimination, ethnic identity, cultural orientation, self-esteem, and depressive symptoms. *J. Adolesc.* **2007**, *30*, 549–567. [CrossRef]
80. Erikson, E.H. *Identity: Youth and Crisis*, 1st ed.; W.W. Norton: New York, NY, USA, 1968. ISBN 978-0-393-09786-3.
81. Phinney, J.S.; Ong, A.D. Conceptualization and measurement of ethnic identity: Current status and future directions. *J. Couns. Psychol.* **2007**, *54*, 271–281. [CrossRef]
82. Hidalgo, M.A.; Cotten, C.; Johnson, A.K.; Kuhns, L.M.; Garofalo, R. 'Yes, I Am More than Just That': Gay/Bisexual Young Men Residing in the United States Discuss the Influence of Minority Stress on their Sexual Risk Behavior Prior to Hiv Infection. *Int. J. Sex. Health* **2013**, *25*, 291–304. [CrossRef]
83. McKeown, E.; Nelson, S.; Anderson, J.; Low, N.; Elford, J. Disclosure, discrimination and desire: Experiences of Black and South Asian gay men in Britain. *Cult. Health Sex.* **2010**, *12*, 843–856. [CrossRef]
84. Souleymanov, R.; Brennan, D.J.; George, C.; Utama, R.; Ceranto, A. Experiences of racism, sexual objectification and alcohol use among gay and bisexual men of colour. *Ethn. Health* **2020**, *25*, 525–541. [CrossRef]
85. Yoo, H.C.; Lee, R.M. Does ethnic identity buffer or exacerbate the effects of frequent racial discrimination on situational well-being of Asian Americans? *J. Couns. Psychol.* **2008**, *55*, 63–74. [CrossRef]
86. McCoy, S.K.; Major, B. Group Identification Moderates Emotional Responses to Perceived Prejudice. *Pers. Soc. Psychol. Bull.* **2003**, *29*, 1005–1017. [CrossRef]
87. Operario, D.; Fiske, S.T. Ethnic Identity Moderates Perceptions of Prejudice: Judgments of Personal Versus Group Discrimination and Subtle Versus Blatant Bias. *Pers. Soc. Psychol. Bull.* **2001**, *27*, 550–561. [CrossRef]
88. Caldwell, C.H.; Kohn-Wood, L.P.; Schmeelk-Cone, K.H.; Chavous, T.M.; Zimmerman, M.A. Racial Discrimination and Racial Identity as Risk or Protective Factors for Violent Behaviors in African American Young Adults. *Am. J. Community Psychol.* **2004**, *33*, 91–105. [CrossRef]
89. Smalls, C.; White, R.; Chavous, T.; Sellers, R. Racial Ideological Beliefs and Racial Discrimination Experiences as Predictors of Academic Engagement Among African American Adolescents. *J. Black Psychol.* **2007**, *33*, 299–330. [CrossRef]
90. Williams, J.L.; Aiyer, S.M.; Durkee, M.I.; Tolan, P.H. The Protective Role of Ethnic Identity for Urban Adolescent Males Facing Multiple Stressors. *J. Youth Adolesc.* **2014**, *43*, 1728–1741. [CrossRef]

91. Toomey, R.B.; Huynh, V.; Jones, S.K.; Lee, S.; Revels-Macalinao, M. Sexual minority youth of color: A content analysis and critical review of the literature. *J. Gay Lesbian Ment. Health* **2017**, *21*, 3–31. [CrossRef]
92. Wilton, L.; Herbst, J.H.; Coury-Doniger, P.; Painter, T.M.; English, G.; Alvarez, M.E.; Scahill, M.; Roberson, M.A.; Lucas, B.; Johnson, W.D.; et al. Efficacy of an HIV/STI Prevention Intervention for Black Men Who Have Sex with Men: Findings from the Many Men, Many Voices (3MV) Project. *AIDS Behav.* **2009**, *13*, 532–544. [CrossRef]
93. Jackson, S.D.; Wagner, K.R.; Yepes, M.; Harvey, T.D.; Higginbottom, J.; Pachankis, J.E. A pilot test of a treatment to address intersectional stigma, mental health, and HIV risk among gay and bisexual men of color. *Psychotherapy* **2022**, *59*, 96–112. [CrossRef]
94. Bogart, L.M.; Dale, S.K.; Daffin, G.K.; Patel, K.N.; Klein, D.J.; Mayer, K.H.; Pantalone, D.W. Pilot intervention for discrimination-related coping among HIV-positive Black sexual minority men. *Cult. Divers. Ethn. Minor. Psychol.* **2018**, *24*, 541–551. [CrossRef]
95. Burton, C.L.; Wang, K.; Pachankis, J.E. Psychotherapy for the Spectrum of Sexual Minority Stress: Application and Technique of the ESTEEM Treatment Model. *Cogn. Behav. Pract.* **2019**, *26*, 285–299. [CrossRef] [PubMed]
96. Pachankis, J.E.; Hatzenbuehler, M.L.; Rendina, H.J.; Safren, S.A.; Parsons, J.T. LGB-affirmative cognitive-behavioral therapy for young adult gay and bisexual men: A randomized controlled trial of a transdiagnostic minority stress approach. *J. Consult. Clin. Psychol.* **2015**, *83*, 875–889. [CrossRef] [PubMed]
97. Jemal, A. Transformative Consciousness of Health Inequities: Oppression Is a Virus and Critical Consciousness Is the Antidote. *J. Hum. Rights Soc. Work* **2018**, *3*, 202–215. [CrossRef] [PubMed]
98. Mosley, D.V.; Hargons, C.N.; Meiller, C.; Angyal, B.; Wheeler, P.; Davis, C.; Stevens-Watkins, D. Critical consciousness of anti-Black racism: A practical model to prevent and resist racial trauma. *J. Couns. Psychol.* **2021**, *68*, 1–16. [CrossRef]
99. Goodkind, S.; Brinkman, B.G.; Elliott, K. Redefining Resilience and Reframing Resistance: Empowerment Programming with Black Girls to Address Societal Inequities. *Behav. Med.* **2020**, *46*, 317–329. [CrossRef]
100. Adames, H.Y.; Chavez-Dueñas, N.Y.; Lewis, J.A.; Neville, H.A.; French, B.H.; Chen, G.A.; Mosley, D.V. Radical healing in psychotherapy: Addressing the wounds of racism-related stress and trauma. *Psychotherapy*, 2022; *ahead of print*. [CrossRef]
101. Nguyen, P.V.; Naleppa, M.; Lopez, Y. Cultural competence and cultural humility: A complete practice. *J. Ethn. Cult. Divers. Soc. Work* **2021**, *30*, 273–281. [CrossRef]
102. Stubbe, D.E. Practicing Cultural Competence and Cultural Humility in the Care of Diverse Patients. *Focus* **2020**, *18*, 49–51. [CrossRef]
103. Lee, R.M.; Yoo, H.C. Structure and Measurement of Ethnic Identity for Asian American College Students. *J. Couns. Psychol.* **2004**, *51*, 263–269. [CrossRef]
104. Arscott, J.; Humphreys, J.; Merwin, E.; Relf, M. "That Guy is Gay and Black. That's a Red Flag." How HIV Stigma and Racism Affect Perception of Risk Among Young Black Men Who Have Sex with Men. *AIDS Behav.* **2020**, *24*, 173–184. [CrossRef]
105. Han, C.-S.; Choi, K.-H. Very Few People Say "No Whites": Gay Men of Color and the Racial Politics of Desire. *Sociol. Spectr.* **2018**, *38*, 145–161. [CrossRef]
106. Tan, J.Y.; Pratto, F.; Operario, D.; Dworkin, S.L. Sexual Positioning and Race-Based Attraction by Preferences for Social Dominance Among Gay Asian/Pacific Islander Men in the United States. *Arch. Sex. Behav.* **2013**, *42*, 1233–1239. [CrossRef] [PubMed]
107. Ang, M.W.; Tan, J.C.K.; Lou, C. Navigating Sexual Racism in the Sexual Field: Compensation for and Disavowal of Marginality by Racial Minority Grindr Users in Singapore. *J. Comput. Commun.* **2021**, *26*, 129–147. [CrossRef]
108. Conner, C.T. How Sexual Racism and Other Discriminatory Behaviors are Rationalized in Online Dating Apps. *Deviant Behav.* 2022, 1–17, *ahead of print*. [CrossRef]
109. Thai, M.; Stainer, M.; Barlow, F.K. The "preference" paradox: Disclosing racial preferences in attraction is considered racist even by people who overtly claim it is not. *J. Exp. Soc. Psychol.* **2019**, *83*, 70–77. [CrossRef]
110. Banks, K.H.; Goswami, S.; Goodwin, D.; Petty, J.; Bell, V.; Musa, I. Interrupting internalized racial oppression: A community based ACT intervention. *J. Context. Behav. Sci.* **2021**, *20*, 89–93. [CrossRef]
111. Ai, A.L.; Nicdao, E.G.; Appel, H.B.; Lee, D.H.J. Ethnic Identity and Major Depression in Asian American Subgroups Nationwide: Differential Findings in Relation to Subcultural Contexts: Asian American Ethnic Identity and Major Depression. *J. Clin. Psychol.* **2015**, *71*, 1225–1244. [CrossRef]
112. Pahl, K.; Way, N. Longitudinal Trajectories of Ethnic Identity Among Urban Black and Latino Adolescents. *Child Dev.* **2006**, *77*, 1403–1415. [CrossRef]
113. Hwang, W.-C.; Ting, J.Y. Disaggregating the effects of acculturation and acculturative stress on the mental health of Asian Americans. *Cult. Divers. Ethn. Minor. Psychol.* **2008**, *14*, 147–154. [CrossRef]
114. Finch, B.K.; Vega, W.A. Acculturation Stress, Social Support, and Self-Rated Health Among Latinos in California. *J. Immigr. Health* **2003**, *5*, 109–117. [CrossRef]
115. Koneru, V.K.; de Mamani, A.G.W.; Flynn, P.M.; Betancourt, H. Acculturation and mental health: Current findings and recommendations for future research. *Appl. Prev. Psychol.* **2007**, *12*, 76–96. [CrossRef]
116. Lara, M.; Gamboa, C.; Kahramanian, M.I.; Morales, L.S.; Hayes Bautista, D.E. Acculturation and Latino Health in the United States: A Review of the Literature and Its Sociopolitical Context. *Annu. Rev. Public Health* **2005**, *26*, 367–397. [CrossRef]
117. Crenshaw, K. Mapping the Margins: Intersectionality, Identity Politics, and Violence against Women of Color. In *The Public Nature of Private Violence*; Routledge: London, UK, 2013; pp. 93–118. [CrossRef]

118. Bauer, G.R.; Churchill, S.M.; Mahendran, M.; Walwyn, C.; Lizotte, D.; Villa-Rueda, A.A. Intersectionality in quantitative research: A systematic review of its emergence and applications of theory and methods. *SSM Popul. Health* **2021**, *14*, 100798. [CrossRef] [PubMed]
119. Bowleg, L. When Black + Lesbian + Woman ≠ Black Lesbian Woman: The Methodological Challenges of Qualitative and Quantitative Intersectionality Research. *Sex Roles* **2008**, *59*, 312–325. [CrossRef]
120. Callaghan, P.; Morrissey, J. Social support and health: A review. *J. Adv. Nurs.* **1993**, *18*, 203–210. [CrossRef]
121. Cohen, S.; Wills, T.A. Stress, social support, and the buffering hypothesis. *Psychol. Bull.* **1985**, *98*, 310–357. [CrossRef] [PubMed]
122. Schaefer, C.; Coyne, J.C.; Lazarus, R.S. The health-related functions of social support. *J. Behav. Med.* **1981**, *4*, 381–406. [CrossRef]
123. Ruez, D. "I never felt targeted as an Asian ... until I went to a gay pub": Sexual racism and the aesthetic geographies of the bad encounter. *Environ. Plan. A Econ. Space* **2017**, *49*, 893–910. [CrossRef]
124. Winder, T.J.A.; Lea, C.H. "Blocking" and "Filtering": A Commentary on Mobile Technology, Racism, and the Sexual Networks of Young Black MSM (YBMSM). *J. Racial Ethn. Health Disparit.* **2019**, *6*, 231–236. [CrossRef]

International Journal of
Environmental Research and Public Health

MDPI

Article

Neighborhood Alcohol Outlet Density, Historical Redlining, and Violent Crime in NYC 2014–2018

Sean J. Haley [1,*], Shari J. Jardine [1,2], Elizabeth A. Kelvin [3,4,5], Christopher Herrmann [6] and Andrew R. Maroko [7]

1 Department of Health Policy and Management, CUNY Graduate School of Public Health and Health Policy, City University of New York, New York, NY 10027, USA
2 Department of Community Health and Social Sciences, CUNY Graduate School of Public Health and Health Policy, City University of New York, New York, NY 10027, USA
3 Department of Epidemiology and Biostatistics, CUNY Graduate School of Public Health and Health Policy, City University of New York, New York, NY 10019, USA
4 CUNY Institute for Implementation Science in Population Health, City University of New York, New York, NY 10027, USA
5 Department of Occupational Health, Epidemiology & Prevention, Donald and Barbara Zucker School of Medicine at Hofstra University/Northwell Health, Hempstead, NY 11549, USA
6 Department of Law & Police Science, John Jay College, City University of New York, New York, NY 10027, USA
7 Department of Environmental, Occupational, and Geospatial Health Sciences, CUNY Graduate School of Public Health and Health Policy, City University of New York, New York, NY 10027, USA
* Correspondence: sean.haley@sph.cuny.edu

Abstract: Alcohol outlets tend to cluster in lower income neighborhoods and do so disproportionately in areas with more residents of color. This study explores the association between on- and off-premise alcohol outlet density and history of redlining with violent crime in New York City between 2014 and 2018. Alcohol outlet density was calculated using a spatial accessibility index. Multivariable linear regression models assess associations between the history of redlining, on-premise and off-premise alcohol outlet density with serious crime. Each unit increase in on- and off-premise alcohol density was associated with a significant increase in violent crime ($\beta = 3.1$, $p < 0.001$ on-premise and $\beta = 33.5$, $p < 0.001$ off premise). In stratified models (redlined vs not redlined community block groups) the association between off-premise alcohol outlet density and violent crime density was stronger in communities with a history of redlining compared to those without redlining ($\beta = 42.4$, $p < 0.001$ versus $\beta = 30.9$, $p < 0.001$, respectively). However, on-premise alcohol outlet density was only significantly associated with violent crime in communities without a history of redlining ($\beta = 3.6$, $p < 0.001$). The violent crime experienced by formerly redlined communities in New York City is likely related to a legacy of racialized housing policies and may be associated with state policies that allow for high neighborhood alcohol outlet density.

Keywords: alcohol; policy; density; redlining; violent crime; policy

Citation: Haley, S.J.; Jardine, S.J.; Kelvin, E.A.; Herrmann, C.; Maroko, A.R. Neighborhood Alcohol Outlet Density, Historical Redlining, and Violent Crime in NYC 2014–2018. *Int. J. Environ. Res. Public Health* **2023**, *20*, 3212. https://doi.org/10.3390/ijerph20043212

Academic Editors: Celia C. Lo, William Ash-Houchen and Tyrone C. Cheng

Received: 7 January 2023
Revised: 7 February 2023
Accepted: 8 February 2023
Published: 12 February 2023

1. Introduction

In the two decades prior to the onset of the COVID-19 pandemic, there was a significant net increase in U.S. alcohol consumption of approximately 3% per decade. Binge drinking increased during the same period by 7.5% per decade [1]. Between 2006 and 2014, there was a 62% increase in alcohol related emergency room visits [2]. Furthermore, according to the National Institute on Alcohol Abuse and Alcoholism, there was a doubling of alcohol-related deaths for those aged 16 and above from 1999 to 2017 (from 35,914 to 72,558), such that the overall age-adjusted death rate increased by 50.9% (from 16.9 to 25.5 per 100,000). Rates increased for all age groups, except for those 75 and older, and increased for all racial and ethnic groups, except among Hispanic males and non-Hispanic Blacks whose rates dipped initially then increased [3].

For over a decade, the Community Preventive Services Task Force has recommended reducing alcohol outlet density to decrease alcohol-related harms [4]. Societal harms associated with alcohol outlet density include greater youth access and underage drinking [5,6], as well as increased instances of violent crime [7]. In New York City (NYC), alcohol outlet density was associated with increased prevalence of alcohol use disorders [8], and cyclist and pedestrian death by a motor vehicle [9]. Off-premise alcohol retail store and on-premise restaurant alcohol outlet density in NYC were significantly associated with street robbery and aggravated assault while on-premise bars/taverns were not [10]. Regulating alcohol outlet density through the reduction or limitation of alcohol licenses remains an important strategy to reduce alcohol-related harms [4].

Consistent with structural frameworks of disease causation [11], alcohol outlets tend to cluster in lower income neighborhoods and do so disproportionately in high poverty areas with more Black, Indigenous, and other residents of color [12,13]. In addition, people living with lower socio-economic status experience nearly twice the mortality from alcohol-attributable causes compared to all other causes of mortality [14,15]. Previous studies found associations between alcohol outlet density and poverty [7,16], as well as associations between alcohol outlet density and the legacy of discriminatory housing practices, including 'redlining' [17].

As a part of the New Deal initiatives during the Great Depression, the Federal Housing Authority supervised the sale of homes constructed with federal dollars and enacted policies that prohibited their sale to 'inharmonious racial groups', citing a potential loss of property values, which would place these federally insured loans at risk of default [18,19]. The Home Owners' Loan Corporation provided risk assessments to the Federal Housing Authority, including color-coded maps. 'Undesirable' neighborhoods were given the letter grade 'D' and colored in red [19,20]. Consequently, federally insured loans included 'restrictive covenant' clauses within mortgage contracts and deeds that prohibited sale or resale to Black families [19], effectively barring Black families from gaining or passing wealth achieved from home ownership to future generations [21]. As such, the Home Owners' Loan Corporation maps serve as a proxy for past racialized government policies. Although outlawed in the 1960s, the laws serve as codified discriminatory policies and are separate from the indicators of the policies' consequences, including racial concentration end economic sedimentation [22]. This study aims to: (1) explore the association of on- and off-premise alcohol outlet density and the history of redlining with violent crime in New York City between 2014 and 2018, and (2) assess whether the associations between alcohol outlet density and violent crime are modified by a history of redlining.

2. Materials and Methods

2.1. Alcohol Outlet Density at the Census Block Group (CBG) Level

Point location data for alcohol outlets were extracted from the New York State Liquor Authority database by utilizing the public license query feature [23]. To minimize the effect of licenses that were newly approved just prior to the start or the end of the study period (2014–2018), licenses with approval dates less than six months prior to the start of 2014, and approval dates within the last six months of 2018 were excluded. License location data were matched to address points using the ArcGIS World Geocoder (n = 11,774). This included both on-premise (n = 6606) and off-premise (n = 5168) alcohol outlets. Wholesale (n = 16), manufacturing (n = 11), and seasonal (n = 27) licenses were excluded. Alcohol outlets with incomplete, unmatched, and/or duplicate addresses were excluded (n = 65, 0.6%).

To calculate alcohol outlet density, the CDC recommends several methods, which fall into four broad categories: count-based, container-based, distance-based, and spatial access-based [24]. This study utilized a spatial accessibility index, which is better suited to assess clustering, measure exposed populations, address access potential, and evaluate harms when compared to simpler container- and distance-based approaches [25]. The spatial accessibility index was calculated by first specifying a "choice set" (the number of outlets used to assess population exposure). The CDC recommends values between five and nine [24]. In this study, we selected nine due to the relatively high population density and concentration of outlets in most NYC boroughs. The Euclidean distance from each CBG centroid (representing population centers) and the nearest nine outlets was then determined. The spatial access score/alcohol outlet density was then calculated as the sum of the inverse distances for all nine alcohol outlets per CBG. As such, the shorter distances to the nearest outlets in a CBG result in larger alcohol outlet density scores.

2.2. *Violent Crime*

Violent crime data were obtained from the New York City Police Department for the years 2014–2018. Violent crime was defined as murder, shooting victim, rape, robbery, or aggravated assault, as these categories are more consistently reported to law enforcement agencies. In New York City, violent crime points were geocoded to the nearest intersection or the midsection of street segments [24]. The geo-coded points were then aggregated to CBG and divided by area to calculate violent crime density (crimes per mi^2) to match the other datasets for analysis.

2.3. *Redlining*

Redlining data were obtained from the Mapping Inequality database and capture data produced between 1935 and 1940 [26]. Using Arc GIS, previously redlined areas were overlayed with current maps of the five boroughs of New York City to align them to current CBG boundaries. CBGs in which greater than 50% of the area was previously redlined were categorized as having a history of redlining.

2.4. *Neighborhood Demographics*

CBG population characteristics were obtained from the 2018 American Community Survey (ACS) 5-year estimates for years 2014–2018 [27]. The population is described in terms of the percent with income below the poverty federal poverty line, percent of adults $\geq$25 years old who did not graduate from high school, population density per mile squared, percent of the population identifying as non-Hispanic Black, percent of the population identifying as Hispanic/Latino, percent of the population that moved in since 2015, percent of housing units that were vacant, and the percent of housing units which were owner-occupied. New York City CBGs served as the unit of analysis. Ninety-six CBGs (populations of fewer than 100 residents including airports, commercial areas, and parks), were excluded from the analysis.

2.5. *Statistical Analysis*

We described the communities overall and stratified on whether they had a history of redlining. The statistical significance of differences in community characteristics by redlining history was assessed with a Wilcoxon rank sum test. We mapped the distribution of the variables of primary interest (density of on-premise, off-premise alcohol outlets, and crime), indicating which neighborhoods had a history of redlining in New York City using ArcGIS Pro version 2.9 [28]. We then ran crude and multivariable linear regression models to assess the crude and adjusted associations between history of redlining, on-premise alcohol outlet density, and off-premise alcohol outlet density with density of serious crime. The multivariable model included all the characteristics of the communities described above. We then added interaction terms for redlining history*on-premise alcohol outlet density and redlining history*off-premise alcohol outlet density to the multivariable model with the understanding that if either interaction term was significant, we would run the multivariable model stratified on redlining history to assess effect modification (i.e., how the association between on- and off-premise alcohol outlet density differs between communities with a history of redlining versus those without such a legacy). All analyses were conducted in R and significance set at $\alpha = 0.05$ for main effects and $\alpha = 0.1$ for effect modification, due to the lower statistical power associated with testing interaction.

3. Results

3.1. Description of the Communities

A total of 6198 CBGs were included in the analyses. Overall, 28.2% of NYC CBGs had at least 50% of their area in historically redlined neighborhoods. The average number of violent crimes per square mile was 2012 in historically redlined CBGs compared to 1166.5 in non-redlined communities ($p < 0.001$). The mean alcohol outlet density for both on- and off-premise outlets was significantly higher in redlined CBGs (14.0 versus 8.7, $p < 0.001$ and 13.0 versus 9.6, $p < 0.001$, respectively) (Figure 1).

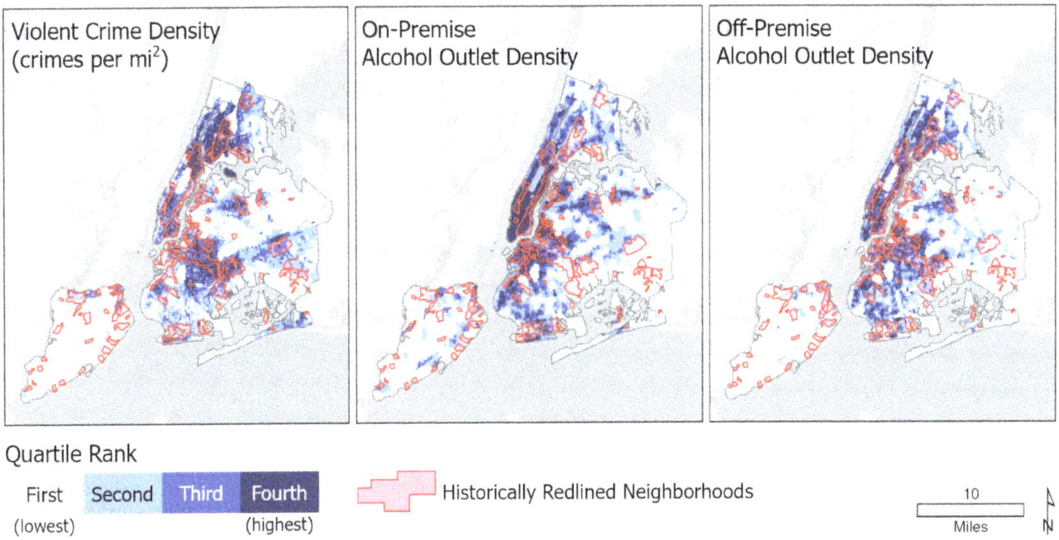

Figure 1. Distribution of violent crime density, on-, and off-premise alcohol outlet density/access score in redlined and non-redlined neighborhoods in New York City.

Other CBG variables, including population density, percent below the federal poverty line, percent of adults 25 years or older without a high school degree, percent of the population identifying as Hispanic/Latino or non-Hispanic Black, percent of the population that moved in since 2015, and percent of homes that were vacant, were all significantly greater in redlined communities. The percent of owner-occupied homes was significantly lower in redlined communities (24.7% versus 39.7%, $p < 0.001$) (Table 1).

Table 1. Description of the Communities overall and by history of redlining.

Variable	Overall	Redline Neighborhood	Non-Redlined Neighborhood	Wilcoxon Rank Sum *p*-Value
Census block groups, n (%)	6198 (100.00)	1750 (28.23)	4448 (71.77)	NA
Density of violent crime per mile^2				<0.001
Mean (SD)	1405.28 (1759.80)	2012.25 (1912.20)	1166.47 (1635.68)	
Median (min, max)	728.85 [0.00, 19720.90]	1462.80 [0.00, 16527.10]	542.85 [0.00, 19720.90]	
On-premises alcohol outlet density				<0.001
Mean (SD)	10.17 (17.11)	14.00 (20.47)	8.67 (15.33)	
Median (min, max)	6.39 [0.78, 786.60]	9.07 [0.97, 454.70]	5.80 [0.78, 786.60]	
Off-premise alcohol outlet density				
Mean (SD)	10.55 (7.20)	12.98 (7.02)	9.60 (7.05)	<0.001
Median (min, max)	9.41 [0.95, 217.55]	12.23 [1.30, 119.34]	8.21 [0.95, 217.55]	
Percent of the population living below the federal poverty line				<0.001
Mean (SD)	18.26 (15.09)	22.42 (17.14)	16.62 (13.87)	
Median (min, max)	14.10 [0.00, 93.50]	18.80 [0.00, 93.50]	12.90 [0.00, 91.60]	

Table 1. *Cont.*

Variable	Overall	Redline Neighborhood	Non-Redlined Neighborhood	Wilcoxon Rank Sum *p*-Value
Percent of the population without a high school degree				0.003
Mean (SD)	18.48 (13.80)	19.87 (15.52)	17.93 (13.03)	
Median (min, max)	16.00 [0.00, 80.60]	17.55 [0.00, 80.60]	15.40 [0.00, 76.30]	
Population density per mile^2				<0.001
Mean (SD)	65596.56 (52965.28)	79200.29 (54825.55)	60244.37 (51240.69)	
Median (min, max)	50829.50 [79.40, 518070.40]	65695.85 [659.10, 490690.70]	45193.00 [79.40, 518070.40]	
Percent of the population identifying as non-Hispanic Black				<0.001
Mean (SD)	21.89 (28.35)	27.61 (29.09)	19.64 (27.73)	
Median (min, max)	6.50 [0.00, 100.00]	15.70 [0.00, 100.00]	5.00 [0.00, 100.00]	
Percent of the population identifying as Hispanic/Latino				0.005
Mean (SD)	27.88 (25.01)	29.35 (25.50)	27.31 (24.79)	
Median (min, max)	19.10 [0.00, 100.00]	21.05 [0.00, 98.30]	18.30 [0.00, 100.00]	
Percent of the population that moved in since 2015				<0.001
Mean (SD)	13.20 (9.22)	14.93 (9.90)	12.52 (8.85)	
Median (min, max)	11.97 [0.00, 81.25]	13.84 [0.00, 59.22]	11.32 [0.00, 81.25]	
Percent of the housing that is vacant				<0.001
Mean (SD)	8.61 (8.13)	9.51 (8.37)	8.26 (8.01)	
Median (min, max)	7.00 [0.00, 67.10]	7.70 [0.00, 51.90]	6.80 [0.00, 67.10]	
Percent of homes owned by the residents				<0.001
Mean (SD)	35.43 (28.07)	24.66 (22.82)	39.67 (28.81)	
Median (min, max)	30.81 [0.00, 100.00]	19.05 [0.00, 100.00]	36.97 [0.00, 100.00]	

3.2. Linear Regression Results

In the crude models, CBGs with a history of redlining had on average 845.8 more violent crimes per square mile than neighborhoods without a history of redlining ($p < 0.001$). Each unit increase in the number of on-premise alcohol outlets per square mile was associated with an increase of 6.9 violent crimes per square mile ($p < 0.001$), and each unit increase in the number of off-premise alcohol outlets per square mile was associated with an increase of 88.6 crimes per square mile ($p < 0.001$) (Table 2).

Table 2. Linear regression models examining the association of redlining, on-premise and off-premise alcohol outlet density, and covariates with crime.

	Crude Models (n = 6198 for All Models)			Multivariable Model (n = 6198)			
Variable	Beta	95% Confidence Interval	*p*-Value	Beta	95% Confidence Interval	*p*-Value	*p*-Value for Interaction W/Redlining Added to Multivariable Model
History of redlining	845.77	750.73, 940.82	<0.001	205.77	128.68, 282.85	<0.001	
On-premise alcohol outlet density	6.92	4.36, 9.47	<0.001	3.08	0.97, 5.18	<0.001	0.090
Off-premise alcohol outlet density	88.62	82.95, 94.29	<0.001	33.50	28.08, 38.92	<0.001	<0.001
Percent of the population below the federal poverty line				15.82	12.83, 18.8	<0.001	
Percent of the population without a high school degree				7.96	4.57, 11.35	<0.001	
Population density per mile^2				0.01	0.01, 0.01	<0.001	
Percent of the population identifying as non-Hispanic Black				15.31	14.08, 16.55	<0.001	
Percent of the population identifying as Hispanic/Latino				16.61	14.85, 18.38	<0.001	
Percent of the population that moved in since 2015				−2.40	−6.36, 1.55	0.230	
Percent of the housing that is vacant				6.34	2.14, 10.55	<0.001	
Percent of homes owned by the resident				−7.45	−9.19, −5.71	<0.001	

After adjusting for community characteristics in the multivariate model, the associations were attenuated but remained significant. Communities with a history of redlining experienced 205.8 more crimes per square mile, on average, than communities without a history of redlining ($p < 0.001$). Each unit increase in on- and off-premise alcohol density was associated with a significant increase in violent crime, although association was stronger for off-premise density ($\beta = 3.1$, $p < 0.001$ and $\beta = 33.5$, $p < 0.001$, respectively) (Table 2). In a test for collinearity, the variable inflation factor (VIF) for the redlining variable was just over 1.1 and VIFs for all the other variables had values below 2.2, well below recommended thresholds.

3.3. *Effect Modification of the Association between On- and Off-Premise Alcohol Outlet Density and Violent Crime Density by History of Redlining*

When interaction terms for history of redlining*alcohol outlet density were added to the multivariate model, both redlining*off-premise alcohol outlet density and redlining*on-premise outlet density were statistically significant at our a priori $\alpha = 0.1$ (interaction term $p < 0.001$ and $p = 0.090$, respectively). We ran the multivariable model stratified on the history of redlining and found that the strength of the association between alcohol outlet density and violent crime density varied by history of redlining, but the direction of the variation differed for on-versus off-premise outlets. As hypothesized, the association between off-premise alcohol outlet density and violent crime density was stronger in communities with a history of redlining compared to those without ($\beta = 42.4$, $p < 0.001$ versus $\beta = 30.9$, $p < 0.001$, respectively). However, on-premise alcohol outlet density was not associated with violent crime in formerly redlined neighborhoods. Rather, the association between on-premise alcohol outlet density and violent crime density was only significant in communities without a history of redlining compared to those with such a legacy ($\beta = 3.6$, $p < 0.001$. versus $\beta = 2.8$, $p = 0.170$, respectively) (Table 3).

Table 3. Multivariable linear regression model stratified on history of redlining.

	Redlined Neighborhoods (n = 1750)			Non-Redlined Neighborhoods (n = 4448)		
Variable	**Beta**	**95% Confidence Interval**	***p*-Value**	**Beta**	**95% Confidence Interval**	***p*-Value**
On-premises alcohol outlet density	2.81	−1.17, 6.79	0.170	3.63	1.14, 6.11	<0.001
Off-premise alcohol outlet density	42.36	30.87, 53.85	<0.001	30.94	24.94, 36.94	<0.001
Percent of the population living below the federal poverty line	15.21	9.36, 21.06	<0.001	14.31	10.86, 17.76	<0.001
Percent of the population without a high school degree	4.98	−2.07, 12.02	0.170	8.49	4.71, 12.27	<0.001
Population density per mile^2	0.01	0.01, 0.01	<0.001	0.01	0.01, 0.01	<0.001
Percent of the population identifying as non-Hispanic Black	20.85	18.03, 23.67	<0.001	13.49	12.15, 14.83	<0.001
Percent of the population identifying as Hispanic/Latino	19.08	15.24, 22.92	<0.001	15.87	13.93, 17.82	<0.001
Percent of the population that moved in since 2015	−4.54	−12.84, 3.77	0.280	−0.20	−4.6, 4.2	0.930
Percent of the housing that is vacant	7.35	−1.54, 16.25	0.110	6.57	1.91, 11.24	0.010
Percent of homes owned by the residents	−16.12	−20.17, −12.06	<0.001	−5.15	−7.02, −3.28	<0.001

4. Discussion

We found that the distribution of on- and off-premise alcohol outlets and of violent crime was denser in communities with a history of redlining. Furthermore, there was a positive association between density of both on- and off-premise alcohol outlets and violent crime. Importantly, the structural effects of redlining are maintained when current socioeconomic indicators are adjusted for, suggesting that formerly redlined areas continue to be associated with crime independent of the current SES indicators that were added to the model. In addition, in the stratified model separating historically redlined neighborhoods from other neighborhoods, we found that the association between off-premise (but not on-premise) alcohol outlet density and violent crime density was significantly stronger in communities with a history of redlining compared to those without this history.

Previous studies found similar associations between alcohol outlet density and violent crime [7,10,14], and alcohol density and redlining [15]. Gorman et al. (2001) assessed the association between alcohol outlet density (measured as total outlets per 100 population) and violent crime in Camden, New Jersey, controlling for poverty and other population characteristics [16]. The study found that total (on-premise + off-premise) alcohol outlet density contributed significantly to violent crime within block groups [16]. Trangenstein et al. (2018) explored the association between access to alcohol outlets and violent crime in Baltimore MD, with attention to outlet characteristics and types of crime [7]. Using a spatial accessibility index, the Trangenstein study found a positive relationship between alcohol outlet density and violent crime. Specifically, the authors found that each 10% increase in alcohol outlet access was associated with a 4.2% increase in violent crime exposure. The authors also identified differential effects, such that a 10% increase in access to off-premise outlets and combined off- and on-premise outlets had a greater association with violent crime than on-premise outlets [7]. In a subsequent Baltimore study, Trangenstein et al. (2020) examined the association between CBG characteristics and alcohol outlet clusters by type of alcohol outlet. The authors found that CBGs that were redlined had 7.3 times the odds of being in an off-premise cluster, 8.1 times the odds of being in an on-premise cluster, and 8.6 times the odds of being in a combined (on- and off-premise) cluster [17].

Feng et al. also used spatial adjustment to assess the association between alcohol outlets and street robberies and aggravated assaults in NYC. They found that among nine categories of alcohol outlets, two on-premise (eateries and restaurants) and two off-premise alcohol outlets (grocery stores and alcohol retail stores) were associated with aggravated assault. In addition, three on-premise (e.g., eateries, bars/taverns, and restaurants) and three off-premise alcohol outlets (e.g., grocery stores, alcohol retail stores, and drug stores) were associated with street robberies. While grocery stores were associated with robberies and assault in all five boroughs, three on-premise venues (e.g., night clubs, hotels, and other eateries) were not associated with robberies or assaults in any borough [10].

Interestingly, while we found that the association between density of off-premise alcohol outlets and violent crime was modified by redlining, the direction of the effect modification for on-premise alcohol outlets was such that the association between on-premise alcohol outlet density and violent crime density was only modified in communities without historical redlining. Our finding may be related to neighborhood variations in economic composition, including rapid neighborhood gentrification in NYC, or to variation in the types of on-premise outlets (hotels vs. nightclubs) within those neighborhoods [15]. Still, although outlawed in the 1960s, redlining codified discriminatory housing policies and continues to be associated with a myriad of health conditions in NYC and elsewhere, suggesting that it has long-lasting impacts [22].

In NY State, Chapter 478 of the Laws of 1934 created the State Liquor Authority and the Division of Alcoholic Beverage Control. According to the law, the State Liquor Authority was established to "regulate and control the manufacture and distribution within the state of alcoholic beverages for the purpose of fostering and promoting temperance in their consumption and respect for and obedience to law; for the primary purpose of promoting health, welfare and safety of the people of the state, and, to the extent possible, supporting economic growth … " The statute also authorizes the State Liquor Authority to "determine whether public convenience and advantage will be promoted by the issuance of licenses to traffic in alcoholic beverages … and to carry out the increase or decrease in the number thereof and the location of premises licensed … in the public interest" [29]. In keeping with its health mandate, results from this paper suggest that the State Liquor Authority might consider limiting the number or licenses in neighborhoods with high outlet density.

Alcohol license applicants in NY State must notify their respective municipalities 30 days in advance of submitting the application. In NYC, the city notifies the appropriate community board. Even though communities can submit a recommendation opposing the alcohol license application, the recommendations are not binding. In 2022 it was revealed that the State Liquor Authority receives 75,000 applications every year and that the average review time is 26 weeks [30,31]. Rather than calling for a review of alcohol outlet density in the face of increasing alcohol related harms, in 2022, Governor Hochul proposed increasing the agency's budget by 2 million dollars to expedite alcohol application processing [31]. Given the results of this and other studies that suggest strong associations between alcohol outlet density and violent crime in NY [7,10,14], the governor's budget request does not appear to align with the NY State Liquor Authority's stated mission of promoting health and safety.

This study has limitations. The analyses used data aggregated to the CBG, and thus the results can only be interpreted as applying to the CBG and not to the individuals living within these communities (i.e., the ecological fallacy whereby population-level correlations are assumed to parallel individual-level correlations) [32]. Although we used a spatial accessibility index as recommended [23], and our analysis relied on Euclidean distances, it is possible that the use of network distances potentially produced slightly different results. As other researchers suggested, there is tremendous variation within categories of on- and off-premise alcohol outlets related to outlet size, capacity, how alcohol is consumed, and whether alcohol consumption by those in the neighborhood is directly related to the violence committed in the defined geographic areas [33]. In addition, the analyses relied on the most recent violent crime data available to the researchers at the time of the study, and the analyses were cross-sectional, such that we cannot determine causation. Furthermore, it is possible that we failed to adjust for all confounders, for example, we did not control for sociodemographic variables in the year 1940 that reflected neighborhood composition to control for differences that pre-dated redlining maps [34]. We might also point out that this analysis was conducted with data from New York City before the COVID-19 pandemic, and it is unclear whether similar associations would be found following the pandemic or in other locations.

Findings from this study add to the growing literature related to the persistent negative health consequences of structural racial discrimination. Although there are a myriad of potential pathways, the effects of legally codified discrimination appear to have sedimentary health effects on the populations who remain [22]. Our findings suggest that the persistent health effects of redlining will not be easily reversed, but that reducing the density of alcohol outlets may serve to ameliorate at least one set of health consequences.

5. Conclusions

Our results suggest that high concentrations of alcohol outlets are associated with violent crimes within low-income neighborhoods. In addition, racialized housing practices appear to have a persistent negative impact on neighborhoods long after such practices are formally abolished. Reducing the concentration of alcohol outlets may be one strategy to reduce violent crime in NYC neighborhoods, the effects of which may be stronger within formerly redlined communities. As such, initiatives addressing neighborhood planning, zoning, and licensing remain the effective approaches to reduce socioeconomic inequalities for alcohol-attributable outcomes [35].

Author Contributions: Conceptualization, S.J.H.; methodology, A.R.M., S.J.J., E.A.K. and C.H.; software, A.R.M.; formal analysis, A.R.M. and C.H.; data curation: A.R.M., S.J.J. and C.H.; writing—original draft preparation, S.J.J. and S.J.H.; writing and editing: all authors; visualization: A.R.M.; project administration: S.J.H. All authors have read and agreed to the published version of the manuscript.

Funding: This research received no external funding.

Institutional Review Board Statement: Not applicable.

Informed Consent Statement: Not applicable.

Data Availability Statement: Publicly available datasets are available as follows: Alcohol outlet locations in NYC: NYS Liquor Authority Mapping Project (LAMP). https://sla.ny.gov. https://lamp.sla.ny.gov (accessed on 8 February 2021). Formerly redlined areas in NYC: Nelson RK, Winling L, Marciano R, Connolly N, et al., "Mapping Inequality," American Panorama, 2017. ed. Robert K. Nelson and Edward L. Ayers. https://dsl.richmond.edu/panorama/redlining/ (accessed on 10 February 2021) [Bronx]. NYC violent crime data: Restrictions apply to the availability of the violent crime data. Although most of the data is available publicly (see: https://compstat.nypdonline.org (accessed on 8 February 2021), to protect the identity of victims, address-level locations of violent crimes are not publicly available. The data may be requested from the NYC Police Department. NYC demographics by US census block groups: Manson S, Schroeder J, Van Riper D, Kugler T, Ruggles S. IPUMS National Historical Geographic Information System: Version 16.0 [dataset]. Minneapolis, MN: IPUMS. 2021. http://doi.org/10.18128/D050.V17.0.

Conflicts of Interest: The authors declare no conflict of interest.

References

1. Grucza, R.A.; Sher, K.J.; Kerr, W.C.; Krauss, M.J.; Lui, C.K.; McDowell, Y.E.; Hartz, S.; Virdi, G.; Bierut, L.J. Trends in Adult Alcohol Use and Binge Drinking in the Early 21st-Century United States: A Meta-Analysis of 6 National Survey Series. *Alcohol. Clin. Exp. Res.* **2018**, *42*, 1939–1950. [CrossRef]
2. White, A.M.; Slater, M.E.; Ng, G.; Hingson, R.; Breslow, R. Trends in Alcohol-Related Emergency Department Visits in the United States: Results from the Nationwide Emergency Department Sample, 2006 to 2014. *Alcohol. Clin. Exp. Res.* **2018**, *42*, 352–359. [CrossRef] [PubMed]
3. White, A.M.; Castle, I.P.; Hingson, R.W.; Powell, P.A. Using Death Certificates to Explore Changes in Alcohol-Related Mortality in the United States, 1999 to 2017. *Alcohol. Clin. Exp. Res.* **2020**, *44*, 178–187. [CrossRef] [PubMed]
4. Task Force on Community Preventive Services. Recommendations for Reducing Excessive Alcohol Consumption and Alcohol-Related Harms by Limiting Alcohol Outlet Density. *Am. J. Prev. Med.* **2009**, *37*, 570–571. [CrossRef]
5. Chen, M.-J.; Gruenewald, P.J.; Remer, L.G. Does Alcohol Outlet Density Affect Youth Access to Alcohol? *J. Adolesc. Health* **2009**, *44*, 582–589. [CrossRef]
6. Chen, M.-J.; Grube, J.W.; Gruenewald, P.J. Community alcohol outlet density and underage drinking. *Addiction* **2010**, *105*, 270–278. [CrossRef] [PubMed]
7. Trangenstein, P.J.; Curriero, F.C.; Webster, D.; Jennings, J.M.; Latkin, C.; Eck, R.; Jernigan, D.H. Outlet Type, Access to Alcohol, and Violent Crime. *Alcohol. Clin. Exp. Res.* **2018**, *42*, 2234–2245. [CrossRef]
8. To, S.E. Alcohol dependence patterns and their impact on New York City. *MedGenMed Medscape Gen. Med.* **2007**, *9*, 23.
9. DiMaggio, C.; Mooney, S.; Frangos, S.; Wall, S. Spatial analysis of the association of alcohol outlets and alcohol-related pedestrian/bicyclist injuries in New York City. *Inj. Epidemiol.* **2016**, *3*, 11. [CrossRef] [PubMed]
10. Feng, S.Q.; Piza, E.L.; Kennedy, L.W.; Caplan, J.M. Aggravating effects of alcohol outlet types on street robbery and aggravated assault in New York City. *J. Crime Justice* **2019**, *42*, 257–273. [CrossRef]
11. Phelan, J.C.; Link, B.G.; Tehranifar, P. Social Conditions as Fundamental Causes of Health Inequalities: Theory, Evidence, and Policy Implications. *J. Health Soc. Behav.* **2010**, *51*, S28–S40. [CrossRef]
12. Romley, J.A.; Cohen, D.; Ringel, J.; Sturm, R. Alcohol and Environmental Justice: The Density of Liquor Stores and Bars in Urban Neighborhoods in the United States. *J. Stud. Alcohol Drugs* **2007**, *68*, 48–55. [CrossRef] [PubMed]
13. Berke, E.M.; Tanski, S.E.; Demidenko, E.; Alford-Teaster, J.; Shi, X.; Sargent, J.D. Alcohol Retail Density and Demographic Predictors of Health Disparities: A Geographic Analysis. *Am. J. Public Health* **2010**, *100*, 1967–1971. [CrossRef] [PubMed]
14. Hay, G.C.; Whigham, P.A.; Kypri, K.; Langley, J.D. Neighbourhood deprivation and access to alcohol outlets: A national study. *Health Place* **2009**, *15*, 1086–1093. [CrossRef]
15. LaVeist, T.A.; Wallace, J.M. Health risk and inequitable distribution of liquor stores in African American neighborhood. *Soc. Sci. Med.* **2000**, *51*, 613–617. [CrossRef] [PubMed]
16. Gorman, D.M.; Speer, P.W.; Gruenewald, P.J.; Labouvie, E.W. Spatial dynamics of alcohol availability, neighborhood structure and violent crime. *J. Stud. Alcohol* **2001**, *62*, 628–636. [CrossRef]
17. Trangenstein, P.J.; Gray, C.; Rossheim, M.E.; Sadler, R.; Jernigan, D.H. Alcohol Outlet Clusters and Population Disparities. *J. Urban Health* **2020**, *97*, 123–136. [CrossRef] [PubMed]
18. FHA Underwriting Manual. Urban Oasis. 1 April 1936. Available online: http://urbanoasis.org/projects/fha/FHAUnderwritingManualPtI.html (accessed on 12 December 2021).
19. Rothstein, R. *The Color of Law: A Forgotten History of How Our Government Segregated America*, 1st ed.; Liveright Publishing Corporation a Division of W.W. Norton & Company: New York, NY, USA, 2017.
20. Home Owners' Loan Corporation (HOLC) Neighborhood Redlining Grade. ARC GIS. Available online: https://gis-for-racialequity.hub.arcgis.com/maps/UrbanObservatory::home-owners-loan-corporation-holc-neighborhood-redlining-grade-1/about (accessed on 12 December 2021).

21. Gross, T.A. "Forgotten History" of How the U.S. Government Segregated America. NPR. 3 May 2017. Available online: https://www.npr.org/2017/05/03/526655831/a-forgotten-history-of-how-the-u-s-government-segregated-america (accessed on 4 November 2021).
22. Krieger, N.; Van Wye, G.; Huynh, M.; Waterman, P.D.; Maduro, G.; Li, W.; Gwynn, R.C.; Barbot, O.; Bassett, M.T. Structural racism, historical redlining, and risk of preterm birth in New York City, 2013–2017. *Am. J. Public Health* **2020**, *110*, 1046–1053. [CrossRef]
23. NYS Liquor Authority Mapping Project (LAMP). Available online: https://sla.ny.gov.. Available online: https://lamp.sla.ny.gov (accessed on 3 April 2022).
24. Centers for Disease Control and Prevention. *Guide for Measuring Alcohol Outlet Density*; Centers for Disease Control and Prevention, US Department of Health and Human Services: Atlanta, GA, USA, 2017.
25. Vogel, M.; Porter, L.C.; McCuddy, T. Hypermobility, Destination Effects, and Delinquency: Specifying the Link between Residential Mobility and Offending. *Soc. Forces* **2017**, *95*, 1261–1284. [CrossRef]
26. Nelson, R.K.; Winling, L.; Marciano, R.; Connolly, N. "Mapping Inequality," American Panorama, 2017 ed. Robert K. Nelson and Edward L. Ayers. Available online: https://dsl.richmond.edu/panorama/redlining/ (accessed on 2 December 2020).
27. Manson, S.; Schroeder, J.; Van Riper, D.; Kugler, T.; Ruggles, S. *IPUMS National Historical Geographic Information System*; Version 16.0 [Dataset]; IPUMS: Minneapolis, MN, USA, 2021. [CrossRef]
28. *ArcGIS Pro [Computer Software]*; Version 2.9; Esri Inc.: New York, NY, USA, 2022.
29. Agency Mission Statement. Available online: https://sla.ny.gov/agency-mission-statement (accessed on 17 August 2022).
30. Raudins, S. New York Liquor License Waits are 26 Weeks—Gov. Hochul Wants to Bulk up the State Liquor Authority to Shorten the Delay. Albany Business Review. 2 March 2022. Available online: https://www.bizjournals.com/albany/news/2022/03/02/hochul-expand-sla-capacity-liquor-license-laws.html (accessed on 17 August 2022).
31. Eisenpress, C. Governor Proposes $2M to Speed up Liquor License Applications. *Crain's New York Business*. 20 January 2022. Available online: https://www.crainsnewyork.com/small-business/governor-proposes-2m-speed-liquor-license-applications (accessed on 17 August 2022).
32. Caputi, T. Medical marijuana laws, substance use treatment admissions and the ecological fallacy. *Addiction* **2019**, *115*, 188–189. [CrossRef]
33. Gmel, G.; Holmes, J.; Studer, J. Are alcohol outlet densities strongly associated with alcohol-related outcomes? A critical review of recent evidence. *Drug Alcohol Rev.* **2016**, *35*, 40–54. [CrossRef] [PubMed]
34. Swope, C.B.; Hernández, D.; Cushing, L.J. The Relationship of Historical Redlining with Present-Day Neighborhood Environmental and Health Outcomes: A Scoping Review and Conceptual Model. *J. Urban Health* **2022**, *99*, 959–983. [CrossRef] [PubMed]
35. Probst, C.; Kilian, C.; Sanchez, S.; Lange, S.; Rehm, J. The role of alcohol use and drinking patterns in socioeconomic inequalities in mortality: A systematic review. *Lancet Public Health* **2020**, *5*, e324–e332. [CrossRef] [PubMed]

International Journal of
Environmental Research and Public Health

MDPI

Article

COVID-19 and Masking Disparities: Qualitative Analysis of Trust on the CDC's Facebook Page

Andrea Laurent-Simpson

Department of Sociology, Dedman College of Humanities and Sciences, Southern Methodist University, Dallas, TX 75205, USA; alaurentsimpson@smu.edu

Abstract: This exploratory paper examines individual levels of risk assessment as impacting institutional trust in the CDC while also contributing to disparities in expressed willingness to mask early in the COVID-19 pandemic. Using both content and thematic analysis of the CDC's Facebook (FB) page from April 2020 and Gidden's modern risk society theory, I consider how social media (SM) users retrospectively perceived a dramatic change in public health (PH) advisory—from the CDC advising against masking in February 2020 (Time 1) to advising the use of "do-it-yourself" (DIY) cloth masking in April 2020 (Time 2)—through a lens of prior, self-guided research. Expressed "knowledge" of masking as preventative (or not) yielded unwavering and sometimes increasing distrust in the CDC based on user perception of the "correct" advisory, regardless of the CDC's position at Time 1 or Time 2. Simultaneously, disparities in masking behaviors appeared to be driven not by CDC guidance but by this same self-guided research. I show this via three themes: (1) claims of ineffectiveness for DIY masking (do not trust CDC now—no masking from the start); (2) conflict between the first and second CDC advisories on masking (do not trust CDC—either already masking anyway or will now); (3) disappointed in the CDC for length of time taken to make a DIY mask recommendation (do not trust CDC—either already masking anyway or will mask now). I discuss the imperative nature of two-way engagement with SM users by PH rather than using SM as a one-way mode of advisory dissemination. This and other recommendations may decrease disparities in preventative behaviors based on individual-level risk assessment as well as increase institutional trust and transparency.

Keywords: risk; institutional trust; COVID-19; emerging infectious disease; social media; masking

Citation: Laurent-Simpson, A. COVID-19 and Masking Disparities: Qualitative Analysis of Trust on the CDC's Facebook Page. *Int. J. Environ. Res. Public Health* **2023**, *20*, 6062. https://doi.org/10.3390/ijerph20126062

Academic Editors: Celia C. Lo, William Ash-Houchen and Tyrone C. Cheng

Received: 7 March 2023
Revised: 25 May 2023
Accepted: 31 May 2023
Published: 6 June 2023

1. Introduction

The original identification of SARS-CoV-2 in Wuhan, China, in December 2019 was followed by fast-paced, global spread of COVID-19. After initially deciding not to label SARS-CoV-2 a Public Health Emergency of International Concern in January 2020, the World Health Organization declared COVID-19 a pandemic in March 2020 [1]. In the United States, the first laboratory confirmed case was identified in Washington in January 2020, and new cases were increasingly discovered in the coming weeks. As the United States Food and Drug Administration began development and dissemination of emergency use tests in early February [1], the United States Centers for Disease Control and Prevention (CDC) was tasked as a public health authority (PHA) with providing prevention guidance to the public. Earliest measures included avoiding close contact with sick people; covering coughs and sneezes; keeping hands away from the face; and staying home when sick [2].

One of the CDC's earliest prevention advisories regarding masking in the context of the pandemic appeared on Facebook (FB) on 27 February 2020 (Time 1), advising U.S. citizens against the use of face masks. The post noted that "only healthcare professionals caring for COVID-19 patients, people who are sick with COVID-19, or in some cases people caring for patients who are sick with COVID-19 need precautions like a facemask to help limit their risk of spreading COVID-19." [3]. By early April (Time 2), emerging research indicated that individuals could be asymptomatic or pre-symptomatic, unknowingly transmitting the virus and dramatically increasing spread [4]. As a result, the CDC changed its guidance, recommending that all citizens wear cloth facemasks "in public settings where other social distancing measures are difficult to maintain (e.g., grocery stores and pharmacies) especially in areas of significant community-based transmission." [5].

1.1. Theory

This research uses a modern risk society lens as a foundation for why differences in institutional trust develop, the context in which individual-level risk assessment emerges, and resulting variance in trust levels. Ulrich Beck has conceptualized risk society as characteristic of modern, post-industrialized societies [6]. Risk society arises in the context of rapidly advancing, modern technologies that usurp institutional ability to calculate risks of new innovations. Whereas members of more traditional societies can lean on local knowledge, religion, and observations of others' habits for behavioral guidance, the modern risk society, by its very nature, forces members to rely upon expert systems of knowledge represented by scientists and other elites whom the average person will never meet [7].

As scientific knowledge is built, expert actors within these systems inevitably disagree on the accuracy of pieces of knowledge as well as how to mitigate the risk that may emerge from technological, and in this case, medical innovation. Anthony Giddens argues that "the fact that experts frequently disagree becomes a familiar terrain for almost everyone [and] ... the claim to universal legitimacy of science becomes much more disputed than before." [8]. A growing inability of science to predict risk (and subsequently develop solutions for society that protect against innovation-driven hazards) creates a social context in which hazardous conditions that emerge due to innovation cannot be effectively planned for in advance [6].

As a result, Giddens has argued that modern risk society emerges in which society's members, once broadly trusting of expert systems, become increasingly aware of the manufactured risk unintentionally created by elite institutional authority [9]. As a result, the general public increasingly doubts expert systems to adequately assess and solve for risk [7]. Individual members feel themselves to be at greater risk as a result of both advancing technology as well as the inability of the institutional structures once trusted to mitigate risk to do so now [9]. Indeed, prior research shows that institutional trust by individuals in the U.S. medical profession, for example, has fallen from 73% in 1966 to 34% in 2012 [10].

Subsequently, and due to this loss of institutional trust, the general public begins to take the task of risk assessment into their own hands in the face of ever-progressing scientific innovation that also creates manmade risk [9]. Individual-level research on particular risks of concern emerges as a way to mitigate personal insecurity. The layperson, attempting to mitigate one's own risk, begins "doing one's own research", including reading peer-reviewed scientific literature; watching and reading the news; or even reaching out to significant, in-group members for their thoughts on the issue to manage one's own risk potential.

1.2. Summary and Grounded Theory Outcomes

In the context of the COVID-19 pandemic and CDC guidance regarding masking, I argue that CDC masking advisories were filtered through individual-level risk assessments already present for users when the CDC posted both the initial as well as the second advisory on the need to (or not to) mask. Figure 1 models the argument that the differences in these pre-existing, individually generated assessments of masking effectiveness created masking disparities. Simultaneously, these same risk assessments impacted levels of trust in the CDC's ability to competently advise the public regarding masking. The perceived necessity for masks during the earliest period of the pandemic in the United States created fluid differences in levels of trust of both the CDC itself as well as its advisories regarding masking. The trustworthiness of the CDC's advisory depended heavily upon whether the current guidance supported a user's own individual-level assessments regarding the efficacy of masking. Ultimately, both masking behaviors and reported trust in the CDC's advisories were filtered through users' individual-level risk assessments rather than the recommendations made by the CDC.

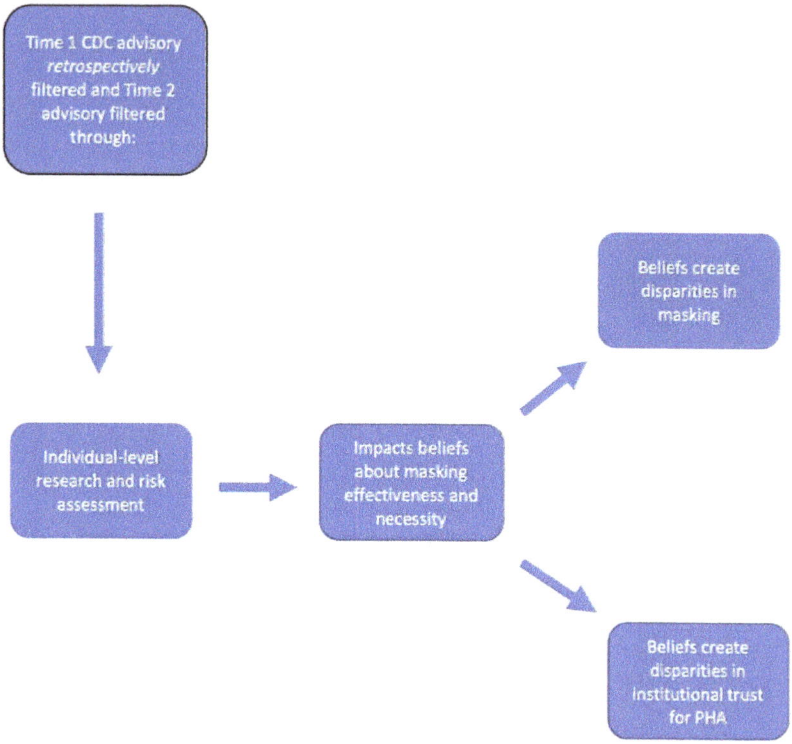

Figure 1. Theoretical argument.

This study has importance to the public health literature for several reasons. First of all, work examining how individual-level research on health influences both trust in PHAs as well as disparities in potential advisory uptake is underdeveloped in the literature [11,12]. Second, existing research examining the use of SM for health-related issues is scant [13,14]. However, we know that the Internet, and SM in particular, are increasingly used by PHAs as widespread dissemination sites of health information [15–17]. As a result, research that uses SM acknowledges these platforms as increasingly important sites of investigation.

Third, existing research on disparities in advisory uptake during COVID-19 and other emerging infectious diseases has focused on demographic variables to explain differences in preventive behavior [12]. These are valuable analyses with respect to the social determinants of health, to be sure. However, it is also important to consider how sociohistorical processes related to innovation risk and the resulting individual reflexivity required to assess risk is contributing to disparities in preventative behavior. Indeed, a large and growing body of literature has examined how self-reflexive research in the era of modern risk has created behavioral disparities and reinforced institutional distrust in many health contexts. This includes emerging infectious disease [11,18,19]; chronic disease [20]; contested illness [21]; and risk language in the media as reinforcing health risks [22]. Using a modern risk society lens to analyze why users on the CDC's FB page felt the need to do their own risk assessments in the first place enables researchers to place these choices in sociohistorical contexts of ever-growing, historical distrust in social institutions.

1.3. Research Objectives and Questions

One of the objectives of this paper is theory generation that can be used in future quantitative work (see Section 2.3 below for more on this). This objective will lead to a better understanding of underlying, and oftentimes hidden, motivations (such as individual-level risk assessment) for the uptake of public health preventative measures (such as masking) that big data and computational and statistical designs might not otherwise pick up in analysis. A second research objective is to explore how individual levels of research on emerging infectious diseases like COVID-19 impact advisory uptake of preventative measures (e.g., masking) as well as how that same research impacts institutional trust.

These research objectives lead to the following questions in this paper: (1) Did individual-level research about COVID-19 and masking efficacy during the pandemic create masking disparities, as self-reported on the CDC's FB page?; (2) How does individual-level research about COVID-19 and masking efficacy during the pandemic impact institutional trust, as expressed on the CDC's FB page, in the CDC as a PHA?

2. Related Works

2.1. Institutional Trust and Rapid Change

As others have noted, prevention of disease spread in society is a fundamental function of PHAs like the CDC, and clear, consistent communication with the public about risk and prevention is key to stemming transmission [23–25]. However, compliance with PH advisories, especially those that require significant changes to daily routines like COVID-19 has, is dependent upon individual risk perception and trust in government, amongst other factors [24,25]. Because of the nature of COVID-19, governments and public health authorities have had to work at break-neck speed to make complex policy decisions in the context of nascent but rapidly evolving science [26]. Often, in the earliest days, these decisions were made, in better scenarios, with pre-print research, and in the worst scenarios, based on what PHAs did not know about the transmission of the virus [26]. As a result, PH guidance in the United States, especially regarding masking, risked the appearance of contradicting itself to the lay public, even while PH researchers were empirically building on recent scientific research. Public trust and cooperation is one of the many variables on which PHAs must depend when working to stem spread of an emerging infectious disease [25,27]. However, the appearance of backtracking on guidance is significant in the public eye and can be viewed as evidence supporting why PHAs should not be trusted. Inconsistent levels of trust from the public can, therefore, create disparities in preventative behavioral outcomes [25].

2.2. COVID-19, Masking, and SM

Extant research examining cross-cultural disparities in masking outcomes during the pandemic has highlighted a multitude of factors impacting this preventive behavior. This work includes the likelihood of masking during COVID-19 as associated with mainstream media or SM viewing [28]; pre-existing attitudes, social pressure, and perceived usefulness and benefits [29,30]; social norms and risk perceptions [30,31]; efficacy perception and prevalence within society [32]; and personalization of masks for identity expression [33].

Recent systematic social scientific research that has specifically explored perceptions of masking from around the world on social media outlets provides a more nuanced understanding of public, digitized debate regarding masking. Indicating the importance of masking discussion to the general public on SM, masking was one of two main prevention methods noted in English language tweets [34]. Further highlighting masking as a significant source of SM commentary, the 30 most frequently shared articles on FB regarding COVID-19 revealed that masking articles were the second most commonly shared articles, bested only by articles that discussed medication [35].

Research specific to increased understanding of how masking was perceived on SM during the pandemic is informative. One large, randomized sample taken from Twitter in June 2020 indicated that the platform was being used to create a community network of clusters with specific influencers, politicians, and general public persons present. User themes and hashtags appeared to center around encouragement to "mask up" [36]. Other research has utilized online experimentation in the U.S. to examine how masking misinformation rebutted by experts impacts user attitudes and perceptions regarding preventative behavior. While expert rebuttals were useful in increasing positive attitudes towards masking, subsequent disputes from SM users worked to create increased negative attitudes towards masking [37]. Still, other quantitative work has focused on public sentiment regarding masking and other preventative measures. Findings indicate that negative sentiment reduced when the current context of the pandemic became more severe (e.g., higher case counts) [38,39].

2.3. Current Methodology Used in SM Analysis of Masking

Most of the existing literature that considers SM, masking, and COVID-19 is classified as quantitative big data analysis that covers one-month time periods with samples ranging from 100,000 to over a million tweets [34,36,38,40]. Very little research exists that is qualitative in nature. More broadly, qualitative work examining the general public's SM response to PH measures exists minimally and with broad thematic sweeps of attitudinal changes across the pandemic [41]. Other work considers healthcare professional response to PPE shortages with SM posts comprising one part of data collection [42]. To the author's knowledge, qualitative work that focuses on SM response to masking as a preventative measure is scant at best. One paper examines tweets over a one-month period to show that pro- and anti-masking positions were both gendered in nature, with anti-masking tweets being more negative towards women's uptake of the preventative measure [43].

Research on methodology may offer reasoning behind why so little qualitative work exists in the realm of SM research in general. Indeed, examining publicly generated content on SM platforms creates voluminous amounts of data. The sheer quantity of posts, regardless of whether the data collection site is FB, Twitter, Weibo, or any other site, lends itself towards fast-paced big data analysis that uses statistical workhorses such as Python and R for analysis. Likewise, researchers who use qualitative measures like thematic or content analysis that require manual coding of data are discouraged by the sheer volume of hundreds of thousands into the millions of data points across one month time periods [44]. However, while leaning on statistical analysis of such data is advantageous for testing hypotheses and predicting probabilities and outcomes, this approach is disadvantaged by the lack of in-depth theory generation that can inform the accurate building of quantitative designs and hypotheses via the self-reports of target populations [45].

As a result, this study uses qualitative content and thematic analysis of data taken from a one-day snapshot of SM posts (with a qualitatively "manageable" $n = 1042$ posts). Analysis examines how users of the CDC's FB page retrospectively perceived the first CDC advisory on masking in the context of an at-the-time change in masking recommendations. Additionally, this paper examines how that change was filtered through users' own risk assessment to impact disparities in reported masking intentions post-change in CDC advisory.

The topic of this paper, in particular, is an important area of research because while research conducted after the second advisory indicated that masking uptake in the U.S. occurred for 62% of the population days after and 76% one month following [46], FB data in this study suggest that choice to follow this preventive measure was moderated by complex patterns of trust in CDC advisories filtered through individual risk assessments. Differences in trust of government agencies and PHAs directed by individual-level risk assessments are an important driver of uptake for prevention strategies [11,12,47]. In this case, prior user-driven research (regarding both masking effectiveness and necessity) guided user-perceived accuracy of both of the CDC's masking advisories. This same user-driven research also created disparities in reported masking outcomes on the CDC's FB page. Examining self-reported levels of trust in PHA advisories is significant to scientific understanding of disparities in preventative behaviors such as masking. For example, a high level of institutional trust was a significant determinant of high levels of preventative behavior during the pandemic in Hubei, China [48]. Other research has shown that blame placed on public health authorities during earlier pandemics promotes distrust in PHAs, potentially eroding PH communication [49] and increasing behavioral disparities in guidance uptake.

3. Data and Methods

3.1. Methods and Data Source

This project asks two questions: (1) Did individual-level research about COVID-19 and masking efficacy during the pandemic create masking disparities, as self-reported on the CDC's FB page?; (2) How does individual-level research about COVID-19 and masking efficacy during the pandemic impact institutional trust, as expressed on the CDC's FB page, in the CDC as a PHA? The nature of both questions demanded a qualitative dataset that would provide substantive narratives highlighting differences in masking and institutional trust. As a result, I used a mixed methods approach for study design, using both conventional and directed content analysis as a means of analyzing data. Conventional content analysis (thematic) was appropriate for this study because it allows for inductive capture of themes in the data [50] that would not have been coded for if I had only been looking for confirmation of modern risk society. For example, locating trust as fluid in the data was one idea that came from this approach. Directed content analysis was also useful here as it allowed for grounding the project in pre-existing categories embedded in modern risk society, such as concrete trust in expert systems [51].

In the United States, the CDC uses multiple avenues of advisory dissemination, including television, radio, and SM contexts. I chose to examine SM data due to the inherent, two-way communication in which users can answer original posts, creating the potential for ongoing dialog regarding a variety of topics [11]. Furthermore, SM is widely used by laypeople as a platform for gathering health information [52]—especially as individuals increasingly seek to conduct their own health risk research—making SM platforms important sites of analysis. I chose the CDC's FB page as the primary data collection site for this project because, in 2020, approximately 69% of American adults reported using FB regularly [53], with 54% of those users noting that they regularly looked for news on the platform [54]. Indeed, with the exception of YouTube, FB is by far the most widely used SM platform in the United States [53]. The CDC was chosen as the key public health authority because its mission, via the United States Public Health Service, is as the "main assessment and epidemiologic unit for the nation ... serving the population as well as providing technical assistance to states and localities." [55].

3.2. Data Collection

As diagrammed in Figure 2, data were collected on the CDC FB page by using the internal FB search tool and the search terms "coronavirus" and (in March 2020) "COVID-19". Especially regarding the search term "coronavirus", the CDC parent post (PP) was then checked to ensure that it was specific to the novel coronavirus (and later COVID-19). Once the PP was verified as relevant, a screenshot and PDF were created for import into NVivo, a qualitative data analysis software program. PPs were pulled within 72 h from FB each time the CDC posted a new advisory or information. User response posts were also pulled in conjunction with each original CDC post. This process began on 28 January 2020, and continued until 10 April 2020, when lockdowns at my home institution made it difficult to continue gathering data. A total of 23 PPs were successfully mined in this manner. This paper focuses on a CDC PP made public on 3 April 2020, with user response posts in the dataset continuing until 7 April 2020. The PP was the CDC's second masking advisory (Time 2) in which mask use for prevention changed from "not necessary except only under very unique circumstances" to "cloth masks should be used by everyone in public settings where social distancing measures are difficult to maintain". Within this PP, 40 user-generated response posts (to the CDC) were made, with an additional 1001 response posts made in response to the 40 user-generated response posts. In total, 1042 posts comprised the data for this project. (For clarity, all user-generated posts, whether they are in direct response to the CDC or to other posters on the CDC FB page, will be referred to as posts or user posts). Users frequently referenced the CDC's initial post (Time 1) in their response posts, and analysis in this project takes those retrospective accounts into consideration. Furthermore, user posts that are used as data points in this paper include a randomly-generated three letter alpha code as an identifier for each user.

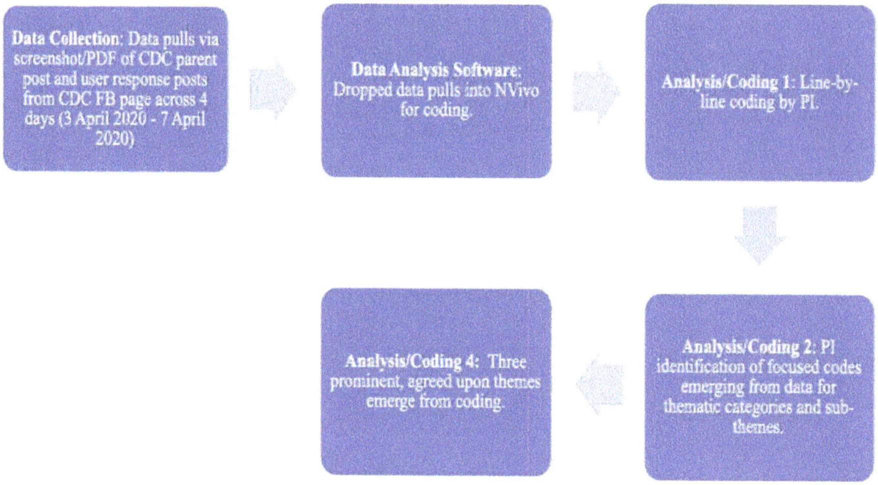

Figure 2. Content Analysis Flowchart.

3.3. Data Analysis

Grounded theory is a widely used qualitative approach that allows researchers to use participant narratives to inductively code data and generate themes [56]. The strength of this kind of analysis is that it offers depth of data that, while not generalizable or replicable in the way quantitative work might be, offers accuracy in analysis [45]. Major thematic content that arises from analysis of grounded theory research is useful in generating theories for future quantitative testing or other qualitative exploration [45]. Systematic line-by-line coding was used to search for substantive themes related to masking and attitudes towards the CDC. This process also allowed for inductive analysis that might reveal implicit meaning formation for users [57]. After identifying initial potential codes arising from the data, I then worked on focused coding—a process that culminated in combining less substantive codes into more powerful, substantive themes representative of the data [57]. This ultimately allowed the identification of three categories of trust in the second CDC advisory on masking aligned with resulting disparities in masking behaviors: (1) claims of ineffectiveness for DIY masking (do not trust CDC now—no masking from the start); (2) conflict between the first and second CDC advisories on masking (do not trust CDC—either already masking anyway or will now); (3) disappointed in the CDC for length of time taken to make a DIY mask recommendation (do not trust CDC—either already masking anyway or will mask now).

Data analysis of the sample of 1042 posts generated 42 initial coding categories with an additional 48 subcategories collapsed under various initial codes. Many of these initial codes did not generate thematic, focused codes (that is, very few pieces of data wound up coded under these categories) and thus were either ultimately abandoned in analysis or were later collapsed into other more precise focused codes that better represented the content of the user's post. For example, one initial code, "Thanks to healthcare workers", ultimately only garnered 6 pieces of data from the entire sample. This category was not deemed as collapsible into other codes while also having too few pieces of evidence to support it as a focused code. As a result, this initial code was abandoned. However, other initial codes, like "CDC lies", were ultimately collapsed under a broader (and ultimately focused) code labelled "CDC not trustworthy". As is typical of coding work in qualitative data analysis [56], sometimes a piece of data might be placed under multiple codes of analysis because the piece of data itself may be representative of more than just one code. In this study, 1042 posts generated a total of 1588 categorizations of data under various initial and, later, focused codes.

Regarding the themes in this paper, Table 1 depicts samples of data points that were categorized under each theme discussed in this paper. Table 1 also provides information on statements of trust (either direct or indirect statements regarding institutional trust in the CDC). Specific criteria were used to determine the inclusion of a piece of data as representative of focused codes. Data that were coded under Theme 1 had to meet at least one of the following parameters: (a) direct questioning of DIY mask as a viable preventative; (b) direct statements that masks do not work; (c) statements that advise, contrary to the Time 2 advisory, people not to mask. Data coded under Theme 2 had to meet at least one of the following parameters: (a) a reference to the Time 1 advisory as ill informed; (b) criticism of the CDC and/or government for not advising masks in Time 1 advisory; (c) direct or indirect statement about trust in the CDC related to conflicting advisories. Finally, data coded under Theme 3 were required to meet at least one of the following parameters: (a) indication that the CDC took too long to recommend DIY masking; (b) indication that individual masking outcomes would have been different if the CDC had told the general public earlier; (c) direct or indirect statement about trust in the CDC as related to length of time to Time 2 advisory. "Direct" or "indirect" statements about trust for each of these themes were determined by assessing if the data point outright noted distrust (direct—e.g., "How can you trust the CDC?") or intimated distrust (indirect—e.g., I wouldn't wear a mask unless I wanted to get sick".) in some way.

Table 1. Themes, sample data points, and N of posts for collected data.

Major Themes	Sample Data Points (by Theme and Trust)	N of Posts
Disparities in Masking and Institutional Trust:		
Dispute Over Effectiveness of DIY Masking (do not trust CDC now, no masking from the start)	"Make sure your [sic] not wearing a mask. They don't protect you."—User KNZ (Indirect distrust) "If COVID can in fact go right through material, then why on earth would anyone settle for a material 'mask?'"—User PMY (Indirect distrust) "They need to address this. It's ridiculous that the CDC does not understand micron sizes of fabric and the size of COVID19. They have to know. It [second advisory] has to be about alleviating fear."—User TKX (Direct distrust) "Making masks[s] will not work [. . .] just stay home now that works." User MKW (Indirect distrust) "Unfortunately homemade masks and clothes likes scarfs [sic] don't protect from particles going through . . . "—User AAV (Indirect distrust)	N = 124
Conflicting Mask Advisories (do not trust CDC—either already masking anyway or will now)	"CDC was irresponsible in telling the general public not to wear masks for the sole reason that they didn't have any [masks]. They should have told people from the beginning to fashion a mask. Instead they shamed people into not wearing them even if they already had one they could have used."—User CIU (Direct distrust) "Really CDC [sic], you are supposed to be the smartest people, hospitals follow your guidelines . . . Before airborne, now droplet. Before no mask now wear mask guidelines. No n95 when in fact that's the best for now to protect the HC [healthcare] workers."—User KGT (Indirect distrust) "The U.S. government knew all of this for months. They didn't prepare and when they realized they were screwed because of inaction they tried to tell us not to wear masks to save them for the medical field. It NEVER made sense not to wear a mask." User TCS (Direct distrust)	N = 74

reviewed, academic work but also on observations of N95 use by medical personnel, hospital policies, and even coaxing from employers.

Perception of risk related to not wearing a mask also appeared to be specifically related to observation of behaviors in Asian countries—especially of PH behaviors in these regions; analysis of financial markers in places including Hong Kong, Singapore, and Japan; as well as previous travel to various Asian locales that had historically worn masks. Indeed, as 51 (5%) posts highlighted these areas as important sources of information, it became clear that they were willing to trust various data flowing from Asia about masking in the pandemic before they would trust the Time 1 recommendation. While the CDC's Time 2 recommendation was in line with pro-masking users' own preventative behavior, the initial conflicting advisory coupled with the second yielded a devolution in institutional trust and accusations about mistakes that had been made by the CDC regarding the pandemic. Furthermore, and in line with the grounded theory in this paper, prior risk assessment that indicated the need for mask wearing created disparities in masking behavior (compared to those who agreed with the CDC's initial advisory) as well as in institutional trust, with one user (User SLK) proud of the fact that they had bucked the CDC's original advice: "I am glad that I've been making my own mask. It doesn't have to be n95. Anything that can contain of protect the virus spreading is better than nothing".

While advisory conflicts such as this were inevitable in the context of a novel pathogen that required rapidly evolving research and outcomes [60], such conflicts were frustrating for the general public. This was especially the case in the United States, a place where one angry poster proclaimed:

> We can no longer trust the CDC ... they are on Trump's payroll. Cloth masks are NOT safe enough!!! Why is the richest and most powerful country in the world telling us how to do DIY life saving measures instead of providing n95 masks for all?? (User EAL)

Indeed, posters saw the CDC's conflicting advisories as proof that an already brewing institutional distrust, coupled with posters' own research, meant that the CDC could not be trusted [60].

4.3. Theme 3—CDC Waited Too Long

A third theme arose in this analysis in which 55 posts (5%) expressed frustration with the Time 2 advisory as well as an emergent distrust in the CDC as a PHA. That is, based on posted self-reports, these users felt that the CDC had waited too long to recommend any kind of masking. While not always apparent if these users had been masking all along, some posts made it clear that they had not been, based on Time 1 guidance, but that they would begin now. For example, one particularly accusatory post (User SCM) noted, "I've been sewing them [masks] like crazy for my family members. I happily would have started sewing them in January if the CDC had been more honest with the public about the necessity of wearing them".

While posts like this indicated that these people would now begin using cloth masks, a sense of emergent betrayal and distrust also seemed apparent. For example, another poster (User NDN) responded, "CDC lied, people died. People could have been fashioning masks 2 months ago." Another poster (User KKD) seemed to blame high testing numbers completely on the CDC while lamenting that people had not been wearing masks all along, saying, "If we would have all worn masks from the beginning the tested positive numbers would be lower. Blame the president all people want [but] this is solely on the CDC".

In line with Gidden's modern risk society lens [8,9], data also indicated that individuals had a responsibility to do their own research so that each person could build individual risk assessments, highlighting the fact that distrust in PHAs had been high from the start of the CDC's Time 1 advisory not to mask. For those users who engaged in their own assessments, the CDC waiting too long to recommend DIY cloth masks did not matter to individual risk. One user matter-of-factly noted:

> . . . just shows how everyone has duty to form [sic] own opinions and look out for themselves. I could not believe the things that were being said by "officials" when I have watched this unfold for months and new [sic] it was all fluff. It's been airborne, it's deadly, it leaves you with impaired lung function. Is it going to wipe out the entire world—no but a lot of people are at risk and warning public in January and taking steps would have made this a lot less deadly. (User EVP)

For this poster, those who trusted macro-level expert system research ("officials") to make individual-level masking decisions experienced a higher risk of death for themselves primarily because the CDC had waited too long to recommend cloth masking. Ultimately, retrospective narratives in this category supported the idea that disparities in masking behavior between Time 1 and Time 2 were rooted in higher levels of institutional trust at the Time 1 advisory (like those whose research did not support masking efficacy). However, a willingness to mask up in the face of the second advisory came alongside waning levels of institutional trust at Time 2.

5. Discussion

Regarding the first research question on the impact of individual-level research during the pandemic as yielding masking disparities, this research found that some posters did lean on their own research to make masking decisions. Indeed, 12% of users claimed that cloth and DIY masking, as recommended by the CDC, was ineffective. Another 7% noted that the CDC was lying about the effectiveness of cloth and DIY masks as a ruse to change the general public's drive to acquire N95 masks. Individual-level research was thematic in these posts as a reason for ignoring the Time 2 advisory that people in the United States turn to masking as a preventative. Thus, disparities in masking arose for those users who leaned on their own research to justify the non-use of DIY and cloth masks.

The second research question asked if individual-level research regarding masking during the pandemic impacted institutional trust in the CDC. The second theme generated in this analysis made it clear that distrust in the CDC was sewn by what appeared to users to be conflicting advisories (Time 1 vs. Time 2). The third theme highlighted a general concern and subsequent distrust over how long the CDC took to finally issue a pro-masking advisory (Time 2). This research started from the position that anti-maskers, those individuals who had never had any intention of wearing masks based on their own research, would socially construct an argument of distrust in the CDC—especially once the CDC moved to recommend cloth face masks. However, inductive analysis of response posts shifted this stance. While FB data certainly supported the presence of an anti-masking contingent that did not believe in the effectiveness of DIY masking, it also laid bare that much of the distrust displayed by users arose in individuals who had been more than willing to wear a mask at Time 1 based on either their own assessments ("conflicting advisories" theme) or existent institutional trust ("waited too long" theme). Indeed, many posters who expressed distrust in the CDC noted that they had been masking all along based on their own research. Furthermore, many posters lamented that, based on their own research, the CDC's incompetence was clear, given that the public had been exposed to images of persons wearing masks in China since January. For example, one person (User SCQ) noted, "Also in early February, Chinese people was [sic] recommended to cover their face in public if they have to go out of their home. I'm so disappointed, that the US government appears to even knew [sic] less than I did".

What are the takeaways of this analysis? First, it is important for PHAs to consider that the individual-level risk assessment inherent in Gidden's modern risk society is one that can create behavioral disparities and devolving levels of trust in and of itself. That is, the propensity for self-driven risk assessment at the individual level is a variable that should be examined alongside other social determinants such as gender, race and ethnicity, and socioeconomic status. In this research, users who leaned on their own research filtered both Time 1 and Time 2 recommendations through self-developed risk assessment lenses. These assessments then guided decisions about masking behaviors, ultimately revealing disparities in preventative behavior founded in how individual research framed the utility of masking. It is possible that creating audience-specific risk and crisis communication would mitigate the kind of behavioral disparities illuminated in this paper and that plagued American masking behaviors early in the pandemic [25].

PHAs might consider offering PH guidance based on a variety of different perspectives that acknowledge the capability of the general public to do its own "homework" regarding illness. This is especially the case when new scientific knowledge appears to contradict itself, leading to potential public confusion and an increased reliance on individual-level research [25]. I am in no way suggesting that laypersons who watch media coverage, peruse peer-reviewed work, and observe other regions' illness response mechanisms are the equivalent of scientific expertise. However, PHAs must realize that a modern risk society inherently guides individuals to seek ontological security for themselves—and if people have become wary of trusting "expert systems" such as the CDC, especially when inevitable scientific conflicts occur, then they will "double down" on their own research to center themselves.

PHAs should not discount this element of self-education as an affront to public health expertise but rather as an opportunity to build on that self-education. For example, the CDC might offer a website in which multiple resources of knowledge, both pro- and con-advisory, are offered for public consumption. This would serve to not only validate self-derived knowledge and risk assessment in the public but also allow individuals to consider, in a non-defensive context, scientific perspectives that vary from their own assessments. This approach would increase PHA transparency (a guiding principle of trust in PHA [61]), acknowledge the potential for members of the modern risk society to research illness, and potentially further minimize disparities in preventative behaviors based on that research.

Second, and related to the above, prior research has noted that healthcare decisions have evolved into a partnership between physicians and patients who have increasingly been encouraged by pharmaceutical companies to do their own research regarding prevention, diagnosis, and treatment [62,63]. Responses to PHA advisories should be viewed in the same way. That is, as researchers work to understand disparities in preventative behaviors such as masking during the pandemic, viewing members of the general public as health consumers who have developed their own risk profiles and tolerances will be important in understanding how to minimize disparities in preventative behaviors. Furthermore, understanding how this "consumer" framework reflects the lens with which the public chooses to (or not to) engage in a recommended preventative behavior, regardless of PHA recommendations, will be an important tool in developing PH strategies that create public trust rather than erode it.

Reflective of the first conclusion above, PHAs should not ignore the power of self-guided research to create disparities in preventative behaviors. Instead, and like the modern physician–patient relationship, these entities should acknowledge a willingness to partner with the citizenry in ways that are not simply "people should partner with us (PHAs) by doing this". Rather, the approach should be "we openly acknowledge and validate the general public's growing ability and desire to make decisions based on self-guided research and we want to partner with you in that endeavor". However, as one poster (User CKR) grumpily noted, "I'm actually tired of hearing the public doesn't know how to use masks and increase [sic] the problem rather than decrease it. You know, we are not stupid. If you learned how to use them, we can too". PHAs like the CDC that express a willingness to partner with the public stand to appear transparent and trusting of an increasingly educated population. These entities may also decrease disparities in preventative behavior uptake by recognizing modern society's relationship to healthcare as consumer based.

Finally, it is important to note that, based on this research, it could be concluded that the CDC, as a PHA, was "damned if it did, damned if it did not" in relation to how posters perceived both the initial and second masking advisories. PHAs have increasingly used SM platforms for the dissemination of recommendations and advisories [15]. As such, agencies involved in public relations must understand the potential benefit to PH of two-way communication with the general public for answering questions, decreasing health behavior disparities, and building trust [11]. While the CDC did use town halls on Twitter as a way of answering questions about the pandemic, these communications were usually very controlled with only particular questions addressed live by experts. SM outlets such as FB offer unique two-way opportunities for PHA to have frequent conversations with far more laypersons who are suspicious or distrusting of the agency. Yet, out of 1042 posts, only one post was made by the CDC—the second advisory that people should begin using DIY cloth masks. Efforts to directly answer even some user-generated concerns might prove fiscally and temporally expensive in terms of manpower, and it has been noted that expert rebuttals can encourage more layperson disputes [37,47]. However, the use of social media as a two-way mode of communication between PHA and the public has been shown to be an effective mode of engagement for mobilizing society during public health emergencies [64]. Addressing concerns posted on SM platforms such as FB is important in decreasing uptake disparities as well as building trust in the general public.

This research is limited in a few ways. The first limitation is encompassed by FB as a data source. While it is true that 80% of adult SM users in the U.S. use SM to gather health information, the demographics of specific users on the FB platform is impossible to determine [65]. The only clearcut identifiers are user-generated FB handles and profile pictures that cannot be gauged for authenticity. Thus, any attempt to analyze this data for demographic purposes would be inaccurate at best. However, as with any disparity in health behaviors, variables such as gender, race and ethnicity, socioeconomic status, and religion are impactful in the formation of attitudes. Religion and political affiliation, for example, have been shown to influence levels of trust in scientific authority [66], and political affiliation may have impacted mask wearing in the United States from the start of the pandemic [59]. Other research has shown that trust in the government varies by race, with whites trusting the government but doubting its competence, while African Americans do not trust the government and doubt its motives [67]. Future research should work to identify how social variables impact the drive to engage in individual-level risk assessment and how resulting assessments can create disparities in both preventative behaviors as well as institutional trust.

Another limitation lies in the fact that CDC FB users who posted regarding the CDC's second masking advisory appeared to submit multiple original and response posts. These more frequent posters were mixed with messages from far less frequent posters. Critics may argue that this concentration of posts from a small contingent of FB users skews the findings of this research. However, this is not unusual, given the nature of SM data in general. Indeed, van Mierlo has noted that 1% of SM users generate the vast majority of user-generated content, with a much smaller minority of posting coming from about 9% of users. The other 90% of users on SM platforms are "lurkers," users who read posts but never generate any of their own content [68]. As with an inability to identify demographic information on users, this is a valid issue when analyzing levels of trust. For example, what are the differences between those users who choose to post condemnation of the CDC (or, alternatively, support for) and those who choose only to read. Future research should consider how these differences may impact the willingness to discuss health behavior outcomes in relationship to individual-level risk assessments and trust in PHAs.

Another limitation can be found in the cross-sectional nature of the data used. It should be reiterated that this exploratory qualitative research analyzed cross-sectional data taken from the Time 2 advisory. This work also analyzed Time 2 posts for retrospective responses to the Time 1 advisory. Based on the findings discussed in this paper, future mixed methods work, bolstered by theory generation taken from qualitative analysis like that in this paper, should explore a quantitatively-driven longitudinal design that allows for analysis of self-guided risk assessment and its impact on the evolution of both preventative behaviors and institutional trust.

It may also be noted that the limited time frame during which data was collected for this paper (4-day window from the CDC's parent post to the last post made) may be a limitation. However, with the understanding that this work is exploratory in nature and specifically built for theory generation to be applied in future research, the small window of data collection may not be considered solely limiting. Rather, consideration of this data as a snapshot of responses, both current and retrospective, allows researchers to observe "in-the-moment" of complete advisory reversal, how prior risk assessments can immediately impact both behavioral outcomes as well as institutional trust. Furthermore, this shortened timeframe may be seen as a tradeoff for the accuracy in analysis of user narratives derived from qualitative content analysis. Indeed, this work provides a strength in the existing literature that is currently steeped in big data, quantitative analyses that, while potentially generalizable in nature, are not terribly accurate or precise with individual-level themes and narratives.

6. Conclusions

This research grows the knowledge that we have regarding how individual-level research regarding health advisories during the COVID-19 pandemic influenced both masking disparities as well as institutional trust in PHAs. As modern risk society posits, citizenry of modern societies initially places high levels of trust in the expert systems that help society progress forward. However, this progress does not come without peril. An inherent lack of expert ability to predict what risks may arise with technological innovation (and what the costs those risks may bring) yields an ever-growing distrust in the expert systems that the general public so readily trusted in the past [9].

In this research, users on the CDC FB page who posted regarding the CDC's second masking advisory demonstrated self-developed risk assessments about mask usage that appear to have been in place prior to the CDC's recommendation for DIY masking. Theory generation from this inductive analysis suggests that individual-level risk assessment is used as a lens through which PH advisories are filtered. As a result, this lens creates disparities in both masking outcomes as well as in levels of institutional trust. Ultimately, this work highlights the need for PH researchers and PHA to include in both future qualitative analysis as well as statistical modeling how individual-level research and subsequent risk assessments factor into health behavior outcomes.

Funding: This research received no external funding.

Institutional Review Board Statement: Data used in this research were publicly available and pre-existing to this research via the social media platform FB. The investigator had no reliable way of identifying posters on this platform. Thus, the research was deemed to be exempt by Southern Methodist University.

Informed Consent Statement: Not applicable.

Data Availability Statement: Data from this research are publicly available on FB and can be retrieved from https://www.facebook.com/cdc/posts/pfbid02nb49qW64gay2Ta7VSNvXd3yRuGe6QHAgggtqB2yoTjB7d1e6kivWGFYcWfVhendjl?comment_id=10157784682631026 (accessed on 9 January 2023).

Conflicts of Interest: The author declares no conflict of interest.

References

1. Centers for Disease Control and Prevention. CDC Museum COVID-19 Timeline. Available online: https://www.cdc.gov/museum/timeline/covid19.html (accessed on 18 August 2022).
2. Centers for Disease Control and Prevention. COVID-19: Stop the Spread of Germs 2020. Available online: https://www.facebook.com/cdc/posts/pfbid02WnY8NnQgA3mqYsgvKorZbGSWDAc8N291YXX9V1iRueFtsH8YQDGVjLdd2tgfuFnJl?__cft__[0]=AZW4oNcre1cENJSydA2njDFw-7csuQFsWvCu-FtBmA9tIcxPYluzVnRldT-QdWIrM3kblA7-oUwQjGswbFUuuufUfT7X0FqN32U3r6rI2kCzlV_R9JoYwHcevoEg1HeRtjPb4G3J-xPYVBpInz48EZ3F&__tn__=%2CO%2CP-R (accessed on 19 August 2022).

3. Centers for Disease Control Facebook Page. Wondering if a Mask Would Protect You from COVID-19? 2020. Available online: https://www.facebook.com/cdc/posts/pfbid02f4JBbsKWeEvZe1c6V1Gsvs1jDixoH9qRpwonebiY4QtaJGVaXs9K4FnNqB91cAm3l?__cft__[0]=AZWtQDpU3TRZ9RTLJrbXWOi98FW5DhWq8Uskn3vssi5Eh_t3VEgPvRH2NGGcIJrcpVwGLFBS-lk3i80XNb7v9dR_N2knM_cpoGlnaIB32ak2QhdrBzTxiC_xSYgwGTTLxc-DYG_nCjemFllecZwyR2vo&__tn__=%2CO%2CP-R (accessed on 18 August 2022).
4. Aguirre-Duarte, N. Can People with Asymptomatic or Pre-Symptomatic COVID-19 Infect Others: A Systematic Review of Primary Data. *Public Glob. Health* **2020**. [CrossRef]
5. Centers for Disease Control and Prevention. CDC's Recommendation Use of Cloth Face Coverings. 2020. Available online: https://www.facebook.com/cdc/posts/pfbid02nQu9YMpKs2VCGykarMGWiybxA48m1s61jWVLUjZaZ3tB1m1kAcp19axGBYD1Qjg1l?comment_id=10157784741681026&reply_comment_id=10157784769721026 (accessed on 18 August 2022).
6. Beck, U. *Risk Society: Towards a New Modernity*; SAGE Publications, Ltd.: London, UK, 1992.
7. Lupton, D. *Risk*, 2nd ed.; Routledge: Abington, UK, 2013.
8. Giddens, A. Risk, Trust, Reflexivity. In *Reflexive Modernization*; Polity Press: Cambridge, UK, 1994; pp. 184–197.
9. Giddens, A. *The Consequences of Modernity*; Stanford University Press: Stanford, CA, USA, 1991.
10. Blendon, R.J.; Benson, J.M.; Hero, J.O. Public Trust in Physicians—U.S. Medicine in International Perspective. *N. Engl. J. Med.* **2014**, *371*, 1570–1572. [CrossRef] [PubMed]
11. Laurent-Simpson, A.; Lo, C.C. Risk society online: Zika virus, social media and distrust in the Centers for Disease Control and Prevention. *Sociol. Health Illn.* **2019**, *41*, 1270–1288. [CrossRef] [PubMed]
12. Lo, C.C.; Laurent-Simpson, A. How SES May Figure in Perceptions of Zika Risks and in Preventive Action. *Sociol. Spectr.* **2018**, *38*, 295–311. [CrossRef]
13. Finney Rutten, L.J.; Blake, K.D.; Greenberg-Worisek, A.J.; Allen, S.V.; Moser, R.P.; Hesse, B.W. Online Health Information Seeking among US Adults: Measuring Progress toward a Healthy People 2020 Objective. *Public Health Rep.* **2019**, *134*, 617–625. [CrossRef]
14. Kontos, E.Z.; Emmons, K.M.; Puleo, E.; Viswanath, K. Communication Inequalities and Public Health Implications of Adult Social Networking Site Use in the United States. *J. Health Commun.* **2010**, *15* (Suppl. 3), 216–235. [CrossRef]
15. Heldman, A.B.; Schindelar, J.; Weaver, J.B. Social Media Engagement and Public Health Communication: Implications for Public Health Organizations Being Truly "Social". *Public Health Rev.* **2013**, *35*, 13. [CrossRef]
16. Liu, B.F.; Fraustino, J.D.; Jin, Y. How Disaster Information Form, Source, Type, and Prior Disaster Exposure Affect Public Outcomes: Jumping on the Social Media Bandwagon? *J. Appl. Commun. Res.* **2015**, *43*, 44–65. [CrossRef]
17. Liu, P.L. COVID-19 information on social media and preventive behaviors: Managing the pandemic through personal responsibility. *Soc. Sci. Med.* **2021**, *277*, 113928. [CrossRef]
18. Loon, J.V. Understanding epidemics in apocalypse culture. In *Risk and Technological Culture*; Routledge: Abington, UK, 2002.
19. Washer, P. Lay perceptions of emerging infectious diseases: A commentary. *Public Underst. Sci.* **2011**, *20*, 506–512. [CrossRef]
20. Wasserman, J.A.; Hinote, B.P. Chronic illness as incalculable risk: Scientific uncertainty and social transformations in medicine. *Soc. Theory Health* **2011**, *9*, 41–58. [CrossRef]
21. Cable, S.; Shriver, T.E.; Mix, T.L. Risk Society and Contested Illness: The Case of Nuclear Weapons Workers. *Am. Sociol. Rev.* **2008**, *73*, 380–401. [CrossRef]
22. Zinn, J.O. Health and illness as drivers of risk language in the news media—A case study of The Times. *Health Risk Soc.* **2020**, *22*, 437–455. [CrossRef]
23. Mykhalovskiy, E.; French, M. COVID-19, public health, and the politics of prevention. *Sociol. Health Illn.* **2020**, *42*, e4–e15. [CrossRef] [PubMed]
24. Giordani, R.C.F.; Giolo, S.R.; Zanoni Da Silva, M.; Muhl, C. Risk perception of COVID-19: Susceptibility and severity perceived by the Brazilian population. *J. Health Psychol.* **2022**, *27*, 1365–1378. [CrossRef]
25. Collins, A.; Florin, M.-V.; Renn, O. COVID-19 risk governance: Drivers, responses and lessons to be learned. *J. Risk Res.* **2020**, *23*, 1073–1082. [CrossRef]
26. Martin, G.P.; Hanna, E.; McCartney, M.; Dingwall, R. Science, society, and policy in the face of uncertainty: Reflections on the debate around face coverings for the public during COVID-19. *Crit. Public Health* **2020**, *30*, 501–508. [CrossRef]
27. Gesser-Edelsburg, A.; Mordini, E.; James, J.J.; Greco, D.; Green, M.S. Risk Communication Recommendations and Implementation during Emerging Infectious Diseases: A Case Study of the 2009 H1N1 Influenza Pandemic. *Disaster Med. Public Health Prep.* **2014**, *8*, 158–169. [CrossRef]
28. Liu, Y.; Duong, H.T.; Nguyen, H.T. Media exposure and intentions to wear face masks in the early stages of the COVID-19 outbreak: The mediating role of negative emotions and risk perception. *Atl. J. Commun.* **2021**, *30*, 467–480. [CrossRef]
29. Zhang, B.; Li, Z.; Jiang, L. The Intentions to Wear Face Masks and the Differences in Preventive Behaviors between Urban and Rural Areas during COVID-19: An Analysis Based on the Technology Acceptance Model. *Int. J. Environ. Res. Public Health* **2021**, *18*, 9988. [CrossRef]
30. Irfan, M.; Akhtar, N.; Ahmad, M.; Shahzad, F.; Elavarasan, R.M.; Wu, H.; Yang, C. Assessing Public Willingness to Wear Face Masks during the COVID-19 Pandemic: Fresh Insights from the Theory of Planned Behavior. *Int. J. Environ. Res. Public Health* **2021**, *18*, 4577. [CrossRef] [PubMed]

31. Cheng, Y.; Liu, R.W.; Foerster, T.A. Predicting intentions to practice COVID-19 preventative behaviors in the United States: A test of the risk perception attitude framework and the theory of normative social behavior. *J. Health Psychol.* **2022**, *27*, 2744–2762. [CrossRef] [PubMed]
32. Bokemper, S.E.; Cucciniello, M.; Rotesi, T.; Pin, P.; Malik, A.A.; Willebrand, K.; Paintsil, E.E.; Omer, S.B.; Huber, G.A.; Melegaro, A. Experimental evidence that changing beliefs about mask efficacy and social norms increase mask wearing for COVID-19 risk reduction: Results from the United States and Italy. *PLoS ONE* **2021**, *16*, e0258282. [CrossRef] [PubMed]
33. Palcu, J.; Schreier, M.; Janiszewski, C. Facial mask personalization encourages facial mask wearing in times of COVID-19. *Sci. Rep.* **2022**, *12*, 891. [CrossRef] [PubMed]
34. Abd-Alrazaq, A.; Alhuwail, D.; Househ, M.; Hamdi, M.; Shah, Z. Top Concerns of Tweeters during the COVID-19 Pandemic: Infoveillance Study. *J. Med. Internet Res.* **2020**, *22*, e19016. [CrossRef]
35. Obiała, J.; Obiała, K.; Mańczak, M.; Owoc, J.; Olszewski, R. COVID-19 misinformation: Accuracy of articles about coronavirus prevention mostly shared on social media. *Health Policy Technol.* **2021**, *10*, 182–186. [CrossRef]
36. Ahmed, W.; Vidal-Alaball, J.; Lopez Segui, F.; Moreno-Sánchez, P.A. A Social Network Analysis of Tweets Related to Masks during the COVID-19 Pandemic. *Int. J. Environ. Res. Public Health* **2020**, *17*, 8235. [CrossRef]
37. Mourali, M.; Drake, C. The Challenge of Debunking Health Misinformation in Dynamic Social Media Conversations: Online Randomized Study of Public Masking During COVID-19. *J. Med. Internet Res.* **2022**, *24*, e34831. [CrossRef]
38. Chum, A.; Nielsen, A.; Bellows, Z.; Farrell, E.; Durette, P.-N.; Banda, J.M.; Cupchik, G. Changes in Public Response Associated with Various COVID-19 Restrictions in Ontario, Canada: Observational Infoveillance Study Using Social Media Time Series Data. *J. Med. Internet Res.* **2021**, *23*, e28716. [CrossRef]
39. Mohammed, F.; Al-Kumaim, N.H.; Alzahrani, A.I.; Fazea, Y. The Impact of Social Media Shared Health Content on Protective Behavior against COVID-19. *Int. J. Environ. Res. Public Health* **2023**, *20*, 1775. [CrossRef]
40. Raskhodchikov, A.N.; Pilgun, M. COVID-19 and Public Health: Analysis of Opinions in Social Media. *Int. J. Environ. Res. Public Health* **2023**, *20*, 971. [CrossRef] [PubMed]
41. Xu, Q.; Shen, Z.; Shah, N.; Cuomo, R.; Cai, M.; Brown, M.; Li, J.; Mackey, T. Characterizing Weibo Social Media Posts from Wuhan, China during the Early Stages of the COVID-19 Pandemic: Qualitative Content Analysis. *JMIR Public Health Surveill.* **2020**, *6*, e24125. [CrossRef] [PubMed]
42. Hoernke, K.; Djellouli, N.; Andrews, L.; Lewis-Jackson, S.; Manby, L.; Martin, S.; Vanderslott, S.; Vindrola-Padros, C. Frontline healthcare workers' experiences with personal protective equipment during the COVID-19 pandemic in the UK: A rapid qualitative appraisal. *BMJ Open* **2021**, *11*, e046199. [CrossRef] [PubMed]
43. Bhasin, T.; Butcher, C.; Gordon, E.; Hallward, M.; LeFebvre, R. Does Karen wear a mask? The gendering of COVID-19 masking rhetoric. *Int. J. Sociol. Soc. Policy* **2020**, *40*, 929–937. [CrossRef]
44. Giglietto, F.; Rossi, L.; Bennato, D. The Open Laboratory: Limits and Possibilities of Using Facebook, Twitter, and YouTube as a Research Data Source. *J. Technol. Hum. Serv.* **2012**, *30*, 145–159. [CrossRef]
45. Fine, G.A.; Elsbach, K.D. Ethnography and Experiment in Social Psychological Theory Building: Tactics for Integrating Qualitative Field Data with Quantitative Lab Data. *J. Exp. Soc. Psychol.* **2000**, *36*, 51–76. [CrossRef]
46. Fisher, K.A.; Barile, J.P.; Guerin, R.J.; Vanden Esschert, K.L.; Jeffers, A.; Tian, L.H.; Garcia-Williams, A.; Gurbaxani, B.; Thompson, W.W.; Prue, C.E. Factors Associated with Cloth Face Covering Use among Adults during the COVID-19 Pandemic—United States, April and May 2020. *MMWR Morb. Mortal. Wkly. Rep.* **2020**, *69*, 933–937. [CrossRef]
47. Malecki, K.M.C.; Keating, J.A.; Safdar, N. Crisis Communication and Public Perception of COVID-19 Risk in the Era of Social Media. *Clin. Infect. Dis.* **2021**, *72*, 697–702. [CrossRef]
48. Wong, L.P.; Wu, Q.; Hao, Y.; Chen, X.; Chen, Z.; Alias, H.; Shen, M.; Hu, J.; Duan, S.; Zhang, J.; et al. The role of institutional trust in preventive practices and treatment-seeking intention during the coronavirus disease 2019 outbreak among residents in Hubei, China. *Int. Health* **2022**, *14*, 161–169. [CrossRef]
49. Joffe, H.; Washer, P.; Solberg, C. Public engagement with emerging infectious disease: The case of MRSA in Britain. *Psychol. Health* **2011**, *26*, 667–683. [CrossRef]
50. Glaser, B.G.; Strauss, A.L. *The Discovery of Grounded Theory: Strategies for Qualitative Research*; 4. Paperback Printing; Aldine: New Brunswick, NJ, USA, 2009.
51. Hsieh, H.-F.; Shannon, S.E. Three Approaches to Qualitative Content Analysis. *Qual. Health Res.* **2005**, *15*, 1277–1288. [CrossRef] [PubMed]
52. Gottfried, J.; Shearer, E. *News Use across Social Medial Platforms 2016*; Pew Research Center: Washington, DC, USA, 2016.
53. Gramlich, J. *10 Facts about Americans and Facebook*; Pew Research Center: Washington, DC, USA, 2021. Available online: https://www.pewresearch.org/fact-tank/2021/06/01/facts-about-americans-and-facebook/ (accessed on 25 August 2022).
54. Walker, M.; Matsa, K.E. *News Consumption across Social Media in 2021*; Pew Research Center: Washington, DC, USA, 2021. Available online: https://www.pewresearch.org/journalism/2021/09/20/news-consumption-across-social-media-in-2021/ (accessed on 25 August 2022).
55. U.S. Institute of Medicine. *The Future of Public Health—Appendix A, Summary of the Public Health System in the United States*; Institute of Medicine (US) Committee for the Study of the Future of Public Health: Washington, DC, USA, 1988. Available online: https://www.ncbi.nlm.nih.gov/books/NBK218212 (accessed on 20 August 2022).

56. Lofland, J. *Analyzing Social Settings: A Guide to Qualitative Observation and Analysis*; Wadsworth/Thomson Learning: Boston, MA, USA, 2006.
57. Charmaz, K. *Constructing Grounded Theory*; SAGE: Thousand Oaks, CA, USA, 2014.
58. Hunter, P. The role of fear in modern societies. *EMBO Rep.* **2021**, *22*, e52157. [CrossRef] [PubMed]
59. Lupton, D.; Southerton, C.; Clark, M.; Watson, A. *The Face Mask in COVID Times: A Sociomaterial Analysis*; De Gruyter: Berlin, Germany, 2021.
60. Baker, D.W. Trust in Health Care in the Time of COVID-19. *JAMA* **2020**, *324*, 2373–2375. [CrossRef] [PubMed]
61. MacKay, M.; Cimino, A.; Yousefinaghani, S.; McWhirter, J.E.; Dara, R.; Papadopoulos, A. Canadian COVID-19 Crisis Communication on Twitter: Mixed Methods Research Examining Tweets from Government, Politicians, and Public Health for Crisis Communication Guiding Principles and Tweet Engagement. *Int. J. Environ. Res. Public Health* **2022**, *19*, 6954. [CrossRef]
62. Conrad, P. The Shifting Engines of Medicalization. *J. Health Soc. Behav.* **2005**, *46*, 3–14. [CrossRef]
63. Conrad, P.; Leiter, V. Medicalization, markets and consumers. *J. Health Soc. Behav.* **2004**, *45*, 158–176.
64. Pang, P.C.-I.; Jiang, W.; Pu, G.; Chan, K.-S.; Lau, Y. Social Media Engagement in Two Governmental Schemes during the COVID-19 Pandemic in Macao. *Int. J. Environ. Res. Public Health* **2022**, *19*, 8976. [CrossRef]
65. Duggan, M.; Ellison, N.B.; Lampe, C.; Lenhart, A.; Madden, M. Social Media Update 2014. Pew Research Center: Internet, Science & Tech. 2015. Available online: http://www.pewinternet.org/2015/01/09/social-media-update-2014 (accessed on 18 May 2018).
66. Gauchat, G. Politicization of Science in the Public Sphere: A Study of Public Trust in the United States, 1974 to 2010. *Am. Sociol. Rev.* **2012**, *77*, 167–187. [CrossRef]
67. Jamison, A.M.; Quinn, S.C.; Freimuth, V.S. "You don't trust a government vaccine": Narratives of institutional trust and influenza vaccination among African American and white adults. *Soc. Sci. Med.* **2019**, *221*, 87–94. [CrossRef]
68. van Mierlo, T. The 1% Rule in Four Digital Health Social Networks: An Observational Study. *J. Med. Internet Res.* **2014**, *16*. [CrossRef]

International Journal of
Environmental Research and Public Health

MDPI

Article

Testing the Multiple Disadvantage Model of Health with Ethnic Asian Children: A Secondary Data Analysis

Tyrone C. Cheng [1,]* and Celia C. Lo [2]

[1] School of Social Work, University of Alabama, Little Hall, Tuscaloosa, AL 35401, USA
[2] Behavioral Research Manager, Peraton, Defense Personnel and Security Research Center, Seaside, CA 93955, USA
* Correspondence: ccheng@sw.ua.edu

Abstract: This study of ethnic Asian children in the United States asked whether their health exhibited relationship with any of six factors: social disorganization, social structural factors, social relationships, the health of their parents, their access to medical insurance, acculturation. The sample of 1350 ethnic Asian children was extracted from the 2018 National Survey of Children's Health. Logistic regression results showed that these children's excellent/very good/good health was associated positively with safe neighborhoods, family incomes, family cohesiveness, family support, and receipt of Temporary Assistance for Needy Families (TANF). In turn, health was associated negatively with single-mother households. Implications of the present results in terms of interventions promoting family support, TANF participation, safe neighborhoods, and professionals' cultural competency are discussed.

Keywords: Asian children; health; multiple disadvantages; welfare

Citation: Cheng, T.C.; Lo, C.C. Testing the Multiple Disadvantage Model of Health with Ethnic Asian Children: A Secondary Data Analysis. *Int. J. Environ. Res. Public Health* **2023**, *20*, 483. https://doi.org/10.3390/ijerph20010483

Academic Editors: Paul B. Tchounwou and Saoirse Nic Gabhainn

Received: 30 September 2022
Revised: 3 December 2022
Accepted: 21 December 2022
Published: 28 December 2022

1. Introduction

Research results have long suggested that, in the United States, child health is associated negatively with minority ethnicity [1–5]. Some studies, nevertheless, have reported anywhere from 78.4% to 96.5% of ethnic Asian children surveyed to have health described as excellent/very good/good [6–9]. In contrast, two published studies found health among ethnic Asian children to be worse than health among white children [10,11], and several studies found no significant differences in health between ethnic Asian children and white children [7,12–14]. It is important, then, to continue examining factors that may be involved in the health of ethnic Asian children.

1.1. Multiple Disadvantage Model

To conduct its investigation of factors in ethnic Asian youngsters' health, the present study applied a theoretical model—the multiple disadvantage model. This model holds that socioeconomic disadvantages and the distress associated with them negatively affect intimate relationships and social relationships. It has been applied to explain children's health as related to maternal health [15]; to explain children's delinquency [16–18]; to explain access to substance use treatment [19]; and to explain racial disparities in victimization [20–22]. The multiple disadvantage model deems historical and structural racism to continually frustrate members of our society who are of minority ethnicity [20]. If these individuals are parents, racism-related frustration may, the model predicts, exhibit a negative influence on their parenting. The literature does offer at least one analysis, though, arguing that to date the search for a racism–health link among children generally (that is, children of all ethnicities) has yielded mixed results [23].

1.1.1. Social Disorganization

In the present study, we applied the multiple disadvantage model to examine how Asian child health might be related to five socioeconomic disadvantages: social disorganization, social structural factors, social relationships, parental health, and medical insurance (see Figure 1). The presence of socioeconomic disadvantages tends to impair both individual physical health and parenting, leading to poor health for children [15]. Prior studies with children in the general population have shown poor health to be linked to social disorganization, for instance to low income and to living in unkempt, unsafe neighborhoods [1,3,24–29]. One study reported a link between ethnic Asian children's poor health, specifically, and the disorganized or materially deprived condition of neighborhoods [30]. For the present study, we speculated that social disorganization factors similar to these are related to health among ethnic Asian children.

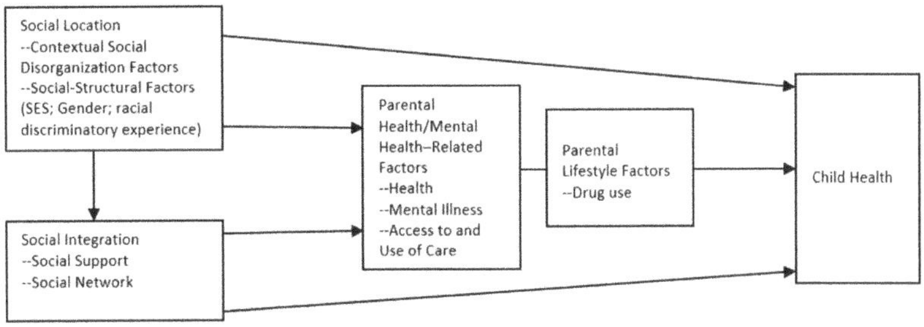

Figure 1. The multiple disadvantage model explaining Asian child health.

1.1.2. Social Structural Factors

We speculated that social structural factors—namely, parents' education, employment status, and income—are, when their attainments are low, a considerable deterrent to the good or excellent health of ethnic Asian children. However, the literature suggests that ethnic Asian children's health is not significantly related to parents' educational attainment [31,32]. On the other hand, research with children of all ethnicities has reported child health to be associated positively with current employment of parents [33,34] and with parents' income [2–4,13,35–37]. While one study reported that receiving public assistance from Temporary Assistance for Needy Families (TANF) or the Supplemental Nutrition Assistance Program (SNAP) is associated positively with children's health [38], another showed a negative association [39]. We ultimately speculated that the health of Asian children would be linked positively to their parents' education, income, and current employment.

1.1.3. Social Relationships

Supportive social relationships can alleviate the distress of Asian parents facing multiple socioeconomic disadvantages. Parents who are supported by strong social networks demonstrate relatively more-effective parenting, according to the literature [40], and that in turn eventually improves children's health [27,41,42]. Two prior studies with a general population of children found poor health to be associated with single-parent families and with parents' separation [36,43]; other studies, however, observed no health-related association either for single-parent households or for support from parents' partner/former partner [4,44]. Additionally, a study in the literature reported no significant relationship between Asian ethnicity and the degree or quality of parents' communication with children's healthcare providers [45]. As well, one published study interestingly reported ethnic Asian children to have received less emotional support from their parents than white children received from theirs [46]. For the present study, we speculated that health among ethnic Asian children would be associated negatively with single-parent households but associated positively with family and social support.

1.1.4. Parental Health

The multiple disadvantage model proposes that facing socioeconomic disadvantages can affect physical health. The literature appears not to address the specific disadvantage of interest to our present study, which would be the physical health of parents of ethnic Asian children. However, studies with a general population of children have indicated that parents in good physical health care relatively effectively for their children [47]. Moreover, published studies also indicate that parents' physical health is associated positively with their children's physical health [15,35,39,48,49]. For this study, we speculated that a positive relationship would be observed between the health of ethnic Asian children and their parents' own health.

1.1.5. Medical Insurance

Lack of medical insurance was the fifth socioeconomic disadvantage affecting families included in our present study. Lack of health coverage can affect children's health, uninsured children reportedly being less healthy than insured children [3,48,49]. For this study, we speculated that a positive relationship would be observed between health among ethnic Asian children and their coverage by medical insurance.

1.2. Acculturation

Another factor we tested as a potential indicator of ethnic Asian children's health was acculturation. Acculturation is the process through which individuals and groups adjust to and/or are changed by a culture beyond their native culture [50], typically as a result of immigration. For Asian individuals and families in the U.S., proficient spoken English is an indicator of acculturation [51]. Studies of ethnic Asian children have concluded that their physical health is associated positively with their English language learning [8,9,52] and moreover is associated negatively with their and/or their parents' having immigrated to the U.S. [6,53,54]. According to one study—and not surprisingly—only 43% of surveyed first-generation Asian immigrants to the U.S. demonstrated proficiency with English [55]. A different study reported finding no significant association between the health of ethnic Asian children and such children's own or their parents' nativity [32].

1.3. Hypotheses

Along with acculturation's role, the present study probed, again, whether facing multiple socioeconomic disadvantages hinders parental/family caregiving for ethnic Asian children, and whether any effect on caregiving seems in turn to diminish children's health. The reviewed literature provided only a small number of studies focusing on factors in the health of ethnic Asian children in the U.S. Based on that modest beginning and applying the multiple disadvantage model, we devised two hypotheses for testing, as follows:

1. Health among ethnic Asian children will be associated positively with safe neighborhood, family income, parents' educational attainment, parents' employment, family support, social support, parents' health, medical coverage, TANF or SNAP enrollment, parents' birth in U.S., children's birth in U.S., and families' English proficiency.
2. Health among ethnic Asian children will be associated negatively with rundown neighborhood, discrimination experience, and single-mother household.

2. Methods

2.1. Sample

This secondary data analysis employed a nationally representative sample of 1350 ethnic Asian children extracted from a public-use data set, the 2018 National Survey of Children's Health (NSCH, Salem, MA, USA). NSCH researchers interviewed 30,530 children and their caregivers, gathering information on health status, insurance coverage, social relationships, family relationships, and neighborhood characteristics [56]. Our sample was limited to participating children of Asian ethnicity and their parents. In our present sample, child's median age was 10 years, and girls constituted nearly 51% of our sample. This study used a public-use data set and was exempted from approval by a university Institutional Review Board.

2.2. Measures

Our outcome variable, child health, was dichotomized as "excellent/very good/good" versus "fair/poor," the latter serving as the reference. In the original NSCH study, participants had been offered the responses "excellent," "very good," "good," "fair," and "poor." Our explanatory variables made up seven groups: social disorganization factors, social structural factors, social relationships and social support, parental health, medical insurance, acculturation factors, and demographic characteristics.

Our social disorganization factors comprised two dichotomous variables and one continuous variable. Rundown neighborhood indicated that a parent had (yes) or had not (no) reported his/her neighborhood (a) to have "litter or garbage on street or sidewalk," (b) to feature "poorly kept or rundown housing," or (c) to feature "vandalism such as broken windows or graffiti." Racial discrimination (yes/no) measured whether his/her parent had reported a participating child to have ever been treated or judged solely on race/ethnicity. Safe neighborhood described how much a participating child's parent agreed that the family's neighborhood was safe for the child, using the offered responses 4 (definitely agree), 3 (somewhat agree), 2 (somewhat disagree), and 1 (definitely disagree).

Our social structural factors included variables measuring parents' educational attainment as well as family income. Parent educational attainment gave the highest level of study completed, using offered responses as follows: 1 (8th grade or below), 2 (9th–12th grade), 3 (graduated high school or GED), 4 (vocational school), 5 (some college), 6 (associate degree), 7 (undergraduate degree), 8 (master's degree), 9 (doctoral or professional degree). Employed parent (yes/no) described parents who had been paid employees during 50 of the 52 weeks preceding NSCH interviews. Family income-to-poverty ratio gave the percentage of federal poverty level that a family's income represented, figures provided in the NSCH data set. Finally, participation in public assistance programs was measured via two variables, receipt of TANF and receipt of SNAP, describing families' receipt of associated benefits during the 12 months preceding interview.

We used six explanatory variables to measure social relationships and social support. Single mother (yes/no) described parents who were single female parents. Next, a response scale was used to measure family cohesiveness and involved two survey items. Parents were asked whether their families drew on strengths that family members possessed, and they were asked whether their families talked together about problems they faced. The response scale comprised 1 (none of the time), 2 (some of the time), 3 (most of the time), and 4 (all the time). Scores for the two items were summed to obtain a total score for each parent, with a higher total score indicating stronger family cohesiveness. The measure yielded a Cronbach's alpha of 0.85.

In addition, we used the dichotomous variable family support to indicate whether a spouse/partner, other family members, or friends were providing a parent with emotional support encouraging his/her parenting efforts. Similarly, the dichotomous variable professional support indicated whether a counselor or other healthcare provider was supplying a surveyed parent with emotional support, and another dichotomous variable peer/religious group support indicated whether a parent had joined a support group of peers or a religious group for the purpose of obtaining emotional support. Finally, neighbor support was measured via a total score from survey items asking parents how much they agreed that adults in the neighborhood (a) know where to get help, (b) watched out for each other's children, and (c) provided help to other parents when requested to. A relatively high total score implied a relatively strong network of supportive neighbors. For all three items, offered responses were 4 (definitely agree), 3 (somewhat agree), 2 (somewhat disagree), and 1 (definitely disagree). The three items yielded a Cronbach's alpha of 0.79.

Resembling our child health outcome variable, our explanatory variable parent health was dichotomized as "excellent/very good/good" versus "fair/poor", the latter serving as the reference. Parent health was a self-reported measure. Our study also considered some variables describing families' participation in public or private medical insurance or assistance programs. Preliminary analysis of a variable indicating private insurance participation, however, suggested the dichotomous variable was vulnerable to singularity, due to our preliminary modeling's inability to estimate the variable's coefficient, or odds ratio. The coefficient could not be estimated because we encountered no cases in which a parent holding private insurance reported a child to be in "fair/poor" health. In light of the real possibility of singularity, our final analysis employed a single dichotomous variable, insured, to indicate a child's coverage by either public or private medical insurance.

We used three dichotomous explanatory variables to measure a family's acculturation: parent born in U.S., child born in U.S., and speaks English at home. The latter variable stated whether or not English was the language largely used in the family's home. We did not include parent's U.S. residence less than five years as a variable because doing so generated singularity in preliminary analysis. Finally, we used three demographic variables as controls in our modeling. The three were parent age (in years), child age (in years), and girl (boy providing the reference).

2.3. Data Analysis

In preparing descriptive statistics, we analyzed categorical variables using frequencies and percentages. Since continuous variables were found not normally distributed, they were analyzed by using medians and interquartile ranges. Because our present study's outcome variable was a binary one, we employed STATA logistic regression to perform linearized variance estimations with robust standard errors, and we added all explanatory variables to the logistic regression model at the same time. In addition, we employed the sampling weights that the NSCH researchers had provided. Our preliminary analyses of tolerance statistics (0.51 or higher) and of correlations ($-0.28 \leq r \leq 0.65$) suggested no multicollinearity problems among the employed explanatory variables.

3. Results

Descriptive analyses demonstrated that a great majority (98.6%) of the ethnic Asian children to have "excellent/very good/good" health (see Table 1). Descriptive statistics also showed 25.9% of these children to live in rundown neighborhoods and 6.2% to have experienced racial discrimination. The median score for safe neighborhood was 4 (i.e., parents reported themselves to "somewhat agree" that their neighborhoods were safe for their children). In this study, the parent's median educational attainment measured 7, or earning of an associate's degree. On average in the study, a family had a median income-to-poverty ratio of 390%. Nearly 82.0% of parents in our study were employed; only 1.2% had received TANF assistance, and 4.3% had received SNAP assistance.

Out of parents of 1350 ethnic Asian children in the present sample, only 5.7% were single mothers. The median score for family cohesiveness was 7 and for neighbor support was 10. Of our sample, 51.9% reported receiving emotional support from members of the family, and 16.4% reported receiving emotional support from healthcare professionals. For 18.9% of parents in our sample, emotional support was provided by a peer/religious group. In addition, 96.5% of parents in our sample reported having "excellent/very good/good" health, while 95.0% of children in our sample had medical insurance. Concerning nativity, 78.4% of children in our sample had been born in the U.S., as had 20.8% of parents in our sample. Furthermore, English was the primary language used at home for 61.1% of families in our sample. Median age of parents in our study was 44.2 years and children 10 years; 50.9% of children in the sample were girls.

Table 1. Descriptive statistics of ethnic Asian children (n = 1350).

	Frequency	Percent	M	IQR
Outcome variable				
Child health (excellent/very good/good)	1331	98.6	N/A	N/A
(fair/poor)	19	1.4	N/A	N/A
Explanatory variables				
Rundown neighborhood (yes)	350	25.9	N/A	N/A
(no)	1000	74.1	N/A	N/A
Racial discrimination (yes)	84	6.2	N/A	N/A
(no)	1266	93.8	N/A	N/A
Safe neighborhood	N/A	N/A	4	1
Parent educational attainment	N/A	N/A	7	8
Employed parent (yes)	1106	81.9	N/A	N/A
(no)	244	18.1	N/A	N/A
Family income-to-poverty ratio (%)	N/A	N/A	390	199
Receipt of TANF (yes)	16	1.2	N/A	N/A
(no)	1334	98.8	N/A	N/A
Receipt of SNAP (yes)	58	4.3	N/A	N/A
(no)	1292	95.7	N/A	N/A
Single mother (yes)	77	43.7	N/A	N/A
(no)	1273	56.3	N/A	N/A
Family cohesiveness	N/A	N/A	7	2
Family support (yes)	700	51.9	N/A	N/A
(no)	650	48.1	N/A	N/A
Professional support (yes)	221	16.4	N/A	N/A
(no)	1129	83.6	N/A	N/A
Peer/religious group support (yes)	255	18.9	N/A	N/A
(no)	1095	81.1	N/A	N/A
Neighbor support	N/A	N/A	10	3
Parent health (excellent/very good/good)	1303	96.5	N/A	N/A
(fair/poor)	47	3.5	N/A	N/A
Insured (yes)	1282	95.0	N/A	N/A
(no)	68	5.0	N/A	N/A
Parent born in U.S. (yes)	281	20.8	N/A	N/A
(no)	1069	79.2	N/A	N/A
Child born in U.S. (yes)	1059	78.4	N/A	N/A
(no)	291	21.6	N/A	N/A
Speaks English at home (yes)	825	61.1	N/A	N/A
(no)	525	38.9	N/A	N/A
Parent age (years)	N/A	N/A	44	10
Child age (years)	N/A	N/A	10	9
Girl	687	50.9	N/A	N/A
Boy	663	49.1	N/A	N/A

Note: M = median; IQR = interquartile range; N/A = not applicable.

Results from multivariate analysis showed the hypothesized model to differ significantly from the null (Wald's χ^2 = 71.15, $p < 0.01$; see Table 2). Specifically, results indicated that residence in a safe neighborhood was associated positively with the likelihood that a child in the sample was in "excellent/very good/good" health (OR = 2.35; $p < 0.05$). Living in rundown neighborhoods and experiencing racial/ethnic discrimination, however, showed no association with children's health in this study. Only two of the tested social structural variables exhibited a significant relationship with our outcome variable—both in positive direction: family income-to-poverty ratio (OR = 1.01, $p < 0.01$) and receipt of TANF (OR = 275.79, $p < 0.05$). In our study, while single motherhood (OR = 0.09, $p < 0.01$) was associated negatively with child health, child's "excellent/very good/good" health was associated positively with family cohesiveness (OR = 2.17, $p < 0.01$) and family support (OR = 15.20, $p < 0.05$). Emotional support (for parents) from healthcare professionals, peer/religious groups, and neighbors did not demonstrate significant effect on child's health in our study. A similar lack of significant association was observed for receipt of

SNAP, for acculturation factors, and for the demographic characteristics age (child's as well as parent's) and gender.

Table 2. Logistic regression results on ethnic Asian child health (excellent/very good/good) (n = 1350).

Variables	OR	RSE	90% Confidence-Interval
Rundown neighborhood (no)	0.73	0.57	0.20–2.65
Racial discrimination (no)	2.27	2.35	0.41–12.43
Safe neighborhood	2.35 *	1.17	1.03–5.33
Parent educational attainment	0.76	0.13	0.57–1.00
Employed parent (no)	0.76	0.84	0.12–4.71
Family income-to-poverty ratio	1.01 **	0.00	1.00–1.01
Receipt of TANF (no)	275.79 *	739.56	3.35–22,708.61
Receipt of SNAP (no)	0.27	0.29	0.05–1.59
Single mother (no)	0.09 **	0.08	0.02–0.40
Family cohesiveness	2.17 **	0.49	1.50–3.14
Family support (no)	15.20 *	20.20	1.71–135.23
Professional support (no)	0.35	0.45	0.04–2.90
Peer/religious group support (no)	0.28	0.38	0.03–2.58
Neighbor support	1.01	0.16	0.78–1.30
Parent health (fair/poor)	4.35	4.77	0.72–26.40
Insured (no)	3.74	3.04	0.98–14.26
Parent born in U.S. (no)	0.74	0.76	0.14–4.01
Child born in U.S. (no)	1.31	1.10	0.33–5.21
Speaks English at home (no)	2.52	2.35	0.54–11.66
Parent age	0.97	0.07	0.86–1.09
Child age	0.97	0.10	0.82–1.16
Girl (boy)	0.39	0.24	0.14–1.08
Wald's χ^2 =	71.15 **		

Notes: ** $p < 0.01$; * $p < 0.05$; OR = odds-ratios; RSE = robust standard errors; reference groups are in parentheses.

4. Discussion

Our study showed over 98% of ethnic Asian children in the sample to be in "excellent/very good/good" health. Moreover, our multivariate analysis findings showed child health to have associations in positive direction with safe neighborhood, family income-to-poverty ratio, receipt of TANF, family cohesiveness, and family support; and associations in negative direction with single mother. No other variables showed significant associations with children's health.

The present study found that the majority of ethnic Asian children in the sample were in "excellent/very good/good" health, a proportion comparable to prior published results [6,7,9]. Our findings, moreover, partially supported our first hypothesis, that the health of ethnic Asian children would be associated positively with safe neighborhoods, family income, parents' educational attainment, parent's employment, family support, social support, parents' health, medical insurance coverage, TANF or SNAP participation, parents' U.S. birth, children's U.S. birth, and families' English proficiency. In the present study, we observed the health of ethnic Asian children to be better with residence in safe neighborhoods. We also observed a relationship in positive direction between their health and their family income, a finding that supports results from prior studies of children in the general population [2–4,13,35–37]. Our study found that receiving TANF was linked to better child health. Unlike a study focused on several cities [38], however, our research found no significant association between ethnic Asian children's health and family participation in SNAP. Thus our overall findings imply that relatively high family incomes and safe neighborhoods facilitate ethnic Asian children's good health and that assistance from TANF has a similar effect among low-income families. Examining our data even more closely showed that merely 9.0% of families in our sample had incomes below federal poverty level; of those, 3.3% participated in TANF, 21.5% participated in SNAP, and 62.8%

had an employed parent. In other words, no TANF or SNAP assistance seems to be sought by the majority of ethnic Asian working-poor families.

In contrast, in line with other prior results for ethnic Asian children [30,31], we found no association between child health and parent's educational background. Our findings additionally showed child health to be associated positively with family cohesiveness and family support. Professionals' provision of emotional support for parents did not change health among the ethnic Asian children in our sample, however; this finding parallels at least one earlier published result [45]. Support for parents from peer-support or religious groups, and from neighbors, similarly lacked demonstrable effect on child health in this study. Such findings suggest that Asian families rely heavily on their relatives and close friends for support, regardless of parents' educational backgrounds.

Like another study [31], our study observed no association between ethnic Asian children's health and the birthplace of their parents or their own birthplace. *Unlike* other studies, though—all of them having small samples, our study indicated no significant association between English proficiency and ethnic Asian children's health [8,51]. While many ethnic Asian families maintain the culture of origin and have difficulties of cultural adjustment [57], our findings found no association between children's health and acculturation.

Our study findings also partially supported our second hypothesis, that the health of ethnic Asian children would be associated negatively with rundown neighborhoods, experiences of racial/ethnic discrimination, and single-parent households. The negative relationship observed, in this study, between child health and households headed by single mothers in particular tends to confirm some prior studies with children in the general population [36,43]. It appears that single mothers can find caring for children to be difficult and stressful; that our outcome (child health) was significantly linked to family support implies that such mothers need a great deal of support from their relatives and close friends. At the same time, we did not observe any significant links, here, between child health and rundown neighborhoods or discrimination experiences. Moreover, close examination of the data revealed that the interaction term between single mother and safe neighborhood (OR = 0.02, $p < 0.05$) yielded a negative association with child health, while interactions terms between single mother and family income-to-poverty ratio, receipt of TANF, family cohesiveness, and family support yielded no significant associations. In fact, many ethnic Asian single mothers report experiencing stigmatization and receiving meager support from family members and peers [58–60]. Such findings suggest that single mothers can have difficulty ensuring their children's health, even with residence in a safe neighborhood.

Our present study had several limitations. The first is inherent in the analyzed data's cross-sectional nature. Because we used cross-sectional data, any causal or directional relationships between tested variables merely reflected theoretical assumptions of the multiple disadvantage model. Second, preliminary analyses we conducted exhibited singularity while examining parent's length of residence in U.S., family mental health problems, and family substance use, impeding our application of the full conceptual framework of the multiple disadvantage model. Third, our present study could not include length of parent's residence in U.S. nor parent's participation Medicaid. Without these two variables, our analysis was unable to examine underlying reasons—such as cultural influences and states' Medicaid policies—for the sampled families' low rate of participation in public assistance. It is important to remember that these limitations, necessitate a cautious approach to any generalization of our findings.

5. Conclusions

Applying the conceptual framework provided by the multiple disadvantage model identified several factors in the health of ethnic Asian children in the U.S., each of those factors describing social disorganization, social structure, or social integration. Most important is the implication from our analysis that interventions would most benefit ethnic Asian families who are impoverished and living in unsafe neighborhoods. Social work professionals should advocate community policing and neighborhood watch groups in ethnic Asian communities, since these constitute effective means of promoting neighborhoods' safety [61,62]. Collaboration of social workers with public-health professionals on one hand and law enforcement professionals on the other should also help create safe Asian neighborhoods [24].

Our findings confirm that TANF assistance is associated with better health among ethnic Asian children. It is thus crucial to raise low-income ethnic Asian families' awareness of TANF and similar programs, especially concerning program eligibility. Public education events organized by community centers and other public-welfare organizations active in Asian communities are one option. To improve health among children of ethnic Asian families headed by single-mothers, social workers and public-health advocates should help the women establish strong social bonds, for example supportive relationships with their relatives and friends. Additionally, those in the helping professions should consistently demonstrate respect for and understanding of Asian cultural assumptions and values concerning children's health and well-being.

Future research in the same vein as the present study might investigate how ethnic Asian children's health is impacted by their parents' participation in public medical insurance programs. As well, many ethnic Asian single mothers may have mood disorders [59], so future research might explore whether and how stress-related mental health or substance use problems they exhibit affect their children's health. Finally, future research might productively involve longitudinal data accommodating analysis of the full conceptual framework of the multiple disadvantage model.

Author Contributions: The authors contributed equally to manuscript preparation and data analysis. All authors have read and agreed to the published version of the manuscript.

Funding: This research received no external funding.

Institutional Review Board Statement: The application of public-use data set is exempted from approval of institutional review.

Informed Consent Statement: Informed consent was obtained by original researchers of the national data set.

Data Availability Statement: This study employed solely public-use data.

Conflicts of Interest: The authors declare no conflict of interest. The company had no role in the design of the study; in the collection, analyses, or interpretation of data; in the writing of the manuscript, or in the decision to publish the results.

References

1. Fan, Y.L.; Chen, Q. Family functioning as a mediator between neighborhood conditions and children's health: Evidence from a national survey in the United States. *Soc. Sci. Med.* **2012**, *74*, 1939–1947. [CrossRef] [PubMed]
2. Stevens, G.D. Gradients in the health status and developmental risks of young children: The combined influences of multiple social risk factors. *Matern. Child Health J.* **2006**, *10*, 187–199. [CrossRef] [PubMed]
3. Larson, K.; Russ, S.A.; Crall, J.J.; Halfon, N. Influence of multiple social risks on children's health. *Pediatrics* **2008**, *121*, 337–344. [CrossRef] [PubMed]
4. Bauman, L.J.; Silver, E.J.; Stein, R.E.K. Cumulative social disadvantage and child health. *Pediatrics* **2006**, *117*, 1321–1328. [CrossRef]
5. Wen, M. Parental Participation in Religious Services and Parent and Child Well-Being: Findings from the National Survey of America's Families. *J. Relig. Health* **2014**, *53*, 1539–1561. [CrossRef]
6. Singh, G.K.; Yu, S.M.; Kogan, M.D. Health, Chronic Conditions, and Behavioral Risk Disparities Among US Immigrant Children and Adolescents. *Public Health Rep.* **2013**, *128*, 463–479. [CrossRef]
7. Flores, G.; Lin, H. Trends in racial/ethnic disparities in medical and oral health, access to care, and use of services in US children: Has anything changed over the years? *Int. J. Equity Health* **2013**, *12*, 10. [CrossRef]
8. Flores, G.; Tomany-Korman, S.C. The language spoken at home and disparities in medical and dental health, access to care, and use of services in US children. *Pediatrics* **2008**, *121*, E1703–E1714. [CrossRef]
9. Yu, S.M.; Huang, Z.J.H.; Schwalberg, R.H.; Overpeck, M.D.; Kogan, M.D. Association of language spoken at home with health and school issues among Asian American adolescents. *J. Sch. Health* **2002**, *72*, 192–198. [CrossRef]
10. Rappaport, E.B.; Robbins, J.M. Overweight in southeastern Pennsylvania children: 2002 household health survey data. *Public Health Rep.* **2005**, *120*, 525–531. [CrossRef]

11. Mehta, N.K.; Lee, H.; Ylitalo, K.R. Child health in the United States: Recent trends in racial/ethnic disparities. *Soc. Sci. Med.* **2013**, *95*, 6–15. [CrossRef] [PubMed]
12. Brewer, M.; Kimbro, R.T.; Denney, J.T.; Osiecki, K.M.; Moffett, B.; Lopez, K. Does neighborhood social and environmental context impact race/ethnic disparities in childhood asthma? *Health Place* **2017**, *44*, 86–93. [CrossRef] [PubMed]
13. Melius, J. Overweight and Obesity in Minority Children and Implications for Family and Community Social Work. *Soc. Work Public Health* **2013**, *28*, 119–128. [CrossRef] [PubMed]
14. Singh, G.K.; Siahpush, M.; Kogan, M.D. Rising Social Inequalities in US Childhood Obesity, 2003-2007. *Ann. Epidemiol.* **2010**, *20*, 40–52. [CrossRef] [PubMed]
15. Cheng, T.C.; Lo, C.C. Racial Disparities in Children's Health: A Longitudinal Analysis of Mothers Based on the Multiple Disadvantage Model. *J. Community Health* **2016**, *41*, 753–760. [CrossRef] [PubMed]
16. Cheng, T.C.; Li, Q. Adolescent delinquency in child welfare system: A multiple disadvantage model. *Child. Youth Serv. Rev.* **2017**, *73*, 205–212. [CrossRef]
17. Cheng, T.C.; Lo, C.C. Social risk and protective factors in adolescents' reduction and cessation of alcohol use. *Subst. Use Misuse* **2017**, *52*, 916–928. [CrossRef]
18. Li, Q.; Cheng, C.T. New evidence in physical violent behaviors among school-aged children: A multiple disadvantages model. *Child. Youth Serv. Rev.* **2017**, *81*, 301–308. [CrossRef]
19. Kedia, S.K.; Schmidt, M.; Dillon, P.J.; Arshad, H.; Yu, X. Substance use treatment in Appalachian Tennessee amid COVID-19: Challenges and preparing for the future. *J. Subst. Abus. Treat.* **2021**, *124*, 108270. [CrossRef]
20. Lo, C.C.; Howell, R.J.; Cheng, T.C. Explaining Black-White Differences in Homicide Victimization. *Aggress. Violent Behav.* **2013**, *18*, 125–134. [CrossRef]
21. Cheng, T.C.; Lo, C.C. Racial disparities in intimate partner violence and in seeking help with mental health. *J. Interpers. Violence* **2015**, *30*, 3283–3307. [CrossRef] [PubMed]
22. Lo, C.C.; Howell, R.J.; Cheng, T.C. Racial Disparities in Age at Time of Homicide Victimization: A Test of the Multiple Disadvantage Model. *J. Interpers. Violence* **2015**, *30*, 152–167. [CrossRef] [PubMed]
23. Priest, N.; Paradies, Y.; Trenerry, B.; Truong, M.; Karlsen, S.; Kelly, Y. A systematic review of studies examining the relationship between reported racism and health and wellbeing for children and young people. *Soc. Sci. Med.* **2013**, *95*, 115–127. [CrossRef] [PubMed]
24. Jackson, D.B.; Posick, C.; Vaughn, M.G. New Evidence of The Nexus Between Neighborhood Violence, Perceptions Of Danger, And Child Health. *Health Aff.* **2019**, *38*, 746–754. [CrossRef] [PubMed]
25. Zuberi, A.; Teixeira, S. Child health in low-income neighborhoods: The unexpected relationship with neighborhood disorder and other aspects of distress. *J. Community Psychol.* **2017**, *45*, 459–472. [CrossRef]
26. Diez Roux, A.V.; Mair, C. Neighborhoods and health. *Ann. N. Y. Acad. Sci.* **2010**, *1186*, 125–145. [CrossRef] [PubMed]
27. Schreier, H.M.C.; Chen, E. Socioeconomic Status and the Health of Youth: A Multilevel, Multidomain Approach to Conceptualizing Pathways. *Psychol. Bull.* **2013**, *139*, 606–654. [CrossRef]
28. Christian, H.; Zubrick, S.R.; Foster, S.; Giles-Corti, B.; Bull, F.; Wood, L.; Knuiman, M.; Brinkman, S.; Houghton, S.; Boruff, B. The influence of the neighborhood physical environment on early child health and development: A review and call for research. *Health Place* **2015**, *33*, 25–36. [CrossRef]
29. Fortson, J.G.; Sanbonmatsu, L. Child Health and Neighborhood Conditions Results from a Randomized Housing Voucher Experiment. *J. Hum. Resour.* **2010**, *45*, 840–864. [CrossRef]
30. Gonzales, F.A.; Jones, R.R.; Deardorff, J.; Windham, G.C.; Hiatt, R.A.; Kushi, L.H. Neighborhood deprivation, race/ethnicity, and urinary metal concentrations among young girls in California. *Environ. Int.* **2016**, *91*, 29–39. [CrossRef]
31. Chen, E.; Martin, A.D.; Matthews, K.A. Understanding health disparities: The role of race and socioeconomic status in children's health. *Am. J. Public Health* **2006**, *96*, 702–708. [CrossRef] [PubMed]
32. Cook, W.K.; Tseng, W. Associations of Asian Ethnicity and Parental Education with Overweight in Asian American Children and Adolescents: An Analysis of 2011–2016 National Health and Nutrition Examination Surveys. *Matern. Child Health J.* **2019**, *23*, 504–511. [CrossRef] [PubMed]
33. Chatterji, P.; Markowitz, S.; Brooks-Gunn, J. Effects of early maternal employment on maternal health and well-being. *J. Popul. Econ.* **2013**, *26*, 285–301. [CrossRef] [PubMed]
34. Kuhlthau, K.A.; Perrin, J.M. Child health status and parental employment. *Arch. Pediatr. Adolesc. Med.* **2001**, *155*, 1346–1350. [CrossRef] [PubMed]
35. Minkovitz, C.S.; O'Campo, P.J.; Chen, Y.H.; Grason, H.A. Associations between maternal and child health status and patterns of medical care use. *Ambul. Pediatr.* **2002**, *2*, 85–92. [CrossRef] [PubMed]
36. Larson, K.; Halfon, N. Family Income Gradients in the Health and Health Care Access of US Children. *Matern. Child Health J.* **2010**, *14*, 332–342. [CrossRef]
37. Currie, J.; Lin, W.C. Chipping away at health: More on the relationship between income and child health. *Health Aff.* **2007**, *26*, 331–344. [CrossRef]
38. de Cuba, S.A.E.; Bovell-Ammon, A.R.; Cook, J.T.; Coleman, S.M.; Black, M.M.; Chilton, M.M.; Casey, P.H.; Cutts, D.B.; Heeren, T.C.; Sandel, M.T.; et al. SNAP, Young Children's Health, and Family Food Security and Healthcare Access. *Am. J. Prev. Med.* **2019**, *57*, 525–532. [CrossRef]

39. Reichman, N.E.; Corman, H.; Noonan, K. Effects of child health on sources of public support. *South. Econ. J.* **2006**, *73*, 136–156. [CrossRef]
40. McConnell, D.; Breitkreuz, R.; Savage, A. From financial hardship to child difficulties: Main and moderating effects of perceived social support. *Child Care Health Dev.* **2011**, *37*, 679–691. [CrossRef]
41. Chen, E.; Hayen, R.; Le, V.; Austin, M.K.; Shalowitz, M.U.; Story, R.E.; Miller, G.E. Neighborhood Social Conditions, Family Relationships, and Childhood Asthma. *Pediatrics* **2019**, *144*, e20183300. [CrossRef] [PubMed]
42. Leininger, L.J.; Ryan, R.M.; Kalil, A. Low-income mothers' social support and children's injuries. *Soc. Sci. Med.* **2009**, *68*, 2113–2121. [CrossRef] [PubMed]
43. Zhang, S.J.; Fuller, T. Neighborhood Disorder and Paternal Involvement of Nonresident and Resident Fathers. *Fam. Relat.* **2012**, *61*, 501–513. [CrossRef]
44. Bass, L.E.; Warehime, M.N. Family Structure and Child Health Outcomes in the United States. *Sociol. Inq.* **2011**, *81*, 527–548. [CrossRef] [PubMed]
45. Wong, M.S.; Showell, N.N.; Bleich, S.N.; Gudzune, K.A.; Chan, K.S. The association between parent-reported provider communication quality and child obesity status: Variation by parent obesity and child race/ethnicity. *Patient Educ. Couns.* **2017**, *100*, 1588–1597. [CrossRef] [PubMed]
46. Lanuza, Y.R. Words and Hugs: Emotional Support for Latino and Asian Children of Immigrants Compared to their White Counterparts with Native-Born Parentage. *Race Soc. Probl.* **2020**, *12*, 112–132. [CrossRef]
47. Ellingsen, R.; Baker, B.L.; Blacher, J.; Crnic, K. Resilient parenting of preschool children at developmental risk. *J. Intellect. Disabil. Res.* **2014**, *58*, 664–678. [CrossRef]
48. Hardie, J.H.; Landale, N.S. Profiles of Risk: Maternal Health, Socioeconomic Status, and Child Health. *J. Marriage Fam.* **2013**, *75*, 651–666. [CrossRef]
49. Akobirshoev, I.; Bowser, D.; Parish, S.L.; Thomas, C.; Bachman, S.S. Does Parental Health Mediate the Relationship between Parental Uninsurance and Insured Children's Health Outcomes? Evidence from a US National Survey. *Health Soc. Work* **2017**, *42*, E68–E76. [CrossRef]
50. Zea, M.C.; Asner-Self, K.K.; Birman, D.; Buki, L.P. The Abbreviated Multidimensional Acculturation Scale: Empirical Validation with Two Latino/Latina Samples. *Cult. Divers. Ethn. Minor. Psychol.* **2003**, *9*, 107–126. [CrossRef]
51. Guerrero, A.D.; Ponce, N.A.; Chung, P.J. Obesogenic Dietary Practices of Latino and Asian Subgroups of Children in California: An Analysis of the California Health Interview Survey, 2007–2012. *Am. J. Public Health* **2015**, *105*, E105–E112. [CrossRef] [PubMed]
52. Chomitz, V.R.; Lee, V.; Must, A.; Chui, K.K.H.; Brown, A. Healthy Living Behaviors Among Chinese-American Preschool-Aged Children: Results of a Parent Survey. *J. Immigr. Minor. Health* **2018**, *20*, 926. [CrossRef] [PubMed]
53. McGee, S.A.; Luz, C. Nativity as a Determinant of Health Disparities Among Children. *J. Immigr. Minor. Health* **2018**, *20*, 517–528. [CrossRef] [PubMed]
54. Hore, P.; Ahmed, M.S.; Sedlar, S.; Saper, R.B.; Nagin, D.; Clark, N. Blood Lead Levels and Potential Risk Factors for Lead Exposures Among South Asians in New York City. *J. Immigr. Minor. Health* **2017**, *19*, 1322–1329. [CrossRef]
55. Ragavan, M.I.; Li, W.D.; Elwy, A.R.; Cowden, J.D.; Bair-Merritt, M. Chinese, Vietnamese, and Asian Indian Parents' Perspectives About Well-Child Visits: A Qualitative Analysis. *Acad. Pediatr.* **2018**, *18*, 628–635. [CrossRef] [PubMed]
56. Child and Adolescent Health Measurement Initiative. *2018 National Survey of Children's Health: SPSS Codebook for Data Users*; U.S. Department of Health and Human Services: Washington, DC, USA, 2020.
57. Tummala-Narra, P.; Sathasivam-Rueckert, N. The Experience of Ethnic and Racial Group Membership Among Immigrant-Origin Adolescents. *J. Adolesc. Res.* **2016**, *31*, 299–342. [CrossRef]
58. Zhang, H. Re-defining stigmatization: Intersectional stigma of single mothers in Thailand. *J. Fam. Stud.* **2022**, 1–27. [CrossRef]
59. Subramaniam, M.; Prasad, R.O.; Abdin, E.; Vaingankar, J.A.; Chong, S.A. Single Mothers Have a Higher Risk of Mood Disorders. *Ann. Acad. Med. Singap.* **2014**, *43*, 145–151. [CrossRef]
60. Pan, E.L.; Farrell, M.P. Ethnic differences in the effects of intergenerational relations on adolescent problem behavior in US single-mother families. *J. Fam. Issues* **2006**, *27*, 1137–1158. [CrossRef]
61. Dukes, R.L.; Portillos, E.; Miles, M. Models of satisfaction with police service. *Polic. Int. J. Police Strateg. Manag.* **2009**, *32*, 297–318. [CrossRef]
62. De Marco, A.; Vernon-Feagans, L. Rural Neighborhood Context, Child Care Quality, and Relationship to Early Language Development. *Early Educ. Dev.* **2013**, *24*, 792–812. [CrossRef] [PubMed]

MDPI
St. Alban-Anlage 66
4052 Basel
Switzerland
www.mdpi.com

International Journal of Environmental Research and Public Health Editorial Office
E-mail: ijerph@mdpi.com
www.mdpi.com/journal/ijerph

www.ingramcontent.com/pod-product-compliance
Lightning Source LLC
Chambersburg PA
CBHW061606210926
51850CB00009B/2232
9783725801473